Essential
McLuhan

Essential
McLuhan

Edited by Eric McLuhan
and Frank Zingrone

Published in 1995 by
House of Anansi Press Limited
895 Don Mills Rd., 400-2 Park Centre
Toronto, ON, M3C 1W3
Tel. (416) 445-3333
Fax (416) 445-5967
www.anansi.ca

Distributed in Canada by
General Distribution Services Ltd.
325 Humber College Blvd.
Etobicoke, ON, M9W 7C3
Tel. (416) 213-1919
Fax (416) 213-1917
E-mail cservice@genpub.com

Electronic Mail Addresses
Eric McLuhan: mcluhane@sympatico.ca
Frank Zingrone: zingf@yorku.ca
The Herbert Marshall McLuhan Foundation, St. Francis Xavier University,
   Antigonish, Nova Scotia: info@Mcluhan.ca
The McLuhan Program in Culture and Technology, University of Toronto,
   Toronto, Ontario: http://www.mcluhan.utoronto.ca

6 5 4 3 2   01 02 03 04 05

National Library of Canada Cataloguing in Publication Data

McLuhan, Eric
Essential McLuhan

Includes index
ISBN 0-88784-565-7

1. McLuhan, Marshall 1911–1980. 2. Mass media.
I. Zingrone, Frank. II. Title.

P92.5.M25M35 1995   302.23'092   C95-930328-6

Cover Design: Bill Douglas/The Bang
Computer Graphics: Tannice Goddard, S.O. Networking

The authors acknowledge the gracious cooperation of Corinne McLuhan, brilliant
publishing expertise of Donald G. Bastian, generous forbearance of Williams Kuhns,
splendid agency of Matie Molinaro, and invaluable editorial assistance of J. P. Zingrone.

Selections for *The Gutenberg Galaxy* used by permission
of the University of Toronto Press.

*We acknowledge for their financial support of our publishing
program the Canada Council for the Arts, the Ontario Arts
Council, and the Government of Canada through the
Book Publishing Industry Development Program (BPIDP).*

THE CANADA COUNCIL | LE CONSEIL DES ARTS
FOR THE ARTS | DU CANADA
SINCE 1957 | DEPUIS 1957

Printed and bound in Canada

Contents

Introduction

I am not a "culture critic" because I am not in any way interested in classifying cultural forms. I am a metaphysician, interested in the life of the forms and their surprising modalities.

(Letters of Marshall McLuhan)

I

Herbert Marshall McLuhan was born in Edmonton, Alberta, on July 21, 1911. He became internationally famous during the 1960s and '70s for his studies of the effects of mass media on thought and social behaviour. After an early flirtation with engineering as a possible vocation, McLuhan's brilliance as a student of literature asserted itself and led him from the University of Manitoba abroad for graduate work (Ph.D., Cambridge, 1943). There he laid the basis of his later work in his erudite and prescient dissertation, "The Place of Thomas Nashe in the Learning of His Time," which examined the modern biases in logic and science that culminated in the triumph of the Newtonian worldview, and its clockwork mechanical perfection, in 19th-century Europe. Beginning with his studies in literature, McLuhan became uniquely alert to the revolutionary threshold of contemporary cultural change.

He returned to North America and teaching posts at the University of Wisconsin (1936) and St. Louis University (1937) before finishing his doctorate at Cambridge. There was a short tenure at Assumption College (now the University of Windsor) in 1944, but by 1946 McLuhan was eagerly conscripted by St. Michael's College, University of Toronto, where he stayed for the rest of his teaching life (except for 1967-68, when he was granted a Schweitzer Chair at Fordham University in New York).

At Cambridge, McLuhan had studied with a breathtakingly luminous faculty: F. R. Leavis, Sir Arthur Quiller-Couch, E. M. W. Tillyard, H. J. Chaytor, and especially the founder of the "New Criticism," I. A. Richards, among other academic celebrities. He learned from them intellectual confidence. Through the years, McLuhan established relations with an array of remarkable people. He had very little to do with the communications pioneer Harold Innis (who had noticed McLuhan's work and was using *The Mechanical Bride* in his classes), but he had strong intellectual acquaintances with Edmund "Ted" Carpenter and Edward T. Hall, cultural anthropologists; the celebrated rhetoric scholar Walter

Ong, S.J.; the artist-critic Wyndham Lewis; Alvin Toffler; Peter Drucker; Jonathan Miller; Eric Havelock; Hugh Kenner; Buckminster Fuller; Pierre Trudeau; the illustrious Canadian pianist Glenn Gould; and the eminent philosopher Etienne Gilson.

His correspondents included many of the most interesting people in the world: for example, the poet Ezra Pound, Woody Allen, John Cage, George Steiner, Clare Boothe Luce, Duke Ellington, Tom Wolfe, Barbara Ward, Jacques Maritain, Wyndham Lewis, Rollo May, Yousuf Karsh, Ann Landers, Jack Paar, Ashley Montagu, Prince Bernhard of the Netherlands, and King Karl Gustav of Sweden.

Before anyone could perceive the electric form of the information revolution, McLuhan was publishing brilliant explanations of the perceptual changes being experienced by the users of mass media. He seemed futuristic to some and an enemy of print and literacy to others. He was, in reality, a deeply literate man of astonishing prescience. Tom Wolfe suggested aloud that McLuhan's work was as important culturally as that of Darwin or Freud. Agreement and scoffing ensued. Increasingly Wolfe's wonder seems justified. Yet, from the start, McLuhan was misunderstood, even purposely, by people with rival agendas or personal turfs to defend; for, truth be known, he was warning everyone how, under electric conditions, their specialist enterprises were obsolescing, just when specialism was being touted as our salvation. As well, the complexity of the ideas and his aphoristic prose style made access to the work seem difficult or elitist in places.

Many, who, for many reasons, misunderstood his work, tried to dismiss him with irrelevant criticisms. His ideas, some complained, were not "logical" enough. Others felt that devaluing the significance of message "content" for media "context" was a threat to civilization. Perhaps most of his critics felt alienated by the tight, imploded aphoristic style that defeated the narrative bias required for argument. McLuhan disliked argument and the protection of intellectual turf. Rather, he saw himself as an explorer "probing" the "psychosocial complex" powerfully changed by the new electric conditions. Electricity continually transforms everything, especially the way people think, and confirms the power of uncertainty in the quest for absolute knowledge. That is revolutionary.

Because of the *decentralizing*, *integrating*, and *accelerating* character of electric process, the emphasis in communication shifts from the specialist "one thing at a time" or linear, logical sequence, to the "all-at-once" simultaneous relations that occur when electronic information approaches the speed of light. Media, as contexts that translate psychological and social experience, eliminate the possibility of simple clear meaning. The environment, overloaded with detailed information, can be ordered meaningfully, McLuhan said, by developing enhanced pattern-recognition skills, the ability to deal with open systems, undergoing continual change, at electric speed. Physical connectedness gives way to the resonant bonds and gigantic open-system patterns of electric information.

The perception of reality now depends upon the structure of information. The form of each medium is associated with a different arrangement, or ratio, among the senses, which creates new forms of awareness. These perceptual transformations, the new ways of experiencing that each medium creates, occur in the user regardless of the program content. This is what the paradox, "the medium is the message," means.

McLuhan's famous distinction between "hot" and "cool" media referred to the different sensory effects associated with media of higher or lower definition. "Hot" media (radio, photography, cinema) are more full of information and allow less involvement of the user; "cool" media (telephone, cartoons, television) are less full of information and allow much greater sensory participation by the user.

II

Since his death in 1980, Marshall McLuhan's reputation has been in a sort of hiatus waiting for electronic reality to catch up. That is happening; a surge of interest in his work emphasizes its usefulness. Not only have his ideas endured, they have retained their primacy in communication theory. Still, no one knows better than he how electric process transforms reality. Now that we too can see so much of what he perceived, it is possible, for example, to discuss "discarnate existence" with a young person who has spent the morning surfing the Internet in search of his invisible friends around the "Global Village," or who appreciates, almost instinctively, how all media translate reality. Several years after his original emphasis on the importance of the "medium" over the "message," it is interesting to note that the most popular shows on television are shows about shows in which the hidden ground of the medium becomes the ironic content of a show without an obvious story line.

Recalling a complaint by Humboldt, Northrop Frye, the other pole in the intellectual field that configured world attention about Toronto during the last 40 years, has marked out the sequence of inhibitions by which our recognition of great minds is averted:

> When you begin a book which is something relatively new, you get first of all a "what nonsense" reaction and then the "many brilliant insights, but of course all wrong" reaction, then finally the "we knew it all along" reaction.
>
> (Toronto, *Globe and Mail*, Feb. 26, 1983, p. 18)

By this measure, McLuhan has evaded the continuing indignity of too much popularity. Strangely, though we have yet to fully comprehend the value of the paradigm of changed reality that he set in motion, his insights are still powerfully valid. This persistent relevance attests to the unavoidable centrality of his ideas for understanding the effects of electric media.

Ironically, few of his critics have read much of his work. There is almost never, for example, any reference to his early groundbreaking articles, scholarly and popular, where many of the ideas first took form, nor even of several of the books. A major intellectual of the 20th century, he is only now on the point of being read comprehensively. This volume of key portions of the McLuhan canon is meant to remedy any continuing shortfall in attention to the work itself.

III

The main effect of electric process, McLuhan discovered, is to retribalize the structure of psychic and social awareness. Millions of people sitting around the TV tube, CNN-style, absorbing the modern equivalent of shamanistic lore from the authorized source is closely analogous to the old tribal relations of tyrannous instruction and control.

The Global Village of corporate consumer values stimulates local peoples to retrieve who they used to be as a protection for their fading identities, for electric process makes us all nobodies desperate for identity. The quest for identity, he warned, always produces violence. The old sensibility, old values, old enmities prevail over larger-scale democratic awareness and commitment. The profound changes to the perceptual apparatus brought about by film, television, and the other mass media return us to conditions so similar to old tribal brutalities that we retrieve the joy in the mystique of violence that governed the lives of preliterate peoples. Electricity takes us back, converts the world into a circuit of neo-tribal resonance. We are replaying the archetypes of deep human experience, the exemplary models of psychic and social reality.

The first accurate descriptions of the transformative effects of major media appeared in *The Gutenberg Galaxy*. Language, speech, grammar, print, books — all the assets of civilized communications are now under pressure from the more primitive forms of electric media, primitive in how they reorganize the sensorium, appealing as they do to feelings rather than thought. Regardless of those readers who thought he approved of the destruction of literate values, McLuhan only sounded the alarm warning of their obsolescence. He would have preferred to keep the agendas for rhetorical and grammatical awareness alive. That is one of the reasons why he wrote in a complex, punning style.

Essentially, McLuhan's unusual prose style involved the discontinuous juxtaposition of witty aphoristic "probes" — his word for investigative statements. This critical approach to discovering meaning is itself an art form. The case can easily be made for McLuhan's being a special sort of artist. His collaboration with Harley Parker suggests that he also saw himself as something of an artist.

In art the importance of the same principle is illustrated by the value of suggestion. In leaving something unsaid, the beholder is given a chance to complete the idea . . .

until you seem to become actually part of it.
(Through the Vanishing Point, 266)

Regarding the artistic merits of the aphorism, McLuhan appears to have taken his cue from Francis Bacon in *The Advancement of Learning* to appreciate its paradoxical spirit: "Knowledge, while in aphorisms and observations (percepts?) . . . is growth." This implies that the wholeness of knowledge is diminished in being defined as concepts. It is this wholeness of percepts that accounts for the perpetual modification and repudiation of all concepts. Knowledge of percepts allows us to anticipate such changes.

McLuhan, rather than engage in arguments based on ideas isolated from real intellectual environments, focuses on their contextual grounds. He forces us to see how our sensory lives change in response to the media we use. Our transformed perception can lead to powerful discoveries. In fact, McLuhan's work explores the paradigm shift in our perceptual values in a way that can't be found elsewhere.

The aphoristic technique makes it possible to present several levels of awareness simultaneously. This return to poetic form is extremely appropriate to the all-at-onceness of electric process. From Cicero and Quintilian to Bacon and Nashe, McLuhan updates the grammarians and rhetoricians as the deep sources of communication theory.

Newspaper ads and television commercials are rooted in the ancient oratorical tradition, as Joyce has shown in the "AEolus," or newspaper, episode of *Ulysses* which features a mass of up-dated rhetorical figures. All communication in any medium carries out a rhetorical agenda. McLuhan's great talent is in exposing these deep grounds to electric conditions.

W. B. Yeats always declined to explain his poems on the grounds that that would tend to limit their suggestibility. He required his readers to get involved with the poetry. Similarly, in all electric media, "the user" must learn to enter into the communication process, to become a sort of co-producer. Under electric conditions, each object is not merely itself but represents a manifold process which evades simple, logical definition, as any astute admirer of Picasso, Klee, or Mondrian knows.

The artist is the man in any field, scientific or humanistic, who grasps the implications of his actions and of new knowledge in his own times. He is the man of integral awareness. (Understanding Media, 65)

In some ways, McLuhan was closer to such artists in his perceptions: a Kandinsky who held that "the environment is the composition," and that "objects have to be considered in the light of the whole." His art, especially apparent in *The Gutenberg Galaxy*, of connecting Medieval and early Renaissance forms to present electric conditions made him seem a spectacular advance on the blindness of specialist scholarship. In the rage against McLuhan and his popularity we often heard howls, inside and out of academe, of ignorance and fear from infuriated minions of a previous century's hold on public consciousness.

The university always wants facts, evidence, and argument. Even the humanists had for too long managed to remain innocent of the implications of the theories of *uncertainty*, *probability*, *complementarity*, and *incompleteness*. This general inheritance from particle physics reinstated the usefulness of paradox for understanding the chaotic array of conflicting truths that interpretive media created.

In the golden groves, the strident debate produced maniacs of Luddite interpretation, some with blood in their eyes. At one point, in the late 1960s, a rumour surfaced that a major U.S. magazine had put out a contract on McLuhan and was offering big money for a name who would "waste" him in print. Hugh Kenner, we know, refused this offer.

The jealousies gelled in a comic aspic of misinterpretations, many critics suspended in postures of arrested awareness, in gestures of alarm and admonition. McLuhan's desire to be perceived, at one level, as a satirist could not have been more deliciously realized. A Dunciad of detractors queued up to rail against what they saw as an assault on civilization. This was the "what nonsense" stage in all its violent petulance. Each adversary looked furiously for the hook of a factual mistake to hang his mad hat on.

McLuhan's sympathies were with the past, with the civilized literate life. He understood better than most that the future is always a new way of retrieving the past. The only rational indictment of his work would be that he relied too much on the past, that his work, in places, was extremely erudite.

His was the first coherent interpretation of the electric world and it required a rethinking of everything. There was resistance. One should not have expected the dinosaurs blissfully to embrace their own ends. No wonder he was not taken immediately unto the culture's bosom, the way he seemed to be trashing traditional views of cultural operation. Specialists who had invested everything in isolated figures, specimens in labs, and who neglected contextual grounds were confused and irate when told they were obsolescent. (What he meant by obsolescence was that the hidden archetypal ground was becoming visible and slowly losing its power over the psyche while becoming clichéd.) Educators were recommending specialist approaches just when think tanks were being formed to solve the complex problems emerging from transformative electric pressure. McLuhan stressed environments and the inter-connectedness of things, the ecology of thought, and the pervasive, inescapable power of electric process to change socio-political existence. Stripped of his playful hyperbole, his vision has been borne out by events.

IV

Literate persons ought to have seen him coming, for he was squarely in the tradition of literary invention that flowed from Joyce, Eliot, Pound, Lewis, and a few others, and he had prepared himself for the battle of the electric mindset by beginning his studies in that other battle between Ancients and Moderns that centred on Harvey and Nashe and that set the grounds for an industrial revolution based on the economics of the Protestant ethic and positivistic science.

While he was telling people that books were being pushed aside by electric media, few noticed that this deeply literate man remained on the side of the Ancients. He had simply gravitated to the points of greatest irritation in cultural change. Embattled readers took him to be a traitor to the cause of literacy; others accused him of technological determinism — as if chance had no place in his (or Innis's) idea of the evolution of communication.

McLuhan seemed to many a paradoxical man. The varied interpretive grounds brought in by mass media suggested that things were true and not true at the same time. The world of print and the world of television are realities apart. He often referred to the cultural transformation in which paradox was degraded in the interests of the growing illusion of clarity demanded by the rational biases of Empiricism. In explaining how electric process reinstates paradox, he approved Rosalie Colie's observation that

> *degradation of paradox is one result of a revolution in thought which valued clarity and exactness above the tricky duplicities of comprehension induced by paradox. In "The Dialogue Concerning the Two World Systems," Galileo's Simplicio points to the dangers involved in favoring "words" over "things" as guides to truth: Once you have denied the principles of sciences and have cast doubt upon the most evident things, everybody knows that you may prove whatever you will, and maintain any paradox.* (Colie, *Paradoxica Epidemica* 1966, 508-20)

Our world is fraught with new paradoxes scientifically produced: the certitude of the last few centuries has been pressed past the limit of its capability and has reversed into its opposite. Uncertainty and probability and the latter's statistical approach to truth are now met by the theories of complexity and chaos. Socially and politically we find it difficult to make sense of paradox: how can everything under the law, for example, be both true and not true at the same time? The law in practice is increasingly circumstantial and relative to media perceptions.

In electric culture we live with the paradox of Simplicio: "only any arbitrary or haphazard odd notion, true or false, unverifiable by experience" (Colie). McLuhan showed that paradox, like metaphor, establishes the ratios of a truth, for truth cannot be just one thing, nor can reality, under electric conditions.

In the information age we should remember Korzybski's notion of a "world of words and a world of not words." Paradox and ambiguity must exist if the interplay between these two worlds is to be balanced humanely. The map is not the territory; the story, not the event; the image, not the thing. The form of presentation may be everything.

V

School, with its lessons, too often ignores this fact. After they escape the Chinese boxes of our education theories, should Yuppie generations unwilling to tolerate rising thresholds of ambiguity surprise us? Paradox should serve as an integrating, ecologizing necessity rather than an annoyance to those who prefer clarity to wonder.

Considering the radical changes brought about by new media, McLuhan set out to discover what the medium actually does to change the mindscape of the user: "the medium is the message." That is, media affect us physically. Sitting for hours in front of a TV set, a cathode ray stimulator, produces a unique and characteristic mental state. It is a state that actually reverses the evolutionary alertness by which we have so far survived extinction. As for message content, if you say "I love you" in person, over the phone, or by billboard, it is likely the medium that most shapes the response you get back. He gave us a way of breaking into the control-room of life's reality studio.

Like a series of Yogic steps to self-awareness, McLuhan's insights can free one from single-minded obsessions with the trivial manipulations of contents. Making humanity whole again seems the objective of all our global aspirations, but the backlash is real and vociferous. A pernicious tribalism is developing worldwide as peoples struggle to forge their identities against the global corporate sameness.

McLuhan arranges his materials in broad patterns of interplaying parts, thus engaging us in larger thought patterns — almost the difference between prose and poetry — which enable us to encounter our own conceptual shortcomings in attempting to expand our perceptual awareness. To move beyond simple facts requires deep involvement in the process of communication; content takes care of itself.

McLuhan has been the subject of a rare act of cultural cannibalism, ingested piecemeal by many who couldn't take him whole. Everywhere glints of his insights shine from the works of others, often unattributed. Borges, in his "Approach to al-Mutasim, or the Game of Shifting Mirrors," has a man trace a soul in the impression it has made on others. It is a serious game in which a greater reality is revealed through fragmented reflections. The physical process of seeing becomes a metaphor for vision. We see because objects reflect light, but it is the light we really seek to see.

McLuhan, at base a grammarian, required absolutely the continual collegial dialogue that was the ground for his work. Even as far back as the group engaged in the *Explorations* project (McLuhan, Tom Easterbrook, Ted Carpenter, and others), the McLuhan style was one of discussion geared to discovery. He was a first-rate investigator who often found meaningful patterns in the work of others that they themselves had not perceived. Most importantly, he thrived on the inputs of the best of those few around him who could play the game close to his level of intensity. You are hereby invited to engage in this process of seeking illumination by learning to probe for underlying structure in information. Read, criticize, and remember that McLuhan was quite prepared to change any statement that didn't hold up under continual probing. Go on to the new places where this material leads.

VI

Essential McLuhan is divided into four sections. Within each division the selections run chronologically. Part I, "Culture as Business," investigates the merger of culture and business in the sense of taking advertising and entertainment seriously as phenomena of fundamental cultural importance. McLuhan was the first systematically to study the shift of business, extended by media, to making and marketing culture. He and his one-time partner, anthropologist Ted Carpenter, along with Edward Hall, used the techniques of modern anthropology to discover the "out-of-awareness" aspects of culture, the "hidden grounds," as McLuhan came to call this domain of the deep underlying structure of information.

"Print and the Electric Revolution," Part II, presents key excerpts of the groundbreaking works on the revolution of literacy that Gutenberg's technology gave the world. That great event is contrasted with formative pieces on the electric revolution and the turbulent shift provoked by this pervasive, globalizing technology. This transformation of all communication systems by electric process is the crux of McLuhan's work and is what we want to represent in these key excerpts. The selections are carefully chosen to epitomize the fundamental contrast between print and its complementary electric mass media.

The "Oral McLuhan" who dominates Part III is closest to the essence of the man himself. He was at his best "dialoguing" with friends and colleagues. The discoveries he made often occurred when in full flight of conversation. Whoever said "I never learn anything when I'm talking," it surely wasn't McLuhan; he always made "breakthroughs" during the high-powered chats some of us were privileged to share. Like Coleridge, McLuhan impressed everyone in person as a man of enormous learning and perception, and by the elegance of his spontaneous speech. The *Playboy* article especially has caught the rhythm of McLuhan's mind in the elegant flow of investigative repartee.

The selections in Part IV, "Culture and Art: Figures and Grounds," exemplify

McLuhan's erudite playfulness. He works a trope or two on Carl Jung and sheds new light on the notion of archetypal power. (Who would have thought anyone could alter the idea of an archetype after the dominance of that area by Jung?) Art is very serious, high-powered play, and the intrusion of popular culture into the arena of art has been one of the most important new aspects of Western culture.

Reading this material requires that the user be willing to unlearn some things that dominate our perceptual lives — for example that logical clarity and narrative sequence are always the index of solid meaning or that the opposite of a great truth is falsity (it may be another great truth). Different media, like styles in painting or literature, are special ways of seeing and induce specific states of mind. Also, the user should remain open to the proposition that much of what is most important, and that works the most powerful changes in our lives, lies outside our general awareness, as environmentally hidden. McLuhan's work is useful and exciting precisely because it is still the best way to discover underlying structure and meaning in a world that most of the time seems impossibly overloaded with conflicting information.

Frank Zingrone
Eric McLuhan

I

Culture as Business

1

American Advertising

A few months ago an American army officer wrote for *Printer's Ink* from Italy. He noted with misgiving that Italians could tell you the names of cabinet ministers but not the names of commodities preferred by Italian celebrities. Furthermore, the wall space of Italian cities was given over to political rather than commercial slogans. Finally, he predicted that there was small hope that Italians would ever achieve any sort of domestic prosperity or calm until they began to worry about the rival claims of cornflakes or cigarettes rather than the capacities of public men. In fact, he went so far as to say that democratic freedom very largely consists in ignoring politics and worrying about the means of defeating underarm odour, scaly scalp, hairy legs, dull complexion, unruly hair, borderline anaemia, athlete's foot, and sluggish bowels, not to mention ferro-nutritional deficiency of the blood, wash-day blues, saggy breasts, receding gums, shiny pants, greying hair, and excess weight. Here we are perhaps in the presence of an excluded middle rather than a *non sequitur*, because American advertising has developed into a jungle of folklore beside which the tales from the Schwartzwald belong with Winnie-the-Pooh.

It is, therefore, quite possible that there is a core of political reality and even health in the wildly proliferating forms of American advertising. The hyperaesthesia of the ad-men's rhetoric has knocked the public into a kind of groggy, slap-happy condition in which perhaps are cushioned a good many of the brutal shocks felt more keenly by the realistic European. Viewed merely as an interim strategy for maintaining hope, tolerance, and good humour in an irrational world, this orgy of irrationalism may not be without its cathartic function. At any rate, the multi-billion dollar, nation-wide educational programmes of the ad-men (dwarfing the outlay on formal education) provide a world of symbols, witticism, and behavior patterns which may or may not be a fatal solvent for the basic political traditions of America, but which certainly do comprise a common experience and a common language for a country whose sectional differences and technological specialisms might easily develop into anarchy. The comedian at the microphone or the professor in the classroom can always be sure of an effective gibe or illustration based on the ads. And both community and communication, in so far as they are managed at all at the popular level, are in the same debt. Moreover, by various means, the whole technique and hallucination of Hollywood has been assimilated to the ads *via* pictorial glamour, so that the two are inseparable. They constitute one world.

It is just as well to preface a glance at American ads with a consideration of the imponderables, because the ads themselves are deceptively easy to assess. A similar abeyance of judgement about the social effects of the sadism purveyed, for example, by thriller and detective literature is indicated. For the extent to which armchair sadism, so fostered, acts as a preservative of good humour in a lethal and chaotic world it is impossible to say. But anybody can check for himself the fact that persons with a penchant for strong-arm political methods are not given to this form of fantasy life. It is, of course, true that the thriller and sleuth fans, from Poe to Ellery Queen, are the willing victims of a psychological trick. By identifying their mental processes with those of the manhunter, the readers achieve a sort of megalomaniac thrill. At the same time they enjoy the illusion of sharing in the scientific techniques of the society which permits them almost no other kind of congenial adjustment or direct participation. "Happiness," said Swift, "is the possession of being perpetually well-deceived." And in a merely political regard we cannot any longer dispense with any source of happiness which will win us a bit of time while we consult the means of survival.

The intellectual claims to perceive and enjoy an order and symmetry in the world and in his own life denied to other men. He arms himself today against the impact of the stereotypes of commercialized culture by keenness of recognition and analysis and engages in a perpetual guerrilla activity. He is a sort of noble savage free-lancing amidst a zombie horde. The dangers attending this mode of existence are obvious. Should he find his energies suddenly depleted or his patience exasperated, he may be tempted to revive them by adopting some lethal myth-mechanism. And at all times he finds it hard to remember the common human nature which persists intact beneath all the modes of mental hysteria rampant from Machiavelli and Calvin until our own day. Yet it is only in the degree to which he is motivated by the benevolence imposed by the perception of the rational form rather than the psychological condition of all men, that he is justified or that he is tolerable. Benda was right. When the intellectual sells out to any brand of social or political neurosis, when fear or loneliness beckon him into some party, he is worse than useless. *Corruptio optimi pessima.*

American "market research," which has developed very rapidly in the past ten years, has a strong totalitarian squint — that of the social engineer. Two recent items will illustrate this. *Time* magazine for 22 July 1946, described a new gadget:

The finished — but still uncut — picture [movie] is given the works with an electrical contraption called the Hopkins Televoting System. Each member of A.R.I.'s [Audience Research Inc.] hand-picked, cross-section audience sits in a wired section of a preview theater. With his eyes on the screen, he clutches a gadget that resembles a flashlight. On the gadget's round face is an indicator that can easily be turned with the fingers. A turn to the right means "Like," further right "Like Very Much." A left twist registers as "Dull" or "Very Dull." The emotional reactions of A.R.I.'s watchers flow into a central machine which combines them all into one big wavy line. This chart, picturing the audience's peaks of ecstasy and valleys of apathy, shows the manufacturer where to trim out dull spots in his picture. It is known as Preview Profile.

Moviemakers used to throw good advertising money after bad to promote an expensive flop. A.R.I. advises just the opposite. If the Preview Profile looks bad, the ad budget might just as well be slashed. If the preview pans out better than expected, the picture is given special treatment and bigger ballyhoo.

Criteria of cinema art aside, this kind of action for direct social control is politics. It aims not only at providing more and more sensation, but at the exploitation of all emotional sets and preferences as just so much raw material to be worked up by centralized control for purposes of super-profits. Clearly the manipulators of such controls are irresponsible and will probably so continue as long as the flow of merchandise and profits remains unchecked.

Meantime, these appetites for private power are inventing the means of possible political power for the future. And even these private activities are obviously political, indirectly. Perhaps, however, the relevant observation here is simply that appetite is essentially insatiable, and where it operates as the criterion of both action and enjoyment (that is, everywhere in the western world since the sixteenth century) it will infallibly discover congenial agencies (mechanical and political) of expression. Almost any political steps taken to curb the A.R.I. type of mind would inevitably transfer this private anarchy into a public tyranny, because that "mind" is not an exceptional one — it is universal. Actually, the A.R.I. type of activity provides our world with a spectacular externalized paradigm of its own inner drives. Creative political activity today, therefore, consists in rational contemplation of these paradigms. Carried out as an educational programme directed toward self-knowledge and self-criticism, the study of these sprightly fantasies of unrestricted appetitive life would constitute precisely that step toward moral and intellectual regeneration which we have always known must precede any sort of genuine improvement. To contemplate the products of our own appetites rather than to anathematize the people who are keen enough to exploit them — that is surely no programme which must await the setting up of committees or social machinery. It is the only form of adult education which could be called realistic and it is instanteously practicable. That the highbrows have been content merely to cock a snoot at the fauna and flora of popular commercial culture is sufficient testimony to the superficiality with which they have envisaged the nature of politics.

In this respect, the American is in a much happier position than the Englishman whose advertisements are such half-hearted and apologetic attempts to externalize his hopes and fears and appetites. American advertising is Cartesian. The English is Baconian. The American responds to showmanship, clarity of layout and distinctness of formulation. The Englishman, to judge by his ads (and I have some scores by me, collected in England over a period of three years), in his timid concern for demure good form falls into the empirical bog of self-defensive puns, archness, and snob-appeal. The American ad-men put on a decisively superior show and provide the analyst with a much greater variety of lively game. But to establish a national pre-eminence in this province is not to make more general claims.

The second item illustrating the totalitarian techniques of American market research occurs in a paper called "New Facts about Radio Research," by Arthur C. Nielsen, president of the A. C. Nielsen Company, "the world's largest marketing research organization." The paper appeared in 1946. It begins:

> A. C. Nielson Company, founded in 1923, provides an example of outstanding success based on long, unswerving and intelligent devotion to a difficult but worthy task. Educated in various branches of engineering and science, and accustomed to dealing with tangible facts, the early leaders of this company were convinced that some means could be found to substitute facts for much of the guesswork then used in guiding corporate marketing operations.
>
> Despite the commercial failure of all methods developed during the first ten years of operation, despite staggering operating losses which twice brought them to the brink of disaster, this group of pioneers persevered — because the great importance of the goal was very clear, and because some of the experiments seemed to show promise.

The tone of austere scientific dedication to a noble task is not phoney in any simple sense. The language of "human service" is rooted in the respectable neurotic formula of Adam Smith — public good through private greed — a face-saving device which developed a complex face of its own in the nineteenth century. In other words, the kind of self-deception in the language of "public service" is no longer private, but is vertically and horizontally effective, in the English-speaking world at least. The Rousseauistic formula to get the good society by liquidating "civilization," or the Marxian formula to get the classless society by liquidating the "middle class," are psychologically analogous — massive mechanisms of evasion and irresponsibility.

Well, the Nielsen Company have now lifted the problem of estimating audience character from the level of conjecture to that of certitude. The advertiser sponsoring any given programme wants to know precisely:

> (a) Average duration of listening; i.e., "holding power" of the programme.
> (b) Variations in audience size at each minute during the broadcast — to permit detection of programme elements which cause audience gains or losses, to locate commercials at moments when the audience is high, etc.

(c) Whether the programme reaches homes that already *use the product, or homes that offer opportunities for* conversion *of new users.*

For this purpose the Nielsen Audimeter has been devised, "the graphic recording instrument installed in a radio receiver in a scientifically selected radio home. By recording every twist of the dial, every minute of the day or night, the Audimeter obtains precious radio data not available through any other means." The Audimeter's data are then tabulated by "The Nielsen Decoder," which is only "one of the many mechanized operations which are producing high values for NIELSEN RADIO INDEX clients." And the installation of audimeters is determined "with utmost care to insure precise proportioning in accordance with a long list of marketing characteristics, including: 1, City size; 2, Family size; 3, Number of rooms; 4, Education; 5, Occupation; 6, Income; 7, Type of dwelling; 8, Number of radio receivers. The characteristics of each N.R.I. home are rechecked monthly, and replacement homes are chosen in a manner which keeps the sample accurately balanced at all times." Moreover, "relations with N.R.I. homes are maintained on such a sound basis that home turnover is limited largely to unavoidable and normal occurrences (e.g., deaths, divorces, fires, removals)."

The direction, as well as the appetitive drive, in this sort of research (the Gallup polls of public opinion are a more obvious but less impressive instance of the same thing) is to be noted in a recent book on *Reaching Juvenile Markets*. Like most American texts on advertising, it was written by a professional psychologist — in this case a child-psychologist. The book points to the enormous proportion of American income which is expended by and for children and analyses a variety of means for bringing child-pressure on the parents to increase and to control such expenditures. Children are more snobbish than adults, more concerned to conform to the tastes of the community in the use of well-known commercial brands, and so on. The schools offer a means for the subtle subsidization of various products. Special Lone Ranger and Superman radio features for children can do much, but the potentialities of this market are only beginning to be appreciated, etc.

A more common type of advertising manual, however, is that represented by *Psychology in Advertising* by A. T. Poffenberger, Ph.D., Sc.D., Professor of Psychology at Columbia University. This sort of book makes available to the copywriter the results of psychiatric research: "The psychoanalysts have made popular the conception of a kind of behavior which is a sort of compromise between the behavior growing out of desire and thinking behavior" (p. 15). To exploit the irrational and, at all times, to avoid the pitfalls of rational "sales resistance" aroused by the inept ad is the first law of advertising dynamics. Forty-four kinds of "attention-getting power" are graded (p. 90) in accordance with their statistically tested potency in an average community. At the top of the list are: Appetite-hunger 9.2; Love of offspring 9.1; Health 9.0; Sex attraction 8.9. And at the end of the list: Amusement 5.8; Shyness 4.2; Teasing 2.6. "Announcing the birth of a Petunia," said an ad in which a man and woman were bent over a flower-pot: "It takes emotion to move merchandise. *Better Homes and Gardens* [a magazine] is perpetual emotion."

Recently, with much public irritation being expressed at the blatancy, duration and frequency of radio commercials, careful tests have been made to determine the effect on the market. The result has been the discovery that irritation has great "attention-getting power" and that those irritated in this respect are reliable customers. Nausea has, therefore, become a new principle of commercial dynam-ics as of esthetics. It is not likely, however, to supplant but to reinforce the more familiar techniques, the most important of which is noted many times by Professor Poffenberger: "An appeal through the visual representation of motion will almost invariably find the nerve paths for that motion open, and is thus bound to get the attention of the reader and to induce in him some form of action" (p. 297). It is in their imaginative grasp of this dramatic principle that the American ad-men are first and the rest nowhere.

"Have you the courage to look ready for Romance: Want to look like a dream walking? . . . Well, you can, so easily! *Just by changing your powder shade*! . . . A delightful 'come hither' look that's so young and feminine — so very invit-ing!" (A bride in wedding-dress is joyfully whispering this to a thoughtful lady.)

A rugged and determined man with a cigar glints at the reader of a full-page ad of a clothing shop: "I'm TOUGH. Panty-waist stuff burns me. Work ten hours a day. Been at it since I was a kid. Gang at the plant call me 'Chief.' Own the place, now. Sure I've made money. Not a million — but enough to buy steak . . . And good clothes. Been getting my duds at Bond's ever since I shed knee pants . . . No big promises. No arty labels dangling high-hat prices. Just good clothes with plenty of guts."

Obviously the dramatic ad is a maker of "patterns of living" as much as the speech and gestures of movie idols. The peculiar idiom of a dead-end kid or a psychological freak may thus be sent up to the firing line of a nationwide adver-tising campaign to provide temporary emotional strategies for millions of adolescents: A wishful but futile gent beside a self-possessed girl on a love-seat: "I love you! said Pete. 'I like you, too!' said Ann. 'Tell me more,' said Pete. 'You look *so* nice, especially around the neck.' 'Ah,' said Pete. 'That is my Arrow Collar.' . . . P.S. Tough, Pete. But remember — where there's an Arrow, can a girl be far behind?" The ads help old and young to "get hep."

An extremely popular technique is the dramatic sequence presented in four or five separate scenes: Tommy comes home from school with a black eye and is questioned by his lovely young mother. He reluctantly tells her that the kids have been taunting him about how his father is going out with other women. He has had to defend his mother's sex-appeal. Mortified, she hastens to get the appropri-ate toothpaste. Next morning, Mom, radiant in panties and bra', brushing her teeth in the bathroom, tells Tommy "it works." Later, Tommy and his friends peek round the corner into the living-room where Dad is waltzing Mom around to radio music. "Gee," says one of the kids, "looks like he's going to haul off and kiss her." "Yep," says Tommy, "you can't say my Dad hangs around with other girls now." This sort of Ad appears in the Sunday Comic Section. Reaching the Juvenile Market.

"Success story of a man in a high position." Picture of blithesome business man seated aloft in the petals of a huge daffodil: "Sitting pretty? You bet . . . this fellow knows how to win and influence customers! He keeps track of their important business events and honors each occasion by sending wonderful fresh flowers by Wire." The wit of the pictorial feature includes an allusion to Jack's bean-stalk.

A nearly nude debutante with zestful abandon applying perfume and sparkling at the reader: "I'm using 'Unconditional Surrender' since he got 6NX Appeal!" "How can *you* get 6NX Appeal? . . . by using the only blades created by the scientific, secret 6NX process. . . . 'Single' men can reach for a star, too!" This is typical of the indirect approach to the American male. Psychological tests prove that he is shy of direct efforts to interest him in glamorizing himself. As social catalysts the ads help also to overcome boy-girl shyness. The girl spots 6NX or some other approved mark of compliance with nationally accredited goods. The boy smells "Unconditional Surrender," and the first thing you know they're able to converse. College courses in "charm" and "gallantry" may soon be unnecessary.

A beautiful girl seated by the telephone while Mom, troubled, hovers in door-way: "Borderline Anaemia deprives a girl of glamor . . . and dates! Medical science says: Thousands who have pale faces — whose strength is at low ebb — may have a blood deficiency. So many girls are 'too tired' to keep up with the crowd — watch romance pass them by because they haven't the energy to make them attractive!"

These ads console and encourage the forlorn by picturing the solitude and neglect suffered by the most ravishing chicks. They analyse the causes of every type of human failure and indicate the scientifically certified formula for "instantaneous or money-back results." The fault is not in our stars but our jars that we are underlings. They display the most ordinary persons surrounded by luxury and old-world charm, suggesting that "a prince and a castle are given away free with every package." The most trashy types of food, crockery, or furniture are exhibited in palatial circumstances. And this "law of association" leads the larger business monopolies to sponsor "the arts" by presenting their product always in conjunction with some aroma of the old masters of paint, pen or music. But just how far these billionaire campaigns of systematic sophistry and hallucination contribute to worsening any given state of affairs would be hard to say. Because there is really nothing in these richly efflorescent ads which has not been deeply wished by the population for a long time. They aren't so much phenomena of a Machiavellian tyranny as the poor man's orchids — both a compensation and a promise for beauty denied. Now, moreover, that the luxuriant and prurient chaos of human passions is thrust forward and gyrated in this way for our daily contemplation, there is the increasing possibility of the recovery of rational detachment. The authors of the Declaration of Independence and the American Constitution were not obsessed with some compulsive psychological strategy for disguising their own irrational wishes or intentions like a Rousseau or a Nietzsche. And their wisdom is far from extinct in the U.S.A. So that, should the energy which activates the ad-men (and the industrial stalks on which they are the passion-flowers) be transferred to the world of political speculation and creation, America could still fulfill many of its broken Utopian promises, because its Jeffersonian tradition is still intact, and likewise its psychological vigour. The two things aren't flowing in the same channels, however, and that is precisely the thing which could be brought about by a frank educational programme based on the curriculum provided by the ad-men.

2

The Mechanical Bride

Preface

Ours is the first age in which many thousands of the best-trained individual minds have made it a full-time business to get inside the collective public mind. To get inside in order to manipulate, exploit, control is the object now. And to generate heat not light is the intention. To keep everybody in the helpless state engendered by prolonged mental rutting is the effect of many ads and much entertainment alike.

Since so many minds are engaged in bringing about this condition of public helplessness, and since these programs of commercial education are so much more expensive and influential than the relatively puny offerings sponsored by schools and colleges, it seemed fitting to devise a method for reversing the process. Why not use the new commercial education as a means to enlightening its intended prey? Why not assist the public to observe consciously the drama which is intended to operate upon it unconsciously?

As this method was followed, "A Descent Into The Maelstrom" by Edgar Poe kept coming to mind. Poe's sailor saved himself by studying the action of the whirlpool and by co-operating with it. The present book likewise makes few attempts to attack the very considerable currents and pressures set up around us today by the mechanical agencies of the press, radio, movies, and advertising. It does attempt to set the reader at the center of the revolving picture created by these affairs where he may observe the action that is in progress and in which everybody is involved. From the analysis of that action, it is hoped, many individual strategies may suggest themselves.

But it is seldom the business of this book to take account of such strategies.

Poe's sailor says that when locked in by the whirling walls and the numerous objects which floated in that environment:

I must *have been delirious, for I even sought* amusement *in speculating upon the relative velocities of their several descents toward the foam below.*

It was this amusement born of his rational detachment as a spectator of his own situation that gave him the thread which led him out of the Labyrinth. And it is in the same spirit that this book is offered as an amusement. Many who are accustomed to the note of moral indignation will mistake this amusement for mere indifference. But the time for anger and protest is in the early stages of a new process. The present stage is extremely advanced. Moreover, it is full, not only of destructiveness but also of promises of rich new developments to which moral indignation is a very poor guide.

Most of the exhibits in this book

21

have been selected because of their typical and familiar quality. They represent a world of social myths or forms and speak a language we both know and do not know. After making his study of the nursery rhyme, "Where are you going, my pretty maid?" the anthropologist C. B. Lewis pointed out that "the folk has neither part nor lot in the making of folklore." That is also true of the folklore of industrial man, so much of which stems from the laboratory, the studio, and the advertising agencies. But amid the diversity of our inventions and abstract techniques of production and distribution there will be found a great degree of cohesion and unity. This consistency is not conscious in origin or effect and seems to arise from a sort of collective dream. For that reason, as well as because of the widespread popularity of these objects and processes, they are here referred to as "the folklore of industrial man." They are unfolded by exhibit and commentary as a single landscape. A whirling phantasmagoria can be grasped only when arrested for contemplation. And this very arrest is also a release from the usual participation.

The unity is not imposed upon this diversity, since any other selection of exhibits would reveal the same dynamic patterns. The fact that the present exhibits are not selected to prove a case but to reveal a complex situation, it is the effort of the book to illustrate by frequent cross-reference to other materials that are not included here. And it is the procedure of the book to use the commentaries on the exhibits merely as a means of releasing some of their intelligible meaning. No effort has been made to exhaust their meaning.

The various ideas and concepts introduced in the commentaries are intended to provide positions from which to examine the exhibits. They are not conclusions in which anybody is expected to rest but are intended merely as points of departure. This is an approach which it is hard to make clear at a time when most books offer a single idea as a means of unifying a troupe of observations. Concepts are provisional affairs for apprehending reality; their value is in the grip they provide. This book, therefore, tries to present at once representative aspects of the reality and a wide range of ideas for taking hold of it. The ideas are very secondary devices for clambering up and over rock faces. Those readers who undertake merely to query the ideas will miss their use for getting at the material.

A film expert, speaking of the value of the movie medium for selling North to South America, noted that:

> *the propaganda value of this simultaneous audio-visual impression is very high, for it standardizes thought by supplying the spectator with a ready-made visual image before he has time to conjure up an interpretation of his own.*

This book reverses that process by providing typical visual imagery of our environment and dislocating it into meaning by inspection. Where visual symbols have been employed in an effort to paralyze the mind, they are here used as a means of energizing it. It is observable that the more illusion and falsehood needed to maintain any given state of affairs, the more tyranny is needed to maintain the illusion and falsehood. Today the tyrant rules not by club or fist, but, disguised as a market researcher, he shepherds his flocks in the ways of utility and comfort.

Because of the circulating point of view in this book, there is no need for it to be read in any special order. Any part of the book provides one or more views of the same social landscape. Ever since Buckhardt saw that the meaning of Machiavelli's method was to turn the state into a work of art by the rational manipulation of power, it has been an open possibility to apply the method of art analysis to the critical evaluation of society. That is attempted here. The Western world, dedicated since the sixteenth century to the increase and consolidation of the power of the state, has developed an artistic unity of effect which makes artistic criticism of that effect quite feasible. Art criticism is free to point to the various means employed to get the effect, as well as to decide whether the effect was worth attempting. As such, with regard to the modern state, it can be a citadel of inclusive awareness amid the dim dreams of collective consciousness.

I wish to acknowledge the advantage I have enjoyed in reading unpublished views of Professor David Riesman on the consumer mentality. To Professor W. T. Easterbrook I owe many enlightening conversations on the problems of bureaucracy and enterprise. And to Professor Felix Giovanelli I am in debt not only for the stimulus of discussion but for his prolonged assistance with the many publishing problems which have attended the entire work.

The Mechanical Bride

Anybody who takes time to study the techniques of pictorial reportage in the popular press and magazines will easily find a dominant pattern composed of sex and technology. Hovering around this pair will usually be found images of hectic speed, mayhem, violence, and sudden death. *Look* and *Life* are only the most obvious places in which to study this cluster of interests. Amid what otherwise may appear as a mere hodgepodge of isolated events, this very consistent pattern stands out. I do not pretend to understand all of it, but it is there for everyone to study, and it is certainly linked to the patterns noted in "Love-Goddess Assembly Line." Many a time have the legs in this exhibit stood on their pedestal by the tall column of *Life's* staff, emblemizing the trick that keeps the big team clicking. They are the slick and visible sign of the dynamo purring contentedly in the Time and Life building, but not only there. And they need to be seen in association with those window displays of car engines on a revolving pedestal, with pistons sliding smoothly

---

Noticed any very spare parts lately?

Have you got what it takes to hook a date? See us for the highest bid on your old model.

"The walk," "the legs," "the body," "the hips," "the look," "the lips." Did she fall off a wall? Call all the king's horses and men.

while a loudspeaker conveys Strauss waltzes to those on the sidewalk.

To the mind of the modern girl, legs, like busts, are power points which she has been taught to tailor, but as parts of the success kit rather than erotically or sensuously. She swings her legs from the hip with masculine drive and confidence. She knows that "a long-legged gal can go places." As such, her legs are not intimately associated with her taste or with her unique self but are merely display objects like the grill work on a car. They are date-baited power levers for the management of the male audience.

Thus, for example, the legs "on a Pedestal" presented by the Gotham Hosiery company are one facet of our "replaceable parts" cultural dynamics. In a specialist world it is natural that we should select some single part of the body for attention. Al Capp expressed this ironically when he had Li'l Abner fall desperately in love with the pictorial scrap of a woman's knee, saying (January 21, 1950), "Why *not*? Some boys fall in love with the expression on a gal's *face*. Ah is a knee man!" Four months and many lethal and romantic adventures later, Li'l Abner was closing in on the owner of the knee.

The "Phantom Pencil Seam Nylons" ad presents another set of spare parts against a romantic landscape. Some people have heard of "Ideas with legs," but everybody today has been brought up on pictures like these, which would rather appear to be "legs with ideas." Legs today have been indoctrinated. They are self-conscious. They speak. They have huge audiences. They are taken on dates. And in varying degrees the ad agencies have extended this specialist treatment to every other segment of the feminine anatomy. A car plus a well-filled pair of nylons is a recognized formula for both feminine and male success and happiness. Ads like these not only express but also encourage that strange dissociation of sex not only from the human person but even from the unity of the body. This visual and not particularly voluptuous character of commercially sponsored glamour is perhaps what gives it so heavy a narcissistic quality. The brittle, self-conscious pose of the mannequin suggests the activities of competitive display rather than spontaneous sensuality. And the smartly turned-out girl walks and behaves like a being who *sees* herself as a slick object rather than is aware of herself as a person. "Ever see a dream walking?" asks a glamour ad. The Hiroshima bomb was named "Gilda" in honor of Rita Hayworth.

Current sociological study of the precocious dating habits of middle-class children reveals that neither sex nor personal interest in other persons is responsible so much as an eagerness to be "in there pitching." This may be reassuring to the parents of the young, but it may create insoluble problems for the same youngsters later on. When sex later becomes a personal actuality, the established feminine pattern of sex as an instrument of power, in an industrial and consumer contest, is a liability. The switch-over from competitive display to personal affec-

tion is not easy for the girl. Her mannequin past is in the way. On the male, this display of power to which he is expected to respond with cars and dates has various effects. The display of current feminine sex power seems to many males to demand an impossible virility of assertion.

*Fair tresses man's imperial race
  ensnare,
And beauty draws us with a single
  hair.*

Men are readily captured by such gentleness and guile, but, surrounded by legs on pedestals, they feel not won but slugged. To this current exaggeration of date-bait some people reply that the glamour business, like the entertainment world, is crammed with both women-haters and men-haters of dubious sex polarity. Hence the malicious insistence on a sort of abstract sex. But whatever truth there may be in this, there is more obvious truth in the way in which sex has been exaggerated by getting hooked to the mechanisms of the market and the impersonal techniques of industrial production.

As early as 1872, Samuel Butler's *Erewhon* explored the curious ways in which machines were coming to resemble organisms not only in the way they obtained power by digestion of fuel but in their capacity to evolve ever new types of themselves with the help of the machine tenders. This organic character of the machines, he saw, was more than matched by the speed with which people who minded them were taking on the rigidity and thoughtless behaviorism of the machine. In a pre-industrial world a great swordsman, horseman, or animal-breeder was expected to take on some of the character of his interests. But how much more is this the case with great crowds of people who spend their waking energies on using and improving machines with powers so very much greater than theirs.

It would be a mistake, therefore, to equate the intensity of the current glamour campaigns and techniques with any corresponding new heights of a man-woman madness. Sex weariness and sex sluggishness are, in measure at least, both the cause and increasingly the outcome of these campaigns. No sensitivity of response could long survive such a barrage. What does survive is the view of the human body as a sort of love-machine capable merely of specific thrills. This extremely behavioristic view of sex, which reduces sex experience to a problem in mechanics and hygiene, is exactly what is implied and expressed on all sides. It makes inevitable both the divorce between physical pleasure and reproduction and also the case for homosexuality. In the era of thinking machines, it would be surprising, indeed, if the love-machine were not thought of as well.

Woman appears as a disagreeable but challenging sex machine in Edmund Wilson's *Memoirs of Hecate County*. But the hero, as an expert sex mechanic, does a skillful job on a variety of these coldly intricate and maxfactorized products of the assembly line. There may be some relation between the fact that England, the first country to develop know-how and industrial technique, was also the first to develop the *ideal* of the frigid woman.

In Budd Schulberg's *What Makes Sammy Run?*, Kit, the heroine, is fascinated by the ferocious little robot that is Sammy. She hates him but is curious to know what it would be like to have this dynamo of pep and drive roaring inside her. With situations of this sort we move over into territory somehow allied to sex and technology but also very closely related to destruction and death. There are some signs that sex weariness may be a factor in the cult of violence, although Wilhelm Reich, the psychologist, argues that it is a mere substitute for sex in those who have acquired the rigidities of a mechanized environment. This view is ably sponsored in G. Legman's *Love and Death*, a study of violence in comic books and literature. And his book certainly doesn't contradict anything said here. But there is surely much to be said also for the view that sadistic violence, real or fictional, in some situations is an attempt to invade persons not only sexually but metaphysically. It is an effort to pass the frontiers of sex, to achieve a more intense thrill than sex affords. There was certainly a good deal of destruction intermixed with the pleasure ideals of the Marquis de Sade.

A news item of March 2, 1950, reported the five-hour flight of a jet Vampire from coast to coast. When the pilot climbed out, he said only that "It

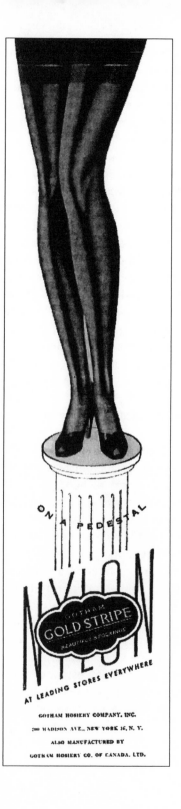

was rather boring." For the satiated, both sex and speed are pretty boring until the element of danger and even death is introduced. Sensation and sadism are near twins. And for those for whom the sex act has come to seem mechanical and merely the meeting and manipulation of body parts, there often remains a hunger which can be called metaphysical but which is not recognized as such, and which seeks satisfaction in physical danger, or sometimes in torture, suicide, or murder. Many of the Frankenstein fantasies depend on the horror of a synthetic robot running amok in revenge for its lack of a "soul." Is this not merely a symbolic way of expressing the actual fact that many people have become so mechanized that they feel a dim resentment at being deprived of full human status?

This is a different way of phrasing what is for Wilhelm Reich only a behavioristic fact. Too simply, he thinks of our machine landscape as an environment which makes people incapable of genital satisfaction. Therefore, he says, they break out in fascist violence. Complete and frequent genital satisfaction from the cradle to the grave is the only way, he suggests, to avoid the recurrence of the age-old vicious circle of patriarchal authority and mechanical servitude. Reflection on *Moby Dick* in his *Studies in Classic American Literature*, D. H. Lawrence saw deeper:

So you see, the sinking of the Pequod was only a metaphysical tragedy, after all. The world goes on just the same. The ship of the soul is sunk. But the machine-manipulating body works just the same: digests, chews gum, admires Botticelli, and aches with amorous love.

Was it not the mistake of D. H. Lawrence to overlook the comedy in a situation of this type? The human person who thinks, works, or dreams himself into the role of a machine is as funny an object as the world provides. And, in fact, he can only be freed from this trap by the detaching power of wild laughter. The famous portrait of a "Nude Descending a Staircase," with its resemblance to an artichoke doing a strip tease, is a cleansing bit of fun intended to free the human robot from his dreamlike fetters. And so with Wyndham Lewis's *The Apes of God*, Picasso's *Doll Women*, and *Finnegans Wake* by James Joyce — the latter especially being a great intellectual effort aimed at rinsing the Augean stables of speech and society with geysers of laughter. It is not a laughter or comedy to be compared with the whimsy-whamsy article of James Thurber or Ogden Nash. For the latter kind is merely a narcotic which confirms the victim in a condition he has neither the energy nor appetite to change.

In a story called "The Girl with the Hungry Eyes," by Fritz Leiber, an ad photographer gives a job to a not too promising model. Soon, however, she is "plastered all over the country" because she has the hungriest eyes in the world. "Nothing vulgar, but just the same they're looking at you with a hunger that's all sex and something more than sex." Something similar may be said of the legs on a pedestal. Abstracted from the body that gives them their ordinary meaning, they become "something more than sex," a metaphysical enticement, a cerebral itch, an abstract torment. Mr. Leiber's girl hypnotizes the country with her hungry eyes and finally accepts the attentions of the photographer who barely escapes with his life. In this vampire, not of the blood but of spirit, he finds "the horror behind the bright billboard. . . . She's the eyes that lead you on and on and then show you death." She says to him: "I want you. I want your high spots. I want everything that's made you happy and everything that's hurt you bad. I want your first girl. . . . I want that licking. . . . I want Betty's legs. . . . I want your mother's death. . . . I want your wanting me. I want your life. Feed me, baby, feed me."

As an instance of how the curious fusion of sex, technology and death persists amid the most unlikely circumstances, the reader may be interested in a display of "Ten Years of *Look*" (October 29, 1946), in which the central picture was a wounded man coming home "to face it all another day down another death-swept road." Flanking him was a sprawling pin-up: "Half a million servicemen wrote in for this one." And underneath him in exactly the same posture of surrender as the pin-up girl was a nude female corpse with a rope around the neck: "Enraged Nazis hanged this Russian guerrilla." If only "for increased reading pleasure" readers should study these editorial ghoul techniques — conscious or not as they may be — and their poetic associations of linked and contrasting imagery.

Perhaps that is what the public wants when it reaches out for the *inside* story smoking hot from the entrails of vice or innocence. That may well be what draws people to the death shows of the speedways and fills the press and magazines with close-ups of executions, suicides, and smashed bodies. A metaphysical hunger to experience everything sexually, to pluck out the heart of the mystery for a super-thrill.

Life, on January 5, 1948, ran a big picture captioned "Ten Seconds Before Death." A Chicago woman called the press and told them she was going to commit suicide. A photographer rushed to her apartment and snapped her. "Just as he took this anguished portrait, she brushed by him, leaped out the third-story window to her death."

This is merely an extreme instance of what is literally ghoulishness. The ghoul tears and devours human flesh in search of he knows not what. His hunger is not earthly. And a very large section of the "human interest" and "true story" activity of our time wears the face of the ghoul and the vampire. That is probably the meaning of the popular phrases "the inside dirt," the "real inside dope." There is very little stress on understanding as compared with the immediate bang of "history in the making." Get the *feel* of it. Put that sidewalk microphone right up against the heart of that school kid who is looking at the Empire State Building for the first time. "Shirley Temple gets her first screen kiss in a picture you'll never forget," and so on.

In all such situations the role of modern technology in providing ever intenser thrills is evident. Mr. Leiber has thus written a very witty parable which shows an intuitive grasp of the mysterious links between sex, technology, and death. Many people were disagreeably surprised by the similar parable of Charlie Chaplin's *Monsieur Verdoux*. The wistful, self-pitying, chivalrous little figure had gone. Here instead was a lady killer in every sense. As Parker Tyler pointed out in his book *Chaplin: Last of the Clowns*, the early Charlie was a man-child seeking the security of the womb in a harsh world. In *Monsieur Verdoux* he in a sense exchanges womb for tomb. In order to have material comfort and security, he is ready to kill. But womb, tomb, and comfort have always been interchangeable symbols in his world. He was the giant killer in his first pictures, the lady killer in his last. The same mechanism of sentimentality dominates both. In other words, his is a popular dream art which works trance-like inside a situation that is never grasped or seen. And this trance seems to be what perpetuated the widely occurring cluster image of sex, technology, and death which constitutes the mystery of the mechanical bride.

From Da Vinci to Holmes

Joyce's famous remark that, "though he might have been more humble, there's no police like Holmes," contains a world of insight. It includes the modern world and elucidates it at the same instant. Joyce explored popular phraseology and heroes with a precision which this book cannot emulate. In the above phrase which refers to "no place like home," Joyce diagnoses the collapse of family life and the rise of the police state amidst a welter of sentiment which is partly rosy and partly lethal. Homes are now a part of a police system. Holmes, the home-hater and woman-hater, is the hero of the "home-loving" and feminized middle class. The arrogant, sterile Holmes and the happy prolific homes of the late Victorian world are fused in a single image which arrests the mind for contemplation and insight. The passion for Holmes and man-hunting literature (which gives the modern world a major point of correspondence with the symbolic figure of Nimrod and the tower of Babel) goes along with the commercial passion for exploiting the values of childhood, femininity, and domesticity. On paper there has never been such a cult of the home. In entertainment there has never been such a cult of the sleuth.

To provide in a few words a pedigree for the figure of the sleuth who dominates thriller fiction may not be very convincing. The quickest way to get a view of the matter is via Holmes, Kipling, and Darwin. However, Kipling's Mowgli and Edgar Queeny's "granitic believer in the law of the jungle," when taken together, open up interrelations between familiar vistas.

In the opening paragraph of Doyle's *A Scandal in Bohemia*, Holmes is described as follows:

He was, I take it, the most perfect reasoning and observing machine that the world has seen; but, as a lover, he would have placed himself in a false position. He never spoke of the softer passions save with a gibe and a sneer . . . Grit in a sensitive instrument, or a crack in one of his own high-power lenses, would not be more disturbing than a strong emotion in a nature such as his.

Here is the split man of the head-versus-heart, thought-versus-feeling type who appeared in the early seventeenth century. But it was not until Darwin that the head (science) became definitely and consciously antisocial. Mr. Queeny derives his "law of the jungle" versus "crusading idealist" from this later nineteenth-century phase of the older split.

Why are both scientist and artist crackpots and pariahs in the popular imagination?

Holmes, Renaissance titan or Last of the Mohicans?

Watson, wife or mother of the virtuoso of crime?

The sleuth cult foreshadows the arrival of the police state?

Could anything exceed the sentimentality or the lavish emotion with which Doyle (and all other writers of crime stories) embellish the figure of the detective? It is through the eyes of some doting Watson, dim of brain, or the dewy eyes of the female secretary, wistfully adoring, that the superman is seen and felt by the reader. This Nietzschean figure achieves his self-dramatization not directly, like the nihilistic malcontents of the Elizabethan stage, but on the inner stage of a mass dream. The sleuth is a recognizable descendant of the heroes who died in the odor of Seneca, but here he lives on, indestructibly, to report his own cause to the unsatisfied. Like the malcontent, the sleuth embodies an attitude, a personal strategy for meeting an opaque and bewildering situation. Both reject the attitude of submission and adjustment to obvious social pressures, affirming themselves as vividly as they can. But where have we met Doyle's description before? Writing in 1868, Thomas Henry Huxley said:

That man, I think, has had a liberal education who has been so trained in his youth that his body is the ready servant of his will, and does with ease and pleasure all the work, that as a mechanism, it is capable of; whose intellect is a clear, cold, logic engine, with all the parts of equal strength, and in smooth working order; ready like a steam engine to be turned to any kind of work. . . .

To many people in 1868 this sentimental robotism didn't seem especially laughable as a "human" ideal. Perhaps not everybody even today would be prepared to recognize it for the lethal formula that it is. The connections between "the law of the jungle," "the spirit of enterprise," and "ringside seat" for the diesel-engine show become evident. Between "The Sparrow versus the Hawk" spirit in education and society, and the Holmes-Huxley-Kipling circuit, the relationship appears in Doyle's views of education in his inventory of Holmes's intellectual tools:

1. Knowledge of Literature — Nil
2. Knowledge of Philosophy — Nil
3. Knowledge of Astronomy — Nil
4. Knowledge of Politics — Feeble
5. Knowledge of Botany — Variable, well up in belladonna, opium and poisons generally
6. Knowledge of Geology — Practical but limited
7. Knowledge of Chemistry — Profound
8. Knowledge of Anatomy — Accurate
9. Knowledge of Sensational Literature — Immense. He appears to know every detail of every horror perpetrated in the century.

In addition, Holmes is a violinist, an all-around athlete, and a lawyer. That is what Doyle considered the ideal mental kit for the man-hunter. Note the slavering chop-smacking stress on Holmes's "immense" erudition in mayhem and murder. That is seemingly the price our world has paid for developing a mind that it sentimentally regards as a cold logic engine. And the curious reader will find it profitable to consult Wyndham Lewis's *Art of Being Ruled* on the nature of the modern scientist's obsession with the romance of destruction.

Let us get the habit of looking very closely at the detached scientific mind, to see whether its boasted detachment amounts to very much besides not choosing to link the significance of one part of its actions to other parts. In short, is its "detachment" just irresponsibility? Sherlock Holmes had about as much detachment as Buck Rogers or those who worked on the first atomic project and later dramatized the business for *The March of Time*, ardently playing themselves in this great melodrama of destruction.

Doyle, in common with his age and ours, was obsessed with the psychic stench that rose from his own splintered ego. This stench was not something that he understood or studied, like a Kirkegaard or a Baudelaire. But in it he lived and wallowed with strictly sensational satisfaction, like that passionate fondler of little girls, Lewis Carroll. A better test case for investigation than the sleuth himself would be hard to find, because by every test he is the superman of our dreams.

Even a Hemingway or a Steinbeck has a firmer grasp of realities and is much less emotionally involved in a merely tiny aspect of human affairs than a Doyle or the typical scientist. And it is worth noting the obvious contrast between the Hemingway hero and the sleuth. The sleuth acts, while the Hemingway hero suffers. The one dishes it out, the other has things done to him. The humanitarian victim type would seem to stem from the period of Don Quixote. His ineffectual benevolence becomes the typical mode of Fielding's *Tcm Jones* as also of the romantic heroes of Scott, Thackeray, and Dickens. Nothing could be less like the aggressive and resourceful sleuth than these familiar figures from romantic fiction past and present. They suffer violence. The modern detective evokes it. So that there is a good deal of point in the claim that detective fiction is scientific. For the popular notion of the scientist as the center of a world of fantastic violence and malignity not only coincides with the world of violence portrayed in detective fiction but with the quality of much scientific vision and speculation.

The superman of thriller fiction, then, is a representative of an attitude for which all classes and conditions in our society have either an open or secret admiration. His pedigree, therefore, must be viewed with some curiosity. Among the common features of all sleuths is, first, their individualism and lonely pride; next, their man-of-the-worldishness; third, their multifarious but specialized learning; and, fourth, their passion for action and excitement. All four of these notes are also features of the Renaissance virtuoso. Since then they have become the marks of "the aristocratic type," especially as embodied in the English public-school boy; but there is no space here to trace the stages by which the intense individualism of this Renaissance scholar-courtier-soldier combination (mainly known to us by Hamlet) became in the Lovelace of Samuel Richardson's *Clarissa* and for the middle classes of the eighteenth century the representative of feudalism and the Devil. Yet the connection for the commercial or trading mind between the haughty aristocrat and the Devil is perfectly plain for the age of the Marquis de Sade, Lord Byron, Poe, and Baudelaire. It would be impossible to exaggerate the fascination which Byron held for the soul of the Watsonian shopkeeper and his family. Byron was the embodiment of the masochistic middle-class dream. The mixture of fear, awe, admiration, and revulsion which he inspired was such that henceforth all rebellion against the spirit of hawking and huckstering takes in large measure the Byronic form. That is how, for example, the image of the disdainful aesthete was achieved — a mold into which the shopkeeper's son could easily pour himself, since it embodies not only disgust with trade but devotion to beauty.

Dupin, the first detective, is thus an aesthete and a dandy. He was created by Poe, himself the aesthete and the dandy. Holmes arrived some decades later. The Byronic markings are strong on Holmes. Also the quarterings of the aesthete in his capricious interest in music, in "murder as a fine art," and his contempt for domesticity. That the preoccupation with crime is, equally in Poe and De Quincey, an expression of sadistic revolt against a sordid world devoted to money and the police protection of "ill-gotten gains," needs very little investigation. That the lonely aesthete-detective is at once a rebel against the crude middle-class conformity and also a type of extreme initiative and the individualism helps however to explain the ambiguity of his appeal for the same middle class. He is at once a type of disinterested aristocratic superiority and of middle-class failure to create new social values. It is easy to note in this the same ambiguity that presides over commercial ads which feature simultaneously quality and cheapness, refinement and availability.

However, a major feature of the modern sleuth notably absent from Poe's Dupin is the quality of the manhunter. The superman features don't change from Da Vinci to Byron and Heathcliff, but the man-hunting proclivities, the endless sniffing out along the road to the supreme metaphysical thrill of murder, are not evident until

Holmes. Byron and Poe were content with the aura of incest as a mark and gesture of antisocial thrill and also of emotional avarice. Baudelaire, Rimbaud, and Wilde explored other sexual variants of the antisocial. But murder, the cerebral itch to hunt down the inmost guilt and secret essence of man, that is the thrill sought by the man-hunter and shared by the thriller fans. Of course, it is vaguely present in all confessional literature of the romantic period, but usually in connection with other interests. Whereas in the literature of crime detection the concentration of specialized thrill is crudely focused on the hunt and the kill.

During the fifty years between Poe's Dupin and the appearance of Holmes, the European cult of Fenimore Cooper's redskins provides the necessary explanation of the rise of that hybrid of aesthete and man-hunter which dominates the popular mind today. The noble savage, utterly above society and commerce, with his unspoiled faculties of a superhuman perfection and keenness, his nose for danger, his eye for clues, and his stomach for scalps — here is the complex image built up sentimentally by Rousseau, digested by Darwin, and expressed by Doyle as the type at once of the sleuth and of the scientific mind.

3

Culture Is Our Business

Invisible Environment

Fish don't know water exists till beached.

A MESSAGE TO THE FISH

I sent a message to the fish,
I told them "this is what I wish" (Through the
Looking-Glass)

The hypnotic effect of yesterday's successes nourishes the
bureaucratic egos.

A newspaper is a corporate symbolist poem,
environmental and invisible, as poem.

Since in any situation 10 percent of the events cause 90 percent, we
ignore the 10 percent and are stunned by the 90 percent. Without
an anti-environment, all environments are invisible. The role of the
artist is to create anti-environments as a means of perception and
adjustment. Hamlet's sleuth technique for coping with the hidden
environment around him was that of the artist: "As I perchance here-
after shall think meet to put an antic disposition on"...
(I, v, 171-72)

Hugh Trevor-Roper explains the process of
making environments invisible and invincible
as follows: "Any society, as long as it is, or
feels itself to be, a working society, tends to
invest in itself: a military society tends to
become more military, a bureaucratic society
more bureaucratic...the dominant military
or official or commercial classes cannot easily
change their orientation...." (The Rise of
Christian Europe, London, Thames and
Hudson, 1965)

"Numbed to death by booze and tranquillizers" is an average
strategy for "keeping in touch" with a runaway world.

WITHOUT CENTERS OR MARGINS

The telegraph press mosaic is acoustic space as much as an electric circus.

One touch of Nature makes the whole world tin.

Auditory and tactile space have always been interleaved. If tactility is the space of the interval, the interval is the cause of closure and rhythm, or upbeat and downbeat.

Acoustic space is totally discontinuous, like touch. It is a sphere without centers or margins, as Professor Botts of the University of Toronto explained a generation ago.

Why was a visually oriented, literate, world indifferent to all but Euclidean space—until Lewis Carroll and Albert Einstein?

Audile-tactile space is the space of involvement. We "lose touch" without it. Visual space is the space of detachment and the public precautions we call "scientific method" and scholarly or citational erudition.

Jazz As Easy As Conversation. (N.Y. Times, Aug. 18/68)

Speech Scientist Wants to Use the Sound of the Human Voice to Help Protect Confidential Information.

Now—answers are friendlier

In fact, everyone in the company has a better outlook with the simple addition of Music by Muzak.*

Every quarter hour of Muzak programming changes by plan. Even your best employees get the lift they need, at the right time, to ease the monotony of daily routine.

Muzak requires no complicated on-premise equipment. No tapes. No records. Muzak programs come from one central distribution point. All you have to do is turn it on. And—your Muzak sound system can be used for paging and public address as well!

Unlike ordinary entertainment music, Muzak is a modern-management tool which improves communications, combats employee fatigue, boredom and tension. The proven way of improving on-time, on-the-job performance. Controlled tests have proved that Muzak programming can increase efficiency 8%, reduce errors over 17%. Write for details. *music by Muzak*

Muzak—A Division of Wrather Corporation, 229 Park Avenue South, New York, N.Y. 10003

GIVE ME
THE MOON FOR A BLANKET

**Soviets say moon soil can shelter men.
(Toronto Globe and Mail, April 10/68)**

A bedbug can detect the presence of a man two whole city blocks away, and a woman—well.... Our society is well known to the bedbug. (Erb, p. 51.)

**"Happiness is for the Pigs" is the title of an
essay by Herman Tennesen. (The Journal of
Existentialism, Winter, 1966)**

Anthony Jay quotes "Pussycat, pussycat, where have you been?" as insight into the tendency of people to reduce all reality to their own dimensions and interests. The cat didn't see the Queen, but saw a little mouse under the royal chair. Such is the clue in the headline: "Did Not Believe Nazis Killing Jews: The German Chancellor heard it all as Allied propaganda." (Kiesinger, Toronto Globe and Mail, July 5/68)

**E. R. Leach, the anthropologist, notes that
mere classification as "immoral" rendered
80,000 elegant London courtesans quite
invisible to Dickens and his readers. They
were a tourist attraction famous throughout
Europe....**

In the same way, both Stalin and Hitler were looked upon as saints by millions of their fellow countrymen, even in the midst of the holocaust... the Russian and German peoples simply "refused to know" what was going on right under their noses." (Runaway World?, Oxford Press, 1968)

**Since Sputnik, the earth has been wrapped in
a dome-like blanket or bubble. Nature ended.
Art took over the ambidextrous universe. We
continue to talk of a machine world.**

It just sits there and does what it's told –

– 230,922 miles away.

Surveyor, designed and built by Hughes

Surveyor, built for NASA and Jet Propulsion Laboratory, responds
immediately to 256 different kinds of commands from earth.

HUGHES
HUGHES AIRCRAFT COMPANY

THE BOOK ARRIVES TOO LATE

The Concept of Dread, by Soren Kierkegaard, appeared in 1844, first year of the commercial telegraph (Baltimore to Washington). It mentions the telegraph as a reason for dread and nowness or existenz.

All the fuss and feathers about existentialism was the direct result of pulling out the connections between events as in a telegraph newspaper, pulling the story line of art as in symbolism.

The existentialist trauma had a physical basis in the first electric extension of our nervous system.

Professor Morse's telegraph is not only an era in the transmission of intelligence, but it has originated in the mind of an entirely new class of ideas, a new species of consciousness. Never before was anyone conscious that he knew with certainty what events were at that moment passing in a distant city—40, 100 or 500 miles off. For example, it is now precisely 11 o'clock. The telegraph announces as follows: 11 o'clock—Senator Walker is now replying to Mr. Butler upon the adoption of the two-thirds rule. It requires no small intellectual effort to realize that this is a fact that now is, and not one that has been. Baltimore is 40 miles from Washington. It is a most wonderful achievement in the arts. (From David Tanner's manuscript on Print Technology in America, to be published by McGraw-Hill)

The New York Review of Books has been called cliquish, intellectual, opinionated and snobbish. For $7.50 a year you can be, too.

For $7.50 a year, you too can be feared and envied.

What will your middle-brow friend say when you point out to him that his two favorite Book-of-the-Month Club authors, Toynbee and Snow, ". . . have one quality in common. They are more highly thought of by readers and by themselves than they are by their colleagues in the literary trade." (You need not credit A. J. P. Taylor for the observation.)

Imagine the reaction of your Jewish friends—any of your friends, for that matter—as you quote I. F. Stone's critique of Zionism in his article on Sartre's important symposium, "Le conflict israélo-arabe."

Or if you want to bring a Molotov cocktail to your next cocktail party, arm yourself with Tom Hayden's "The Occupation of Newark," in which the establishment version of what went on there is blown to bits by fact after carefully-aimed fact.

But controversial opinion isn't the only trouble you'll buy for your $7.50.

Could you admit to an ugly mob of Robert Lowell enthusiasts, his brand-new *Prometheus Bound* clutched, hard-covered, to their breasts, that you'd read the complete text last year in The New York Review?

Obviously, life as a New York Review reader isn't for everybody. Even some who become subscribers are going to be sorry.

To ease your regret if you should happen to be one of these, we've written an unusual offer into our coupon: a no-questions-asked refund of the entire annual subscription fee, that you can call for any time you feel like it during the life of the subscription.

Any time, that is, that you feel like thumbing your nose at us.

I wouldn't mind being looked up to as an intellectual snob. I want to become a subscriber for the year ahead at only $7.50, saving $2.10 from the newsstand price.

But if—for any reason, at any time during the life of my subscription—I want to go back to the security and comfort of my former days as a non-subscriber, I'll let you know, and this coupon constitutes your agreement to refund my entire annual fee and stop sending The New York Review.

☐ Send bill. ☐ $7.50 enclosed. Please add an extra month for saving bookkeeping costs.

NAME _____

ADDRESS _____

CITY _____

STATE _____ ZIP _____

The New York Review of Books
Subscriber Service Department, E-1
P.O. Box 79, Des Moines, Iowa 50301

FREEDOM FROM THE PRESS

Are you brushing your teeth with secondhand water?

A good lie can travel half around the world before the truth can get out of bed. (Mark Twain)

Thanks eversore much, Point Carried! I can't say if it's the weight you strike me to the quick or that red mass I was looking at...Honours to you and may you be commended for our exhibitiveness! (FW)

British sociologist D. G. MacRae says the reason why the huge potential of the ad world has not been tapped by his colleagues is that "we do not want our prejudices disturbed by knowledge." If ads disappeared, so would most of our information service environment—the Muzak of the eye.

Like George Washington, Thomas Jefferson had a bad press. In 1807 he observed: "Nothing can now be believed which is seen in a newspaper. Truth itself becomes suspicious by being put in that polluted vehicle. I will add that the man who never looks at a newspaper is better informed than he who reads them...."

Death and taxes: Remember when you could be sure of them?

"Unless you've tried our embalming fluid, you haven't lived." (Ad in Casket and Sunnyside)

Creative advertising, creative journalism and creative readership, combined into one powerful selling force.

THE WALL STREET JOURNAL

Editions published: Eastern, Midwest, Pacific Coast and Southwest/Distributed everywhere every business day.

Media Mix

Having adapted Beethoven's Sixth Symphony for "Fantasia," Walt Disney commented: "Gee! This'll make Beethoven."

THE FURLOINED EMPIRE

In his <u>History of the Fur Trade</u>, H. A. Innis explains how the North American colonies, British and American, were deeply indebted to the fur traders for their origins.

Washington and Jefferson were land surveyors eager to advance settlement of the fur traders' territories. Hence conflict. Settlers ruined trap lines. The igloo was also a fur-lined job. Until the trapper got the Eskimo on the trail, there were no igloos. The Eskimos still live in stone houses, ignored by cameramen as not photogenic. Multi-sensuous hunters, they proved the greatest mechanics at Gander, to the surprise of the American Air Force.

As the totem pole is tied to the lineality of the missionaries' Bible, so the igloo was made possible by the primus stove.

The Eskimo, like any pre-literate, leaps easily from the Paleolithic stone age to the electric age, by-passing the Neolithic specialism.

WHAT BECOMES A LEGEND MOST?

An exquisite extra-dark
natural mink called
BLACKGLAMA®
bred only by
Great Lakes Mink men
and designed by
Bonwit Teller

"WE'RE SURE GOING
TO HAVE SOME WRECKS NOW!"

Disneyland is itself a wondrous media mix. Cartoons drove the photo back to myth and dream screen. E. S. Carpenter, in his review of The Disney Version (Richard Schickel, Simon and Schuster), points to another media mix in Disney's life: "The only splash of color in Disney's private life was a model train that circled his home.... Much of his social life consisted of donning an engineer's cap.... He enjoyed planning wrecks....'Boy, we're sure going to have some wrecks now!'"

The N.Y. Times of July 16/68, under the head "Steaming Along," shows "Rhodesia's Hot Prospect for the Olympic Marathon" training for the event by puffing along beside a full-size steam locomotive. As media mix this has all the pathos of The Loneliness of the Long Distance Runner.

The present ad mixes a dozen media but leaves us in doubt as to whether the commuter has slaughtered the plane pilot or the ticket agent.

After TWA Blue Chip Service, you arrive ready to do business in Chicago.

Aren't you a little tired of feeling like a commuter?

OXford 5-6000. Jets every hour on the half hour.

TELEVISION KILLS
TELEPHONY IN BROTHERS' BROIL (FW)

The present ad is more concerned with smothering than brothering and is as rich an example of media illiteracy as could be asked for.

"It's what's happening so don't fight it, baby!"

TV is not only an X-ray "zerothruster" or fire god like Zoroaster, but it is entirely subliminal in its impact, as is the case with all other new media.

The Reader's Digest portrays Prince Hamlet holding aloft a TV set on the platform of Elsinore as if he had encountered a spirit: Tv or not Tv? That's Not the Question. The reason it is not the question, of course, is that The Reader's Digest offers the advertiser a bigger market.

Medea Mystery: McLuhan's phone call from Roy Thompson (owner of the London Times) for a private chat about media. Chat blossoms (unbeknownst to McLuhan) into BBC show, also televised across U.S.A.

Some emotional arguments you hear about TV vs. magazines.

1. **Pictures in TV commercials move.** That's true. And there's a lot of excitement and drama in that. On the other hand, magazine pictures *stand still.* In case you have to sneeze. Or leave the room. And by the by, do you know who really invented the video-playback? Magazines did. We call it: Looking-At-The-Ad-A-Second-Time.

2. **TV is colorful and has impact for everybody.** Right. Magazine impact is limited to the audience you're trying to reach. Like, for example, women who want to read about products and ideas that help make them more efficient homemakers—and more attractive wives. They turn on Good Housekeeping Magazine for the precise purpose of doing just that. As to color: magazine color reaches 100% of the homes that own color-vision eyes.

3. **TV packs a lot into a minute.** It has to. At rates up to $1,000 per second.

4. **TV is the proven medium for new products.** What percentage of them, with TV as the dominant or only medium, survive the test market stage? We don't know. But in the past 4 years, 190 products have been introduced in test market editions of Good Housekeeping (all, of course, covered by our Consumers' Guaranty Seal); and of these, 73 have already gone regional or national.

5. **TV is easier to look at.** Agreed. With a magazine on your lap, you either concentrate or converse. *Not both.* You're involved. Or you aren't. And speaking of involvement, did you ever get involved with a magazine that reprinted last winter's entire issue as a "summer-replacement re-run"?

6. **With TV they can't turn the page and skip your ad.** No. But they can turn the dial. Or turn to human conversation. And besides, no advertising medium can make ineffective advertising effective. But the right environment in magazines can give effective advertising its maximum opportunity to be read, thought about, believed, and acted upon. Most important: when the audience goes out and plunks down 50¢ for that environment they're going to be doing some reading. Even if that magazine stays around the house awhile. And it does. As proven by voluminous research. And a gadget called: the magazine rack.

* * * * *

Now that we've given vent to our emotions, let's agree that of course TV, when it's at its best, is a powerful medium that does stand alone in many areas of entertainment and impact. But in advertising it works best as part of a well-balanced media mix.

That's why so many advertisers depend on magazines *and* TV. Selective magazines such as Good Housekeeping. Each month, nearly 13,000,000 women seek out Good Housekeeping. They seek out the advertising. They believe it. They respond to it.

To advertising men who are also businessmen there is no emotional argument. No argument at all.

If you haven't already taken it, the next step is as clear as these words before your eyes.

Good Housekeeping

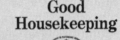

"IF IT WEREN'T FOR EDISON, WE'D BE WATCHING TV BY CANDLELIGHT"

The invisibility of color TV, the supposition that it has some relation to black-and-white TV has proved a corker. Siegfried Giedion's phrase: "anonymous history" (in introducing Space-Time & Architecture) was an attempt to cope with the difficulty of introducing a new design form to people imbued with many unconscious habits of perception. Color is not so much a visual as a tactile medium (as Harley Parker and I explain in To the Vanishing Point: Space in Poetry and Painting).

The cones of the eye in interface create the experience of color: "The center or macula lutea of the eye is responsive to hue and texture. The periphery, on the other hand, is concerned with darkness and lightness and also with movement. . . .The macula and the periphery work in tandem. However, peripheral vision can exist by itself. While color vision is inclusive, black-and-white is partial. (The potential of any technology is always dissipated by its user's involvement in its predecessor.) The iconic thrust of color TV will be buried under mountains of old pictorial space."

On the back of this ad from TV Guide (June 8/68) Neil Hickey reports that "television is under attack for failing to communicate with the Negro;..."

Color TV, far more than black-and-white, gives the Negro easy dominance over the white man's image. Hickey is doing the usual. Ignoring the medium and watching the content.

A color TV set is only as good as the picture tube.

Most picture tubes look alike. And just as a pretty cabinet can enclose a poor set, so can a look-alike tube enclose a poor picture.

That's where Sylvania comes in. When we developed the original Color Bright 85® it was the brightest picture tube ever made. Richer reds, brighter blues, glowier greens.

And you still can't buy a better replacement tube. At any price.

So why take chances?

And just as tubes look alike, so do servicemen. But some don't always have what you need. And others are hard to find. The servicemen shown here install Color Bright 85. So when you have to replace the most important part of your set, don't let appearances fool you.

COLOR TELEVISION BY

SYLVANIA
A SUBSIDIARY OF
GENERAL TELEPHONE & ELECTRONICS

SHEEP IN WOLFE'S CLOTHING

Tramp covered with newspapers on park bench to buddy: "As a former media man, I use newspapers for coverage in depth and radio to find out what's going on." (Broadcasting, February 19/68)

At the beginning of his very flattering essay on myself in <u>The Pump House Gang</u> (Farrar, Straus & Giroux), Tom Wolfe has a drawing of me which at once suggests another title for his essay ("What if he's right?"), namely, "I'd Rather Be Wrong." At the end of his essay he confronts me with a waitress in a topless restaurant to whom I uttered the assurance: "The topless waitress is the thin edge of a trial balloon!" (I.e., the silicone bust.)

Anthropologist Leach is quite right in pointing out that the TV generation is "growing more conformist, not less." But it is not a visual or pictorial conformity that is developing. The hairless ape has begun to attach a great significance to his hair. "Fair tresses man's imperial rod and snare, And beauty draws us with a single hair." He points out that: "quite a lot of alarm is generated by sheep in wolves' clothing."

The young are really the hairs to a generation of incompetence.

The young are really the hairs to a generation of incompetence.

HURRY UP, PLEASE, IT'S TIME!

"Assuary as there's a bonum in your ossthealogy!" (FW)

Time was perhaps the first magazine to apply the format of the telegraph press (i.e., the mosaic of items without connection) to the periodical. Just a dateline. The Time formula of mosaic in place of connected editorial features permits the juxtaposition of esoteric and trival — the formula for creating environments, not just a point of view.

Mosaic transparency and simultaneity appears in the ad itself. The mosaic as such is an acoustic, tribal form, feathers in the hat of Time.

"Only Time lets advertisers select three occupational cross-sections of its readers ... (Note how the tribal caste system here bloometh.)

Only TIME offers this new kind of marketing selectivity: Demographic Editions

Only TIME lets advertisers select three occupational cross-sections of its readers and advertise just to them, with no wastage.

Like TIME's National Edition, all three Demographics go to the better-off, better-positioned Chiefs in their respective fields. Each Demographic Edition carries the same editorial and advertising contents as the National Edition except for additional pages of advertising addressed to the occupational group you want to reach.

As in the past, of course, if your primary market is Chiefs in every field... use TIME's National Edition.

Demographic Edition	Rate Base	Cost per B&W page
Doctors'	75,000	$1500
College Students'	250,000	$3125
Educators'	125,000	$1500

4

Joyce, Mallarmé, and the Press

Declining to write for the *Revue Européenne* in 1831, Lamartine said to its editor:

> *Do not perceive in these words a superb disdain for what is termed journalism. Far from it; I have too intimate a knowledge of my epoch to repeat this absurd nonsense, this impertinent inanity against the Periodical Press. I know too well the work Providence has committed to it. Before this century shall run out journalism will be the whole press — the whole human thought. Since that prodigious multiplication which art has given to speech — multiplication to be multiplied a thousand-fold yet — mankind will write their books day by day, hour by hour, page by page. Thought will be spread abroad in the world with the rapidity of light; instantly conceived, instantly written, instantly understood at the extremities of the earth — it will spread from pole to pole. Sudden, instant, burning with the fervor of soul which made it burst forth, it will be the reign of the human soul in all its plenitude. It will not have time to ripen — to accumulate in a book; the book will arrive too late. The only book possible from today is a newspaper.*

It is strange that the popular press as an art form has often attracted the enthusiastic attention of poets and aesthetes while rousing the gloomiest apprehensions in the academic mind. The same division of opinion can be traced in the sixteenth century concerning the printed book. Two thousand years of manuscript culture were abruptly dissolved by the printing press. Failure to understand this arises from various overriding assumptions about the universal benefits of print. But today when technology has conferred ascendancy on pictorial and radio communication it is easy to detect the peculiar limitations and bias of the four-century span of book culture which is coming to a close.

In her recent study of George Herbert, Rosamund Tuve stressed the extent to which metaphysical conceits were direct translations into verbal terms of popular pictorial imagery of the late middle ages. She was able to show that the characteristic conceits of Herbert and others arose from the meeting of the old manuscript culture (with its marginal pictures) and the new printed medium. In the same way, many others have argued that the peculiar richness of effect of Elizabethan and Jacobean language was the result of a meeting of the oral tradition and the new printed culture. Mere literature didn't begin until the oral tradition was entirely subordinated to the silent and private studies of the bookman. It was the lifelong claim of W. B. Yeats that in Ireland this conquest over the spoken word was less complete than elsewhere in Anglo-Saxony.

So, if the metaphysicals owe much to their adaptation of medieval pictographs to the printed medium, it could be suggested that modern poetry with its elaborate mental landscapes owes much to the new pictorial technology which fascinated Poe and Baudelaire and on which Rimbaud and Mallarmé built much of their aesthetics. If the Jacobeans were receding from a pictographic culture toward the printed page, may we not meet them at the point where we are receding from the printed word under the impetus of pictorial technology? Manuscript technology fostered a constellation of mental attitudes and skills of which the modern world has no memory. Plato foresaw some of them with alarm in the *Phaedrus*:

> *The specific which you have discovered is an aid not to memory, but to reminiscence, and you give your disciples not truth but only the semblance of truth; they will be hearers of many things and will have learned nothing; they will appear omniscient and will generally know nothing; they will be tiresome company, having the show of wisdom without the reality.*

Plato is speaking for the oral tradition before it was modified by literacy. He saw writing as a mainly destructive revolution. Since then we have been through enough revolutions to know that every medium of communication is a unique art form which gives salience to one set of human possibilities at the expense of another set. Each medium of expression profoundly modifies human sensibility in mainly unconscious and unpredictable ways. Alphabetic communication brings about an inevitable psychic withdrawal, as H. J. Chaytor showed in *From Script to Print*, with a train of personal and social maladjustments. But it secures a host of advantages. Psychic withdrawal is automatic because the process of literacy is the process of setting up the interior monologue. It is the problem of translation of the auditory into the visual and back again, which is the process of writing and reading, that brings the interior monologue into existence, as can be observed in the study of pre-literate cultures today. This introversion with its consequent weakening of sense perception also creates inattention to the speech of others and sets up mechanisms which interfere with verbal recall. Exact verbal recall is scarcely a problem for pre-literate cultures.

Throughout *Finnegans Wake* Joyce plays some of his major variations on his theme of "abcedmindedness" in "those pagan ironed times of the first city . . . when a frond was a friend." His "verbivocovisual" presentation of an "all nights newsery reel" is the first dramatization of the very media of communication as both form and vehicle of the flux of human cultures. Most of the problems of reading the *Wake* dissolve when it is seen that he is using the media themselves as art forms as in a "phantom city phaked of philm pholk." The lights go up in his "Feenichts Playhouse" as the sun dips at the end of the Anna Livia section, and he is ready to mime the war of light and dark, of Michael, the Devil, and the maggies in a zodiacal dance of the witches ("monthage") "with nightly redistribution of parts and players by the puppetry producer."

Throughout the *Wake* this interior "tubloid" or tale of a tub is linked both to the cabbalistic significance of the letters of the alphabet and to the psychological effect of literacy in creating a general "abcedmindedness" in human society.

But the arrest of the flux of thought and speech which is the written page permits that prolonged analysis of thought processes from which arise the structures of science. Pictographic Chinese culture, for example, would seem to stand midway between the extremes of our abstract written tradition and the plenary oral tradition with its stress on speech as gesture and gesture as "phatic communion." And it is perhaps this medial position between the noncommunicating extremes of print and pictorial technology which attracts us today to the Chinese ideogram.

A principal feature of manuscript culture was its relative unity. The rarity and inaccessibility of manuscript books fostered a habit of encyclopedism. And where scholars were not numerous there were additional reasons for each of them to be acquainted with the entire range of authors. Moreover, manuscripts were studied slowly and aloud. Silent reading was impossible until the presses created the macadamized highways of print. The handwritten book was a broken road which was traveled slowly and infrequently. It kept the reader close to the dimensions of oral discourse. The publication of a poem consisted in reading or reciting it to a small audience. The promulgation of ideas was by public disputation.

Print multiplied scholars, but it also diminished their social and political importance. And it did the same for books. Unexpectedly, print fostered nationalism and broke down international communication because publishers found that the vernacular audience was larger and more profitable. As H. A. Innis has shown in *The Bias of Communication*, the printed word has been a major cause of international disturbance and misunderstanding since the sixteenth century. But pictorial communication is relatively international and hard to manipulate for purposes of national rivalry. H. A. Innis has been the great pioneer in opening up the study of the economic and social consequences of the various media of communication; so that today any student of letters is necessarily indebted to him for insight into changing attitudes to time and space which result from shifting media. In particular his studies of the newspaper as a major branch of the technology of print are relevant to the study of modern literature. Beginning as an economic historian, Innis was gradually impelled to consider not just the external trade routes of the world but also the great trade routes of the mind. He became aware that the modern world, having solved the problem of commodities, had turned its technology to the packaging of information and ideas.

If the manuscript tradition encouraged encyclopedism, book culture naturally tended to specialism. There were enough books to make reading a full-time occupation and to ensure an entirely withdrawn and private existence for the whole class of bookmen. Eventually there were enough books to splinter the reading public into dozens of noncommunicating groups. This has meant a large degree of unawareness in our culture of the meaning and drift of its most obvious developments. The bookman as such is not easily interested even in the technology and art of the book form of communication. And as this form has been modified by the popular press, and later developments, the exponents of book culture have registered various emotions but little curiosity. It is not, therefore, incongruous that real understanding of the changes in modern communication should have come mainly from the resourceful technicians among modern poets and painters.

Much of the novelty of the *Portrait*, *Ulysses*, and the *Wake* is an illusion resulting from inattention to technical developments in the arts since Newton. That manipulation of a continuous parallel between modern Dublin and ancient Ithaca which Mr. Eliot has noted as the major resource of *Ulysses* was a transfer to the time dimension of a "double-plot," a technique which had been the staple of all picturesque art for two hundred years. De Gourmont observed that one achievement of Flaubert had been the transfer of Chateaubriand's panoramic art from nature and history to the industrial metropolis. And Baudelaire had matched Flaubert in this witty reversal of the role of picturesque landscape. But English landscape art in painting, poetry, and the novel was decades in advance of France and Europe, a fact which was inseparable from English industrial experiment and scientific speculation. In her fascinating book *Newton Demands the Muse*, Marjorie Nicolson records the impact of Newtonian optics on the themes of the poets. But the techniques of rendering experience were equally modified in the direction of an inclusive image of society and consciousness. The new vision of space and light as outer phenomena which were precisely correlative to our inner faculties gave a new meaning and impetus to the juxtaposition of images and experiences. The taste for the discontinuities of Gothic art was one with the new interest in the juxtaposition of various social classes in the novels of the road (Fielding, Smollett, Mackenzie) and in the juxtaposition of historical epochs as well as primitive and sophisticated experience in Scott and Byron. More subtle was the juxtaposition of various states of the same mind in *Tristram Shandy* and the sleuthlike quest for the origins of such states on the part of Sterne and later of Wordsworth.

But the parallel development of the arts of spatial manipulation of mental states which was occurring in the popular press has been given no attention. Innis has shown how the new global landscapes of the press were not only geared to industry but were themselves the means of paying for new roads, for railway and telegraph and cable. The physical landscape of the earth was changed very quickly by the landscapes of the newspaper, even though the political scene has not yet caught up. The networks of news, trade, and transport were one. And newspapermen like Dickens who had no stake in established literary decorum were quick to adapt the technology of print to art and entertainment. Well before the French impressionists and symbolists had discovered the bearings for art of modern technology, Dickens had switched the picturesque perspectives of the eighteenth-century novel to the representation of the new industrial slums. Neurotic eccentricity in the sub-world of the metropolis he proved to be a much richer source for the rendering of mania and manic states of mind than the crofters of Scott or the yokels of Wordsworth. And Dostoevsky mined from Dickens freely, as G. B. Shaw did later still. But just how valid were the impressionist techniques of the picturesque kind familiar to the news reporter appears in the notable essay of Eisenstein in *Film Form* where he shows the impact of Dickens on the art of D. W. Griffith.

How deeply English artists had understood the principles of picturesque art by 1780 appears from the invention of cinema at that time. In 1781 De Loutherbourg, the theatrical scene-painter, contrived in London a panorama which he called the "Eidophusikon" so as "to realize pictures in all four dimensions." His "various Imitations of Natural Phenomena, Represented by Moving Pictures" were advertised in these words and caused a sensation. Gainsborough, we are told by a contemporary, "was so delighted that for a time he thought of nothing else, talked of nothing else, and passed his evenings at the exhibition in long succession." He even made one of these machines for himself capable of showing sunrise and moonrise as well as storms and ships at sea. Gainsborough through this cinema was experiencing the novelty of cubism with "*lo spettatore nel centro del quadro.*"

Another familiar instance of the abrupt newspaper juxtaposition of events in "picturesque perspective" is *The Ring and the Book*, an explicitly newspaperish crime report given as a series of "inside stories," each one contained within another like Chinese boxes. But it was Mallarmé who formulated the lessons of the press as a guide for the new impersonal poetry of suggestion and implication. He saw that the scale of modern reportage and of the mechanical multiplication of messages made personal rhetoric impossible. Now was the time for the artist to intervene in a new way and to manipulate the new media of communication by a precise and delicate adjustment of the relations of words, things, and events. His task had become not self-expression but the release of the life in things. *Un Coup de Dés* illustrates the road he took in the exploitation of all things as gestures of the mind, magically adjusted to the secret powers of being. As a vacuum tube is used to shape and control vast reservoirs of electric power, the artist can manipulate the low current of casual words, rhythms, and resonances to evoke the primal harmonies of existence or to recall the dead. But the price he must pay is total self-abnegation.

The existentialist metaphysic latent in Mallarmé's aesthetics was stated in

1924 in *In Praise of Newspapers* by Karel Čapek:

> *The newspaper world like that of the wild beasts exists solely in the present; Press consciousness (if one can speak of consciousness) is circumscribed by simple present time extending from the morning on to the evening edition, or the other way round. If you read a paper a week old you feel as if you were turning the pages of Dalimil's chronicle: no longer is it a newspaper but a memorial. The ontological system of newspapers is actualized realism: what is just now exists . . . literature is the expression of old things in eternally new forms, while newspapers are eternally expressing new realities in a stabilized and unchangeable form.*

By extending the technique of reporting the coexistence of events in China and Peru from global space to the dimension of time, Joyce achieved the actualized realism of a continuous present for events past, present, and future. In reverse, it is only necessary to remove the dateline from any newspaper to obtain a similar if less satisfactory model of the universe. That is what R. L. Stevenson meant when he said he could make an epic a newspaper if he knew what to leave out. Joyce knew what to leave out.

For that school of thought for which the external world is an opaque prison, art can never be regarded as a source of knowledge but only as a moral discipline and a study of endurance. The artist is not a reader of radiant signatures on *materia signata* but the signer of a forged check on our hopes and sympathies. This school has supported the idea of the function of art as catharsis which, as G. R. Levy shows in *The Gate of Horn*, was a preparation for the lesser Greek mysteries. But if the world is not opaque and if the mind is not of the earth earthy, then this moral view of art should yield to the cognitive view. However that may be, the cathartic, ethical view of art has led to a doctrinaire hostility to the use of discontinuity in art (the theme of Arnold's preface to *Poems*, 1853) and indifference to all popular art. And in the past century with every technological device advancing the discontinuous character of communication the stand taken by the cathartic and ethical school has enveloped the entire world of popular culture in a haze of esoteric nescience, disguised, however, as a profound moral concern with the wider hope and the higher things. Joyce had a phrase for this anti-cognitive attitude, "the cultic twalette."

Moral and aesthetic horror at the ignobility of the popular scene gave way to an opposite attitude in the symbolists, and Mallarmé is, before Joyce, the best spokesman of the new approach. In his *Shop-Windows* (*Étalages*), while analyzing the aesthetics of commercial layout, he considers the relations between poetry and the press.

A shop window full of new books prompts his reflection that the function of the ordinary run of books is merely to express the average degree of human boredom and incompetence, to reduce to a written form the horizon of the human scene in all its abounding banality. Instead of deploring this fact as literary men tend to do, the artist should exploit it: "The vague, the commonplace, the smudged and defaced, not banishment of these, occupation rather! Apply them as to a patrimony."

Only by a conquest and occupation of these vast territories of stupefaction can the artist fulfill his culturally heroic function of purifying the dialect of the tribe, the Herculean labor of cleaning the Augean stables of speech, of thought and feeling. Turning directly to the press, Mallarmé designates it as "a traffic, an epitomization of enormous and elementary interests . . . employing print for the propagation of opinions, the recital of divers facts, made plausible, in the Press, which is devoted to publicity, by the omission, it would seem, of any art." He delights in the dramatic significance of the fact that in the French press, at least, the literary and critical features form a section at the base of the first page. And even more delightful:

> *Fiction properly so called, or the imaginative tale, frolics across the average daily paper, enjoying the most prominent spots even to the top of the page, dislodging the financial feature and pushing actuality into second place. Here, too, is the suggestion and even the lesson of a certain beauty: that today is not only the supplanter of yesterday or the presager of tomorrow but issues from time, in general, with an integrity bathed and fresh. The vulgar placard, bawled . . . at the street corner thus sustains this reflection . . . on the political text. Such experience leaves some people cold because they imagine that while there may be a little more or less of the sublime in these pleasures tasted by the people, the situation as regards that which alone is precious and immeasurably lofty, and which is known by the name of Poetry, that this situation remains unchanged. Poetry (they suppose) will always be exclusive and the best of its pinions will never approach those pages of the newspaper where it is parodied, nor are they pleased by the spread of wings in our hands of those vast improvised sheets of the daily paper.*

Mallarmé is laughing at these finicky and unperceptive people for whom the press appears as a threat to "real culture"; and continues:

> *To gauge by the extraordinary, actual superproduction, through which the Press intelligently yields its average, the notion prevails, nonetheless, of something very decisive which is elaborating itself: a prelude to an era, a competition for the foundation of the popular modern Poem, at the very least of innumerable Thousand and One Nights: by which the majority of readers will be astonished at the sudden invention. You are assisting at a celebration, all of you, right now, amidst the contingencies of this lightning achievement!*

The author of *Ulysses* was the only person to grasp the full artistic implications of this radically democratic aesthetic elaborated by the fabulous artificer, the modern Daedalus, Stéphane Mallarmé. But Joyce was certainly assisted by Flaubert's *Sentimental Education* and *Bouvard and Pécuchet* in adapting Mallarmé's insights to his own artistic purposes. A very little reflection on the scrupulously banal character of Flaubert's epics about industrial man illuminates much of the procedure in *Ulysses* and the *Wake*.

Crise de Vers, *Étalages*, and *Le Livre, Instrument Spirituel* all belong to the last few years of Mallarmé's life, representing his ultimate insights (1892-1896). And in each of these essays he is probing the aesthetic consequences and possibilities of the popular arts of industrial man. In *Le Livre* he turns to scrutinize the press once more, opening with the proposition, self-evident to him, that the whole world exists in order to result in a book. This is a matter of metaphysical fact, that all existence cries out to be raised to the level of scientific or poetic intelligibility. In this sense "the book" confers on things and persons another mode of existence which helps to perfect them. And it is plain that Mallarmé regarded the press as this ultimate encyclopedic book in its most rudimentary form. The almost superhuman range of awareness of the press now awaits only the full analogical sense of exact orchestration to perfect its present juxtaposition of items and themes. And this implies the complete self-effacement of the writer, for "this book does not admit of any signature." The job of the artist is not to sign but to read signatures. Existence must speak for itself. It is already richly and radiantly signed. The artist has merely to reveal, not to forge the signatures of existence. But he can only put these in order by discovering the orchestral analogies in things themselves. The result will be "the hymn, harmony and joy, as a pure ensemble ordered in the sharpest and most vivid circumstance of their interrelations. Man charged with divine vision has no other mode of expression save the parallelism of pages as a means of expressing the links, the whims, the limpidity on which he gazes."

All those pseudo-rationalisms, the forged links and fraudulent intelligibility which official literature has imposed on existence must be abandoned. And this initial step the press has already taken in its style of impersonal juxtaposition which conveys such riches to the writer. This work of "popular enchantment" which is the daily paper is not lacking in moral edification, for the hubbub of appetites and protests to be found among the advertisements and announcements proclaims each day the "original servitude" of man and the confusion of tongues of the tower of Babel. But the very format of the press resembles "a retracted wing which is ready to spread itself," awaiting only the "intervention of folding or of rhythm" in order to rid us of all that passes for "literature."

Mallarmé sees this impersonal art of juxtaposition as revolutionary and democratic also in the sense that it enables each reader to be an artist: "Reading becomes a solitary, tacit concert given to itself by the mind which recaptures significance from the least sonorities." It is the rhyming and orchestrating of things themselves which releases the maximum intelligibility and attunes the ears of men once more to the music of the spheres. We are finished, he says, with that custom of an official literary decorum by which poets sang in chorus, obliterating with their personal forgeries the actual signatures of things. In fact, the new poet will take as much care to avoid a style that is not in things themselves as literary men have in the past sought to achieve and impose one.

In approaching the structure of *Ulysses* as a newspaper landscape it is well to call to mind a favorite book of Joyce's, *The Purple Island* of Phineas Fletcher, the author's name suggesting Finn the arrow-maker. Fletcher presents the anatomy and labyrinths of the human body in terms of an enchanted Spenserian landscape. Many have pointed out the importance of the human form of the sleeping giant, the collective consciousness, as the structure of the *Wake*. And Joyce was careful to instruct his readers in the relation between the episodes of *Ulysses* and our bodily organs. (In 1844 the American press greeted the telegraph as "the first definite pulsation of the real nervous system of the world.") In *Ulysses* in episode seven we find ourselves in a newspaper office in "the heart of the Hibernian metropolis." For Joyce the press was indeed a "microchasm" of the world of man, its columns unchanging monuments to the age-old passions and interests of all men, and its production and distribution a drama involving the hands and organs of the entire "body politic." With its dateline June 16, 1904, *Ulysses* is, newspaperwise, an abridgement of all space in a brief segment of time, as the *Wake* is a condensation of all time in the brief space of "Howth castle and environs."

The dateline of *Ulysses*, the day of the end of the drought in the land of "The Dead," the day of the meeting of Joyce and Nora Barnacle, was the day that Joyce was to preserve in exile as Aeneas carried to New Troy the ashes and huturn of his ancestors (Fustel de Coulanges' *The Ancient City* is a useful introduction to this aspect of Joyce's filial piety). But whereas the techniques of the *Wake* are "telekinetic" and are explicitly specified as those of radio, television, newsreel, and the stuttering verbal gestures of H. C. E., it is the newspaper as seen by Mallarmé that provides most of the symbolist landscapes of *Ulysses*. As a daily cross-section of the activities and impulses of the race the press is an inclusive image affording possibilities of varied orchestration. A passage in *Stephen Hero* suggests the direction in which Joyce has modified the superficial cross-section of the popular press:

> *The modern spirit is vivisective. Vivisection itself is the most modern process one can conceive. . . . All modern political and religious criticism dispenses with presumptive states. . . . It examines the entire community in action and reconstructs the spectacle of redemption. If you were an esthetic philosopher you would take note of all my vagaries because here you have the spectacle of the esthetic instinct in action. The philosophic college should spare a detective for me.*
> (p. 186)

The key terms here, vivisection, community in action, reconstruction, detection, are related to every phase of Joyce's aesthetic. In *Modern Painters* Ruskin discusses the discontinuous picturesque techniques in medieval and modern art under the term "grotesque," noting it as the avenue by which popular and democratic expression enters the serious levels of art:

> A fine grotesque is the expression, in a moment, by a series of symbols thrown together in bold and fearless connection of truths which it would have taken a long time to express in any verbal way, and of which the connection is left for the beholder to work out for himself, the gaps, left or overleaped by the haste of the imagination, forming the grotesque character. . . . Hence it is an infinite good to mankind when there is a full acceptance of the grotesque . . . an enormous amount of intellectual power is turned to use, which in this present century of ours, evaporates in street gibing. . . . It is with a view to the reopening of this great field of human intelligence, long entirely closed, that I am striving to introduce Gothic architecture . . . and to revive the art of illumination . . . the distinctive difference between illumination and painting proper, being, that illumination admits no shadows, but only gradations of pure colour.

Ruskin in describing the grotesque gives the very formula for "vivisection" or the community in action, though he hadn't the faintest idea of how to adapt this ideal to contemporary art. It was not misleading on Joyce's part, therefore, when he spoke of his work as a Gothic cathedral or to the *Wake* as an activated page of the Book of Kells. In presenting "history as her is harped," Joyce concludes: "And so the triptych vision passes out of a hillside into a hillside. Fairshee fading. Again am I deliciated by the picaresqueness of your irmages." (*Wake*, 486). It is the Mallarméan method of orchestration of the qualities of ordinary speech and experience that recurs, again, and again in the *Wake*:

> and inform to the old sniggering publicking press and its nation of sheepcopers about the whole plighty troth between them, malady of milady made melody of malodi, she, the lalage of lyonesses, and him, her knave errant . . . for all within crystal range.

The last "crystal" image gives the typical translation of the auditory into the visual, music into color, the harp of Aeolus into the harp of Memnon, time into space, which is the kind of metamorphosis which is going on everywhere in the *Wake*.

But the world of *Ulysses*, being primarily a modulation of space, is relatively static and newspaperish in its landscapes. It stands as inferno to the purgatorio of the *Wake*. However, in the Aeolus section of *Ulysses*, which is governed specifically by the organ "lungs" and the art of rhetoric, "everything," as Bloom says, "speaks for itself." The sheets of the newspaper become the tree harp for the wind of rhetoric. And the tree harp of the newspaper office is appropriately located beside the rock pillar of the hero:

Before Nelson's Pillar, trams glowed, shunted, changed trolley, started for Blackrock.

The trams with their rows of cast steel provide a parallel network to the linotype machines and the rows of printed matter. But if the tree and pillar provide the true image of a hero cult, the rhetoric that blows through the leaves of this tree is that of an alien speech. Much is made of this contretemps throughout the episode, and the climax brings this dramatic conflict to an issue. J. J. O'Malloy recites John F. Taylor's defense of the Gaelic revival, the theme of which is the Mosaic refusal to accept the gods and cult of the dominant Egyptians, a refusal which made possible his descent from Sinai "bearing in his arms the tables of the law graven in the language of the outlaw." This passage, the only one Joyce seems to have recorded from *Ulysses*, has an obvious bearing on the relation of his own art to English culture.

In his *Dialogue de l' Arbre* Valéry expounds the Aeolian cosmology of trees, roots, trunks, branches, leaves:

Chacun dit son nom. . . . O langage confus, langage qui t'agites, je veux foudre toutes tes voix. Cent mille feuilles mues font ce que le rêveur murmure aux puissances du songe.

And he proceeds to contemplate the tree as a labyrinth merging with river and sea yet remaining a giant. In the same way the Aeolean tree music of the press "reamalgemerges" with the Mosaic eloquence of Sinai and the mountain, just as Anna Livia is also ALP (and Aeolus was a volcano spirit, that is, a cyclopean or mountain figure. He was the reputed father of Ulysses and hence of Bloom). The cyclopean aspect of Aeolus and the press provides an important motif, that of crime detection and the private eye. The press man as a "Shaun the cop" or cyclops type ("though he might have been more humble there's no police like Holmes") is presented in this episode as a parody or ape of the artist. Editor Myles Crawford, soliciting the services of Stephen, boasts of the sleuthing feats of "we'll paralyze Europe" Ignatius Gallaher. Gallaher's idea of scare journalism is paralysis as opposed to the artist's idea of awakening. Gallaher reconstructed the pattern of the Phoenix Park murders to paralyze Europe; the artist reconstructs the crime of history as a means of awakening the dead. As "bullock-befriending bard," Stephen is the threader of that Labyrinth described by Vergil in the fourth Georgic, the fable of the ox and of the bees of poetic inspiration.

Nevertheless Joyce is not questioning the parallel between journalism and art in respect to the retracing process. The very conditions of journalism fostered insight into artistic production, because daily or periodic publication led to a great deal of serial composition. This in turn compelled authors to write their stories backwards. Edgar Poe, a journalist, in "The Philosophy of Composition," begins:

> Charles Dickens, in a note now lying before me, alluding to an examination I once made of the mechanism of Barnaby Rudge, says — "By the way, are you aware that Godwin wrote his Caleb Williams backwards?"

Poe then develops the familiar symbolist doctrine of poem as an art situation which is the formula for a particular effect. The same method of composition in reverse enabled Poe to pioneer the detective story. There is nothing accidental, therefore, about the Aeolus episode being crammed with instances of reversal and reconstruction. Applying the same principle to language yields, in the *Wake*, a reconstruction of all the layers of culture and existence embedded in the present forms of words and speech gesture.

It was natural that eighteenth-century writers should have been attracted to the retracing and reconstruction principle of art, which made Horace Walpole say of *Tristram Shandy* that it was the first book which consists "in the whole narrative going backwards." A little later Dr. Thomas Brown in Edinburgh argued that the poet's imagination differed from the ordinary man's by the power of reversing the direction of association. Once picturesque art, following the spectroscope, had broken up the continuum of linear art and narrative the possibility of cinematic montage emerged at once. And montage has to be arranged forwards or backwards. Forwards it yields narrative. Backwards it is reconstruction of events. Arrested it consists of the static landscape of the press, the co-existence of all aspects of community life. This is the image of the city presented in *Ulysses*.

5

Letter to Harold Adams Innis

St. Michael's College
March 14/51

Dear Innis[1]

Thanks for the lecture re-print. This makes an opportunity for me to mention my interest in the work you are doing in communication study in general. I think there are lines appearing in *Empire and Communications* [1950], for example, which suggest the possibility of organizing an entire school of studies. Many of the ancient language theories of the Logos type which you cite in [*Empire and Communications*][2] for their bearings on government and society have recurred and amalgamated themselves today under the auspices of anthropology and social psychology. Working concepts of "collective consciousness" in advertizing agencies have in turn given salience and practical effectiveness to these "magical" notions of language.

But it was most of all the esthetic discoveries of the symbolists since Rimbaud and Mallarmé (developed in English by Joyce, Eliot, Pound, Lewis and Yeats) which have served to recreate in contemporary consciousness an awareness of the *potencies* of language such as the Western world has not experienced in 1800 years.

Mallarmé saw the modern press as a magical institution born of technology.[3] The discontinuous juxtaposition of unrelated items made necessary by the influx of news stories from every quarter of the world, created, he saw, a symbolic landscape of great power and importance. (He used the word "symbol" in the strict

---

[1]The manuscript of this letter is headed in the upper-left corner: "Rewrite of letter for mimeograph HMM". The original letter was written some weeks previously because it was acknowledged by Innis on February 26 (with apologies for not doing so earlier). Innis said he had been "very much interested" in McLuhan's letter and that he would like to have it typed and circulated to "one or two of our mutual friends", adding that he wished to receive the "mimeographed sheet" referred to. Innis wrote over the body of the letter: "Memorandum on humanities".

[2]Added by Innis.

[3]McLuhan read Stéphane Mallarmé — who saw an art form in the daily newspaper — in the *Oeuvres Complètes* (Gallimard, 1945), in which the press is discussed in "Etalages" (pp. 375-6), "Le Livre

---

Greek sense sym-ballein, to pitch together, physically and musically). He saw at once that the modern press was not a rational form but a magical one so far as communication was concerned. Its very technological form was bound to be *efficacious* far beyond any informative purpose. Politics were becoming musical, jazzy, magical.

The same symbolist perception applied to cinema showed that the *montage* of images was basically a return via technology to age-old picture language. S. Eisenstein's *Film Form* and *Film Technique* explore the relations between modern developments in the arts and Chinese ideogram, pointing to the common basis of ideogram in modern art[,] science and technology.

One major discovery of the symbolists which had the greatest importance for subsequent investigation was their notion of the learning process as a labyrinth of the senses and faculties whose retracing provided the *key* to all arts and sciences (basis of myth of Daedalus, basic for the dreams and schemes of Francis Bacon, and, when transferred by [Giovanni Battista] Vico[4] to philology and history of culture, it also forms the basis of modern historiography, archaeology, psychology and artistic procedures alike.[)] Retracing becomes in modern historical scholarship the technique of reconstruction. The technique which Edgar Poe first put to work in his detective stories.[5] In the arts this discovery has had all those astonishing results which have seemed to separate the ordinary public from what it regards as esoteric magic. From the point of view of the artist however the business of art is no longer the communication of thoughts or feelings which are to be conceptually ordered, but a direct participation in an experience. The whole tendency of modern communication whether in the press, in advertizing or in the high arts is towards participation in a process, rather than apprehension of concepts. And this major revolution, intimately linked to technology, is one whose consequences have not begun to be studied although they have begun to be felt.

One immediate consequence, it seems to me, has been the decline of literature. The hypertrophy of letter-press, at once the cause and effect of universal literacy, has produced a spectacular decline of attention to the printed or written word. As you have shown in *Empire and Communications*, ages of literature

---

Instrument spirituel" (p. 378 ff.) and "Deuil" (pp. 523-4). See the first article in *The Mechanical Bride*: "Front Page", opposite a reproduction of the April 20, 1950 front page of *The New York Times*. Here McLuhan says that "any paper today is a collective work of art, a daily 'book' of industrial man, an Arabian night's entertainment. . . . Notoriously it is the visual technique of a Picasso, the literary technique of James Joyce." See also McLuhan's essay "Joyce, Mallarmé and the Press" (which first appeared in *The Sewanee Review*, vol. 62, no. 1, Winter 1954) in Eugene McNamara, ed., *The Interior Landscape: The Literary Criticism of Marshall McLuhan* (1969).

[4]For Vico, see page 339, note 3.

[5]See page 271, note 4.

have been few and brief in human history. The present literary epoch has been of exceptional duration — 400 years. There are many symptoms that it is at an end. The comic book for example has been seen as a degenerate literary form instead of as a nascent pictorial and dramatic form which has sprung from the new stress on visual-auditory communication in the magazines, the radio and television. The young today cannot follow narrative but they are alert to drama. They cannot bear description but they love landscape and action.

If literature is to survive as a scholastic discipline except for a very few people, it must be by a transfer of its techniques of perception and judgement to these new media. The new media, which are already much more constitutive educationally than those of the class-room, must be inspected and discussed in the class-room if the class-room is to continue at all except as a place of detention. As a teacher of literature it has long seemed to me that the *functions* of literature cannot be maintained in present circumstances without radical alteration of the procedures of teaching. Failure in this respect relegated Latin and Greek to the specialist; and English literature has already become a category rather than an interest in school and college.

As mechanical media have popularized and enforced the presence of the arts on all people it becomes more and more necessary to make studies of the function and effect of communication on society. Present ideas of such effects are almost entirely in terms of mounting or sagging sales curves resulting from special campaigns of commercial education. Neither the agencies nor the consumers know anything about the social or cultural effects of this education.

Deutsch's interesting pamphlet on communication is thoroughly divorced from any sense of the social functions performed by communication.[6] He is typical of a school likewise in his failure to study the matter in the *particular*. He is the technician interested in power but uncritical and unconcerned with social effect. The diagnosis of his type is best found, so far as I know, in Wyndham Lewis's *The Art of Being Ruled*. That pamphlet [*sic*] is probably the most radical political document since Machiavelli's *Prince*. But whereas Machiavelli was concerned with the use of society as raw material for the arts of power, Lewis reverses the perspective and tries to discern the human shape once more in a vast technological landscape which has been ordered on Machiavellian lines.

The fallacy in the Deutsch-Wiener[7] approach is its failure to understand the techniques and functions of the traditional arts as the essential type of all human

---

[6]Karl Deutsch's paper (written for a 1951 conference), "Communication in Self-governing Organizations: Notes on Autonomy, Freedom and Authority in the Growth of Social Groups", was published in Lyman Bryson, ed., *Conference on Science, Philosophy and Religion in Their Relation to the Democratic Way of Life. 12 Session. Freedom and Authority in Our Time* (1953).

[7]Norbert Wiener, *The Human Use of Human Beings: Cybernetics and Society* (1950).

communication. It is instead a dialectical approach born of technology and quite unable of itself to see beyond or around technology. The Medieval schoolmen ultimately ended up on the same dialectical reef.

As Easterbrook may have told you I have been considering an experiment in communication which is to follow the lines of this letter in suggesting means of linking a variety of specialized fields by what might be called a method of esthetic analysis of their common features. This method has been used by my friend Siegfried Giedion in *Space, Time and Architecture* and in *Mechanization Takes Command*. What I have been considering is a single mimeographed sheet to be sent out weekly or fortnightly to a few dozen people in different fields, at first illustrating the underlying unities of form which exist where diversity is all that meets the eye. Then, it is hoped there will be a feedback of related perception from various readers which will establish a continuous flow.

It seems obvious to me that Bloor St.[8] is the one point in this University where one might establish a focus of the arts and sciences. And the organizing concept would naturally be "Communication Theory and practice". A simultaneous focus of current and historical forms. Relevance to be given to selection of areas of study by dominant artistic and scientific modes of the particular period. Arts here used as providing criteria, techniques of observation, and bodies of recorded, *achieved*, experience. Points of departure but also return.

For example the actual techniques of economic study today seem to me to be of genuine relevance to anybody who wishes to grasp the best in current poetry and music. And vice versa. There is a real, living unity in our time, as in any other, but it lies submerged under a superficial hubbub of sensation. Using Frequency Modulation techniques one can slice accurately through such interference, whereas Amplitude Modulation leaves you bouncing on all the currents.

University of Toronto Archives   Marshall McLuhan

---

[8]The Economics Building at 273 Bloor Street West, Toronto. It originally housed McMaster University and is now occupied by the Royal Conservatory of Music.

6

Postures and Impostures
of Managers Past

Maneggiare (Italian) — to handle, especially to manage or train horses.
Ménager (French) — to use carefully, to husband, to spare.
Diehard — His not to reason why; breakdown by keeping uptight.
Dropout — His but to reason why; breakthrough by keeping in touch.

Politics and morals are divorced. Each of the two has its own ends, each its own
means. They are not reconcilable. There is no middle position of compromise.
(Niccolò Machiavelli, *The Prince*)

I put no ceiling on progress.
(Alfred P. Sloan, Jr.)

History is bunk.
(Henry Ford)

History has many cunning passages, contrived corridors
And issues, deceives with whispering ambitions,
Guides us by vanities.
(T. S. Eliot, *"Gerontion"*)

History is not a compilation of facts, but an insight into a moving process of life.
*(*S. Giedion, *Space, Time and Architecture*)

History as Observatory of Change

Today the cultural historian can reveal the hidden factors in the cultures of the past, just as the programmes of innovational processes have the means of seeing the effects of any action before it begins. The approach is that of the instantaneous testing of processes under controlled conditions. *When we push our paradigms back, we get "history"; when we push them forward, we get "science."* The historian, such as Eric Havelock in his *Preface to Plato*, has now the same power to recall ancient events. History offers the controlled conditions of a laboratory for observing patterns of change, much as primitive societies living in prehistory (preliteracy) give postliterate man the means of observing the action of the latest technologies.

Such instant retrieval joins prehistory and posthistory in an inclusive now of all traditions.

> *The providence that's in a watchful state*
> *Knows almost every grain of Plutus' gold,*
> *Finds bottom in the uncomprehensive deeps,*
> *Keeps place with thought, and almost, like the gods,*
> *Does thoughts unveil in their dumb cradles.*
>
> (Shakespeare, *Troilus and Cressida*)

The American executive now experiences the European "existential" anguish in the clash between job and role. The more responsible he is, the less power he has — the more involved, the less freedom.

With the acceleration of change, management now takes on entirely new functions. While navigation amidst the unknown is becoming the normal role of the executive, the new need is not merely to navigate but to anticipate effects with their causes. At instant speeds in our resonant Echoland, it is fatal to "wait and see." "Feedback" relying on experience is now too slow. We must know in advance of action. The "feedforward" of knowledge based on pattern recognition of process is essential for reprogramming beyond ideologies. What had always appeared inevitable can thus be bypassed.

THERE IS NO LONGER ANY NEED TO BACK INTO A PROPHYLACTIC FUTURE WITH MILDEWED HINDSIGHT.

1. Role Becomes Job

THE PRESIDENT

The academic historians of Ford's time strove to make history into a science by a *matching* process. Henry Ford turned to *making* history by scrapping the agrarian world around him. He was one of the greatest creators of new social clothing and service environments. While altering every pattern of the contemporary world and of history, he resolutely averted his gaze from the past and present alike. It was in a spirit of somnambulistic compensation that he built Greenfield Village in the eye of the industrial maelstrom.

Henry Ford, one of the most antiquated and tribalistic of all industrial managers, was "*The* President." There were no other members of the hierarchy.

In dispensing with the conventional organizational hierarchy, Ford naturally resorted to the tribal form of government by Mafia methods. He was ahead of his time. He could afford to junk history, since he *was* history.

At the other extreme in the motor industry was Alfred P. Sloan, Jr., of General Motors, whose very conventional hierarchical organization is portrayed in detail by Peter Drucker in *Concept of the Corporation.* With his archaic dream of decentralization for General Motors, Sloan involuntarily restored the baronial pattern of managerial bosses and autonomous groupings in his empire. This pattern readily enabled his representatives to see themselves as "knights in shining armor." This "Court of King Arthur" sort of world was seen by Henry Ford, through the spectacles of Mark Twain, as pure bunkum.

The Rear-View Mirror

Henry Ford teamed up with Thomas Edison to build Greenfield Village, a nostalgic RVM evocation of the agrarian world that they had junked by their innovations. Daniel J. Boorstin, in *The Image: Or, What Happened to the American Dream,* need have gone no further than Greenfield Village to reconstruct the stages of slaughter, interment, and monumentality, by which Bonanzaland became a universal parking lot. The extreme forms of urban decentralism created by the car led swiftly to extreme forms of managerial centralism. Ford and Sloan split apart over this. Ford saw it as a means of strengthening centralist control, while Sloan chose the strategy of decentralism as in accord with the mobility of the car.

Having already stated the contrast between oral and written patterns of social and legal procedures of the past, it is possible to see these traditionally opposed forms of order once more in the center of the management dramas of our present world.

Mini-Mafia

Oozing charm from every pore
He oiled his way across the floor
(My Fair Lady)

The effect of satellites is the conversion of the planet into a global theater that demands spectacular programming beyond anything conceived by the old Hollywood. The global theater demands the world population not only as audience but as a cast of participants.

In *Fortune* Magazine, July, 1969, Tom Alexander wrote on "The Unexpected Payoff of Project Apollo." He describes, on the one hand, the extreme fragmented hierarchical and specialized organization that went into the project, and, on the other hand, the emergency of an integral "musical" organization of all these components into an unexpected kind of "NASA Mafia."

Horse Collar and Stirrup as Extensions of Man

Machiavelli is now as obsolete as Gutenberg from whom he stems. "Old Nick" was among the first to observe the psychic and social fracturing that resulted from the alphabet ("alforabit") when speeded by the new press. Let us ask what sort of a pamphlet might have been written by an equally sharp observer when the stirrup and the horse collar were new. Lynn White has detailed the political and urban revolutions that proceeded from those medieval innovations, in *Medieval Technology and Social Change*. The stirrup created the feudal system, revolutionizing landholding and all the structures of social power. The knight became the invincible tank.

With the horse collar came "horsepower" and the agricultural and transportation revolutions. New cities, new markets, Gutenberg, and gunpowder shot these structures to pieces by sheer speed-up and specialism. From the most ancient times the perfections of natural beauty had been the supreme focus of intellectual contemplation by those in power. The break from regarding nature as beauty to exploiting nature as a source of power and wealth came suddenly. It gathered momentum in the sixteenth century with the press and was dominant until the turn of the nineteenth century.

Humpty Dumpty: China Egg on the Magazine Wall

. . . a break-through after a long accumulation of tension, as a swollen river breaks through its dikes, or in the manner of a cloudburst . . . Applied to human conditions, it refers to the time when inferior people gradually begin to disappear. Their influence is on the wane; as a result of resolute action, a change in conditions occurs, a break-through. . . .

(I Ching)

The story of the fall of Humpty Dumpty, as it were, is recorded in all the classics of the sixteenth century, from More's *Utopia*, and *Don Quixote* to Shakespeare. The entire works of Shakespeare are concerned with the unhappy dissolution of personal faith and loyalty and the rise of the Machiavellian Iagos, Edmunds, and Macbeths. Calculating adventurers, usurpers, and opportunists seemed to Shakespeare to have succeeded an age of harmony and music:

> *O! when degree is*
> *shak'd,*
> *Which is the ladder to all high designs,*
> *The enterprise is sick. How could communities,*
> *Degrees in schools, and brotherhoods in cities,*
> *Peaceful commerce from dividable shores,*
> *The primogenitive and due of birth,*
> *Prerogative of age, crowns, sceptres, laurels,*
> *But by degree, stand in authentic place?*
> *Take but degree away, untune that string,*
> *And hark! what discord follows; each thing meets*
> *In mere oppugnancy.*
>   (Shakespeare, *Troilus and Cressida*)

The pre-Gutenberg world assumed resonance and music as the physical basis of social order. The shift to individual self-interest and private goals instead of corporate role playing was a sixteenth-century drama that is being played backward today. The return to resonance as the physical basis of being itself is now asserted by science and implemented by instant electric circuitry.

The timeless appeal of Prince Hamlet as a chief of state lies in his being torn between his corporate princely role and the new private-power politics of the strong-arm Fortinbras types. "Moreness" went with the divide-and-rule tactics of the new print age of mass production. Machiavelli saw that the uniform repetitive products of the press created the universal market of uniform pricing. He saw that the principle would also extend to ambitious people engaged in specialist activities created by the Gutenberg technology: "Every man has his price." This was not a cynical observation under the circumstances.

Lear's Dilemma

King Lear is like Hamlet, trying to play it both ways, the pathetic case of a man seeking to be "with it" but lacking awareness of the Machiavellian consequences of the new forms of delegated authority.

"L'esprit de Quantité"

The villain Edmund is the Machiavelli of the play. He is imbued with the new idea of *moreness* as power goal (*l'esprit de quantité*), which became the basis of the new idea of "sovereign states." Whereas the medieval monarch had "put on" his subjects as his "corporate mask," the Renaissance prince saw his people contained within visual and geographic boundaries.

KING LEAR IS A WORKING MODEL OF THE PROCESS
OF DENUDATION BY WHICH MEN TRANSLATED THEMSELVES
FROM A WORLD OF ROLES TO A WORLD OF JOBS.

*King Lear is a kind of elaborate case history of people translating themselves out
of a world of roles into the new world of jobs. This is a process of denudation
which does not occur instantly except in artistic vision. But Shakespeare saw that
it had happened in his time. He was not talking about the future. However, the
older world of roles had lingered on as a ghost just as after a century of electricity
the West still feels the presence of the older values of literacy and privacy and separateness.*

(Marshall McLuhan, *The Gutenberg Galaxy*)

The State as a Work of Art

As the old medieval world of organic coherence fell open, many, like
Machiavelli, saw the possibility of dealing with the state as a work of art. Jacob
Burckhardt spent a volume on this theme without knowing that any old structure
automatically becomes a work of art. In a word, the Machiavellis were looking
back to the medieval times through Renaissance glasses. All utopias are images
of the immediately preceding society projected into the future. Such is More's
Utopia as much as Orwell's anti-utopia *1984*. Samuel Butler saw the dilemma in
his title *Erewhon* by spelling his utopia backward. All power became a masquerade of fakes and fictions. Loss of the traditional forms of identity and loyalty
freed everybody to become an isolated person in somebody's game. The popular
name for these new adventurers was "honest men." Shakespeare has typified
them in "honest Iago," the "honest engine" of power and intrigue, the fabricator
of "ocular proof."

2. New Resumes Old

The A-Stone-Aged Manager

Having scrapped the medieval world, the Gutenberg technology extended man's
powers of retrieval by speed-up. The medieval scriptorium had no means of coping with the whole of antiquity, but the Gutenberg press dumped all the ancient
classics into the Renaissance lap. There was an orgy of paganism and miming of
ancient styles of prose and dress and art.

Pope, in *The Dunciad*, records the ultimate development of Gutenberg as a
kind of supermarket abundance of books, which swamped the human intelligence and befogged the wits of men in clouds of ink. The seventeenth-century
"balance" between "hardware" and "software" yielded quickly to the eighteenth-

century triumph of "hardware," familiar to every schoolboy who reads Goldsmith's *Deserted Village*. William Blake, however, took an even grimmer view of the change than that expressed in the pastoral lament of the genial Irishman.

U.S.A. as Laboratory for Social Experiments, Past and Present

is the theme of Peter Farb's *Man's Rise to Civilization as Shown by the Indians of North America from Primeval Times to the Coming of the Industrial State:*

> North America is the place in the world most nearly ideal to observe the evolution of human societies and customs, institutions and beliefs, for these are revealed there with all the clarity of a scientific experiment. The story of the Indians in North America provides modern man with a living test tube, in which the major ingredients that went into the experiment, the intermediate reactions that took place, and the final results are largely known.

The electrotechnic age, having rendered obsolete the age of industrial "hardware" and its organization chart, has unexpectedly retrieved the most primitive and archaic cultures of many times and places. We now are swamped by a new environment of preliterate forms. This brings us full circle on our tour with

OFF-Again — ON-Again — FINN-Again

There are only two basic extreme forms of human organization. They have innumerable variants or "parti-colored" forms. The extreme forms are the *civilized* and the *tribal* (eye and ear): the Cromwellian specialist and the Celtic involved. Only the civilized form is fragmented in action, whether in business or in politics or in entertainment. Hence the anarchy of the contemporary world where all these forms coexist.

Dependent upon the materials and hence the technologies available to mankind, the pattern of social organization and management swings violently from stress on the entrepreneur and the virtues of the lonely individualist to the close-knit and emotionally involved group. In the diversified scope of modern business structures, these extremes can express themselves at different levels of the same organization. Tribal cliques can grow in the shade of the old organization tree. The telephone can foster such groups, especially when the "bugging" of the phones is on a large scale. The oral substructure *ground* quickly undermines the organization "tree."

By the law of change, whatever has reached its extreme must turn back.

(I Ching)

It is explained in the same context of this 4,000-year-old management manual that innovation "does indeed guide all happenings, but it never behaves outwardly as the leader. Thus true strength is that strength which, mobile as it is hidden, concentrates on the work without being outwardly visible." What is actually visible in new situations is the ghost of old ones. It is the movie that *appears* on TV. It is the old written word that *appears* on Telex. The hidden force of change is the new speed that alters all configurations of power. The new speed creates a new hidden *ground* against which the old *ground* becomes the *figure* of the dropout. The function of the dropout is to reveal the new hidden *ground* or environment. This development can occur either as individual or corporate. The role of the typical "drop-in" or consultant is to prop up the collapsing foundations. Freud arrived too late to save the nuclear family. He was dumped by the nuclear age.

THE HIDDEN PERSUADERS AND THE FRUSTRATED RADICALS

All management theories and political ideologies follow an involuntary procedure. The idealists share with the experienced and practical men of their time the infirmity of substituting concepts for percepts. Both concentrate on a clash between past experience and future goals that black out the usual but hidden processes of the present. Both ignore the fact that *dialogue* as a process of creating the new came before, and goes beyond, the *change* of "equivalents" that merely reflect or repeat the old.

Pastimes Are Past Times

The new expert, along with the old executive, has been swept away in a flood of comedies. New environments of information and enterprise have revealed the contours of these obsolescent types, even as the satellite has created a sudden and universal awareness of "pollution."

MEN OF EXTINCTION UNITE; WITH HARDENINGOF THE CATEGORIES YOU'VE NOTHING TO LOSE BUT THE CHANGE.

Lost Interface

The French revolutionaries were determined to abolish the *ancient regime* that had become a rococo masquerade long before 1789. The old feudal hierarchy of costumes and roles had to be scrapped at any cost. *Le grand monarque*, with his surround of china shepherdesses, was swept aside to make way for *l'empereur*, whose enormous centralist power was derived, not from the feudal pennies of the peasantry, but from the cannon and "hardware" of the new middle-class manufacturers. The puny and slow-moving bureaucracy of the Bourbons was replaced by the speed of production and road movement of Napoleon's legions. Napoleon introduced a semaphore telegraph system that gave him four-hour intervals of intercom with Rome. He ran the army and the country as a centralized industrial corporation. He invented the rule of using the right-hand side of the road to create traffic speed and conformity. He introduced the fragmented uniformity of the "metric" system and the speedy Code Napoleon. The old common law disappeared under a monumental catafalque of classical solemnity and senatorial dignity. The egalitarian dreams of the Jacobins were gaily sacrificed, to *la gloire et l'honneur de la patrie*. The idealists had fought for liberty and equality, and they got a military state with careers open to talents. Napoleon anticipated the later organization chart with "staff and line," proclaiming the right of every private to envisage a marshal's baton in his old kit bag.

These were the visible developments that reversed the dreams of the *avant-garde*. A far more insidious force was inherent in the entire speed-up of the new industrial "hardware" complex.

3. "Ground" Remakes "Figure"

Hidden Environments Reshape Their Makers

In Europe and in England alike the extreme specialism of the industrial revolution created a massive retrieval of medieval sensibility in the arts and crafts, and in religion. This was the new hidden *ground* that entered into abrasive interface with the pronounced *figure* of the dominant new industrialisms. This hidden action in the later nineteenth century has its parallel at present in the retribalizing process of electrotechniques. While detribalizing is assigned top priority for civilized advance in all backward areas, regardless of geography or ideology, there is also occurring a complementary and hidden process of retribalization that is independent of either plotters or planners, ideology or geography. The most archaic societies now begin with our latest electric technology. They by-pass the civilized phase that occupied Western energies for thousands of years and plunge even deeper into their own tribal traditions.

The Renaissance or the rebirth of pagan antiquity was the unexpected consequence of demolishing the feudal system. The return of the pagan gods and pagan humanism had not been the objective of any of the reformers. The Luthers and Calvins had sought to purge the church of its accretion of political impurities. Driving toward primal simplicity, they encountered innumerable schisms and doctrinal specialisms as the dominant *figure* of their actions. The hidden *ground* was the overwhelming new retrieval of pagan antiquity via print technology. The very technological instrument of individual "inner light" and liberation immersed them in a new environment of merely utilitarian objectives.

> *The hateful siege of contraries.*
> (Milton, *Paradise Lost*)

In our own century the same siege of hateful contraries and dramatic reversals was played out in the Eastern medieval theater of the Romanoffs. The Russians sloughed off the feudal hegemony of the Romanoffs and grasped the latest means of Western organization of industrial production. The slogan was:

CATCH UP AND SURPASS!

Just when the West was plunging Eastward, and when the enlightened spirits had either booked a passage to India or, like Yeats, were already on the iconic route to Byzantium, cultural anthropologists like Sir James Frazer set out to retrieve the Great Mother and the mythic figures of archaic consciousness. But the anthropologists failed to note that these forms of awareness had become totally pervasive even before the jazz age of the 1920's. The instant telegraph had established modes of social order that radio broadcasting pushed all the way to Hitler's ovens.

The same cruel paradox involves the American Negro, whose jazz rhythms integrated the cultures of the entire world for the first time in history or before. The same Negro is now expected to "integrate" with the subculture of literacy after having created a universal culture of tribal jazz.

James Joyce put it all in a phrase about the heroine of *Finnegans Wake*. She is Anna Livia Plurabelle, musical mother of all forms, the hidden *ground* of being:

> *Sheshell ebb music wayriver she flows.*

The hidden *ground* and force of the anthropological enterprise, as much as the business world of the consumer-producer, lay in the power of instant electric communication to restore all things to an inclusive present. By involving all men in all men, by the electric extension of their own nervous systems, the new technology turns the *figure* of the primitive society into a universal *ground* that buries all previous *figures*. The naïveté of the anthropologists, "secure" in a civilized literate stockade, is matched again and again by would-be innovators who head for specific goals:

The author of Perry Mason often felt the irony of his situation. Having set out to write, that he might have leisure for hunting and fishing, he spent his life dictating to a team of secretaries. The hidden *ground* of his plight was precisely hunting and fishing. His hero, Perry Mason, is a full-time hunter and fisher of men and clues. The sleuth, the undercover man, is a major posture of the hunter against the new electric *ground* of the telephone and TV.

Man Hunter and Sleuth: Posture and Imposture

In one of Sherlock Holmes's adventures his quarry demurs when Holmes declares that he had seen him at a particular spot. The quarry retorts that "I saw nobody following me there." And Holmes comments, "That is what you may expect to see when I follow you."

Half the world today is engaged in keeping the other half "under surveillance." This, in fact, is the hang-up of the age of "software" and information. In the preceding "hardware" age the "haves" of the world had kept the "have-nots" under "surveillance." This old beat for flatfoots has now been relegated to the world of popular entertainment. *The police state is no work of art, a bureaucratic ballet of undulating sirens.* That is a way of seeing that the espionage activities of our multitudinous man hunters "crediting" agencies are not only archaic, but redundant and irrelevant.

GALLUPING ESPIONAGE CREATES THE UNPERSON:
THE MAN THAT NEVER WAS

POSTURE AND IMPOSTURE AS WAYS OF LIFE
NOW MERGE IN THE GLOBAL THEATER

Print and the
Electric Revolution

7

Media and Cultural Change

For anyone acquainted with poetry since Baudelaire and with painting since Cézanne, the later world of Harold A. Innis is quite readily intelligible. He brought their kinds of contemporary awareness of the electric age to organize the data of the historian and the social scientists. Without having studied modern art and poetry, he yet discovered how to arrange his insights in patterns that nearly resemble the art forms of our time. Innis presents his insights in a mosaic structure of seemingly unrelated and disproportioned sentences and aphorisms. Such is page 108, for example, with its scholarly footnote that will certainly bear looking into. Anybody who has looked up the reference material that Innis cites so frequently, will be struck by the skill with which he has extracted exciting facts from dull expositions. He explored his source material with a "geiger counter," as it were. In turn, he presents his finds in a pattern of insights that are not packaged for the consumer palate. He expects the reader to make discovery after discovery that he himself had missed. His view of the departmentalized specialisms of our Universities as ignoble monopolies of knowledge is expressed on page 194: "Finally we must keep in mind the limited role of Universities and recall the comment that 'the whole external history of science is a history of the resistance of academies and Universities to the progress of knowledge.'"

One can say of Innis what Bertrand Russell said of Einstein on the first page of his *A B C of Relativity* (1925): "Many of the new ideas can be expressed in non-mathematical language, but they are none the less difficult on that account. What is demanded is a change in our imaginative picture of the world." The "later Innis" who dominates *The Bias of Communication* had set out on a quest for the causes of change. The "early Innis" of *The Fur Trade in Canada* had conformed a good deal to the conventional patterns of merely reporting and narrating change. Only at the conclusion of the fur trade study did he venture to interlace or link complex events in a way that reveals the causal processes of change. His insight that the American Revolution was in large part due to a clash between the interests of the settlers on one hand and the interests of the fur traders on the other is the sort of vision that becomes typical of the later Innis. He changed his procedure from working with a "point of view" to that of the generating of insights by the method of "interface," as it is named in chemistry. "Interface" refers to the interaction of substances in a kind of mutual irritation. In art and poetry this is precisely the technique of "symbolism" (Greek "symballein" — to throw together) with its paratactic procedure of juxtaposing without connectives. It is the natural form of conversation or dialogue rather than of written discourse. In writing, the tendency is to isolate an aspect of some matter and to direct steady attention upon that aspect. In dialogue there is an equally natural interplay of multiple aspects of any matter. This interplay of aspects can generate insights or discovery. By contrast, a point of view is merely a way of *looking at* something. But an insight is the sudden awareness of a complex process of interaction. An insight is a contact with the life of forms. Students of computer programming have had to learn how to approach all knowledge structurally. In order to transfer any kind of knowledge to tapes it is necessary to understand the form of that knowledge. This has led to the discovery of the basic difference between classified knowledge and pattern recognition. It is a helpful distinction to keep in mind when reading Innis since he is above all a recognizer of patterns. Dr. Kenneth Sayre explains the matter as follows in his *The Modelling of Mind* (University of Notre Dame Press, 1963), p. 17: "Classification is a *process*, something which takes up one's time, which one might do reluctantly, unwillingly, or enthusiastically, which can be done with more or less success, done very well or very poorly. Recognition, in sharp contrast, is not time-consuming. A person may spend a long while looking before recognition occurs, but when it occurs it is "instantaneous." When recognition occurs, it is not an act which would be said to be performed either reluctantly or enthusiastically, compliantly or under protest. Moreover, the notion of recognition being unsuccessful, or having been done very poorly, seems to make no sense at all."

In this book Innis has much to say about the oral as opposed to the written methods of approaching the learning process. In the paper titled "A Critical Review" he explains: "My bias is with the oral tradition, particularly as reflected in Greek civilization, and with the necessity of recapturing something of its spirit." (p. 190) E. A. Havelock, a former colleague of Innis, has recently devoted an entire study to the clash of the old oral and the new written culture of Greece. His *Preface to Plato* (Harvard, 1963) would have delighted Innis, and there are very many sentences in Innis which should become the subject of such full investigations.

I am pleased to think of my own book *The Gutenberg Galaxy* (University of Toronto Press, 1962) as a footnote to the observations of Innis on the subject of the psychic and social consequences, first of writing and then of printing. Flattered by the attention that Innis had directed to some work of mine, I turned for the first time to his work. It was my good fortune to begin with the first essay in this book: "Minerva's Owl." How exciting it was to encounter a writer whose every phrase invited prolonged meditation and exploration: "Alexandria broke the link between science and philosophy. The library was an imperial instrument to offset the influence of Egyptian priesthood." (p. 10)

Innis takes much time to read if he is read on his own terms. That he deserves to be read on his own terms becomes obvious as soon as that experiment is tried even once. So read, he takes time but he also saves time. Each sentence is a compressed monograph. He includes a small library on each page, and often incorporates a small library of references on the same page in addition. If the business of the teacher is to save the student's time, Innis is one of the greatest teachers on record. The two sentences just quoted imply and invite an awareness of the specific structural forms of science and philosophy as well as of the structural nature and functions of empires, libraries, and priesthoods. Most writers are occupied in providing accounts of the contents of philosophy, science, libraries, empires, and religions. Innis invites us instead to consider the formalities of power exerted by these structures in their mutual interaction. He approaches each of these forms of organized power as exercising a particular kind of force upon each of the other components in the complex. All of the components exist by virtue of processes going on within each and among them all. Just what "science" or "philosophy" was at this time will be manifested by what each does to the other in their encounter in the social and historic process. And so with the other components. They explain themselves by their behaviour in a historic action. Innis had hit upon the means of using history as the physicist uses the cloud chamber. By bouncing the unknown form against known forms, he discovered the nature of the new or little known form.

This use of history as a scientific laboratory, as a set of controlled conditions within which to study the life and nature of forms, is very far removed from the conventional narrative of a Toynbee. Toynbee is like the announcer of a sporting event. He tells a good deal about what is happening. His tone of earnest concern indicates to the reader or listener that the events have some significance. In the same situation Innis would have observed that the form of the sporting event was an interesting model of perception, giving us an immediate image of the motives and patterns of the society that had invented this corporate extension of itself. He would then explain that his role of announcer, like that of the audience at the sporting event, was part of the structure of the game, having a distorting bias of perception and amplification that gave the game in question a great deal of political and commercial force.

As soon as the reader grasps that Innis is concerned with the unique power of each form to alter the action of other forms it encounters, he will be able to proceed as Innis did. He can begin to observe and estimate the action and counteraction of forms past and present. He will discover that Innis never repeats himself, but that he never ceases to test the action of oral forms of knowledge and social organization in different social contexts. Innis tests the oral form as it reacts in many different written cultures, just as he tests the effects of time-structured institutions in their varieties of contact with space-oriented societies.

It would be a mistake to suppose that Innis has garnered most of the available insights from any given historical test that he happens to run. In the same way, he is quite capable of inaccurate observation during the running of his tests of the interactions of social forms, though this in no way impairs the validity of his way of testing the structural properties of social forms. For example, he notes that: "The Greeks took over the alphabet and made it a flexible instrument suited to the demands of a flexible oral tradition by the creation of words." (p. 7) The alphabet is a technology of visual fragmentation and specialism, and it led the Greeks quickly to the discovery of classifiable data. Havelock clarifies this at length in his *Preface to Plato*. As long as the oral culture was not overpowered by the technological extension of the visual power in the alphabet, there was a very rich cultural result from the interplay of the oral and written forms. The revival of oral culture in our own electric age now exists in a similar fecund relation with the still powerful written and visual culture. We are in our century "winding the tape backwards." The Greeks went from oral to written even as we are moving from written to oral. They "ended" in a desert of classified data even as we could "end" in a new tribal encyclopedia of auditory incantation.

Innis sometimes mistook the interplay of written and oral forms, ascribing to the written form itself what was a hybrid product of its interaction with oral culture: "The alphabet borrowed from the Phoenicians was given vowels and adapted to the demands of speech. The ear replaced the eye. With the spread of writing the oral tradition developed fresh powers of resistance evident in the flowering of Greek culture in the sixth and fifth centuries." (p. 136) Had Innis made a more intense analysis of the visual modalities inherent in the phonetic alphabet, or a more thorough study of the dynamics of oral forms, he would have avoided some of these slips. But the method he discovered remains. He had discovered a means of using historical situations as a lab in which to test the character of technology in the shaping of cultures.

Innis taught us how to use the bias of culture and communication as an instrument of research. By directing attention to the bias or distorting power of the dominant imagery and technology of any culture, he showed us how to understand cultures. Many scholars had made us aware of the "difficulty of assessing the quality of a culture of which we are a part or of assessing the quality of a culture of which we are not a part." (p. 132) Innis was perhaps the first to make of this vulnerable fact of all scholarly outlook the prime opportunity for research and discovery. Peter F. Drucker in *Managing for Results* (Harper and Row, 1964) has shown how in any human organization or situation 90 per cent of the events are caused by 10 per cent. Most human attention is allocated to the 90 per cent area which is the area of problems. The 10 per cent area is the area of irritation and also of opportunity. It was the genius of Harold Innis that refused to be distracted by the 90 per cent area of problems. He went straight to the 10 per cent core of opportunity and sought insight into the causes that underlay the whole situation. For example, he writes: "We are perhaps too much a part of the civilization which followed the printing industry to be able to detect its characteristics. Education in the words of Laski became the art of teaching men to be deceived by the printed word." (p. 139)

Once Innis had ascertained the dominant technology of a culture he could be sure that this was the cause and shaping force of the entire structure. He could also be sure that this dominant form and all its causal powers were necessarily masked from the attention of that culture by a psychic mechanism of "protective inhibition" as it were. At a stroke he had solved two major problems that are forever beyond the power of the "nose-counters" and of statistical researchers. First, he knew what the pattern of any culture had to be, both physically and socially, as soon as he had identified its major technological achievements. Second, he knew exactly what the members of that culture would be ignorant of in their daily lives. What has been called "the nemesis of creativity" is precisely a blindness to the effects of one's most significant form of invention.

A good example of this technological blindness in Innis himself was his mistake in regarding radio and electric technology as a further extension of the patterns of mechanical technology: "The radio appealed to vast areas, overcame the division between classes in its escape from literacy, and favoured centralization and bureaucracy." (p. 82) Again: "Competition from the new medium, the radio involved an appeal to the ear rather than to the eye and consequently an emphasis on centralization." (p. 188) This is an example of Innis failing to be true to his own method. After many historical demonstrations of the space-binding power of the eye and the time-binding power of the ear, Innis refrains from applying these structural principles of the action of radio. Suddenly, he shifts the ear world of radio into the visual orbit, attributing to radio all the centralizing powers of the eye and of visual culture. Here Innis was misled by the ordinary consensus of his time. Electric light and power, like all electric media, are profoundly decentralizing and separatist in their psychic and social consequences. Had he not been hypnotized by his respect for the pervasive conventional view on this question, Innis could have worked out the new electric pattern of culture quite easily.

What is rare in Innis occurs in his mention of the views of Wyndham Lewis: "Wyndham Lewis has argued that the fashionable mind is the time-denying mind." He is referring to *Time and Western Man* which is devoted to a denunciation of the obsession with time as a religious mystique in the work of Bergson, Alexander, Whitehead, and others. Because of his own deep concern with the values of tradition and temporal continuity, Innis has managed to misread Wyndham Lewis radically. Earlier, in the same essay, "A Plea for Time," he raises an issue that may bear on the occasional miscarriage of his own structural method of analysis. Speaking of the unfortunate effects of the extreme impact of print development on our twentieth century culture, he observes: "Communication based on the eye in terms of printing and photography had developed a monopoly which threatened to destroy Western civilization first in war and then in peace." (p. 80) Innis did not like monopolies in any form. He saw that they bred violent reactions: "The disastrous effect of the monopoly of communication based on the eye hastened the development of a competitive type of communication based on the ear, in the radio and in the linking of sound to the cinema and to television. Printed material gave way in effectiveness to the broadcast and to the loud speaker." (p. 81) What Innis has failed to do in this part of his essay is to make a structural analysis of the modalities of the visual and the audible. He is merely assuming that an extension of information in space has a centralizing power regardless of the human faculty that is amplified and extended. But whereas the visual power extended by print does indeed extend the means to organize a spatial continuum, the auditory power extended electrically does in effect abolish space and time alike. Visual technology creates a centre-margin pattern of organization whether by literacy or by industry and a price system. But electric technology is instant and omnipresent and creates multiple centres-without-margins. Visual technology whether by literacy or by industry creates nations as spatially uniform and homogeneous and connected. But electric technology creates not the nation but the tribe — not the superficial association of equals but the cohesive depth pattern of the totally involved kinship groups. Visual technologies, whether based on papyrus or paper, foster fragmentation and specialism, armies, and empires. Electric technology favours not the fragmentary but the integral, not the mechanical but the organic. It had not occurred to Innis that electricity is in effect an extension of the nervous system as a kind of global membrane. As an economic historian he had such a rich experience of the technological extensions of the bodily powers that it is not surprising that he failed to note the character of this most recent and surprising of human extensions.

There is one department in which Innis never fails, and in which the flavour of Inniscence is never lost — his humour. Humour is of the essence of his aphoristic association of incongruities. His technique of discovery by the juxtaposition of forms lends itself everywhere to a series of dramatic surprises. On page 77 in the midst of considering the revolt of the American colonies and nineteenth century wars he suddenly observes a parallel with the press wars of Hearst and Pulitzer as related to the emergence of the comic strip. He is unrivalled in his power to discover choice items in contemporary history to illuminate grave matters of archaeology. Referring to the neglect of the horse as a factor in military history, he recalls that "E. J. Dillon remarked concerning a mounted policeman that he was always surprised by the look of intelligence on the horse's face." (p. 95) The mosaic structure of insights employed in the work of the later Innis is never far removed from the comic irony of an Abraham Lincoln. Innis found that his technique of insight engendered a perpetual entertainment of surprises and intellectual comedy.

To record the intellectual influences that shaped the work of Innis would be a large, if rewarding, task. His studies at the University of Chicago after the First

World War occurred at a most favourable time. The work of Emile Durkheim, Max Weber, and John Dewey had fecundated a new group of economic and social studies that flowered in the writings of Thorstein Veblen, George Herbert Mead, and Robert Ezra Park. These men created an atmosphere at Chicago in the 1920's that attracted and inspired many able students. Most of these men had, like Innis, spent their youth in small towns. The speedy growth of the metropolis after the first war presented an inexhaustible subject for these sociologists, and much of their work was directed to urban study and analysis, using the small town as a basis for comparison and contrast. Innis tended to follow another pattern, though, as we shall see, he was deeply in debt to Robert Ezra Park. Durkheim, the late nineteenth century founder of analytic sociology, dealt with whole populations. The Chicago school dealt with local communities. Innis is European rather than American in his choice of the larger themes. From Park, however, he learned how to identify the control mechanisms by which a heterogeneous community yet manages to arrange its affairs with some degree of uniformity. Perhaps Innis was aided in this choice by his familiarity with the staple economy of Canada. A semi-industrialized country, rich in major resources like wheat, lumber, minerals, fur, fish, and wood pulp has a peculiar economic and social life compared to a more diversified and developed economy. Innis seized the opportunity to deal with this unique pattern of a staple economy and was not led to follow the popular pattern of urban studies that was being pursued by the exciting and productive Chicago group. I suggest that Innis made the further transition from the history of staples to the history of the media of communication quite naturally. Media are major resources like economic staples. In fact, without railways, the staples of wheat and lumber can scarcely be said to exist. Without the press and the magazine, wood pulp could not exist as a staple either.

In May, 1940, the *Canadian Journal of Economics and Political Science* published an article by Robert Park entitled "Physics and Society" (reprinted in *Society* by Robert Ezra Park [Free Press of Glencoe, 1955], pp. 301-21). Park began by citing Walter Bagehot to the effect that society is a social organism maintained by a social process. The theme of his essay is recapitulated this way: "I have gone into some detail in my description of the role and function of communication because it is so obviously fundamental to the social process, and because extensions and improvements which the physical sciences have made to the means of communications are so vital to the existence of society and particularly to that more rationally organized form of society we call civilization." (*Society*, p. 314)

The ideas of Park seem to have appealed more to the mind of Harold Innis than to any other student of Robert Park. Anybody can hear the Innis note in such observations by Park as the following: "Technological devices have naturally changed men's habits and in doing so, they have necessarily modified the structure and functions of society." (p. 308) Again: "From this point of view it seems that every technical device, from the wheelbarrow to the aeroplane, in so far as it provided a new and more effective means of locomotion, has, or should have, marked an epoch in society. This is so far true as most other important changes in the means of transportation and communication. It is said likewise that every civilization carries in itself the seeds of its own destruction. Such seeds are likely to be the technical devices that introduce a new social order and usher out an old." (*Society*, pp. 309-10) In the same year as his "Physics and Society" article, Park published "News as a Form of Knowledge": "I have indicated the role which news plays in the world of politics in so far as it provides the basis for the discussions in which public opinion is formed. The news plays quite as important a role in the world of economic relations, since the price of commodities, including money and securities, as registered in the world market and in every local market dependent upon it, is based on the news." (p. 86)

These ideas were not lost on Harold Innis. Indeed, Innis developed them much further than Park did, and should be considered as the most eminent of the Chicago group headed by Robert Park.

8

The Gutenberg Galaxy

Prologue

The present volume is in many respects complementary to *The Singer of Tales* by Albert B. Lord. Professor Lord has continued the work of Milman Parry, whose Homeric studies had led him to consider how oral and written poetry naturally followed diverse patterns and functions. Convinced that the poems of Homer were oral compositions, Parry "set himself the task of proving incontrovertibly if it were possible, the oral character of the poems, and to that end he turned to the study of the Yugoslav epics." His study of these modern epics was, he explained, "to fix with exactness the *form* of oral story poetry. . . . Its method was to observe singers working in a thriving tradition of unlettered song and see how the form of their songs hangs upon their having to learn and practice their art without reading and writing."[1]

Professor Lord's book, like the studies of Milman Parry, is quite natural and appropriate to our electric age, as *The Gutenberg Galaxy* may help to explain. We are today as far into the electric age as the Elizabethans had advanced into the typographical and mechanical age. And we are experiencing the same confusions and indecisions which they had felt when living simultaneously in two contrasted forms of society and experience. Whereas the Elizabethans were poised between medieval corporate experience and modern individualism, we reverse their pattern by confronting an electric technology which would seem to render individualism obsolete and the corporate interdependence mandatory.

Patrick Cruttwell had devoted an entire study (*The Shakespearean Moment*) to the artistic strategies born of the Elizabethan experience of living in a divided world that was dissolving and resolving at the same time. We, too, live at such a moment of interplay of contrasted cultures, and *The Gutenberg Galaxy* is intended to trace the ways in which the *forms* of experience and of mental outlook and expression have been modified, first by the phonetic alphabet and then by printing. The enterprise which Milman Parry undertook with reference to the contrasted *forms* of oral and written poetry is here extended to the *forms* of thought and the organization of experience in society and politics. That such a study of the divergent nature of oral and written social organization has not been

---

[1] Quoted in *The Singer of Tales*, p. 3.

carried out by historians long ago is rather hard to explain. Perhaps the reason for the omission is simply that the job could only be done when the two conflicting forms of written and oral experience were once again co-existent as they are today. Professor Harry Levin indicates as much in his preface to Professor Lord's *The Singer of Tales* (p. xiii):

> *The term "literature," presupposing the use of letters, assumes that verbal works of imagination are transmitted by means of writing and reading. The expression "oral literature" is obviously a contradiction in terms. Yet we live at a time when literacy itself has become so diluted that it can scarcely be invoked as an esthetic criterion. The Word as spoken or sung, together with a visual image of the speaker or singer, has meanwhile been regaining its hold through electrical engineering. A culture based upon the printed book, which has prevailed from the Renaissance until lately, has bequeathed to us — along with its immeasurable riches — snobberies which ought to be cast aside. We ought to take a fresh look at tradition, considered not as the inert acceptance of a fossilized corpus of themes and conventions, but as an organic habit of re-creating what has been received and is handed on.*

The omission of historians to study the revolution in the *forms* of thought and social organization resulting from the phonetic alphabet has a parallel in socio-economic history. As early as 1864-67 Karl Rodbertus elaborated his theory of "Economic Life in Classical Antiquity." In *Trade and Market in the Early Empires* (p. 5), Harry Pearson describes his innovation as follows:

> *This remarkably modern view of the social function of money has not been suffi-ciently appreciated. Rodbertus realized that the transition from a "natural economy" to a "money economy" was not simply a technical matter, which resulted from a substitution of money purchase for barter. He insisted instead that a monetarized economy involved a social structure entirely different from that which went with an economy in kind. It was this change in the social structure accompa-nying the use of money rather than the technical fact of its use which ought to be emphasized, he thought. Had this point been expanded to include the varying social structures accompanying trading activity in the ancient world the contro-versy might have been resolved before it began.*

In other words, had Rodbertus further explained that different forms of money and exchange structured societies in varying ways, generations of confused con-troversy might have been avoided. The matter was finally explained when Karl Bucher approached the classical world not from our conventional mode of historical retrospect but from the primitive side. By starting with non-literate societies and moving toward the classical world, "he suggested that ancient economic life might better be understood if viewed from the perspective of primitive rather than modern society."[2]

Such a reverse perspective of the literate Western world is the one afforded to the reader of Albert Lord's *Singer of Tales*. But we also live in an electric or post-literate time when the jazz musician uses all the techniques of oral poetry. Empathic identification with all the oral modes is not difficult in our century.

In the electronic age which succeeds the typographic and mechanical era of the past five hundred years, we encounter new shapes and structures of human interdependence and of expression which are "oral" in form even when the components of the situation may be non-verbal. This question is raised more fully in the concluding section of *The Gutenberg Galaxy*. It is not a difficult matter in itself, but it does call for some reorganization of imaginative life. Such a change of modes of awareness is always delayed by the persistence of older patterns of perception. The Elizabethans appear to our gaze as very medieval. Medieval man thought of himself as classical, just as we consider ourselves to be modern men. To our successors, however, we shall appear as utterly Renaissance in character, and quite unconscious of the major new factors which we have set in motion during the past one hundred and fifty years.

Far from being deterministic, however, the present study will, it is hoped, elucidate a principal factor in social change which may lead to a genuine increase in human autonomy. Peter Drucker writing on "The Technological Revolution" of our time in *Technology and Culture* (vol. II, no. 4, 1961, p. 348) states: "There is only one thing we do not know about the Technological Revolution — but it is essential: What happened to bring about the basic change in attitudes, beliefs, and values which released it? 'Scientific progress', I have tried to show, had little to do with it. But how responsible was the great change in world outlook which, a century earlier, had brought about the great Scientific Revolution?" *The Gutenberg Galaxy* at least attempts to supply the "one thing we do not know." But even so, there may well prove to be some other things!

The method employed throughout this study is directly related to what Claude Bernard presented in his classic introduction to *The Study of Experimental Medicine*. Observation, Bernard explains (pp. 8-9) consists in noting phenomena without disturbing them, but: "Experiment, according to the same physiologists, implies, on the contrary, the idea of a variation or disturbance that an investigator brings into the conditions of natural phenomena. . . . To do this, we suppress an organ in the living subject, by a section or ablation; and from the disturbance produced in the whole organism or in a special function, we deduce the function of the missing organ."

The work of Milman Parry and Professor Albert Lord was directed to

---

[2]*Trade and Market in the Early Empires*, p. 5.

observing the entire poetic process under oral conditions, and in contrasting that result with the poetic process which we under written conditions, assume as "normal." Parry and Lord, that is, studied the poetic organism when the auditory function was suppressed by literacy. They might also have considered the effect on the organism when the visual function of language was given extraordinary extension and power by literacy. And this is a factor in the experimental method which may have been overlooked just because it was inconvenient to manage. But given intense and exaggerated action, "the disturbance produced in the whole organism or in a special function" is equally observable.

Man the tool-making animal, whether in speech or in writing or in radio, has long been engaged in extending one or another of his sense organs in such a manner as to disturb all of his other senses and faculties. But having made these experiments, men have consistently omitted to follow them with observations.

J. Z. Young, writing on *Doubt and Certainty in Science*, notes (pp. 67-8):

The effect of stimulations, external or internal, is to break up the unison of action of some part or the whole of the brain. A speculative suggestion is that the distur- bance in some way breaks the unity of the actual pattern that has been previously built up in the brain. The brain then selects those features from the input that tend to repair the model and to return the cells to their regular synchronous beating. I cannot pretend to be able to develop this idea of models in our brain in detail, but it has great possibilities in showing how we tend to fit ourselves to the world and the world to ourselves. In some way the brain initiates sequences of actions that tend to return it to its rhythmic pattern, this return being the act of consummation, or completion. If the first action performed fails to do this, fails that is to stop the original disturbance, then other sequences may be tried. The brain runs through its rules one after another, matching the input with its various models until some- how unison is achieved. This may perhaps only be after strenuous, varied, and prolonged searching. During this random activity further connexions and action patterns are formed and they in turn will determine future sequences.

The inevitable drive for "closure," "completion," or equilibrium occurs both with the suppression and the extension of human sense or function. Since *The Gutenberg Galaxy* is a series of historical observations of the new cultural com- pletions ensuing upon the "disturbances," first of literacy, and then of printing, the statement of an anthropologist may assist the reader at this point:

Today man has developed extensions for practically everything he used to do with his body. The evolution of weapons begins with the teeth and the fist and ends with the atom bomb. Clothes and houses are extensions of man's biological temperature- control mechanisms. Furniture takes the place of squatting and sitting on the ground. Power tools, glasses, TV, telephones, and books which carry the voice across both time and space are examples of material extensions. Money is a way of extending and storing labor. Our transportation networks now do what we used to do with our feet and backs. In fact, all man-made material things can be treated as extensions of what man once did with his body or some specialized part of his body.[3]

That outering or uttering of sense which is language and speech is a tool which "made it possible for man to accumulate experience and knowledge in a form that made easy transmission and maximum use possible."[4]

Language is metaphor in the sense that it not only stores but translates experience from one mode into another. Money is metaphor in the sense that it stores skill and labour and also translates one skill into another. But the principle of exchange and translation, or metaphor, is in our rational power to translate all of our senses into one another. This we do every instant of our lives. But the price we pay for special technological tools, whether the wheel or the alphabet or radio, is that these massive *extensions* of sense constitute *closed* systems. Our private senses are not closed systems but are endlessly translated into each other in that experience which we call con-sciousness. Our extended senses, tools, technologies, through the ages, have been closed systems incapable of interplay or collective awareness. Now, in the electric age, the very instantaneous nature of co-existence among our technological instruments has created a crisis quite new in human history. Our extended faculties and senses now constitute a single field of experience which demands that they become collectively conscious. Our technologies, like our private senses, now demand an interplay and ratio that makes *rational* co-existence possible. As long as our technologies were as slow as the wheel or the alphabet or money, the fact that they were separate, closed systems was socially and psychically supportable. This is not true now when sight and sound and movement are simultaneous and global in extent. A ratio of interplay among these extensions of our human functions is now as necessary collectively as it has always been for our private and personal rationality in terms of our private senses or "wits," as they were once called.

Hitherto historians of culture have tended to isolate technological events much in the way that classical physics dealt with physical events. Louis de Broglie, describing *The Revolution in Physics*, makes much of this limitation of the Cartesian and Newtonian procedures which are so near those of the historians using an individual "point of view" (p. 14):

Faithful to the Cartesian ideal, classical physics showed us the universe as being analogous to an immense mechanism which was capable of being described with

---

[3]Edward T. Hall, *The Silent Language*, p. 79.

[4]Leslie A. White, *The Science of Culture*, p. 240.

complete precision by the localization of its parts in space and by their change in the course of time. . . . But such a conception rested on several implicit hypotheses which were admitted almost without our being aware of them. One of these hypotheses was that the framework of space and time in which we seek almost instinctively to localize all of our sensations is a perfectly rigid and fixed framework where each physical event can, in principle, be rigorously localized independently of all the dynamic processes which are going on around it.

We shall see how not only Cartesian but Euclidean perceptions are constituted by the phonetic alphabet. And the revolution that de Broglie describes is a derivative not of the alphabet but of the telegraph and of radio. J. Z. Young, a biologist, makes the same point as de Broglie. Having explained that electricity is not a thing that "flows" but is "the condition we observe when there are certain spatial relations between things," he explains (p. 111):

Something similar has happened as physicists have devised ways of measuring very small distances. It has been found no longer possible to use the old model of supposing that what was being done was to divide up something called matter into a series of bits, each with definite properties called size, weight, or position. Physicists do not now say that matter 'is made' of bodies called atoms, protons, electrons, and so on. What they have done is to give up the materialist method of describing their observations in terms of something made as by a human process of manufacture, like a cake. The word atom or electron is not used as the name of a piece. It is used as part of the description of the observations of physicists. It has no meaning except as used by people who know the experiments by which it is revealed.

And, he adds, "it is important to realize that great changes in ways of *ordinary* human speaking and acting are bound up with the adoption of new instruments." Had we meditated on such a basic fact as that long ago, we might easily have mastered the nature and effects of all our technologies, instead of being pushed around by them. At any rate, *The Gutenberg Galaxy* is a prolonged meditation on that theme of J. Z. Young.

Nobody has been more conscious of the futility of our closed systems of historical writing than Abbot Payson Usher. His classic, *A History of Mechanical Inventions*, is an explanation of why such closed systems cannot make contact with the facts of historical change: "The cultures of antiquity do not fit the patterns of the linear sequences of social and economic evolution developed by the German Historical Schools. . . . If linear concepts of development are abandoned and the development of civilization is viewed frankly as a multilinear process much can be done toward the understanding of the history of Western culture as a progressive integration of many separate elements" (pp. 30-1).

A historical "point of view" is a kind of closed system that is closely related to typography, and flourishes where the unconscious effects of literacy flourish without countervailing cultural forces. Alexis de Tocqueville, whose literacy was much modified by his oral culture, seems to us now to have had a kind of clairvoyance concerning the patterns of change in the France and America of his time. He did not have a point of view, a fixed position from which he filled in a visual perspective of events. Rather he sought the operative dynamic in his data:

> But if I go further and seek among these characteristics the principal one, which includes almost all the rest, I discover that in most of the operations of the mind each American appeals only to the individual effort of his own understanding.
>
> America is therefore one of the countries where the precepts of Descartes are least studied and are best applied. . . . Everyone shuts himself tightly up within himself and insists upon judging the world from there.[5]

His skill in creating interplay between the written and oral modes of perceptual structure enabled de Tocqueville to achieve "scientific" insights into psychology and politics. By this interplay of two modes of perception he achieved prophetic understanding while other observers were merely expressing their private viewpoints. De Tocqueville knew well that typographic literacy had not only produced the Cartesian outlook but also the special traits of American psychology and politics. By his method of interplay among divergent perceptual modes, de Tocqueville was able to react to his world, not in sections but as a whole, and as to an open *field*. And such is the method which A. P. Usher notes has been absent from the study of cultural history and change. De Tocqueville had employed a procedure such as J. Z. Young describes (p. 77): "It may be that a great part of the secret of the brain's powers is the enormous opportunity provided for interaction between the effects of stimulating each part of the receiving fields. It is this provision of interacting-places or mixing-places that allows us to react to the world *as a whole* to much greater degree than other animals can do." But our technologies are by no means uniformly favourable to this organic function of interplay and of interdependence. To investigate this question with respect to alphabetic and typographic culture is the task of the present book. And it is today a quest which cannot but be undertaken in the light of new technologies which deeply affect the traditional operation and achieved values of alphabetic literacy and typographic culture.

There is a recent work that seems to me to release me from the onus of mere eccentricity and novelty in the present study. It is *The Open Society and Its Enemies* by Karl R. Popper, a work devoted to the study of aspects of

---

[5]*Democracy in America*, part II, book I, chap. I.

detribalization in the ancient world and of retribalization in the modern world. For the "open society" was effected by phonetic literacy, as will shortly appear, and is now threatened with eradication by electric media, as will be discussed in the conclusion of this study. Needless to say, the "is," rather than the "ought," of all these developments, is alone being discussed. Diagnosis and description must precede valuation and therapy. To substitute moral valuation for diagnosis is a natural and common enough procedure, but not necessarily a fruitful one.

Karl Popper devotes the first part of his large study to the detribalization of ancient Greece and the reaction to it. But neither in Greece nor in the modern world does he give any consideration to the dynamics of our technologically extended senses as factors either in the opening or closing of societies. His descriptions and analyses follow an economic and political point of view. The passage below is especially relevant to *The Gutenberg Galaxy* because it begins with the interplay of cultures *via* commerce and ends with the dissolution of the tribal state, even as it is dramatized by Shakespeare in *King Lear*.

It is Popper's view that tribal or closed societies have a biological unity and that "our modern open societies function largely by way of abstract relations, such as exchange of co-operation." That the abstracting or opening of closed societies is the work of the phonetic alphabet, and not of any other form of writing or technology, is one theme of *The Gutenberg Galaxy*. On the other hand, that closed societies are the product of speech, drum, and ear technologies, brings us at the opening of the electronic age to the sealing of the entire human family into a single global tribe. And this electronic revolution is only less confusing for men of the open societies than the revolution of phonetic literacy which stripped and streamlined the old tribal or closed societies. Popper offers no analysis of the causes of such change, but he does give (p. 172) a description of the situation that is very relevant to *The Gutenberg Galaxy*:

> *By the sixth century B.C., this development had led to the partial dissolution of the old ways of life, and even to a series of political revolutions and reactions. And it had led not only to attempts to retain and to arrest tribalism by force, as in Sparta, but also to that great spiritual revolution, the invention of critical discussion, and in consequence of thought that was free from magical obsessions. At the same time we find the first symptoms of a new uneasiness.* The strain of civilization was beginning to be felt.*
>
> *This strain, this uneasiness, is a consequence of the breakdown of the closed society. It is still felt even in our day, especially in times of social change. It is the strain created by the effort which life in an open and partially abstract society continually demands from us — by the endeavor to be rational, to forego at least some of our emotional social needs, to look after ourselves, and to accept responsibilities. We must, I believe, bear this strain as the price to be paid for every increase in knowledge, in reasonableness in co-operation and in mutual help, and*

consequently in our chances of survival, and in the size of the population. It is the price we have to pay for being human.

The strain is most closely related to the problem of the tension between the classes which is raised for the first time by the breakdown of the closed society. The closed society itself does not know this problem. At least to its ruling members, slavery, caste, and class rule are 'natural' in the sense of being unquestionable. But with the breakdown of the closed society, this certainty disappears, and with it all feeling of security. The tribal community (and later the 'city') is the place of security for the member of the tribe. Surrounded by enemies and by dangerous or even hostile magical forces, he experiences the tribal community as a child experiences his family and his home, in which he plays his definite part; a part he knows well, and plays well. The breakdown of the closed society, raising as it does the problem of class and other problems of social status, must have had the same effect upon the citizens as a serious family quarrel and the breaking up of the family home is liable to have on children. Of course, this kind of strain was felt by the privileged classes, now that they were threatened, more strongly than by those who had formerly been suppressed; but even the latter felt uneasy. They also were frightened by the breakdown of their 'natural' world. And though they continued to fight their struggle, they were often reluctant to exploit their victories over their class enemies who were supported by tradition, the status quo, *a higher level of education, and a feeling of natural authority.*

These observations lead us straight on to a consideration of *King Lear* and the great family quarrel in which the sixteenth century found itself involved early in the Gutenberg Era.

The Gutenberg Galaxy

When King Lear proposes "our darker purpose" as the subdivision of his kingdom, he is expressing a politically daring and *avant-garde* intent for the early seventeenth century:

> *Only we still retain*
> *The name, and all th' additions to a king. The sway,*
> *Revenue, execution of the rest,*
> *Beloved sons, be yours; which to confirm,*
> *This coronet part betwixt you.*[1]

Lear is proposing an extremely modern idea of delegation of authority from centre to margins. His "darker purpose" would have been recognized at once as left-wing Machiavellianism by an Elizabethan audience. The new patterns of power and organization which have been discussed during the preceding century were now, in the early seventeenth century, being felt at all levels of social and private life. *King Lear* is a presentation of the new strategy of culture and power as it affects the state, the family, and the individual psyche:

> *Meantime we shall express our darker purpose.*
> *Give me the map there. Know we have divided*
> *In three our kingdom. . . .*

The map was also a novelty in the sixteenth century, age of Mercator's projection, and was key to the new vision of peripheries of power and wealth. Columbus had been a cartographer before he was a navigator; and the discovery that it was possible to continue in a straight-line course, as if space were uniform and continuous, was a major shift in human awareness in the Renaissance. More important, the map brings forward at once a principal theme of King Lear, namely the isolation of the visual sense as a kind of blindness.

It is in the first scene of the play that Lear expresses his "darker purpose," using the Machiavellian cant term. Earlier in the first scene the darkness of Nature, as it were, is shown in the boasting of Gloucester about the illegitimacy

---

[1] *The Complete Works of Shakespeare*, ed. G. L. Kittredge. All quotations from *King Lear*, unless otherwise noted, are from Act I, scene i. Kittredge's edition is cited throughout.

of his handsome love-child Edmund: "But I have, sir, a son by order of law, some year older than this, who is yet no dearer in my account." The gaiety with which Gloucester alludes to the begetting of Edmund is later alluded to by Edgar:

The dark and vicious place where thee he got
Cost him his eyes. (V, iii)

Edmund, the love-child, opens the second scene of the play with:

Thou, Nature, art my goddess; to thy law
My services are bound. Wherefore should I
Stand in the plague of custom, and permit
The curiosity of nations to deprive me,
For that I am some twelve or fourteen moonshines
Lag of a brother?

Edmund has *l'esprit de quantité* so essential to tactile measurement and to the impersonality of the empirical mind. Edmund is presented as a force of nature, eccentric to mere human experience and "the curiosity of nations." He is a prime agent in the fragmentation of human institutions. But the great fragmenter is Lear himself, with his inspired idea of setting up a constitutional monarchy by means of delegating by authority. His plan for himself is that he become a specialist: Only we still retain "The name, and all th' additions to a King."

Following his specialist cue, Goneril and Regan leap into the act of filial devotion with specialist and competitive intensity. It is Lear who fragments them by insisting on a divisive eulogistic competition:

Tell me, my daughters
(Since now we will divest us, both of rule,
Interest of territory, cares of state),
Which of you shall we say doth love us most?
That we our largest bounty may extend
Where nature doth with merit challenge. Goneril
Our eldest-born, speak first.

Competitive individualism had become the scandal of a society long invested with corporate and collective values. The role played by print in instituting new patterns of culture is not unfamiliar. But one natural consequence of the specializing action of the new forms of knowledge was that all kinds of power took on a strongly centralist character. Whereas the role of the feudal monarch had been inclusive, the king actually including in himself all his subjects, the Renaissance prince tended to become an exclusive power centre surrounded by his individual subjects. And the result of such centralism, itself dependent on many new developments in roads and commerce, was the habit of delegation of powers and the specializing of many functions in separate areas and individuals. In *King Lear*, as in other plays, Shakespeare shows an utter clairvoyance concerning the social and personal consequences of denudation and stripping of attributes and functions for the sake of speed, precision, and increased power. His insights appear so richly in his lines that it is very difficult to select among them. But with the very opening words of Goneril's aria we are deep in them:

> *I love you more than words can wield the matter;*
> *Dearer than eyesight, space, and liberty:*

The stripping of the very human senses themselves will be one of the themes of this play. The separation of sight from the other senses has already been stressed in Lear's expression of his "darker purpose" and his resort to the mere visual map. But whereas Goneril is ready to strip off sight as an expression of devotion, Regan rallies to her challenge with:

>   *. . . I profess*
> *Myself an enemy to all other joys*
> *Which the most precious square of sense professes, . . .*

Regan will strip off all the human senses so long as she possesses Lear's love.

The allusion to "the most precious square of sense" shows Shakespeare doing an almost scholastic demonstration of the need for a ratio and interplay among the senses as the very constitution of rationality. His theme in Lear is that of John Donne in *An Anatomy of the World*:

> *'Tis all in pieces, all coherence gone;*
> *All just supply, and all Relation:*
> *Prince, subject, Father, Son, are things forgot,*
> *For every man alone thinks he hath got*
> *To be a Phoenix . . .*

The breaking of "the most precious square of sense" means the isolation of one sense from another by separate intensities with the ensuing irrationality and clash among wits and persons and functions. This breaking of the ratios among wits (or senses) and persons and functions is the theme of the later Shakespeare.

As Cordelia observes the flash agility of those specialists in filial piety, Goneril and Regan, she says:

>   *... I am sure my love's*
> *More richer than my tongue.*

Her rational fulness is as nothing to the specialism of her sisters. She has no fixed point of view from which she can launch bolts of eloquence. Her sisters are cued for particular occasions, streamlined by fragmentation of sense and motive for exact calculation. They are like Lear, *avant-garde* Machiavels, able to deal explicitly and scientifically with occasions. They are resolute and consciously liberated not only from the square of sense but from its moral analogate, "conscience." For that ratio among motives "does make cowards of us all." And Cordelia is a coward hindered from specialist action by the complexities of her conscience, her reason, and her role.

King Lear is a working model of the process of denudation by which men translated themselves from a world of roles to a world of jobs.

King Lear is a kind of elaborate case history of people translating themselves out of a world of roles into the new world of jobs. This is a process of stripping and denudation which does not occur instantly except in artistic vision. But Shakespeare saw that it had happened in his time. He was not talking about the future. However, the older world of roles had lingered on as a ghost just as after a century of electricity the West still feels the presence of the older values of literacy and privacy and separateness.

Kent, Edgar, and Cordelia are "out of phase" in the language of W. B. Yeats. They are "feudal" in their total loyalty which they consider merely natural to their *roles*. In role they exercise no delegated authority or powers. They are autonomous centres. As Georges Poulet in his *Studies in Human Time* points out (p. 7): "For the man of the Middle Ages, then, there was not one duration only. There were *durations*, ranked one above another, and not only in the universality of the exterior world but within himself, in his own nature, in his own human existence." The easy habit of configuration which had lasted through several centuries yields with the Renaissance to continuous, lineal, and uniform sequences for time and space and personal relationships alike. And the analogous world of roles and ratios is suddenly succeeded by a new lineal world, as in *Troilus and Cressida* (III, iii):

>   *Take the instant way;*
> *For honour travels in a strait so narrow*
> *Where one but goes abreast. Keep then the path,*

For emulation hath a thousand sons
That one by one pursue. If you give way,
Or hedge aside from the direct forthright,
Like to an ent'red tide, they all rush by,
And leave you hindmost . . .

The idea of homogeneous segmentation of persons and relations and functions could only appear to the sixteenth century as the dissolution of all bonds of sense and reason. *King Lear* offers a complete demonstration of how it felt to live through the change from medieval to Renaissance time and space, from an inclusive to an exclusive sense of the world. His changed attitude to Cordelia exactly reflects the idea of the Reformers concerning fallen nature. Poulet says (p. 10):

> *For them, too, both man and nature were divinely animated. For them also there had been a time when nature and man had participated in the creative power. . . . But that time existed for them no longer. The time when nature was divine was now succeeded by the time of fallen nature; fallen by its own fault, by the free act in consequence of which it had separated itself from its origin, cut itself off from its source, denied God. And from that moment on, God had withdrawn from nature and from man.*

Lear is quite explicit in designating Cordelia as a Puritan:

> *Let pride, which she calls plainness, marry her.*

The Reformers in their stress on individual function and independence naturally saw no point in all the formalities that belong to quite impersonal roles in society. It is clear to the audience, however, that it is rather Cordelia's dedication to her traditional role that makes her so helpless in the presence of the new individualism both of Lear and her sisters:

> *I love your Majesty*
> *According to my bond; no more nor less.*

She well knows that her devoted *role* adds up to "nothing" in terms of the new shrill and expansive individualism. Poulet describes (p. 9) this new world as "no longer anything more than an immense organism, a gigantic network of interchanges and reciprocal influences which was animated, which was guided interiorly in its cyclical development by a force everywhere the same and perpetually diversified, that could be called indiscriminately God, or Nature, or the Soul of the World, or Love."

The anguish of the third dimension is given its first verbal manifestation in poetic history in *King Lear*.

Shakespeare seems to have missed due recognition for having in *King Lear* made the first, and so far as I know, the only piece of verbal three-dimensional perspective in any literature. It is not again until Milton's *Paradise Lost* (II, 11. 1-5) that a fixed visual point of view is deliberately provided for the reader:

> *High on a Throne of Royal State, which far*
> *Outshon the wealth of* Ormus *and* Ind,
> *Or where the gorgeous East with richest hand*
> *Showrs on her Kings* Barbaric *Pearl and Gold,*
> *Satan exalted sat,* . . .

The arbitrary selection of a single static position creates a pictorial space with vanishing point. This space can be filled in bit by bit, and is quite different from non-pictorial space in which each thing simply resonates or modulates its own space in visually two-dimensional form.

Now the unique piece of three-dimensional verbal art which appears in *King Lear* is in Act IV, scene vi. Edgar is at pains to persuade the blinded Gloucester to believe the illusion that they are at the edge of a steep cliff:

> *Edgar.* . . . *Hark, do you hear the sea?*
> *Gloucester.*   *No, truly.*
> *Edgar. Why then, your other senses grow imperfect*
>   *By your eyes' anguish.* . . .
>   *Come on, sir; here's the place. Stand still. How fearful*
>   *And dizzy 'tis to cast one's eyes so low!*

The illusion of the third dimension is discussed at length in E. H Gombrich's *Art and Illusion*. Far from being a normal mode of human vision, three-dimensional perspective is a conventionally acquired model of seeing, as much acquired as is the means of recognizing the letters of the alphabet, or of following chronological narrative. That it was an acquired illusion Shakespeare helps us to see by his comments on the other senses in relation to sight. Gloucester is ripe for illusion because he has suddenly lost his sight. His power of visualization is not quite separate from his other senses. And it is the sense of sight in deliberate isolation from the other senses that confers on man the illusion of the third dimension, as Shakespeare makes explicit here. There is also the need to fix the gaze:

Come on, sir; here's the place. Stand still. How fearful
And dizzy 'tis to cast one's eyes so low!
The crows and choughs that wing the midway air
Show scarce so gross as beetles. Halfway down
Hangs one that gathers sampire — dreadful trade!
Methinks he seems no bigger than his head.
The fishermen that walk upon the beach,
Appear like mice; and yond tall anchoring bark,
Diminish'd to her cock; her cock, a buoy
Almost too small for sight. The murmuring surge,
That on th' unnumb'red idle pebbles chafes,
Cannot be heard so high. I'll look no more,
Lest my brain turn, and the deficient sight
Topple down headlong.

What Shakespeare does here is to place five flat panels of two-dimensions, one behind the other. By giving these flat panels a diagonal twist they succeed each other, as it were, in a perspective from the "stand still" point. He is utterly aware that the disposition to this kind of illusionism results from the separation of the senses. Milton learned to make the same kind of visual illusion after his blindness. And by 1709 Bishop Berkeley in his *New Theory of Vision* was denouncing the absurdity of Newtonian visual space as a mere abstract illusion severed from the sense of touch. The stripping of the senses and the interruption of their interplay in tactile synesthesia may well have been one of the effects of the Gutenberg technology. This process of separation and reduction of functions had certainly reached a critical point by the early seventeenth century when *King Lear* appeared. But to determine how far such a revolution in the human sense life could have proceeded from Gutenberg technology calls for a somewhat different approach from merely sampling the sensibility of a great play of the critical period.

King Lear is a kind of medieval sermon-exemplum or inductive reasoning to display the madness and misery of the new Renaissance life of action. Shakespeare explains minutely that the very principle of *action* is the splitting up of social operations and of the private sense life into specialized segments. The resulting frenzy to discover a new over-all interplay of forces ensures a furious activation of all components and persons affected by the new stress.

Cervantes had a similar awareness, and his *Don Quixote* is galvanized by the new form of the book as much as Machiavelli had been hypnotized by the special segment of experience that he had chosen to step up to the highest intensity of awareness. Machiavelli's abstraction of the entity of personal power from the social matrix was comparable to the much earlier abstraction of *wheel* from animal form. Such abstraction ensures a great deal more movement. But the Shakespeare-Cervantes vision is of the futility of such movement and of action deliberately framed on a fragmentary or specialist bias.

W. B. Yeats has an epigram which puts the themes of *King Lear* and *Don Quixote* in cryptic form:

Locke sank into a swoon
The garden died
God took the spinning jenny
Out of his side.

The Lockean swoon was the hypnotic trance induced by stepping up the visual component in experience until it filled the field of attention. Psychologists define hypnosis as the filling of the field of attention by one sense only. At such a moment "the garden" dies. That is, the garden indicates the interplay of all the senses in haptic harmony. With the instressed concern with one sense only, the mechanical principle of abstraction and repetition emerges into explicit form. Technology is explicitness, as Lyman Bryson said. And explicitness means the spelling out of one thing at a time, one sense at a time, one mental or physical operation at a time. Since the object of the present book is to discern the origins and modes of the Gutenberg configuration of events, it will be well to consider the effects of the alphabet on native populations today. For as they *are* in relation to the phonetic alphabet, so we once *were*.

The interiorization of the technology of the phonetic alphabet translates man from the magical world of the ear to the neutral visual world.

J. C. Carothers, writing in *Psychiatry* (November, 1959) on "Culture, Psychiatry and the Written Word," set forth a number of observations contrasting non-literate natives with literate natives, and the non-literate man with the Western man generally. He starts (p. 308) with the familiar fact that

> *by reason of the type of educational influences that impinge upon Africans in infancy and early childhood, and indeed throughout their lives, a man comes to regard himself as a rather insignificant part of a much larger organism — the family and the clan — and not as an independent, self-reliant unit; personal initiative and ambition are permitted little outlet; and a meaningful integration of a man's experience on individual, personal lines is not achieved. By contrast to the constriction at the intellectual level, great freedom is allowed for at the temperamental level, and a man is expected to live very much in the "here and now," to be highly extraverted, and to give very free expression to his feelings.*

113

In a word, our notions of the "uninhibited" native ignore the utter inhibition and suppression of his mental and personal life which is unavoidable in a non-literate world:

> *Whereas the Western child is early introduced to building blocks, keys in locks, water taps, and a multiplicity of items and events which constrain him to think in terms of spatiotemporal relations and mechanical causation, the African child receives instead an education which depends much more exclusively on the spoken word and which is relatively highly charged with drama and emotion. (p. 308)*

That is, a child in any Western milieu is surrounded by an abstract explicit visual technology of uniform time and uniform continuous space in which "cause" is efficient and sequential, and things move and happen on single planes and in successive order. But the African child lives in the implicit, magical world of the resonant oral word. He encounters not efficient causes but formal causes of configurational field such as any non-literate society cultivates. Carothers repeats again and again that "rural Africans live largely in a world of sound — a world loaded with direct personal significance for the hearer — whereas the Western European lives much more in a visual world which is on the whole indifferent to him." Since the ear world is a hot hyperesthetic world and the eye world is relatively a cool, neutral world, the Westerner appears to people of ear culture to be a very cold fish indeed.[2]

Carothers reviews the familiar non-literate idea of the "power" of words where thought and behaviour depend upon the magical resonance in words and their power to impose their assumptions relentlessly. He cites Kenyatta concerning love magic among the Kikuyu:

> *It is very important to acquire the correct use of magical words and their proper intonations, for the progress in applying magic effectively depends on uttering these words in their ritual order. . . . In performing these acts of love magic the performer has to recite a magical formula. . . . After this recitation he calls the name of the girl loudly and starts to address her* as though she were listening. (p. 309)

It is a matter of "rite words in rote order," as Joyce put it. But once more any Western child today grows up in this kind of magical repetitive world as he hears advertisements on radio and TV.

Carothers next asks (p. 310) how literacy in a society might operate to effect the change from the notion of words as resonant, live, active, natural forces to the

---

[2]See chapter on "Acoustic Space" by E. Carpenter and H. M. McLuhan in *Explorations in Communication*, pp. 65-70.

notion of words as "meaning" or "significance" for minds:

> *I suggest that it was only when the written, and still more the printed, word appeared on the scene that the stage was set for words to lose their magic powers and vulnerabilities. Why so?*
>
> *I developed the theme in an earlier article with reference to Africa, that the nonliterate rural population lives largely in a world of sound, in contrast to western Europeans who live largely in a world of vision. Sounds are in a sense dynamic things, or at least are always indicators of dynamic things — of movements, events, activities, for which man, when largely unprotected from the hazards of life in the bush or the veldt, must be ever on the alert. . . . Sounds lose much of this significance in western Europe, where man often develops, and must develop, a remarkable ability to disregard them. Whereas for Europeans, in general, "seeing is believing," for rural Africans reality seems to reside far more in what is heard and what is said. . . . Indeed, one is constrained to believe that the eye is regarded by many Africans less as a receiving organ than as an instrument of the will, the ear being the main receiving organ.*

Carothers reiterates that the Westerner depends on a high degree of visual shaping of spatio-temporal relations without which it is impossible to have the mechanistic sense of causal relations so necessary to the order of our lives. But the quite different assumptions of native perceptual life have led him to ask (p. 311) what has been the possible role of written words in shifting habits of perception from the auditory to visual stress:

> *When words are written, they become, of course, a part of the visual world. Like most of the elements of the visual world, they become static things and lose, as such, the dynamism which is so characteristic of the auditory world in general, and of the spoken word in particular. They lose much of the personal element, in the sense that the heard word is most commonly directed at oneself, whereas the seen word most commonly is not, and can be read or not as whim dictates. They lose those emotional overtones and emphases which have been described, for instance, by Monrad-Krohn . . . Thus, in general, words, by becoming visible, join a world of relative indifference to the viewer — a world from which the magic "power" of the word has been abstracted.*

Carothers continues his observations into the area of "free ideation" permitted to literate societies and quite out of the question for oral, non-literate communities:

> *The concept that verbal thought is separable from action, and is, or can be, ineffective and contained within the man . . . has important sociocultural implications, for it is only in societies which recognize that verbal thoughts can be so*

contained, and do not of their nature emerge on wings of power, that social
constraints can, in theory at least, afford to ignore ideation. (p. 311)

Thus, in a society still so profoundly oral as Russia, where spying is done by ear and not by eye, at the memorable "purge" trials of the 1930's Westerners expressed bafflement that many confessed total guilt not because of what they had done but what they had thought. In a highly literate society, then, visual and behavioural conformity frees the individual for inner deviation. Not so in an oral society where inner verbalization is effective social action:

In these circumstances it is implicit that behaviour constraints must include
constraint of thought. Since all behaviour in such societies is governed and
conceived on highly social lines, and since directed thinking can hardly be other
than personal and unique for each individual, it is furthermore implicit in the
attitude of these societies that the very possibility of such thinking is hardly to be
recognized. Therefore, if and when such thinking does occur, at other than strictly
practical and utilitarian levels, it is apt to be seen as deriving from the devil or
from other external evil influences, and as something to be feared and shunned as
much in oneself as in others. (p. 312)

It is, perhaps, a little unexpected to hear the compulsive and rigid patterns of a deeply oral-aural community referred to as "governed and conceived on highly social lines." For nothing can exceed the automatism and rigidity of an oral, non-literate community in its non-personal collectivity. As Western literate communities encounter the various "primitive" or auditory communities still remaining in the world, great confusion occurs. Areas like China and India are still audile-tactile in the main. Such phonetic literacy as has penetrated there has altered very little. Even Russia is still profoundly oral in bias. Only gradually does literacy alter substructures of language and sensibility.

Alexander Inkeles in his book on *Public Opinion in Russia* (p. 137) gives a useful account of how the ordinary and unconscious bias, even of the Russian literate groups, has a direction quite counter to anything a long-literate community would consider "natural." The Russian attitude, like that of any oral society, reverses our stress:

In the United States and England it is the freedom of expression, the right itself in
the abstract, that is valued. . . . In the Soviet Union, on the other hand, the results
of exercising freedom are in the forefront of attention, and the preoccupation with
the freedom itself is secondary. It is for this reason that the discussions between
Soviet and Anglo-American representatives characteristically reach absolutely no
agreement on specific proposals, although both sides assert that there should be
freedom of the press. The American is usually talking about freedom of expression,

the right to say or not to say certain things, a right which he claims exists in the United States and not in the Soviet Union. The Soviet representative is usually talking about access to the means of expression, not to the right to say things at all, and this access he maintains is denied to most in the United States and exists for most in the Soviet Union.

Soviet concern with media *results* is natural to any oral society where interdependence is the result of instant interplay of cause and effect in the total structure. Such is the character of a village, or, since electric media, such is also the character of global village. And it is the advertising and PR community that is most aware of this basic new dimension of global interdependence. Like the Soviet Union, they are concerned about *access* to the media and about *results*. They have no concern whatever about self-expression and would be shocked by any attempt to take over, say, a public advertisement for oil or coke as a vehicle of private opinion or personal feeling. In the same way the literate bureaucrats of the Soviet Union cannot imagine anybody wanting to use public media in a private way. And this attitude has just nothing to do with Marx, Lenin, or Communism. It is a normal tribal attitude of any oral society. The Soviet press is their equivalent of our Madison Avenue in shaping production and social processes.

Schizophrenia may be a necessary consequence of literacy.

Carothers stresses that until phonetic writing split apart thought and action, there was no alternative but to hold all men responsible for their thoughts as much as their actions. His great contribution has been to point to the breaking apart of the magical world of the ear and the neutral world of the eye, and to the emergence of the detribalized individual from this split. It follows, of course, that literate man, when we meet him in the Greek world, is a split man, a schizophrenic, as all literate men have been since the invention of the phonetic alphabet. Mere writing, however, has not the peculiar power of the phonetic technology to detribalize man. Given the phonetic alphabet with its abstraction of meaning from sound and the translation of sound into a visual code, and men were at grips with an experience that transformed them. No pictographic or ideogrammic or hieroglyphic mode of writing has the detribalizing power of the phonetic alphabet. No other kind of writing save the phonetic has ever translated man out of the possessive world of total interdependence and interrelation that is the auditory network. From that magical resonating world of simultaneous relations that is the oral and acoustic space there is only one route to the freedom and independence of detribalized man. That route is *via* the phonetic alphabet, which lands men at once in varying degrees of dualistic schizophrenia. Here is how Bertrand Russell describes (in his *History of Western Philosophy*, p. 39) this condition of the Greek world in the early throes of dichotomy and the trauma of literacy:

> *Not all of the Greeks, but a large proportion of them, were passionate, unhappy, at war with themselves, driven along one road by the intellect and along another by the passions, with the imagination to conceive heaven and the wilful self-assertion that creates hell. They had a maxim "nothing too much", but they were in fact excessive in everything — in pure thought, in poetry, in religion, and in sin. It was the combination of passion and intellect that made them great, while they were great. . . . There were, in fact, two tendencies in Greece, one passionate, religious, mystical, other worldly, the other cheerful, empirical, rationalistic, and interested in acquiring knowledge of a diversity of facts.*

The division of faculties which results from the technological dilation or externalization of one or another sense is so pervasive a feature of the past century that today we have become conscious, for the first time in history, of how these mutations of culture are initiated. Those who experience the first onset of a new technology, whether it be alphabet or radio, respond most emphatically because the new sense ratios set up at once by the technological dilation of eye or ear, present men with a surprising new world, which evokes a vigorous new "closure," or novel pattern of interplay, among all of the senses together. But the initial shock gradually dissipates as the entire community absorbs the new habit of perception into all of its areas of work and association. But the real revolution is in this later and prolonged phase of "adjustment" of all personal and social life to the new model of perception set up by the new technology.

The Romans carried out the alphabetic translation of culture into visual terms. The Greeks, whether ancient or Byzantine, clung to much of the older oral culture with its distrust of action and applied knowledge. For applied knowledge, whether in military structure or industrial organization, depends upon uniformity and homogenization of populations. "It is certain," wrote the symbolist Edgar Allan Poe, "that the mere act of inditing tends in a great degree to the logicalization of thought." Lineal, alphabetic inditing made possible the sudden invention of "grammars" of thought and science by the Greeks. These grammars or explicit spellings out of personal and social processes were visualizations of non-visual functions and relations. The functions and processes were not new. But the means of arrested visual analysis, namely the phonetic alphabet, was as new to the Greeks as the movie camera in our century.

We can ask ourselves later why the fanatic specialism of the Phoenicians, which hacked the alphabet out of the hieroglyphic culture, did not release any further intellectual or artistic activity in them. Meantime, it is relevant to note that Cicero, the encyclopedic synthesizer of the Roman world, when surveying the Greek world, reproves Socrates for having been the first to make a split between mind and heart. The pre-Socratics were still mainly in a non-literate culture. Socrates stood on the border between that oral world and the visual and literate culture. But he wrote nothing. The Middle Ages regarded Plato as the mere scribe or amanuensis of Socrates. And Aquinas considered that neither Socrates nor Our Lord committed their teaching to writing because the kind of interplay of minds that is in teaching is not possible by means of writing.[3]

Does the interiorization of media such as letters *alter the ratio among our senses and change mental processes?*

What concerned Cicero, the practical Roman, was that the Greeks had put difficulties in the way of his own program for the *doctus orator*. In chapters xv-xxiii of the third book of the *De oratore*, he offers a history of philosophy from the beginning to his own time, trying to explain how it came about that the professional philosophers had made a breach between eloquence and wisdom, between practical knowledge and knowledge which these men professed to follow for its own sake. Before Socrates learning had been the preceptress of living rightly and speaking well. But with Socrates came the division between the tongue and the heart. That the eloquent Socrates should have been of all people the one to initiate a division between thinking wisely and speaking well was inexplicable: ". . . quorum princeps Socrates fuit, is, qui omnium eruditorum testimonio totiusque judicio Graeciae cum prudentia et acumine et venustate et subtilitate, tum vero eloquentia, varietate, copia, quam se cumque in partem dedisset omnium fuit facile princeps . . ."

But after Socrates things became much worse in Cicero's opinion. The Stoics, despite a refusal to cultivate eloquence, have alone of all the philosophers declared eloquence to be a virtue and wisdom. For Cicero, wisdom is eloquence because only by eloquence can knowledge be applied to the minds and hearts of men. It is applied knowledge that obsesses the mind of Cicero the Roman as it did the mind of Francis Bacon. And for Cicero, as for Bacon, the technique of application depends upon the Roman brick procedure of uniform repeatability and homogeneous segments of knowledge.

If a technology is introduced either from within or from without a culture, and if it gives new stress or ascendancy to one or another of our senses, the ratio among all of our senses is altered. We no longer feel the same, nor do our eyes

---

[3]Utrum Christus debuerit doctrinam Suam Scripto tradere. *Summa Theologica*, part III, q. 42, art. 4.

and ears and other senses remain the same. The interplay among our senses is perpetual save in conditions of anesthesia. But any sense when stepped up to high intensity can act as an anesthetic for other senses. The dentist can now use "audiac" — induced noise — to remove tactility. Hypnosis depends on the same principle of isolating one sense in order to anesthetize the others. The result is a break in the ratio among the senses, a kind of loss of identity. Tribal, non-literate man, living under the intense stress on auditory organization of all experience, is, as it were, entranced.

Plato, however, the scribe of Socrates as he seemed to the Middle Ages, could in the act of writing[4] look back to the non-literate world and say:

It would take a long time to repeat all that Thamus said to Theuth in praise or blame of the various arts. But when they came to letters, This, said Theuth, will make the Egyptians wiser and give them better memories; it is a specific both for the memory and for the wit. Thamus replied: O most ingenious Theuth, the parent or inventor of an art is not always the best judge of the utility or inutility of his own inventions to the users of them. And in this instance, you who are the father of letters, from a paternal love of your own children have been led to attribute to them a quality which they cannot have; for this discovery of yours will create forgetfulness in the learners' souls, because they will not use their memories; they will trust to the external written characters and not remember of themselves. The specific which you have discovered is an aid not to memory, but to reminiscence, and you give your disciples not truth, but only the semblance of truth; they will be hearers of many things and will have learned nothing; they will appear to be omniscient and will generally know nothing; they will be tiresome company, having the show of wisdom without the reality.

Plato shows no awareness here or elsewhere of how the phonetic alphabet had altered the sensibility of the Greeks; nor did anybody else in his time or later. Before his time, the myth-makers, poised on the frontiers between the old oral world of the tribe and the new technologies of specialism and individualism, had foreseen all and said all in a few words. The myth of Cadmus states how this King who had introduced the Phoenician script, or the phonetic alphabet to Greece, had sown the dragon's teeth and they had sprung up armed men. This, as with all myth, is a succinct statement of a complex social process that had occurred over a period of centuries. But it was only in recent years that the work of Harold Innis opened up the Cadmus myth fully. (See, for example, *The Bias of Communication* and *Empire and Communications*.) The myth, like the aphorism and maxim, is characteristic of oral culture. For, until literacy deprives language

---

[4]*Phaedrus*, trans. B. Jowett, 274-5. All quotations from Plato are from Jowett's translation.

of its multi-dimensional resonance, every word is a poetic world unto itself, a "momentary deity" or revelation, as it seemed to non-literate men. Ernst Cassirer's *Language and Myth* presents this aspect of non-literate human awareness, surveying the wide range of current study of language origins and development. Towards the end of the nineteenth century numerous students of non-literate societies had begun to have doubts about the *a priori* character of logical categories. Today, when the role of phonetic literacy in the creating of the techniques of enunciation of propositions ("formal logic") is well known, it is still supposed, even by some anthropologists, that Euclidean space and three-dimensional visual perception is a universal datum of mankind. The absence of such space in native art is considered by such scholars to be owing to lack of artistic skill. Cassirer, reporting on the notion of words as myth (the etymology of *mythos* indicates that it means "word") says (p. 62):

> *According to Usener, the lowest level to which we can trace back the origin of religious concepts is that of "momentary gods", as he calls those images which are born from the need or the specific feeling of a critical moment . . . and still bearing the mark of all its pristine volatility and freedom. But it appears that the new findings which ethnology and comparative religion have put at our disposal during the three decades since the publication of Usener's work enable us to go back one step further yet.*

Civilization gives the barbarian or tribal man an eye for an ear and is now at odds with the electronic world.

This step takes to a more generalized sense of the manifestations of divine potency, away from particular, individualized "archetypes" and epiphanies of "momentary deities." It must often have puzzled the scholars and physicists of our time that just in the degree to which we penetrate the lowest layers of non-literate awareness we encounter the most advanced and sophisticated ideas of twentieth-century art and science. To explain that paradox will be an aspect of the present book. It is a theme around which much emotion and controversy are daily engendered as our world shifts from a visual to an auditory orientation in its electric technology. The controversy, of course, ignores the cause of the process altogether and clings to the "content." Setting aside the effects of the alphabet in creating Euclidean space for the Greek sensibility, as well as the simultaneous discovery of perspective and chronological narrative, it will be necessary to return briefly to the native world with J. C. Carothers. For it is in the non-literate world that it is easiest to discern the operation of phonetic letters in shaping our Western world.

That the Greeks were able to do more with the written word than other communities such as the Babylonian and Egyptian was, according to H. A. L. Fisher (*A History of Europe*, p. 19) that they were not under "the paralysing control of organized priestcraft." But even so, they had only a brief period of exploration and discovery before settling into a *clichéd* pattern of repetitive thought. Carothers feels that the early Greek intelligentsia not only had the stimulus of sudden access to the acquired wisdom of other peoples, but, having none of its own, there were no vested interests in acquired knowledge to frustrate the immediate acceptance and development of the new. It is this very situation which today puts the Western world at such a disadvantage, as against the "backward" countries. It is our enormous backlog of literate and mechanistic technology that renders us so helpless and inept in handling the new electric technology. The new physics is an auditory domain and long-literate society is not at home in the new physics, nor will it ever be.

This, of course, is to overlook the utter discrepancy between the phonetic alphabet and any other kind of writing whatever. Only the phonetic alphabet makes a break between eye and ear, between semantic meaning and visual code; and thus only phonetic writing has the power to translate man from the tribal to the civilized sphere, to give him an eye for an ear. The Chinese culture is considerably more refined and perceptive than the Western world has ever been. But the Chinese are tribal, people of the ear. "Civilization" must now be used technically to mean detribalized man for whom the visual values have priority in the organization of thought and action. Nor is this to give any new meaning or value to "civilization" but rather to specify its character. It is quite obvious that most civilized people are crude and numb in their perceptions, compared with the hyperesthesia of oral and auditory cultures. For the eye has none of the delicacy of the ear. Carothers goes on (p. 313) to observe that:

> *So far as Plato's thinking can be considered representative of the thinking of the Greeks, it is very clear that the word, whether thought or written, still retained, for them, and from our point of view, vast powers in the 'real' world. Although at last it was seen as nonbehavioural itself, it now came to be regarded as the fount and origin not only of behaviour but of all discovery: it was the only key to knowledge, and thought alone — in words or figures — could unlock all doors for understanding the world. In a sense, indeed, the power of words or other visual symbols became greater than before . . . now verbal and mathematical thought became the only truth, and the whole sensory world came to be regarded as illusory, except insofar as thoughts were heard or seen.*

In his dialogue of the *Cratylus*, named for his teacher of language and grammar, Plato has Socrates say (438):

But if these things are only to be known through names, how can we suppose that the givers of names had knowledge, or were legislators before there were names at all, and therefore before they could have known them?

Cratylus: I believe, Socrates, the true account of the matter to be, that a power more than human gave things their first names, and that the names which were thus given are necessarily their true names.

This view of Cratylus was the basis of most language study until the Renaissance. It is rooted in the old oral "magic" of the "momentary deity" kind such as is favoured again today for various reasons. That it is most alien to merely literary and visual culture is easily found in the remarks of incredulity which Jowett supplies as his contribution to the dialogue.

Carothers turns to David Riesman's *The Lonely Crowd* (p. 9) for further orientation in his queries concerning the effects of writing on non-literate communities. Riesman had characterized our own Western world as developing in its "typical members a social character whose conformity is insured by their tendency to acquire early in life an internalized set of goals." Riesman made no effort to discover why the manuscript culture of the ancient and medieval worlds should not have conferred inner direction, nor why a print culture should inevitably confer inner direction. That is part of the business of the present book. But it can be said at once that "inner direction" depends upon a "fixed point of view." A stable, consistent character is one with an unwavering outlook, an almost hypnotized visual stance, as it were. Manuscripts were altogether too slow and uneven a matter to provide either a fixed point of view or the habit of gliding steadily on single planes of thought and information. As we shall see, manuscript culture is intensely audile-tactile compared to print culture; and that means that detached habits of observation are quite uncongenial to manuscript cultures, whether ancient Egyptian, Greek, or Chinese or medieval. In place of cool visual detachment the manuscript world puts empathy and participation of all the senses. But non-literate cultures experience such an overwhelming tyranny of the ear over the eye that any balanced interplay among the senses is unknown at the auditory extreme, just as balanced interplay of the senses became extremely difficult after print stepped up the visual component in Western experience to extreme intensity.

The modern physicist is at home with oriental field theory.

Carothers finds Riesman's classification of "tradition-directed" peoples as corresponding "quite closely to those areas occupied by societies which are non-literate or in which the great majority of the population has been untouched by literacy" (p. 315). It should be understood that to be "touched" by literacy is not a very sudden affair, nor is it a total matter at any time or in any place. That should become very clear as we move through the sixteenth and later centuries. But today, as electricity creates conditions of extreme interdependence on a global scale, we move swiftly again into an auditory world of simultaneous events and over-all awareness. Yet the habits of literacy persist in our speech, our sensibilities, and in our arrangement of the spaces and times of our daily lives. Short of some catastrophe, literacy and visual bias could bear up for a long time against electricity and "unified field" awareness. And the same is true the other way around. Germans and the Japanese, while far-advanced in literate and analytic technology, retained the core of auditory tribal unity and total togetherness. The advent of radio, and electricity generally, was not only for them but for all tribal cultures a most intense experience. Long-literate cultures have naturally more resistance to the auditory dynamic of the total electric field culture of our time.

Riesman, referring to tradition-directed people, says (p. 26):

Since the type of social order we have been discussing is relatively unchanging, the conformity of the individual tends to be dictated to a very large degree by power relations among the various age and sex groups, the clans, castes, professions, and so forth — relations which have endured for centuries and are modified but slightly, if at all, by successive generations. The culture controls behaviour minutely, and, . . . careful and rigid etiquette governs the fundamentally influential sphere of kin relationships. . . . Little energy is directed toward finding new solutions of the age-old problems . . .

Riesman points out that to meet even the rigid demands of complex religious ritual and etiquette "individuality of character need not be highly developed." He speaks as a highly literate man for whom "development" means having a private point of view. High development as it might appear to a native would not be accessible to our visual mode of awareness. We can get some idea of the attitude of a member of a tradition-directed society to technological improvements from a story related by Werner Heisenberg in *The Physicist's Conception of Nature*. A modern physicist with his habit of "field" perception, and his sophisticated separation from our conventional habits of Newtonian space, easily finds in the pre-literate world a congenial kind of wisdom.

Heisenberg is discussing "science as a part of the interplay between man and Nature" (p. 20):

In this connection it has often been said that the far-reaching changes in our environment and in our way of life wrought by this technical age have also changed dangerously our ways of thinking, and that here lie the roots of the crises which have shaken our times and which, for instance, are also expressed in modern art. True, this objection is much older than modern technology and science, the use of implements going back to man's earliest beginnings. Thus, two and a half thousand years ago, the Chinese sage Chuang-Tzu spoke of the danger of the machine when he said:

'As Tzu-Gung was travelling through the regions north of the river Han, he saw an old man working in his vegetable garden. He had dug an irrigation ditch. The man would descend into the well, fetch up a vessel of water in his arms and pour it out into the ditch. While his efforts were tremendous the results appeared to be very meagre.

'Tzu-Gung said, "There is a way whereby you can irrigate a hundred ditches in one day, and whereby you can do much with little effort. Would you not like to hear of it?" Then the gardener stood up, looked at him and said, "And what would that be?"

'Tzu-Gung replied, "You take a wooden lever, weighted at the back and light in front. In this way you can bring up water so quickly that it just gushes out. This is called a draw-well."

'Then anger rose up in the old man's face, and he said, "I have heard my teacher say that whoever uses machines does all his work like a machine. He who does his work like a machine grows a heart like a machine, and he who carries the heart of a machine in his breast loses his simplicity. He who has lost his simplicity becomes unsure in the strivings of his soul. Uncertainty in the strivings of the soul is something which does not agree with honest sense. It is not that I do not know of such things: I am ashamed to use them."'

Clearly this ancient tale contains a great deal of wisdom, for "uncertainty in the strivings of the soul" is perhaps one of the aptest descriptions of man's condition in our modern crisis; technology, the machine, has spread through the world to a degree that our Chinese sage could not even have suspected.

The sort of "simplicity" envisaged by the sage is a more complex and subtle product than anything that occurs in a society with specialized technology and sense life. But perhaps the real point of the anecdote is that it appealed to Heisenberg. It would not have interested Newton. Not only does modern physics abandon the specialized visual space of Descartes and Newton, it re-enters the subtle auditory space of the non-literate world. And in the most primitive society, as in the present age, such auditory space is a total field of simultaneous relations in which "change" has as little meaning and appeal as it had for the mind of Shakespeare or the heart of Cervantes. All values apart, we must learn today that our electric technology has consequences for our most ordinary perceptions and habits of action which are quickly recreating in us the mental processes of the most primitive men. These consequences occur, not in our thoughts or opinions, where we are trained to be critical, but in our most ordinary sense life, which creates the vortices and the matrices of thought and action. This book will try to explain why print culture confers on man a language of thought which leaves him quite unready to face the language of his own electro-magnetic technology. The strategy any culture must resort to in a period like this was indicated by Wilhelm von Humboldt:

> *Man lives with his objects chiefly — in fact, since his feeling and acting depends on his perceptions, one may say exclusively — as language presents them to him. By the same process whereby he spins language out of his own being, he ensnares himself in it; and each language draws a magic circle round the people to which it belongs, a circle from which there is no escape save by stepping out of it into another.*[5]

Such awareness as this has generated in our time the technique of the suspended judgment by which we can transcend the limitations of our own assumptions by a critique of them. We can now live, not just amphibiously in divided and distinguished worlds, but pluralistically in many worlds and cultures simultaneously. We are no more committed to one culture — to a single ratio among the human senses — any more than to one book or to one language or to one technology. Our need today is, culturally, the same as the scientist's who seeks to become aware of the bias of the instruments of research in order to correct that bias. Compartmentalizing of human potential by single cultures will soon be as absurd as specialism in subject or discipline has become. It is not likely that our age is more obsessional than any other, but it has become sensitively aware of the conditions and fact of obsession beyond any other age. However, our fascination with all phases of the unconscious, personal and collective, as with all modes of primitive awareness, began in the eighteenth century with the first violent revulsion against print culture and mechanical industry. What began as a "Romantic reaction" towards organic wholeness may or may not have hastened the discovery of electro-magnetic waves. But certainly the electro-magnetic discoveries have recreated the simultaneous "field" in all human affairs so that the human family now exists under conditions of a "global village." We live in a single constricted space resonant with tribal drums. So that concern with the "primitive" today is as banal as nineteenth-century concern with "progress," and as irrelevant to our problems.

---

[5] Quoted by Cassirer in *Language and Myth*, p. 9.

The new electronic interdependence recreates the world in the image of a global village.

It would be surprising, indeed, if Riesman's description of tradition-directed people did not correspond to Carothers' knowledge of African tribal societies. It would be equally startling were the ordinary reader about native societies not able to vibrate with a deep sense of affinity for the same, since our new electric culture provides our lives again with a tribal base. There is available the lyrical testimony of a very Romantic biologist, Pierre Teilhard de Chardin, in his *Phenomenon of Man* (p. 240):

> *Now, to the degree that — under the effect of this pressure and thanks to their psychic permeability — the human elements infiltrated more and more into each other, their minds (mysterious coincidence) were mutually stimulated by proximity. And as though dilated upon themselves, they each extended little by little the radius of their influence upon this search which, by the same token, shrank steadily. What, in fact, do we see happening in the modern paroxysm? It has been stated over and over again. Through the discovery yesterday of the railway, the motor car and the aeroplane, the physical influence of each man, formerly restricted to a few miles, now extends to hundreds of leagues or more. Better still: thanks to the prodigious biological event represented by the discovery of electromagnetic waves, each individual finds himself henceforth (actively and passively) simultaneously present, over land and sea, in every corner of the earth.*

People of literary and critical bias find the shrill vehemence of de Chardin as disconcerting as his uncritical enthusiasm for the cosmic membrane that has been snapped round the globe by the electric dilation of our various senses. This externalization of our senses creates what de Chardin calls the "noosphere" or a technological brain for the world. Instead of tending towards a vast Alexandrian library the world has become a computer, an electronic brain, exactly as in an infantile piece of science fiction. And as our senses have gone outside us, Big Brother goes inside. So, unless aware of this dynamic, we shall at once move into a phase of panic terrors, exactly befitting a small world of tribal drums, total interdependence, and superimposed co-existence. It is easy to perceive signs of such panic in Jacques Barzun who manifests himself as a fearless and ferocious Luddite in his *The House of the Intellect*. Sensing that all he holds dear stems from the operation of the alphabet on and through our minds, he proposes the abolition of all modern art, science, and philanthropy. This trio extripated, he feels we can slap down the lid on Pandora's box. At least Barzun localizes his problem even if he has no clue as to the kind of agency exerted by these forms. Terror is the normal state of any oral society, for in it everything affects everything all the time.

Reverting to the earlier theme of conformity, Carothers continues (pp. 315-16): "Thought and behavior are not seen as separate; they are both seen as behavioral. Evil-willing is, after all the most fearful type of "behavior" known in many of these societies, and a dormant or awakening fear of it lies ever in the minds of all their members." In our long striving to recover for the Western world a unity of sensibility and of thought and feeling we have no more been prepared to accept the tribal consequences of such unity than we were ready for the fragmentation of the human psyche by print culture.

Literacy affects the physiology as well as the psychic life of the African.

Carothers concludes his discussion of the effects of phonetic writing on Africans with an excerpt (pp. 317-18) from an article that appeared in a Kenya daily newspaper, the *East African Standard*. The author, a missionary doctor, headed his article "How Civilization Has Affected the African."

The purpose of this article is to show that through a very little education a remarkably rapid and far-reaching change has taken place in African boys and girls, so much so that in a generation, human characteristics and reactions have altered to a degree which one would have expected to have taken centuries.

The high qualities of the African untouched by missions or education impress nearly everyone. Those of this district are good workers, cheerful, uncomplaining, unaffected by monotony or discomforts, honest and usually remarkably truthful. But it is not uncommon to hear uncomplimentary comparisons made between those Africans and those born of Christian parents or those who started school at an early age. A writer, however, who visited schools in Madagascar says that these untouched children are naturally lethargic. They sit still too long: the impulse to play seems to be dormant. They are impervious to monotony and their mental lethargy enables them to perform, for children, prodigious acts of endurance. These children naturally develop into the uneducated African, who is incapable of filling any skilled post. At the most he can be trained to carry out work that requires no reasoning. That is the penalty paid for his good qualities.

The African will remain in permanent servitude if only to ignorance unless there is willingness to risk the destruction of those qualities in the changes education brings and a desire to face building up his character again but with a totally different mentality. This different mentality may show itself in a shirking of work, trouble over food or in a desire to have his wife living with him however difficult for the employer. The reasons are clear; the African's whole capacity for interest, pleasure and pain are immensely increased through even a little education.

For the educated African (using this term for even the comparatively low stan-
dard achieved by the average African schoolboy) the sense of interest has been
aroused through the new variety of life and monotony has become a trial to him as
it is to the normal European. It takes greater will-power for him to be faithful to
uninteresting work, and lack of interest brings fatigue.

The author next turned to the changed attitudes to taste and sex and pain resulting from literacy:

I suggest also that the nervous system of the untouched African is so lethargic that
he needs little sleep. Many of our workmen walk some miles to their jobs, work
well all day and then return home and spend most of the night sitting up guarding
their gardens against the depredations of wild pigs. For weeks on end they sleep
only two or three hours a night.

The important moral inference from all this is that the African of the old gener-
ation with whom we have nearly all worked, will never be seen again. The new
generation is completely different, capable of rising to greater heights and of
descending to greater depths. They deserve a more sympathetic knowledge of their
difficulties and their far greater temptations. African parents need to be taught
this before it is too late so that they may realize that they are dealing with finer
bits of mechanism than they themselves were.

Carothers stresses the fact that it is indeed a very little literacy that produces these effects, "some familiarity with written symbols — in reading, writing and arithmetic."

Finally (p. 318), Carothers turns for a moment to China, where printing had been invented in the seventh or eighth century and yet "seems to have had little effect in emancipating thought." He calls in the testimony of Kenneth Scott Latourette, who writes in *The Chinese, Their History and Culture* (p. 310):

The hypothetical visitor from Mars might well have expected the Industrial
Revolution and the modern scientific approach to have made their first
appearance in China rather than the Occident. The Chinese are so industrious,
and have shown such ingenuity in invention and by empirical processes have
forestalled the West in arriving at so much useful agricultural and medical lore
that they, rather than the nations of the West, might have been looked to as the
forerunners and leaders in what is termed the scientific approach towards the
understanding and mystery of man's natural environment. It is little short of
amazing that a people who pioneered in the invention of paper, printing, gunpow-
der, and the compass — to speak only of some of their best known innovations —
did not also take precedence in devising the power loom, the steam engine, and
the other revolutionary machines of the eighteenth and nineteenth centuries.

The purpose of printing among the Chinese was not the creation of uniform repeatable products for a market and a price system. Print was an alternative to their prayer-wheels and was a visual means of multiplying incantatory spells, much like advertising in our age.

But we can learn much about print from the Chinese attitude towards it. For the most obvious character of print is repetition, just as the obvious effect of repetition is hypnosis or obsession. Moreover, printing ideograms is totally different from typography based on the phonetic alphabet. For the ideograph even more than the hieroglyph is a complex *Gestalt* involving all of the senses at once. The ideogram affords none of the separation and specialization of sense, none of the breaking apart of sight and sound and meaning which is the key to the phonetic alphabet. So that the numerous specializations and separations of function inherent in industry and applied knowledge simply were not accessible to the Chinese. Today they appear to be proceeding along the lines of the phonetic alphabet. This ensures that they will liquidate their present and traditional culture *in toto*. They will then proceed by the paths of schizophrenia and multiply dichotomies in the direction of physical power and aggressive organization, on a centre-margin or Roman pattern.

The quite irrelevant ground that Carothers assigns to explaining the earlier Chinese indifference to industrialism is that Chinese writing — or printing — requires much erudition for its understanding. The same is true in varying degrees of all non-alphabetic forms of writing. The comment of Latourette on this point will help here as well as later:

The greater part of the voluminous literature in Chinese has been written in the classical style . . . The Chinese classical language presents difficulties. It is highly artificial. It is often replete with allusions and quotations and to appreciate and even to understand much of it the reader has to bring to it a vast store of knowledge of existing literature . . . It is only by going through a prodigious amount of literature and especially by memorising quantities of it that the scholar obtains a kind of sixth sense which enables him to divine which of several readings is correct. Even the perusal of the classical language, therefore, requires long preparation. Composition is still more of a task. Few Occidentals have achieved an acceptable style and many a modern Chinese who is the finished product of the present-day curriculum is far from adept.

The concluding observation of Carothers is that genetic studies of human groups offer no certainty and very small data, indeed, compared to cultural and environmental approaches. My suggestion is that cultural ecology has a reasonably stable base in the human sensorium, and that any extension of the sensorium by technological dilation has a quite appreciable effect in setting up new ratios or proportions among all the senses. Languages being that form of technology constituted by dilation or uttering (outering) of all of our senses at once, are themselves immediately subject to the impact or intrusion of any mechanically extended sense. That is, writing affects speech directly, not only its accidence and syntax but also its enunciation and social uses.[6]

Why non-literate societies cannot see films or photos without much training.

Since the present object is to elucidate the effective causality of phonetic writing in setting up new kinds of perception, let us turn to a paper[7] by Professor John Wilson of the African Institute of London University. For literate societies it is not easy to grasp why non-literates cannot see in three dimensions or perspective. We assume that this is normal vision and that no training is needed to view photos or films. Wilson's experiences arose from trying to use film in teaching natives to read:

> *The next bit of evidence was very, very interesting. This man — the sanitary inspector — made a moving picture, in very slow time, very slow technique, of what would be required of the ordinary household in a primitive African village in getting rid of standing water — draining pools, picking up all empty tins and putting them away, and so forth. We showed this film to an audience and asked them what they had seen, and they said they had seen a chicken, a fowl, and we didn't know that there was a fowl in it! So we very carefully scanned the frames one by one for this fowl, and, sure, enough, for about a second, a fowl went over the corner of the frame. Someone had frightened the fowl and it had taken flight, through the right-hand, bottom segment of the frame. This was all that had been seen. The other things he had hoped they would pick up from the film they had not picked up at all, and they had picked up something which we didn't know was in the film until we inspected it minutely. Why? We developed all sorts of theories. Perhaps it was the sudden movement of the chicken. Everything else was done in slow technique — people going forward slowly picking up the tin, demonstrating and all the rest of it, and the bird was apparently the one bit of reality for them. For them there was another theory that the fowl had religious significance, which we rather dismissed.*
>
> Question: *Could you describe in more detail the scene in the film?*
>
> Wilson: *Yes, there was very slow movement of a sanitary laborer coming along and seeing a tin with water in it, picking the tin up and very carefully pouring the water out and then rubbing it into the ground so no mosquito could breed and very carefully putting this tin in a basket on the back of a donkey. This was to*

---

[6]H. M. McLuhan, "The Effect of the Printed Book on Language in the Sixteenth Century," in *Explorations in Communication*, pp. 125-35.

[7]"Film Literacy in Africa," *Canadian Communications*, vol. I, no. 4, summer, 1961, pp. 7–14.

show how you disposed of rubbish. It was like the man in the park with a spiked
stick, picking up the bits of paper and putting them in the sack. All this was done
very slowly to show how important it was to pick up those things because of
mosquitoes breeding in standing water. The cans were all very carefully taken
away and disposed of in the ground and covered up so there would be no more
standing water. The film was about five minutes long. The chicken appeared for a
second in this kind of setting.

Question: *Do you literally mean that when you talked with the audience you*
came to believe that they had not seen anything else but the chicken?

Wilson: *We simply asked them: What did you see in this film?*

Question: *Not what did you think?*

Wilson: *No, what did you see?*

Question: *How many people were in the viewing audience of whom you asked*
this question?

Wilson: *30-odd.*

Question: *No one gave you a response other than "We saw the chicken"?*

Wilson: *No, this was the first quick response — "We saw a chicken."*

Question: *They did see a man, too?*

Wilson: *Well, when we questioned them further they had seen a man, but what*
was really interesting was they hadn't made a whole story out of it, and in point of
fact, we discovered afterwards that they hadn't seen a whole frame — they had
inspected the frame for details. Then we found out from the artist and an eye
specialist that a sophisticated audience, an audience that is accustomed to the
film, focuses a little way in front of the flat screen so that you take in the whole
frame. In this sense, again, a picture is a convention. You've got to look at the
picture as a whole first, and these people did not do that, not being accustomed to
pictures. When presented with the picture they began to inspect it, rather as the
scanner of a television camera, and go over it very rapidly. Apparently, that is
what the eye unaccustomed to pictures does — scans the picture — and they hadn't
scanned one picture before it moved on, in spite *of the slow technique of the film.*

The key facts are at the end of the passage. Literacy gives people the power to
focus a little way in front of an image so that we take in the whole image or
picture at a glance. Non-literate people have no such acquired habit and do not
look at objects in our way. Rather they scan objects and images as we do the
printed page, segment by segment. Thus they have no detached point of view.
They are wholly *with* the object. They go emphatically into it. The eye is used,
not in perspective but tactually, as it were. Euclidean spaces depending on much
separation of sight from touch and sound are not known to them.

Further difficulties which these natives had with film will help us to see how
many of the conventions of literacy are built into even non-verbal forms like film:

My point is that I think we've got to be very wary of pictures; they can be interpreted in the light of your experience. Now, next we thought that if we are going to use these films we've got to have some sort of process of education and we've got to have some research. We found also some fascinating things in this research process. We found that the film is, as produced in the West, a very highly conventionalized piece of symbolism although it looks very real. For instance, we found that if you were telling a story about two men to an African audience and one had finished his business and he went off the edge of the screen, the audience wanted to know what had happened to him; they didn't accept that this was just the end of him and that he was of no more interest in the story. They wanted to know what happened to this fellow, and we had to write stories that way, putting in a lot of material that wasn't to us necessary. We had to follow him along the street until he took a natural turn — he mustn't walk off the side of the screen, but must walk down the street and make a natural turn. It was quite understandable that he could disappear around the turn. The action had to follow a natural course of events.

Panning shots were very confusing because the audience didn't realize what was happening. They thought the items and details inside the picture were literally moving. You see, the convention was not accepted. Nor was the idea of a person sitting still while the camera was brought in to a close-up; this was a strange thing, this picture growing bigger in your presence. You know the common way of starting a film: show the city, narrow it down to a street, narrow it down to one house, take your camera in through the window, etc. This was literally interpreted as you walking forward and doing all those things until you were finally taken in through the window.

All of this meant that to use the film as a really effective medium we had to begin a process of education in useful conventions and make those films which would educate people to one convention, to the idea, for example, of a man walking off the side of the screen. We had to show that there was a street corner and have the man walk around the street corner and then in the next part of the film show him walking away, and then cut the scene.

African audiences cannot accept our passive consumer role in the presence of film.

A basic aspect of any literate audience is its profound acceptance of a passive consumer role in the presence of book or film. But an African audience had had no training in the private and silent following of a narrative process.

This is an important matter. An African audience does not sit silently without participating. They like to participate, so the person who shows the films and makes the live commentary must be flexible, stimulating, and get responses. If

there is a situation where a character sings a song, the song is sung and the audi-
ence is invited to join in. This audience participation had to be thought of as the
film was made and opportunities provided for it. Live commentators who presented
the films had to be trained to the last degree in what the film meant and in their
interpretation of the film for different audiences. They were Africans taken out of
the teaching profession and trained for this business.

But even when trained to follow film the native of Ghana cannot accept a film
about Nigerians. He cannot generalize his experience from film to film, such is
the depth of involvement in particular experiences. This empathic involvement,
natural to the oral society and the audile-tactile man, is cracked by the phonetic
alphabet which abstracts the visual component from the sensory complex. This
leads to one further point of Wilson's. He explained the relevance of Chaplin's
technique in making films for native audiences. The story was in the gestures,
and the gestures were complex and precise. Wilson noted the inability of
Africans to follow complex narratives but also their subtlety in dramatization:

One thing we were ignorant of at this time, and something we ought to have
known a lot more about is that those African audiences are very good at role-
playing. Part of a child's education in a pre-literate society is role-playing; he's
got to learn to play the role of elders in certain given situations. One thing fortu-
nately we did discover was that the cartoon went down very well. This puzzled us
until we found out that puppetry is quite a common pastime.

But there is more to this point than Wilson supposes. Had TV been available he
would have been amazed to discover how much more readily the Africans took
to it than they did to film. For with film you are the camera and the non-literate
man cannot use his eyes like a camera. But with TV you are the screen. And TV
is two-dimensional and sculptural in its tactile contours. TV is not a narrative
medium, is not so much visual as audile-tactile. That is why it is empathic, and
why the optimal mode of TV image is the cartoon. For the cartoon appeals to
natives as it does to our children, because it is a world in which the visual component is so small that the viewer has as much to do as in a crossword puzzle.[8]
   More important still, with the bounding line of a cartoon, as with a cave painting, we tend to be in an area of the interplay of the senses, and hence of strongly
haptic or tactile character. That is to say, the art of the draughtsman and the *cela-*
tor alike is a strongly tactile and tangible art. And even Euclidean geometry is by
modern standards very tactile.

-----

[8]For more data on the new space orientation in TV-viewing, see H. M. McLuhan, "Inside the Five Sense
Sensorium," *Canadian Architect*, June, 1961, vol. 6, no. 6, pp. 49–54.

This is a matter discussed by William Ivins, Jr., in *Art and Geometry: A Study in Space Intuitions*. He explains the unverbalized assumptions of Greek space awareness: "The Greeks never mentioned among the axioms and postulates of their geometry their basic assumption of congruence, and yet . . . it is among the most fundamental things in Greek geometry, and plays a determining role in its form, its power, and its limitations." (p. x) Congruence was a new and exciting visual dimension, unknown to audile-tactile cultures. As Ivins says in this regard, "Unlike the eye, the unaided hand is unable to discover whether three or more objects are on a line." (p. 7) It is very obvious why Plato might have insisted that "no one destitute of geometry enter" his academy. A similar motive leads the Viennese musician Carl Orff to forbid children to study music in his school if they have already learned to read and write. The visual bias so attained he feels makes it quite hopeless to develop their audile-tactile powers in music. Ivins goes on to explain why we have the illusion of space as a kind of independent container, whereas in fact space is "a quality or relationship of things and has no existence without them." (p. 8) Yet in comparison with later centuries, "the Greeks were tactile minded and . . . whenever they were given the choice between a tactile or a visual way of thought they instinctively chose the tactile one." (pp. 9-10) Such remained the case until well after Gutenberg in Western experience. Considering the history of Greek geometry, Ivins observes: ". . . again and again during a period of six or seven centuries they went right up to the door of modern geometry, but that, inhibited by their tactile-muscular, metrical ideas, they were never able to open that door and pass out into the great open spaces of modern thought." (p. 58)

When technology extends one of our senses, a new translation of culture occurs as swiftly as the new technology is interiorized.

Although the main theme of this book is the Gutenberg Galaxy or a configuration of events, which lies far ahead of the world of alphabet and of scribal culture, it needs to be known why, without alphabet, there would have been no Gutenberg. And, therefore, we must get some insight into the conditions of culture and perception that make first, writing, and then, perhaps, alphabet possible at all.[9]

---

[9]The Koreans by 1403 were making cast-metal type by means of punches and matrices (*The Invention of Printing in China and its Spread Westward* by T. F. Carter). Carter had no concern with the alphabet relation to print and was probably unaware that the Koreans are reputed to have a phonetic alphabet.

Wilson's account of the years of perceptual training needed to enable adult Africans to be able to see movies has its exact analogue in the difficulties which Western adults have with "abstract" art. In 1925 Bertrand Russell wrote his *ABC of Relativity*, pointing out on the first page that:

> *Many of the new ideas can be expressed in non-mathematical language, but they are none the less difficult on that account. What is demanded is a change in our imaginative picture of the world. . . . The same sort of change was demanded by Copernicus, when he taught that the earth is not stationary . . . To us now there is no difficulty in this idea, because we learned it before our mental habits had become fixed. Einstein's ideas, similarly, will seem easier to generations which grow up with them; but for us a certain effort of imaginative reconstruction is unavoidable.*

It is simpler to say that if a new technology extends one or more of our senses outside us into the social world, then new ratios among all of our senses will occur in that particular culture. It is comparable to what happens when a new note is added to a melody. And when the sense ratios alter in any culture then what had appeared lucid before may suddenly be opaque, and what had been vague or opaque will become translucent. As Heinrich Wolfflin stated the matter in 1915, in his revolutionary *Principles of Art History* (p. 62) "the effect is the thing that counts, not the sensuous facts." Wolfflin began working from the discoveries of the sculptor Adolf von Hildebrand, whose *Problem of Form in the Figurative Arts* had first clearly explained the disorder in ordinary human sense perception, and the role of art in clarifying this confusion. Hildebrand had shown how tactility was a kind of synesthesia or interplay among the senses, and as such, was the core of the richest art *effects*. For the low definition imagery of the tactile mode compels the viewer into an active participant role. When Africans watch movies as if they were low definition forms for active participation, we are amused by the incongruity. Working from effect rather than from cause, which we have already seen as native to the Russian, was for us a novel mode of procedure in the later nineteenth century, and will come in for fuller discussion later in this book.

A recent work by Georg von Bekesy, *Experiments in Hearing*, offers an exactly reverse answer to the problem of space to the one which Carothers and Wilson have just given us. Whereas they are trying to talk about the perception of non-literate people in terms of literate experience, Professor von Bekesy chooses to begin his discussion of acoustical space on its own terms. As one proficient in auditory spaces, he is keenly aware of the difficulty of talking about the space of hearing, for the acoustical is necessarily a world in "depth."[10] It is of the utmost interest that

---

[10]See "Acoustic Space."

in trying to elucidate the nature of hearing and of acoustic space, Professor von Bekesy should deliberately avoid viewpoint and perspective in favour of mosaic field. And to this end he resorts to two-dimensional painting as a means of revealing the resonant depth of acoustic space. Here are his own words (p. 4):

> It is possible to distinguish two forms of approach to a problem. One, which may be called the theoretical approach, is to formulate the problem in relation to what is already known, to make additions or extensions on the basis of accepted principles, and then to proceed to test these hypotheses experimentally. Another, which may be called the mosaic approach, takes each problem for itself with little reference to the field in which it lies, and seeks to discover relations and principles that hold within the circumscribed area.

Von Bekesy then proceeds to introduce his two paintings:

> A close analogy to these two approaches may be found in the field of art. In the period between the eleventh and seventeenth centuries the Arabs and the Persians developed a high mastery of the arts of description. . . . Later, during the Renaissance, a new form of representation was developed in which the attempt was made to give unity and perspective to the picture and to represent the atmosphere. . . .
>
> When in the field of science a great deal of progress has been made and most of the pertinent variables are known, a new problem may most readily be handled by trying to fit it into the existing framework. When, however, the framework is uncertain and the number of variables is large the mosaic approach is much the easier.

The mosaic approach is not only "much the easier" in the study of the simultaneous which is the auditory field; it is the only relevant approach. For the "two-dimensional" mosaic or painting is the mode in which there is muting of the visual as such, in order that there may be maximal interplay among all of the senses. Such was the painterly strategy "since Cézanne," to paint as if you held, rather than as if you saw, objects.

A theory of cultural change is impossible without knowledge of the changing sense ratios effected by various externalizations of our senses.

It is very much worth dwelling on this matter, since we shall see that from the invention of the alphabet there has been a continuous drive in the Western world towards the separation of the senses, of functions, of operations, of states emotional and political, as well as of tasks — a fragmentation which terminated, thought Durkheim, in the *anomie* of the nineteenth century. The paradox presented by Professor von Bekesy is that the two-dimensional mosaic is, in fact, a multidimensional world of interstructural resonance. It is the three-dimensional world of pictorial space that is, indeed, an abstract illusion built on the intense separation of the visual from the other senses.

There is here no question of values or preferences. It is necessary, however, for any other kind of understanding to know why "primitive" drawing is two-dimensional, whereas the drawing and painting of literate man tends towards perspective. Without this knowledge we cannot grasp why men ever ceased to be "primitive" or audile-tactile in their sense bias. Nor could we ever understand why men have "since Cézanne" abandoned the visual in favour of the audile-tactile modes of awareness and of organization of experience. This matter clarified, we can much more easily approach the role of alphabet and of printing in giving a dominant role to the visual sense in language and art and in the entire range of social and of political life. For until men have up-graded the visual component communities know only a tribal structure. The detribalizing of the individual has, in the past at least, depended on an intense visual life fostered by literacy, and by literacy of the alphabetic kind alone. For alphabetic writing is not only unique but late. There had been much writing before it. In fact, any people that ceases to be nomadic and pursues sedentary modes of work is ready to invent writing. No merely nomadic people ever had writing any more than they ever developed architecture or "enclosed space." For writing is a visual enclosure of non-visual spaces and senses. It is, therefore, an abstraction of the visual from the ordinary sense interplay. And whereas speech is an outering (utterance) of all our senses at once, writing abstracts from speech.

At the present time it is easier to grasp this specific technology of writing. The new institutes for teaching speeded-up reading habits work on the separation of eye-movements from inner verbalization. It will be indicated later that all reading in the ancient and medieval worlds was reading aloud. With print the eye speeded up and the voice quieted down. But inner verbalizing was taken for granted as inseparable from the horizontal following of the words on the page. Today we know that the divorce of reading and verbalizing can be made by vertical reading. This, of course, pushes the alphabetic technology of the separation of the senses to an extreme of inanity, but it is relevant to an understanding of how writing of any sort gets started.

In a paper entitled "A History of the Theory of Information," read to the Royal Society in 1951, E. Colin Cherry of the University of London, observed that "Early invention was greatly hampered by an inability to dissociate mechanical structure from animal form. The invention of the wheel was one outstanding early effort of such dissociation. The great spurt in invention which began in the sixteenth century rested on the gradual dissociation of the machine from animal form." Printing was the first mechanization of an ancient handicraft and led easily to the further mechanization of all handicrafts. The modern phases of this process are the theme of *Mechanization Takes Command* by Siegfried Giedion.

However, Giedion is concerned with a minute tracing of the stages by which in the past century we have used mechanism to recover organic form:

> *In his celebrated studies of the 'seventies on the motions of men and animals, Edward Muybridge set up a series of thirty cameras at twelve-inch intervals, releasing their shutters electromagnetically as soon as the moving object passed before the plate. . . . Each picture showed the object in an isolated phase as arrested by each camera. (p. 107)*

That is to say, the object is translated out of organic or simultaneous form into a static or pictorial mode. By revolving a sequence of such static or pictorial spaces at a sufficient speed, the illusion of organic wholeness, or interplay of spaces, is created. Thus, the wheel finally becomes the means of moving our culture away from the machine. But it was by means of electricity applied to the wheel that the wheel merges once more with animal form. In fact, the wheel is now an obsolete form in the electric-missile age. But hyper-trophy is the mark of obsolescence, as we shall see again and again. Just because wheel is now returning to organic form in the twentieth century it is quite easy for us to understand how primitive man "invented" it. Any creature in motion is a wheel in that repetition of movement has a cyclic and circular principle in it. Thus the melodies of literate societies are repeatable cycles. But the music of non-literate people has no such repetitive cyclic and abstract form as melody. Invention, in a word, is translation of one kind of space into another.

Giedion devotes some time to the work of the French physiologist, Etienne Jules Morey (1830-1904), who devised the myograph for recording the movements of muscles: "Morey quite consciously looks back to Descartes, but instead of graphically representing sections he translates organic movement into graphic form." (p. 19)

The twentieth century encounter between alphabetic and electronic faces of culture confers on the printed word a crucial role in staying the return to the Africa within.

The invention of the alphabet, like the invention of the wheel, was the translation or reduction of a complex, organic interplay of spaces into a single space. The phonetic alphabet reduced the use of all the senses at once, which is oral speech, to a merely visual code. Today, such translation can be effected back and forth through a variety of spatial forms which we call the "media of communication." But each of these spaces had unique properties and impinges upon our other senses or spaces in unique ways.

Today, then, it is easy to understand the invention of the alphabet because, as A. N. Whitehead pointed out in *Science and the Modern World* (p. 141) the great discovery of the nineteenth century was the discovery of the method of discovery:

> *The greatest invention of the nineteenth century was the invention of the method of invention. A new method entered into life. In order to understand our epoch, we can neglect all the details of change, such as railways, telegraphs, radios, spinning machines, synthetic dyes. We must concentrate on the method in itself; that is the real novelty which has broken up the foundations of the old civilization . . . . One element in the new method is just the discovery of how to set about bridging the gap between the scientific ideas, and the ultimate product. It is a process of disciplined attack upon one difficulty after another.*

The method of invention, as Edgar Poe demonstrated in his "Philosophy of Composition," is simply to begin with the solution of the problem or with the effect intended. Then one backtracks, step by step, to the point from which one must begin in order to reach the solution or effect. Such is the method of the detective story, of the symbolist poem, and of modern science. It is, however, the twentieth century step beyond this method of invention which is needed for understanding the origin and the action of such forms as the wheel or the alphabet. And that step is not the backtracking from *product* to starting point, but the following of *process* in isolation from product. To follow the contours of process as in psychoanalysis provides the only means of avoiding the product of process, namely neurosis or psychosis.

It is the purpose of the present book to study primarily the print phase of alphabetic culture. The print phase, however, has encountered today the new organic and biological modes of the electronic world. That is, it is now interpenetrated at its extreme development of mechanism by the electro-biological, as de Chardin has explained. And it is this reversal of character which makes our age "connatural," as it were, with non-literate cultures. We have no more difficulty in understanding the native or non-literate experience, simply because we have recreated it electronically within our own culture. (Yet post-literacy is a quite different mode of interdependence from pre-literacy.) So my dwelling upon the earlier phases of alphabetic technology is not irrelevant to an understanding of the Gutenberg era.

Colin Cherry had this to say about early writing:

> *A detailed history of spoken and written languages would be irrelevant to our present subject, but nevertheless there are certain matters of interest which may be taken as a starting-point. The early writings of Mediterranean civilizations were*

in picture, or "logographic" script: simple pictures were used to represent objects and also, by association, ideas, actions, names, and so on. Also, what is much more important, phonetic writing was developed, in which sounds were given symbols. With the passage of time, the pictures were reduced to more formal symbols as determined by the difficulty of using a chisel, or a reed brush, while the phonetic writing simplified into a set of two or three dozen alphabetic letters, divided into consonants and vowels.

In Egyptian hieroglyphics we have a supreme example of what is now called redundancy *in languages and code; one of the difficulties in deciphering the Rosetta stone lay in the fact that a polysyllabic word might give each syllable not one symbol but a number of different ones in common use, in order that the word should be thoroughly understood. (The effect when literally transcribed into English is one of stuttering.) On the other hand the Semitic languages show an early recognition of redundancy. Ancient Hebrew script had no vowels: modern Hebrew has none, too, except in children's books. Many other ancient scripts have no vowels. Slavonic Russian went a step further in condensation: in religious texts, commonly used words were abbreviated to a few letters, in a manner similar to our present-day use of the ampersand, abbreviations such as lb and the increasing use of initials, e.g., U.S.A., Unesco, O.K.*

It is not the avoidance of redundancy that is the key to the phonetic alphabet and its effects on person and society. "Redundancy" is a "content" concept, itself a legacy of alphabetic technology. That is, any phonetic writing is a visual code for speech. Speech is the "content" of phonetic writing. But it is not the content of any other kind of writing. Pictographic and ideographic varieties of writing are *Gestalts* or snapshots of various situations, personal or social. In fact, we can get a good idea of non-alphabetic forms of writing from modern mathematical equations like $E = MC^2$ or from the ancient Greek and Roman "figures of rhetoric." Such equations or figures have no content but are structures like an individual melody which evoke their own world. The figures of rhetoric are postures of the mind, as hyperbole, or irony, or litotes, or simile, or paranomasia. Picture writing of all kinds is a ballet of such postures which delights our modern bias towards synesthesia and audile-tactile richness of experience, far more than does the bare, abstract alphabetic form. It would be well today if children were taught a good many Chinese ideograms and Egyptian hieroglyphs as a means of enhancing their appreciation of our alphabet.

Colin Cherry, then, misses the point about the unique character of our alphabet, namely that it dissociates or abstracts, not only sight and sound, but separates all meaning from the sound of the letters, save so far as the meaningless letters relate to the meaningless sounds. So long as any other meaning is vested in sight or sound, the divorce between the visual and the other senses remains incomplete, as is the case in all forms of writing save the phonetic alphabet.

Current concern with reading and spelling reform steers away from visual to auditory stress.

It is interesting that today there is a growing unrest about our alphabetic dissociation of the senses. On page 143 there is a sample of a recent attempt at a new alphabet that would restore more phonic character to our script. The most notable thing about the sample is that it has the highly textural and tactile quality of an ancient manuscript page. In our desire to restore some unity of interplay among our senses we grope towards ancient manuscript forms which must be read aloud to be read at all. Side by side with this extreme development is that of the new institutes for speeded-up reading. There they are taught how to use the eye on the page so as to avoid all verbalization and all incipient movements of the throat which accompany our cinematic chase from left to right, in order to create the mental sound movie which we call reading.

The most definitive work we have on the phonetic letters is *The Alphabet* by David Diringer. He begins his story as follows (p. 37):

The alphabet is the last, the most highly developed, the most convenient and the most easily adaptable system of writing. Alphabetic writing is now universally employed by civilized peoples; its use is acquired in childhood with ease. There is an enormous advantage, obviously, in the use of letters which represent single sounds rather than ideas or syllables; no sinologist knows all the 80,000 or so Chinese symbols, but it is also far from easy to master the 9,000 or so symbols actually employed by Chinese scholars. How far simpler is it to use 22 or 24 or 26 signs only! The alphabet may also be passed from one language to another without great difficulty; the same alphabet is used now for English, French, Italian, German, Spanish, Turkish, Polish, Dutch, Czech, Croatian, Welsh, Finnish, Hungarian and others, and has derived from the alphabet once used by the ancient Hebrews, Phoenicians, Aramaeans, Greeks, Etruscans and Romans.

Thanks to the simplicity of the alphabet, writing has become very common; it is no longer a more or less exclusive domain of the priestly or other privileged classes, a it was in Egypt, or Mesopotamia, or China. Education has become largely a matter of reading and writing, and is possible for all. The fact that alphabetic writing has survived with relatively little change for three and a half millennia, notwithstanding the introduction of printing and the typewriter, and the extensive use of shorthand-writing, is the best evidence for its suitability to serve the needs of the whole modern world. It is this simplicity, adaptability and suitability which have secured the triumph of the alphabet over the other systems of writing.

Alphabetic writing and its origin constitute a story in themselves; they offer a new field for research which American scholars are beginning to call

helpiŋ ɟhe bliend man

loŋ agœ ɟhær livd a
bliend man. hee livd whær
treeʒ and flouerʒ grœ; but
ɟhe bliend man cœd not see
ɟhe treeʒ or flouerʒ.

ɟhe pœr man had tœ feel
ɟhe wæ to gœ wiɟh hiʒ stick.
tap-tap-tap went hiʒ stick on
ɟhe rœd. hee waukt slœly.

The New York Times

NEW 43-UNIT ALPHABET: This is a page from a work called "Jesus the Helper," printed in the experimental augmented Roman alphabet in Britain. The alphabet, based largely on phonetics, contains the conventional alphabet with letters "q" and "x" discarded and nineteen new letters added. There are no capital letters. Under the system, the letter "o" is unchanged in the sound of "long," but "ago" is spelled "agoe" with the "o" and "e" joined. Another new letter is an inverted "z," for sounds like "trees." The conventional "s" is used in words like "see." Other new letters include "i" and "e" joined by a cross-bar for words like "blind;" "o" and "u" joined for words like "flowers," and two "o's" that are joined together. In September, about 1,000 British children will start to learn to read with this phonetic, experimental alphabet.

Figure 1, from the *New York Times*, July 20, 1961.

"alphabetology." No other system of writing has had so extensive, so intricate and so interesting a history.

Diringer's observation that the alphabet is "now universally employed by civilized peoples" is a bit tautological since it is by alphabet alone that men have detribalized or individualized themselves into "civilization." Cultures can rise far above civilization artistically but without the phonetic alphabet they remain tribal, as do the Chinese and the Japanese. It is necessary to stress that my concern is with the process of separation of sense by which the detribalizing of men is achieved. Whether such personal abstraction and social detribalization be a "good thing" is not for any individual to determine. But a recognition of the process may disembarrass the matter of the miasmal moral fogs that now invest it.

The alphabet is an aggressive and militant absorber and transformer of cultures, as Harold Innis was the first to show.

Another observation of Diringer's that deserves comment is the acceptability among all peoples of a technology that uses letters to "represent single sounds rather than ideas or syllables." Another way of putting this is to say that any society possessing the alphabet can translate any adjacent cultures into its alphabetic mode. But this is a one-way process. No non-alphabetic culture can take over an alphabetic one, because the alphabet cannot be assimilated; it can only liquidate or reduce. However, in the electronic age we may have discovered the limits of the alphabet technology. It need no longer seem strange that peoples like the Greeks and Romans, who had experienced the alphabet, should also have been driven in the direction of conquest and organization-at-a-distance. Harold Innis, in *Empire and Communications*, was the first to pursue this theme and to explain in detail the simple truth of the Cadmus myth. The Greek King Cadmus, who introduced the phonetic alphabet to Greece, was said to have sown the dragon's teeth and that they sprang up armed men. (The dragon's teeth may allude to the old hieroglyphic forms.) Innis also explained why print causes nationalism and not tribalism; and why print causes price systems and markets such as cannot exist without print. In short, Harold Innis was the first person to hit upon the *process* of change as implicit in the *forms* of media technology. The present book is a footnote of explanation to his work.

Diringer is emphatic about only one thing concerning the alphabet. No matter how or when it was achieved:

At any rate, it must be said that the great achievement of the invention was not the creation of the signs. It lies in the adoption of a purely alphabetic system, which, moreover, denoted each sound by one sign only. For this achievement, simple as it now seems to us, the inventor, or the inventors are to be ranked among the greatest benefactors of mankind. No other people in the world has been able to develop a true alphabetic writing. The more or less civilized peoples of Egypt, Mesopotamia, Crete, Asia Minor, Indus Valley, China, Central America, reached an advanced stage in the history of writing, but could not get beyond the transitional stage. A few peoples (the ancient Cypriotes, the Japanese and others), developed a syllabary. But only the Syro-Palestinian Semites produced a genius who created the alphabetic writing, from which have descended all past and present alphabets.

Each important civilization modifies its script and time may make its relation to some of its near relatives quite unrecognizable. Thus, the Brahmi, the great mother-script of India, the Korean alphabet, the Mongolian scripts are derived from the same source as the Greek, the Latin, the Runic, the Hebrew, the Arabic, the Russian alphabet, although it is practically impossible for a layman to see a real resemblance between them. (pp. 216-17)

By the meaningless sign linked to the meaningless sound we have built the shape and meaning of Western man. Our next concern will be to trace somewhat sketchily the effects of the alphabet in manuscript culture in the ancient and medieval world. After that, we shall look much more closely at the transformation of alphabetic culture, by the printing press.

The Homeric hero becomes a split-man as he assumes an individual ego.

In his *Art and Illusion*, E. H. Gombrich writes (p. 116):

If I had to reduce the last chapter to a brief formula it would be "making comes before matching." Before the artist ever wanted to match the sights of the visible world he wanted to create things in their own right. . . . The very violence with which Plato denounces this trickery reminds us of the momentous fact that at the time he wrote, mimesis was a recent invention. There are many critics now who share his distaste, for one reason or another, but even they would admit there are few more exciting spectacles in the whole history of art than the great awakening of Greek sculpture and painting between the sixth century and the time of Plato's youth toward the end of the fifth century B.C.

Etienne Gilson makes much of the distinction between making and matching in his *Painting and Reality*. And whereas till Giotto a painting was a thing, from

Giotto till Cézanne painting became the representation of things. See his chapter VIII on "Imitation and Creation."

There was, of course, the same development towards representation and direct lineal narrative in poetry and prose, as we shall see. What is essential for understanding this process, however, is that *mimesis* in Plato's (not Aristotle's) sense is the necessary effect of separating out the visual mode from the ordinary enmeshment with the audile-tactile interplay of senses. It is this process, brought about by the experience of phoentic literacy, that hoicks societies of the world of "sacred" or cosmic space and time into the detribalized or "profane" space and time of civilized and pragmatic man. Such is the theme of *The Sacred and The Profane: The Nature of Religion* by Mircea Eliade.

In *The Greeks and the Irrational*, E. R. Dodds discusses the emotional instability and manias of the Homeric heroes: "And we may also ask ourselves why a people so civilised, clear-headed, and rational as the Ionians did not eliminate from their national epics these links with Borneo and the primitive past, just as they eliminated the fear of the dead . . ." (p. 13) But it is his next page that is especially helpful:

"His own behaviour . . . has become alien to him. He cannot understand it. It is for him no part of his Ego." This is a perfectly true observation, and its relevance to some of the phenomena we have been considering cannot, I think, be doubted. Nilsson is also, I believe, right in holding that experiences of this sort played a part — along with other elements, such as the Minoan tradition of protecting goddesses — in building up that machinery of physical intervention to which Homer resorts so constantly and, to our thinking, often so superfluously. We find it superfluous because the divine machinery seems to us in many cases to do no more than duplicate a natural psychological causation. But ought we not perhaps to say rather that the divine machinery "duplicates" a psychic intervention — that is, presents it in a concrete pictorial form? This was not superfluous; for only in this way could it be made vivid to the imagination of the hearers. The Homeric poets were without the refinements of language which would have been needed to "put across" adequately a purely psychological miracle. What more natural than that they should first supplement, and later replace, an old unexciting threadbare formula like μένος ἔμβαλε Θυμῷ *by making the god appear as a physical presence and exhort his favourite with the spoken word? How much more vivid than a mere inward monition is the famous scene in* Iliad *I where Athena plucks Achilles by the hair and warns him not to strike Agamemnon! But she is visible to Achilles alone: "none of the others saw her." That is a plain hint that she is projection, the pictorial expression, of an inward monition — a monition which Achilles might have described by such a vague phrase as* ἐνέπνευσεν φρεσὶ δαίμων. *And I suggest that in general the inward monition, or the sudden unaccountable feeling of power, or the sudden unaccountable loss of judgement, is the germ out of which the divine machinery developed.*

The hero has become a split man as he moves towards the possession of an individual ego. And the "split" is manifest as pictorialized models or "machinery" of complex situations such as tribal, auditory man had made no effort to visualize. That is to say, detribalization, individualization, and pictorialization are all one. The magical mode disappears in proportion as interior events are made visually manifest. But such manifestation is also reduction and distortion of complex relations which are more fully sensed when there is full interplay of all the senses at once.

Mimesis to Plato had appeared, quite understandably, as varieties of representation, especially visual. In his *Poetics* 4, Aristotle made mimesis central to his entire cognitive and epistemological world, not limiting it to any one sense. But the first onset of literacy, and, therefore, of visuality as abstracted from the other senses, seemed to Plato a diminution of ontological awareness, or an impoverishment of Being. Bergson somewhere asks, how should we be able to know if some agent could double the speed of *all* events in the world? Quite simply, he answered. We would discern a great loss of richness in experience. Such seems to have been Plato's attitude towards literacy and visual mimesis.

Gombrich begins his tenth chapter of *Art and Illusion* with further observations on visual mimesis:

> *The last chapter has led this inquiry back to the old truth that the discovery of appearances was not due so much to a careful observation of nature as to the invention of pictorial effects. I believe indeed that the ancient writers who were still filled with a sense of wonder at man's capacity to fool the eye came closer to an understanding of this achievement than many later critics . . . but if we discard Berkeley's theory of vision, according to which we "see" a flat field but "construct" a tactile space, we can perhaps rid art history of its obsession with space and bring other achievements into focus, the suggestion of light and texture, for instance, or the mastery of physiognomic expression.*

Berkeley's *New Theory of Vision* (1709) is now favoured by psychologists of our sense lives. But Berkeley was concerned to refute Descartes and Newton, who had wholly abstracted the visual sense from the interaction of the other senses. On the other hand, the suppression of the visual sense in favour of the audile-tactile complex, produces the distortions of tribal society, and of the configuration of jazz and primitive art imitations which broke upon us with radio, but not just "because" of radio.[11]

---

[11]Georg von Bekesy's article on "Similarities between Hearing and Skin Sensations" (*Psychological Review*, Jan., 1959, pp. 1-22) provides a means of understanding why no sense can function in isolation nor can be unmodified by the operation and diet of the other senses.

Gombrich not only has all the most relevant information about the rise of the pictorial mode; he has all the right difficulties. He ends his *Art and Illusion* by commenting (pp. 117-18):

> *There is finally the history of Greek painting as we can follow it in painted pottery, which tells of the discovery of foreshortening and the conquest of space early in the fifth century and of light in the fourth. . . . Emanuel Loewy at the turn of the century first developed his theories about the rendering of nature in Greek art that stressed the priority of conceptual modes and their gradual adjustment to natural appearances. . . . But in itself it explains very little. For why was it that this process started comparatively so late in the history of mankind? In this respect our perspective has very much changed. To the Greeks the archaic period represented the dawn of history, and classical scholarship has not always shaken off this inheritance. From this point of view it appeared quite natural that the awakening of art from primitive modes should have coincided with the rise of all those other activities, that, for the humanist, belong to civilization: the development of philosophy, of science, and of dramatic poetry.*

9

Understanding Media

Introduction

James Reston wrote in *The New York Times* (July 7, 1957):

> *A health director . . . reported this week that a small mouse, which presumably had been watching television, attacked a little girl and her full-grown cat. . . . Both mouse and cat survived, and the incident is recorded here as a reminder that things seem to be changing.*

After three thousand years of explosion, by means of fragmentary and mechanical technologies, the Western world is imploding. During the mechanical ages we had extended our bodies in space. Today, after more than a century of electric technology, we have extended our central nervous system itself in a global embrace, abolishing both space and time as far as our planet is concerned. Rapidly, we approach the final phase of the extensions of man — the technological simulation of consciousness, when the creative process of knowing will be collectively and corporately extended to the whole of human society, much as we have already extended our senses and our nerves by the various media. Whether the extension of consciousness, so long sought by advertisers for specific products, will be "a good thing" is a question that admits of a wide solution. There is little possibility of answering such questions about the extensions of man without considering all of them together. Any extension, whether of skin, hand, or foot, affects the whole psychic and social complex.

Some of the principal extensions, together with some of their psychic and social consequences, are studied in this book. Just how little consideration has been given to such matters in the past can be gathered from the consternation of one of the editors of this book. He noted in dismay that "seventy-five per cent of your material is new. A successful book cannot venture to be more than ten per cent new." Such a risk seems quite worth taking at the present time when the stakes are very high, and the need to understand the effects of the extensions of man becomes more urgent by the hour.

In the mechanical age now receding, many actions could be taken without too much concern. Slow movement insured that the reactions were delayed for considerable periods of time. Today the action and the reaction occur almost at the same time. We actually live mythically and integrally, as it were, but we continue to think in the old, fragmented space and time patterns of the pre-electric age.

Western man acquired from the technology of literacy the power to act without reacting. The advantages of fragmenting himself in this way are seen in the case of the surgeon who would be quite helpless if he were to become humanly involved in his operation. We acquired the art of carrying out the most dangerous social operations with complete detachment. But our detachment was a posture of noninvolvement. In the electric age, when our central nervous system is technologically extended to involve us in the whole of mankind and to incorporate the whole of mankind in us, we necessarily participate, in depth, in the consequences of our every action. It is no longer possible to adopt the aloof and dissociated role of the literate Westerner.

The Theater of the Absurd dramatizes this recent dilemma of Western man, the man of action who appears not to be involved in the action. Such is the origin and appeal of Samuel Beckett's clowns. After three thousand years of specialist explosion and of increasing specialism and alienation in the technological extensions of our bodies, our world has become compressional by dramatic reversal. As electrically contracted, the globe is no more than a village. Electric speed in bringing all social and political functions together in a sudden implosion has heightened human awareness of responsibility to an intense degree. It is this implosive factor that alters the position of the Negro, the teen-ager, and some other groups. They can no longer be *contained*, in the political sense of limited association. They are now *involved* in our lives, as we in theirs, thanks to the electric media.

This is the Age of Anxiety for the reason of the electric implosion that compels commitment and participation, quite regardless of any "point of view." The partial and specialized character of the viewpoint, however noble, will not serve at all in the electric age. At the information level the same upset has occurred with the substitution of the inclusive image for the mere viewpoint. If the nineteenth century was the age of the editorial chair, ours is the century of the psychiatrist's couch. As extension of man the chair is a specialist ablation of the posterior, a sort of ablative absolute of backside, whereas the couch extends the integral being. The psychiatrist employs the couch, since it removes the temptation to express private points of view and obviates the need to rationalize events.

The aspiration of our time for wholeness, empathy and depth of awareness is a natural adjunct of electric technology. The age of mechanical industry that preceded us found vehement assertion of private outlook the natural mode of expression. Every culture and every age has its favorite model of perception and knowledge that it is inclined to prescribe for everybody and everything. The mark of our time is its revulsion against imposed patterns. We are suddenly eager to have things and people declare their beings totally. There is a deep faith to be found in this new attitude — a faith that concerns the ultimate harmony of all being. Such is the faith in which this book has been written. It explores the contours of our own extended beings in our technologies, seeking the principle of intelligibility in each of them. In the full confidence that it is possible to win an understanding of these forms that will bring them into orderly service, I have looked at them anew, accepting very little of the conventional wisdom concerning them. One can say of media as Robert Theobald has said of economic depressions: "There is one additional factor that has helped to control depressions, and that is a better understanding of their development." Examination of the origin and development of the individual extensions of man should be preceded by a look at some general aspects of the media, or extensions of man, beginning with the never-explained numbness that each extension brings about in the individual and society.

The Medium Is the Message

In a culture like ours, long accustomed to splitting and dividing all things as a means of control, it is sometimes a bit of a shock to be reminded that, in operational and practical fact, the medium is the message. This is merely to say that the personal and social consequences of any medium — that is, of any extension of ourselves — result from the new scale that is introduced into our affairs by each extension of ourselves, or by any new technology. Thus, with automation, for example, the new patterns of human association tend to eliminate jobs, it is true. That is the negative result. Positively, automation creates roles for people, which is to say depth of involvement in their work and human association that our preceding mechanical technology had destroyed. Many people would be disposed to say that it was not the machine, but what one did with the machine, that was its meaning or message. In terms of the ways in which the machine altered our relations to one another and to ourselves, it mattered not in the least whether it turned out cornflakes or Cadillacs. The restructuring of human work and association was shaped by the technique of fragmentation that is the essence of machine technology. The essence of automation technology is the opposite. It is integral and decentralist in depth, just as the machine was fragmentary, centralist, and superficial in its patterning of human relationships.

The instance of the electric light may prove illuminating in this connection. The electric light is pure information. It is a medium without a message, as it were, unless it is used to spell out some verbal ad or name. This fact, characteristic of all media, means that the "content" of any medium is always another medium. The content of writing is speech, just as the written word is the content of print, and print is the content of the telegraph. If it is asked, "What is the content of speech?," it is necessary to say, "It is an actual process of thought, which is in itself nonverbal." An abstract painting represents direct manifestation of creative thought processes as they might appear in computer designs. What we are considering here, however, are the psychic and social consequences of the designs or patterns as they amplify or accelerate existing process. For the "message" of any medium or technology is the change of scale or pace or pattern that it introduces into human affairs. The railway did not introduce movement or transportation or wheel or road into human society, but it accelerated and enlarged the scale of previous human functions, creating totally new kinds of cities and new kinds of work and leisure. This happened whether the railway functioned in a tropical or a northern environment, and is quite independent of the freight or content of the railway medium. The airplane, on the other hand, by accelerating the rate of transportation, tends to dissolve the railway form of city, politics, and association, quite independently of what the airplane is used for.

Let us return to the electric light. Whether the light is being used for brain surgery or night baseball is a matter of indifference. It could be argued that these activities are in some way the "content" of the electric light, since they could not exist without the electric light. This fact merely underlines the point that "the medium is the message" because it is the medium that shapes and controls the scale and form of human association and action. The content or uses of such media are as diverse as they are ineffectual in shaping the form of human association. Indeed, it is only too typical that the "content" of any medium blinds us to the character of the medium. It is only today that industries have become aware of the various kinds of business in which they are engaged. When IBM discovered that it was not in the business of making office equipment or business machines, but that it was in the business of processing information, then it began to navigate with clear vision. The General Electric Company makes a considerable portion of its profits from electric light bulbs and lighting systems. It has not yet discovered that, quite as much as A.T.&T., it is in the business of moving information.

The electric light escapes attention as a communication medium just because it has no "content." And this makes it an invaluable instance of how people fail to study media at all. For it is not till the electric light is used to spell out some brand name that it is noticed as a medium. Then it is not the light but the "content" (or what is really another medium) that is noticed. The message of the electric light is like the message of electric power in industry, totally radical, pervasive, and decentralized. For electric light and power are separate from their uses, yet they eliminate time and space factors in human association exactly as do radio, telegraph, telephone, and TV, creating involvement in depth.

A fairly complete handbook for studying the extensions of man could be made up from selections from Shakespeare. Some might quibble about whether or not he was referring to TV in these familiar lines from *Romeo and Juliet*:

But soft! what light through yonder window breaks?
It speaks, and yet says nothing.

In *Othello*, which, as much as *King Lear*, is concerned with the torment of people transformed by illusions, there are these lines that bespeak Shakespeare's intuition of the transforming powers of new media:

> *Is there not charms*
> *By which the property of youth and maidhood*
> *May be abus'd? Have you not read Roderigo,*
> *Of some such thing?*

In Shakespeare's *Troilus and Cressida*, which is almost completely devoted to both a psychic and social study of communication, Shakespeare states his awareness that true social and political navigation depend upon anticipating the consequences of innovation:

> *The providence that's in a watchful state*
> *Knows almost every grain of Plutus' gold,*
> *Finds bottom in the uncomprehensive deeps,*
> *Keeps place with thought, and almost like the gods*
> *Does thoughts unveil in their dumb cradles.*

The increasing awareness of the action of media, quite independently of their "content" or programming, was indicated in the annoyed and anonymous stanza:

> *In modern thought, (if not in fact)*
> *Nothing is that doesn't act,*
> *So that is reckoned wisdom which*
> *Describes the scratch but not the itch.*

The same kind of total, configurational awareness that reveals why the medium is socially the message has occurred in the most recent and radical medical theories. In his *Stress of Life*, Hans Selye tells of the dismay of a research colleague on hearing of Selye's theory:

> *When he saw me thus launched on yet another enraptured description of what I had observed in animals treated with this or that impure, toxic material, he looked at me with desperately sad eyes and said in obvious despair: "But Selye, try to realize what you are doing before it is too late! You have now decided to spend your entire life studying the pharmacology of dirt!"*

As Selye deals with the total environmental situation in his "stress" theory of disease, so the latest approach to media study considers not only the "content" but the medium and the cultural matrix within which the particular medium operates.

The older unawareness of the psychic and social effects of media can be illustrated from almost any of the conventional pronouncements.

In accepting an honorary degree from the University of Notre Dame a few years ago, General David Sarnoff made this statement: "We are too prone to make technological instruments the scapegoats for the sins of those who wield them. The products of modern science are not in themselves good or bad; it is the way they are used that determines their value." That is the voice of the current somnambulism. Suppose we were to say, "Apple pie is in itself neither good nor bad; it is the way it is used that determines its value." Or, "The smallpox virus is in itself neither good nor bad, it is the way it is used that determines its value." Again, "Firearms are in themselves neither good nor bad; it is the way they are used that determines their value." That is, if the slugs reach the right people firearms are good. If the TV tube fires the right ammunition at the right people it is good. I am not being perverse. There is simply nothing in the Sarnoff statement that will bear scrutiny, for it ignores the nature of the medium, of any and all media, in the true Narcissus style of one hypnotized by the amputation and extension of his own being in a new technical form. General Sarnoff went on to explain his attitude to the technology of print, saying that it was true that print caused much trash to circulate, but it had also disseminated the Bible and the thoughts of seers and philosophers. It has never occurred to General Sarnoff that any technology could do anything but *add* itself on to what we already are.

Such economists as Robert Theobald, W. W. Rostow, and John Kenneth Galbraith have been explaining for years how it is that "classical economics" cannot explain change or growth. And the paradox of mechanization is that although it is itself the cause of maximal growth and change, the principle of mechanization excludes the very possibility of growth or the understanding of change. For mechanization is achieved by fragmentation of any process and by putting the fragmented parts in a series. Yet, as David Hume showed in the eighteenth century, there is no principle of causality in a mere sequence. That one thing follows another accounts for nothing. Nothing follows from following, except change. So the greatest of all reversals occurred with electricity, that ended sequence by making things instant. With instant speed the causes of things began to emerge to awareness again, as they had not done with things in sequence and in concatenation accordingly. Instead of asking which came first, the chicken or the egg, it suddenly seemed that a chicken was an egg's idea for getting more eggs.

Just before an airplane breaks the sound barrier, sound waves become visible on the wings of the plane. The sudden visibility of sound just as sound ends is an apt instance of that great pattern of being that reveals new and opposite forms just as the earlier forms reach their peak performance. Mechanization was never so vividly fragmented or sequential as in the birth of the movies, the moment that translated us beyond mechanism into the world of growth and organic interrelation. The movie, by sheer speeding up the mechanical, carried us from the world of sequence and connections into the world of creative configuration and structure. The message of the movie medium is that of transition from lineal connections to configurations. It is the transition that produced the now quite correct observation: "If it works, it's obsolete." When electric speed further takes over from mechanical movie sequences, then the lines of force in structures and in media become loud and clear. We return to the inclusive form of the icon.

To a highly literate and mechanized culture the movie appeared as a world of triumphant illusions and dreams that money could buy. It was at this moment of the movie that cubism occurred, and it has been described by E. H. Gombrich (*Art and Illusion*) as "the most radical attempt to stamp out ambiguity and to enforce one reading of the picture — that of a man-made construction, a colored canvas." For cubism substitutes all facets of an object simultaneously for the "point of view" or facet of perspective illusion. Instead of the specialized illusion of the third dimension on canvas, cubism sets up an interplay of planes and contradiction or dramatic conflict of patterns, lights, textures that "drives home the message" by involvement. This is held by many to be an exercise in painting, not in illusion.

In other words, cubism, by giving the inside and outside, the top, bottom, back, and front and the rest, in two dimensions, drops the illusion of perspective in favor of instant sensory awareness of the whole Cubism, by seizing on instant total awareness, suddenly announced that *the medium is the message*. Is it not evident that the moment that sequence yields to the simultaneous, one is in the world of the structure and of configuration? Is that not what has happened in physics as in painting, poetry, and in communication? Specialized segments of attention have shifted to total field, and we can now say, "The medium is the message" quite naturally. Before the electric speed and total field, it was not obvious that the medium is the message. The message, it seemed, was the "content," as people used to ask what a painting was *about*. Yet they never thought to ask what a melody was about, nor what a house or a dress was about. In such matters, people retained some sense of the whole pattern, of form and function as a unity. But in the electric age this integral idea of structure and configuration has become so prevalent that educational theory has taken up the matter. Instead of working with specialized "problems" in arithmetic, the structural approach now follows the lines of force in the field of number and has small children meditating about number theory and "sets."

Cardinal Newman said of Napoleon, "He understood the grammar of gunpowder." Napoleon had paid some attention to other media as well, especially the semaphore telegraph that gave him a great advantage over his enemies. He is on record for saying that "Three hostile newspapers are more to be feared than a thousand bayonets."

Alexis de Tocqueville was the first to master the grammar of print and typography. He was thus able to read off the message of coming change in France and

America as if he were reading aloud from a text that had been handed to him. In fact, the nineteenth century in France and in America was just such an open book to de Tocqueville because he had learned the grammar of print. So he, also, knew when that grammar did not apply. He was asked why he did not write a book on England, since he knew and admired England. He replied:

> One would have to have an unusual degree of philosophical folly to believe one-self able to judge England in six months. A year always seemed to me too short a time in which to appreciate the United States properly, and it is much easier to acquire clear and precise notions about the American Union than about Great Britain. In America all laws derive in a sense from the same line of thought. The whole of society, so to speak, is founded upon a single fact; everything springs from a simple principle. One could compare America to a forest pierced by a multitude of straight roads all converging on the same point. One has only to find the center and everything is revealed at a glance. But in England the paths run criss-cross, and it is only by travelling down each one of them that one can build up a picture of the whole.

De Tocqueville, in earlier work on the French Revolution, had explained how it was the printed word that, achieving cultural saturation in the eighteenth century, had homogenized the French nation. Frenchmen were the same kind of people from north to south. The typographic principles of uniformity, continuity, and lineality had overlaid the complexities of ancient feudal and oral society. The Revolution was carried out by the new literati and lawyers.

In England, however, such was the power of the ancient oral traditions of common law, backed by the medieval institution of Parliament, that no uniformity or continuity of the new visual print culture could take complete hold. The result was that the most important event in English history has never taken place; namely, the English Revolution on the lines of the French Revolution. The American Revolution had no medieval legal institutions to discard or to root out, apart from monarchy. And many have held that the American Presidency has become very much more personal and monarchical than any European monarch ever could be.

De Tocqueville's contrast between England and America is clearly based on the fact of typography and of print culture creating uniformity and continuity. England, he says, has rejected this principle and clung to the dynamic or oral common-law tradition. Hence the discontinuity and unpredictable quality of English culture. The grammar of print cannot help to construe the message of oral and nonwritten culture and institutions. The English aristocracy was properly classified as barbarian by Matthew Arnold because its power and status had nothing to do with literacy or with the cultural forms of typography. Said the Duke of Gloucester to Edward Gibbon upon the publication of his *Decline and Fall*: "Another damned fat book, eh, Mr. Gibbon? Scribble, scribble, scribble, eh,

Mr. Gibbon?" De Tocqueville was a highly literate aristocrat who was quite able to be detached from the values and assumptions of typography. That is why he alone understood the grammar of typography. And it is only on those terms, standing aside from any structure or medium, that its principles and lines of force can be discerned. For any medium has the power of imposing its own assumption on the unwary. Prediction and control consist in avoiding this subliminal state of Narcissus trance. But the greatest aid to this end is simply in knowing that the spell can occur immediately upon contact, as in the first bars of a melody.

A Passage to India by E. M. Forster is a dramatic study of the inability of oral and intuitive oriental culture to meet with the rational, visual European patterns of experience. "Rational," of course, has for the West long meant "uniform and continuous and sequential." In other words, we have confused reason with literacy, and rationalism with a single technology. Thus in the electric age man seems to the conventional West to become irrational. In Forster's novel the moment of truth and dislocation from the typographic trance of the West comes in the Marabar Caves. Adela Quested's reasoning powers cannot cope with the total inclusive field of resonance that is India. After the Caves: "Life went on as usual, but had no consequences, that is to say, sounds did not echo nor thought develop. Everything seemed cut off at its root and therefore infected with illusion."

A Passage to India (the phrase is from Whitman, who saw America headed Eastward) is a parable of Western man in the electric age, and is only incidentally related to Europe or the Orient. The ultimate conflict between sight and sound, between written and oral kinds of perception and organization of existence is upon us. Since understanding stops action, as Nietzsche observed, we can moderate the fierceness of this conflict by understanding the media that extend us and raise these wars within and without us.

Detribalization by literacy and its traumatic effects on tribal man is the theme of a book by the psychiatrist J. C. Carothers, *The African Mind in Health and Disease* (World Health Organization, Geneva, 1953). Much of his material appeared in an article in *Psychiatry* magazine, November, 1959: "The Culture, Psychiatry, and the Written Word." Again, it is electric speed that has revealed the lines of force operating from Western technology in the remotest areas of bush, savannah, and desert. One example is the Bedouin with his battery radio on board the camel. Submerging natives with floods of concepts for which nothing has prepared them is the normal action of all of our technology. But with electric media Western man himself experiences exactly the same inundation as the remote native. We are no more prepared to encounter radio and TV in our literate milieu than the native of Ghana is able to cope with the literacy that takes him out of his collective tribal world and beaches him in individual isolation. We are as numb in our new electric world as the native involved in our literate and mechanical culture.

Electric speed mingles the cultures of prehistory with the dregs of industrial marketeers, the nonliterate with the semiliterate and the postliterate. Mental breakdown of varying degrees is the very common result of uprooting and inundation with new information and endless new patterns of information. Wyndham Lewis made this a theme of his group of novels called *The Human Age*. The first of these, *The Childermass*, is concerned precisely with accelerated media change as a kind of massacre of the innocents. In our own world as we become more aware of the effects of technology on psychic formation and manifestation, we are losing all confidence in our right to assign guilt. Ancient prehistoric societies regard violent crime as pathetic. The killer is regarded as we do a cancer victim. "How terrible it must be to feel like that," they say. J. M. Synge took up this idea very effectively in his *Playboy of the Western World*.

If the criminal appears as a nonconformist who is unable to meet the demand of technology that we behave in uniform and continuous patterns, literate man is quite inclined to see others who cannot conform as somewhat pathetic. Especially the child, the cripple, the woman, and the colored person appear in a world of visual and typographic technology as victims of injustice. On the other hand, in a culture that assigns roles instead of jobs to people — the dwarf, the skew, the child create their own spaces. They are not expected to fit into some uniform and repeatable niche that is not their size anyway. Consider the phrase "It's a man's world." As a quantitative observation endlessly repeated from within a homogenized culture, this phrase refers to the men in such a culture who have to be homogenized Dagwoods in order to belong at all. It is in our I.Q. testing that we have produced the greatest flood of misbegotten standards. Unaware of our typographic cultural bias, our testers assume that uniform and continuous habits are a sign of intelligence, thus eliminating the ear man and the tactile man.

C. P. Snow, reviewing a book of A. L. Rowse (*The New York Times Book Review*, December 24, 1961) on *Appeasement* and the road to Munich, describes the top level of British brains and experience in the 1930s. "Their I.Q.'s were much higher than usual among political bosses. Why were they such a disaster?" The view of Rowse, Snow approves: "They would not listen to warnings because they did not wish to hear." Being anti-Red made it impossible for them to read the message of Hitler. But their failure was as nothing compared to our present one. The American stake in literacy as a technology or uniformity applied to every level of education, government, industry, and social life is totally threatened by the electric technology. The threat of Stalin or Hitler was external. The electric technology is within the gates, and we are numb, deaf, blind, and mute about its encounter with the Gutenberg technology, on and through which the American way of life was formed. It is, however, no time to suggest strategies when the threat has not even been acknowledged to exist. I am in the position of Louis Pasteur telling doctors that their greatest enemy was quite invisible, and quite unrecognized by them. Our conventional response to all media, namely that it is how they are used that counts, is the numb stance of the technological idiot. For the "content" of a medium is like the juicy piece of meat carried by the burglar to distract the watchdog of the mind. The effect of the medium is made strong and intense just because it is given another medium as "content." The content of a movie is a novel or a play or an opera. The effect of the movie form is not related to its program content. The "content" of writing or print is speech, but the reader is almost entirely unaware either of print or of speech.

Arnold Toynbee is innocent of any understanding of media as they have shaped history, but he is full of examples that the student of media can use. At one moment he can seriously suggest that adult education, such as the Workers Educational Association in Britain, is a useful counterforce to the popular press. Toynbee considers that although all of the oriental societies have in our time accepted the industrial technology and its political consequences: "On the cultural plane, however, there is no uniform corresponding tendency." (Somervell, I. 267) This is like the voice of the literate man, floundering in a milieu of ads, who boasts, "Personally, I pay no attention to ads." The spiritual and cultural reservations that the oriental peoples may have toward our technology will avail them not at all. The effects of technology do not occur at the level of opinions or concepts, but alter sense ratios or patterns of perception steadily and without any resistance. The serious artist is the only person able to encounter technology with impunity, just because he is an expert aware of the changes in sense perception.

The operation of the money medium in seventeenth-century Japan had effects not unlike the operation of typography in the West. The penetration of the money economy, wrote G. B. Sansom (in *Japan*, Cresset Press, London, 1931) "caused a slow but irresistible revolution, culminating in the breakdown of feudal government and the resumption of intercourse with foreign countries after more than two hundred years of seclusion." Money has reorganized the sense life of peoples just because it is an *extension* of our sense lives. This change does not depend upon approval or disapproval of those living in the society.

Arnold Toynbee made one approach to the transforming power of media in his concept of "etherialization," which he holds to be the principle of progressive simplification and efficiency in any organization or technology. Typically, he is ignoring the *effect* of the challenge of these forms upon the response of our senses. He imagines that it is the response of our opinions that is relevant to the effect of media and technology in society, a "point of view" that is plainly the result of the typographic spell. For the man in a literate and homogenized society ceases to be sensitive to the diverse and discontinuous life of forms. He acquires the illusion of the third dimension and the "private point of view" as part of his Narcissus fixation, and is quite shut off from Blake's awareness or that of the Psalmist, that we become what we behold.

Today when we want to get our bearings in our own culture, and have need to stand aside from the bias and pressure exerted by any technical form of human expression, we have only to visit a society where that particular form has not been felt, or a historical period in which it was unknown. Professor Wilbur

Schramm made such a tactical move in studying *Television in the Lives of Our Children*. He found areas where TV had not penetrated at all and ran some tests. Since he had made no study of the peculiar nature of the TV image, his tests were of "content" preferences, viewing time, and vocabulary counts. In a word, his approach to the problem was a literary one, albeit unconsciously so. Consequently, he had nothing to report. Had his methods been employed in 1500 A.D. to discover the effects of the printed book in the lives of children or adults, he could have found out nothing of the changes in human and social psychology resulting from typography. Print created individualism and nationalism in the sixteenth century. Program and "content" analysis offer no clues to the magic of these media or to their subliminal charge.

Leonard Doob, in his report *Communication in Africa*, tells of one African who took great pains to listen each evening to the BBC news, even though he could understand nothing of it. Just to be in the presence of those sounds at 7 P.M. each day was important for him. His attitude to speech was like ours to melody — the resonant intonation was meaning enough. In the seventeenth century our ancestors still shared this native's attitude to the forms of media, as is plain in the following sentiment of the Frenchman Bernard Lam, expressed in *The Art of Speaking* (London, 1696):

> *'Tis an effect of the Wisdom of God, who created Man to be happy, that whatever is useful to his conversation (way of life) is agreeable to him . . . because all victual that conduces to nourishment is relishable, whereas other things that cannot be assimulated and be turned into our substance are insipid. A Discourse cannot be pleasant to the Hearer that is not easie to the Speaker; nor can it be easily pronounced unless it be heard with delight.*

Here is an equilibrium theory of human diet and expression such as even now we are only striving to work out again for media after centuries of fragmentation and specialism.

Pope Pius XII was deeply concerned that there be serious study of the media today. On February 17, 1950, he said:

> *It is not an exaggeration to say that the future of modern society and the stability of its inner life depend in large part on the maintenance of an equilibrium between the strength of the techniques of communication and the capacity of the individual's own reaction.*

Failure in this respect has for centuries been typical and total for mankind. Subliminal and docile acceptance of media impact has made them prisons without walls for their human users. As A. J. Liebling remarked in his book *The Press*, a man is not free if he cannot see where he is going, even if he has a gun to help him get there. For each of the media is also a powerful weapon with which to clobber other media and other groups. The result is that the present age has been one of multiple civil wars that are not limited to the world of art and entertainment. In *War and Human Progress*, Professor J. U. Nef declared: "The total wars of our time have been the result of a series of intellectual mistakes . . . "

If the formative power in the media are the media themselves, that raises a host of large matters that can only be mentioned here, although they deserve volumes. Namely, that technological media are staples or natural resources, exactly as are coal and cotton and oil. Anybody will concede that society whose economy is dependent upon one or two major staples like cotton, or grain, or lumber, or fish, or cattle is going to have some obvious social patterns of organization as a result. Stress on a few major staples creates extreme instability in the economy but great endurance in the population. The pathos and humor of the American South are embedded in such an economy of limited staples. For a society configured by reliance on a few commodities accepts them as a social bond quite as much as the metropolis does the press. Cotton and oil, like radio and TV, become "fixed charges" on the entire psychic life of the community. And this pervasive fact creates the unique cultural flavor of any society. It pays through the nose and all its other senses for each staple that shapes its life.

That our human senses, of which all media are extensions, are also fixed charges on our personal energies, and that they also configure the awareness and experience of each one of us, may be perceived in another connection mentioned by the psychologist C. G. Jung:

> *Every Roman was surrounded by slaves. The slave and his psychology flooded ancient Italy, and every Roman became inwardly, and of course unwittingly, a slave. Because living constantly in the atmosphere of slaves, he became infected through the unconscious with their psychology. No one can shield himself from such an influence.*
>
> (*Contributions to Analytical Psychology*, London, 1928)

Media Hot and Cold

"The rise of the waltz," explained Curt Sachs in the *World History of the Dance*, "was a result of that longing for truth, simplicity, closeness to nature, and primitivism, which the last two-thirds of the eighteenth century fulfilled." In the century of jazz we are likely to overlook the emergence of the waltz as a hot and explosive human expression that broke through the formal feudal barriers of courtly and choral dance styles.

There is a basic principle that distinguishes a hot medium like radio from a cool one like the telephone, or a hot medium like the movie from a cool one like

TV. A hot medium is one that extends one single sense in "high definition." High definition is the state of being well filled with data. A photograph is, visually, "high definition." A cartoon is "low definition," simply because very little visual information is provided. Telephone is a cool medium, or one of low definition, because the ear is given a meager amount of information. And speech is a cool medium of low definition, because so little is given and so much has to be filled in by the listener. On the other hand, hot media do not leave so much to be filled in or completed by the audience. Hot media are, therefore, low in participation, and cool media are high in participation or completion by the audience. Naturally, therefore, a hot medium like radio has very different effects on the user from a cool medium like the telephone.

A cool medium like hieroglyphic or ideogrammic written characters has very different effects from the hot and explosive medium of the phonetic alphabet. The alphabet, when pushed to a high degree of abstract visual intensity, became typography. The printed word with its specialist intensity burst the bonds of medieval corporate guilds and monasteries, creating extreme individualist patterns of enterprise and monopoly. But the typical reversal occurred when extremes of monopoly brought back the corporation, with its impersonal empire over many lives. The hotting-up of the medium of writing to repeatable print intensity led to nationalism and the religious wars of the sixteenth century. The heavy and unwieldy media, such as stone, are time binders. Used for writing, they are very cool indeed, and serve to unify the ages; whereas paper is a hot medium that serves to unify spaces horizontally, both in political and entertainment empires.

Any hot medium allows of less participation than a cool one, as a lecture makes for less participation than a seminar, and a book for less than dialogue. With print many earlier forms were excluded from life and art, and many were given strange new intensity. But our own time is crowded with examples of the principle that the hot form excludes, and the cool one includes. When ballerinas began to dance on their toes a century ago, it was felt that the art of the ballet had acquired a new "spirituality." With this new intensity, male figures were excluded from ballet. The role of women had also become fragmented with the advent of industrial specialism and the explosion of home functions into laundries, bakeries, and hospitals on the periphery of the community. Intensity or high definition engenders specialism and fragmentation in living as in entertainment, which explains why any intense experience must be "forgotten," "censored," and reduced to a very cool state before it can be "learned" or assimilated. The Freudian "censor" is less of a moral function than an indispensable condition of learning. Were we to accept fully and directly every shock to our various structures of awareness, we would soon be nervous wrecks, doing double-takes and pressing panic buttons every minute. The "censor" protects our central system of values, as it does our physical nervous system by simply cooling off the onset of experience a great deal. For many people, this cooling system brings on a life-long state of psychic *rigor mortis*, or of somnambulism, particularly observable in periods of new technology.

An example of the disruptive impact of a hot technology succeeding a cool one is given by Robert Theobald in *The Rich and the Poor*. When Australian natives were given steel axes by the missionaries, their culture, based on the stone axe, collapsed. The stone axe had not only been scarce but had always been a basic status symbol of male importance. The missionaries provided quantities of sharp-steel axes and gave them to women and children. The men had even to borrow these from the women, causing a collapse of male dignity. A tribal and feudal hierarchy of traditional kind collapses quickly when it meets any hot medium of the mechanical, uniform, and repetitive kind. The medium of money or wheel or writing, or any other form of specialist speed-up of exchange and information, will serve to fragment a tribal structure. Similarly, a very much greater speed-up, such as occurs with electricity, may serve to restore a tribal pattern of intense involvement such as took place with the introduction of radio in Europe, and is now tending to happen as a result of TV in America. Specialist technologies detribalize. The nonspecialist electric technology retribalizes. The process of upset resulting from a new distribution of skills is accompanied by much culture lag in which people feel compelled to look at new situations as if they were old ones, and come up with ideas of "population explosion" in an age of implosion. Newton, in an age of clocks, managed to present the physical universe in the image of a clock. But poets like Blake were far ahead of Newton in their response to the challenge of the clock. Blake spoke of the need to be delivered "from single vision and Newton's sleep," knowing very well that Newton's response to the challenge of the new mechanism was itself merely a mechanical repetition of the challenge. Blake saw Newton and Locke and others as hypnotized Narcissus types quite unable to meet the challenge of mechanism. W. B. Yeats gave the full Blakean version of Newton and Locke in a famous epigram:

Locke sank into a swoon;
The garden died;
God took the spinning jenny
Out of his side.

Yeats presents Locke, the philosopher of mechanical and lineal associationism, as hypnotized by his own image. The "garden," or unified consciousness, ended. Eighteenth-century man got an extension of himself in the form of the spinning machine that Yeats endows with its full sexual significance. Woman, herself, is thus seen as a technological extension of man's being.

Blake's counterstrategy for his age was to meet mechanism with organic myth. Today, deep in the electric age, organic myth is itself a simple and automatic

163

response capable of mathematical formulation and expression, without any of the imaginative perception of Blake about it. Had he encountered the electric age, Blake would not have met its challenge with a mere repetition of electric form. For myth *is* the instant vision of a complex process that ordinarily extends over a long period. Myth is contraction or implosion of any process, and the instant speed of electricity confers the mythic dimension on ordinary industrial and social action today. We *live* mythically but continue to think fragmentarily and on single planes.

Scholars today are acutely aware of a discrepancy between their ways of treating subjects and the subject itself. Scriptural scholars of both the Old and New Testaments frequently say that while their treatment must be linear, the subject is not. The subject treats of the relations between God and man, and between God and the world, and of the relations between man and his neighbor — all these subsist together, and act and react upon one another at the same time. The Hebrew and Eastern mode of thought tackles problem and resolution, at the outset of a discussion, in a way typical of oral societies in general. The entire message is then traced and retraced, again and again, on the rounds of a concentric spiral with seeming redundancy. One can stop anywhere after the first few sentences and have the full message, if one is prepared to "dig" it. This kind of plan seems to have inspired Frank Lloyd Wright in designing the Guggenheim Art Gallery on a spiral, concentric basis. It is a redundant form inevitable to the electric age, in which the concentric pattern is imposed by the instant quality, and overlay in depth, of electric speed. But the concentric with its endless intersection of planes is necessary for insight. In fact, it is the technique of insight, and as such is necessary for media study, since no medium has its meaning or existence alone, but only in constant interplay with other media.

The new electric structuring and configuring of life more and more encounters the old lineal and fragmentary procedures and tools of analysis from the mechanical age. More and more we turn from the content of messages to study total effect. Kenneth Boulding put this matter in *The Image* by saying, "The meaning of a message is the change which it produces in the image." Concern with *effect* rather than *meaning* is a basic change of our electric time, for effect involves the total situation, and not a single level of information movement. Strangely, there is a recognition of this matter of effect rather than information in the British idea of libel: "The greater the truth, the greater the libel."

The effect of electric technology had at first been anxiety. Now it appears to create boredom. We have been through the three stages of alarm, resistance, and exhaustion that occur in every disease or stress of life, whether individual or collective. At least, our exhausted slump after the first encounter with the electric has inclined us to expect new problems. However, backward countries that have experienced little permeation with our own mechanical and specialist culture are much better able to confront and to understand electric technology. Not only have backward and nonindustrial cultures no specialist habits to overcome in their encounter with electromagnetism, but they have still much of their traditional oral culture that has the total, unified "field" character of our new electromagnetism. Our old industrialized areas, having eroded their oral traditions automatically, are in the position of having to rediscover them in order to cope with the electric age.

In terms of the theme of media hot and cold, backward countries are cool, and we are hot. The "city slicker" is hot, and the rustic is cool. But in terms of the reversal of procedures and values in the electric age, the past mechanical time was hot, and we of the TV age are cool. The waltz was a hot, fast mechanical dance suited to the industrial time in its moods of pomp and circumstance. In contrast, the Twist is a cool, involved and chatty form of improvised gesture. The jazz of the period of the hot new media of movie and radio was hot jazz. Yet jazz of itself tends to be a casual dialogue form of dance quite lacking in the repetitive and mechanical forms of the waltz. Cool jazz came in quite naturally after the first impact of radio and movie had been absorbed.

In the special Russian issue of *Life* magazine for September 13, 1963, it is mentioned in Russian restaurants and night clubs, "though the Charleston is tolerated, the Twist is taboo." All this is to say that a country in the process of industrialization is inclined to regard hot jazz as consistent with its developing programs. The cool and involved form of the Twist, on the other hand, would strike such a culture at once as retrograde and incompatible with its new mechanical stress. The Charleston, with its aspect of a mechanical doll agitated by strings, appears in Russia as an avant-garde form. We, on the other hand, find the *avant-garde* in the cool and the primitive, with its promise of depth involvement and integral expression.

The "hard" sell and the "hot" line become mere comedy in the TV age, and the death of all the salesmen at one stroke of the TV axe has turned the hot American culture into a cool one that is quite unacquainted with itself. America, in fact, would seem to be living through the reverse process that Margaret Mead described in *Time* magazine (September 4, 1954): "There are too many complaints about society having to move too fast to keep up with the machine. There is great advantage in moving fast if you move completely, if social, educational, and recreational changes keep pace. You must change the whole pattern at once and the whole group together — and the people themselves must decide to move."

Margaret Mead is thinking here of change as uniform speed-up of motion or a uniform hotting-up of temperatures in backward societies. We are certainly coming within conceivable range of a world automatically controlled to the point where we could say, "Six hours less radio in Indonesia next week or there will be a great falling off in literary attention." Or, "We can program twenty more hours of TV in South Africa next week to cool down the tribal temperature raised by radio last week." Whole cultures could now be programmed to keep their emotional climate stable in the same way that we have begun to know something about maintaining equilibrium in the commercial economies of the world.

In the merely personal and private sphere we are often reminded of how changes of tone and attitude are demanded of different times and seasons in order to keep situations in hand. British clubmen, for the sake of companionship and amiability, have long excluded the hot topics of religion and politics from mention inside the highly participational club. In the same vein, W. H. Auden wrote, ". . . this season the man of goodwill will wear his heart up his sleeve, not on it. . . . the honest manly style is today suited only to Iago" (Introduction to John Betjeman's *Slick But Not Streamlined*). In the Renaissance, as print technology hotted up the social *milieu* to a very high point, the gentleman and the courtier (Hamlet-Mercutio style) adopted, in contrast, the casual and cool nonchalance of the playful and superior being. The Iago allusion of Auden reminds us that Iago was the *alter ego* and assistant of the intensely earnest and very non-nonchalant General Othello. In imitation of the earnest and forthright general, Iago hotted up his own image and wore his heart on his sleeve, until General Othello read him loud and clear as "honest Iago," a man after his own grimly earnest heart.

Throughout *The City in History*, Lewis Mumford favors the cool or casually structured towns over the hot and intensely filled-in cities. The great period of Athens, he feels, was one during which most of the democratic habits of village life and participation still obtained. Then burst forth the full variety of human expression and exploration such as was later impossible in highly developed urban centers. For the highly developed situation is, by definition, low in opportunities of participation, and rigorous in its demands of specialist fragmentation from those who would control it. For example, what is known as "job enlargement" today in business and in management consists in allowing the employee more freedom to discover and define his function. Likewise, in reading a detective story the reader participates as co-author simply because so much has been left out of the narrative. The open-mesh, silk stocking is far more sensuous than the smooth nylon, just because the eye must act as hand in filling in and completing the image, exactly as in the mosaic of the TV image.

Douglas Cater in *The Fourth Branch of Government* tells how the men of the Washington press bureaus delighted to complete or fill in the blank of Calvin Coolidge's personality. Because he was so like a mere cartoon, they felt the urge to complete his image for him and his public. It is instructive that the press applied the word "cool" to Cal. In the very sense of a cool medium, Calvin Coolidge was so lacking in any articulation of data in his public image that there was only one word for him. He was real cool. In the hot 1920s, the hot press medium found Cal very cool and rejoiced in his lack of image, since it compelled the participation of the press in filling in an image of him for the public. By contrast, F. D. R. was a hot press agent, himself a rival of the newspaper medium and one who delighted in scoring off the press on the rival hot medium of radio. Quite in contrast, Jack Paar ran a cool show for the cool TV medium, and became a rival for the patrons of the night spots and their allies in the gossip columns. Jack Paar's war with the gossip columnists was a weird example of clash between a hot and cold medium such as had occurred with the "scandal of the rigged TV quiz shows." The rivalry between the hot press and radio media, on one hand, and TV on the other, for the hot ad buck, served to confuse and to overheat the issues in the affair that pointlessly involved Charles van Doren.

An Associated Press story from Santa Monica, California, August 9, 1962, reported how

Nearly 100 traffic violators watched a police traffic accident film today to atone for their violations. Two had to be treated for nausea and shock. . . .

Viewers were offered a $5.00 reduction in fines if they agreed to see the movie, Signal 30, *made by Ohio State police.*

It showed twisted wreckage and mangled bodies and recorded the screams of accident victims.

Whether the hot film medium using hot content would cool off the hot drivers is a moot point. But it does concern any understanding of media. The effect of hot media treatment cannot include much empathy or participation at any time. In this connection an insurance ad that featured Dad in an iron lung surrounded by a joyful family group did more to strike terror into the reader than all the warning wisdom in the world. It is a question that arises in connection with capital punishment. Is a severe penalty the best deterrent to serious crime? With regard to the bomb and the cold war, is the threat of massive retaliation the most effective means to peace? Is it not evident in every human situation that is pushed to a point of saturation that some precipitation occurs? When all the available resources and energies have been played up in an organism or in any structure there is some kind of reversal of pattern. The spectacle of brutality used as deterrent can brutalize. Brutality used in sports may humanize under some conditions, at least. But with regard to the bomb and retaliation as deterrent, it is obvious that numbness is the result of any prolonged terror, a fact that was discovered when the fall-out shelter program was broached. The price of eternal vigilance is indifference.

Nevertheless, it makes all the difference whether a hot medium is used in a hot or a cool culture. The hot radio medium used in cool or nonliterate cultures has a violent effect, quite unlike its effect, say in England or America, where radio is felt as entertainment. A cool or low literacy culture cannot accept hot media like movies or radio as entertainment. They are, at least, as radically upsetting for them as the cool TV medium has proved to be for our high literacy world.

And as for the cool war and the hot bomb scare, the cultural strategy that is desperately needed is humor and play. It is play that cools off the hot situations of actual life by miming them. Competitive sports between Russia and the West will hardly serve that purpose of relaxation. Such sports are inflammatory, it is plain. And what we consider entertainment or fun in our media inevitably appears as violent political agitation to a cool culture.

One way to spot the basic difference between hot and cold media uses is to compare and contrast a broadcast of a symphony performance with a broadcast of a symphony rehearsal. Two of the finest shows ever released by the CBC were of Glenn Gould's procedure in recording piano recitals, and Igor Stravinsky's rehearsing the Toronto symphony in some of his new work. A cool medium like TV, when really used, demands this involvement in process. The neat tight package is suited to hot media, like radio and gramophone. Francis Bacon never tired of contrasting hot and cool prose. Writing in "methods" or complete packages, he contrasted with writing in aphorisms, or single observations such as "Revenge is a kind of wild justice." The passive consumer wants packages, but those, he suggested, who are concerned in pursuing knowledge and in seeking causes will resort to aphorisms just because they are incomplete and require participation in depth.

The principle that distinguishes hot and cold media is perfectly embodied in the folk wisdom: "Men seldom make passes at girls who wear glasses." Glasses intensify the outward-going vision, and fill in the feminine image exceedingly, Marion the Librarian notwithstanding. Dark glasses, on the other hand, create the inscrutable and inaccessible image that invites a great deal of participation and completion.

Again, in a visual and highly literate culture, when we meet a person for the first time his visual appearance dims out the sound of the name, so that in self-defense we add: "How do you spell your name?" Whereas, in an ear culture, the *sound* of a man's name is the overwhelming fact, as Joyce knew when he said in *Finnegans Wake*, "Who gave you that numb?" For the name of a man is a numbing blow from which he never recovers.

Another vantage point from which to test the difference between hot and cold media is the practical joke. The hot literary medium excludes the practical and participant aspect of the joke so completely that Constance Rourke, in her *American Humor*, considers it as no joke at all. To literary people, the practical joke with its total physical involvement is as distasteful as the pun that derails us from the smooth and uniform progress that is typographic order. Indeed, to the literary person who is quite unaware of the intensely abstract nature of the typographic medium, it is the grosser and participant forms of art that seem "hot," and the abstract and intensely literary form that seems "cool." "You may perceive, Madam," said Dr. Johnson, with a pugilistic smile, "that I am well-bred to a degree of needless scrupulosity." And Dr. Johnson was right in supposing that "well-bred" had come to mean a white-shirted stress on attire that rivaled the rigor of the printed page. "Comfort" consists in abandoning a visual arrangement in favor of one that permits casual participation of the senses, a state that is excluded when any one sense, but especially the visual sense, is hotted up to the point of dominant command of a situation.

On the other hand, in experiments in which all outer sensation is withdrawn, the subject begins a furious fill-in or completion of senses that is sheer hallucination. So the hotting up of one sense tends to effect hypnosis, and the cooling of all senses tends to result in hallucination.

Reversal of the Overheated Medium

A headline for June 21, 1963, read:

**WASHINGTON-MOSCOW HOT LINE
TO OPEN IN 60 DAYS**

The Times of London Service, Geneva:
The agreement to establish a direct communication link between Washington and Moscow for emergencies was signed here yesterday by Charles Stelle of the United States and Semyon Tsarapkin of the Soviet Union. . . .
The link, known as the hot line, will be opened within sixty days, according to U.S. officials. It will make use of leased commercial circuits, one cable and the other wireless, using teleprinter equipment.

The decision to use the hot printed medium in place of the cool, participational, telephone medium is unfortunate in the extreme. No doubt the decision was prompted by the literary bias of the West for the printed form, on the ground that it is more impersonal than the telephone. The printed form has quite different implications in Moscow from what it has in Washington. So with the telephone. The Russians' love of this instrument, so congenial to their oral traditions, is owing to the rich nonvisual involvement it affords. The Russian uses the telephone for the sort of effects we associate with the eager conversation of the lapel-gripper whose face is twelve inches away.

Both telephone and teleprinter as amplifications of the unconscious cultural bias of Moscow, on one hand, and of Washington, on the other, are invitations to monstrous misunderstandings. The Russian bugs rooms and spies by ear, finding this quite natural. He is outraged by our visual spying, however, finding this quite unnatural.

The principle that during the stages of their development all things appear under forms opposite to those that they finally present is an ancient doctrine. Interest in the power of things to reverse themselves by evolution is evident in a great diversity of observations, sage and jocular. Alexander Pope wrote

Vice is a monster of such frightful mien
As to be hated needs but to be seen;
But seen too oft, familiar with its face,
We first endure, then pity, then embrace.

A caterpillar gazing at the butterfly is supposed to have remarked, "Waal, you'll never catch me in one of those durn things."

At another level we have seen in this century the changeover from the debunking of traditional myths and legends to their reverent study. As we begin to react in depth to the social life and problems of our global village, we become reactionaries. Involvement that goes with our instant technologies transforms the most "socially conscious" people into conservatives. When Sputnik had first gone into orbit a schoolteacher asked her second-graders to write some verse on the subject. One child wrote:

The stars are so big,
The earth is so small,
Stay as you are.

With man his knowledge and the process of obtaining knowledge are of equal magnitude. Our ability to apprehend galaxies and subatomic structures, as well, is a movement of faculties that include and transcend them. The second-grader who wrote the words above *lives* in a world much vaster than any which a scientist today has instruments to measure, or concepts to describe. As W. B. Yeats wrote of this reversal, "The visible world is no longer a reality and the unseen world is no longer a dream."

Associated with this transformation of the real world into science fiction is the reversal now proceeding apace, by which the Western world is going Eastern, even as the East goes Western. Joyce encoded this reciprocal reverse in his cryptic phrase:

The West shall shake the East awake
While ye have the night for morn.

The title of his *Finnegans Wake* is a set of multi-leveled puns on the reversal by which Western man enters his tribal, or Finn, cycle once more, following the track of the old Finn, but wide awake this time as we re-enter the tribal night. It is like our contemporary consciousness of the Unconscious.

The stepping-up of speed from the mechanical to the instant electric form reverses explosion into implosion. In our present electric age the imploding or contracting energies of our world now clash with the old expansionist and traditional patterns of organization. Until recently our institutions and arrangements, social, political, and economic, had shared a one-way pattern. We still think of it as "explosive," or expansive; and though it no longer obtains, we still talk about the population explosion and the explosion in learning. In fact, it is not the increase of numbers in the world that creates our concern with population. Rather, it is the fact that everybody in the world has to live in the utmost proximity created by our electric involvement in one another's lives. In education, likewise, it is not the increase in numbers of those seeking to learn that creates the crisis. Our new concern with education follows upon the changeover to an interrelation in knowledge, where before the separate subjects of the curriculum had stood apart from each other. Departmental sovereignties have melted away as rapidly as national sovereignties under conditions of electric speed. Obsession with the older patterns of mechanical, one-way expansion from centers to margins is no longer relevant to our electric world. Electricity does not centralize but decentralizes. It is like the difference between a railway system and an electric grid system: the one requires railheads and big urban centers. Electric power, equally available in the farmhouse and the Executive Suite, permits any place to be a center, and does not require large aggregations. This reverse pattern appeared quite early in electrical "labor-saving" devices, whether a toaster or washing machine or vacuum cleaner. Instead of saving work, these devices permit everybody to do his own work. What the nineteenth century had delegated to servants and housemaids we now do for ourselves. This principle applies *in toto* in the electric age. In politics, it permits Castro to exist as independent nucleus or center. It would permit Quebec to leave the Canadian union in a way quite inconceivable under the regime of the railways. The railways require a uniform political and economic space. On the other hand, airplane and radio permit the utmost discontinuity and diversity in spatial organization.

Today the great principle of classical physics and economics and political science, namely that of the divisibility of each process, has reversed itself by sheer extension into the unified field theory; and automation in industry replaces the divisibility of process with the organic interlacing of all functions in the complex. The electric tape succeeds the assembly line.

In the new electric Age of Information and programmed production, commodities themselves assume more and more the character of information, although this trend appears mainly in the increasing advertising budget. Significantly, it is those commodities that are most used in social communication, cigarettes, cosmetics, and soap (cosmetic removers) that bear much of the burden of the upkeep of the media in general. As electric information levels rise, almost any kind of material will serve any kind of need or function, forcing the intellectual more and more into the role of social command and into the service of production.

It was Julien Benda's *Great Betrayal* that helped to clarify the new situation in which the intellectual suddenly holds the whip hand in society. Benda saw that the artists and intellectuals who had long been alienated from power, and who since Voltaire had been in opposition, had now been drafted for service in the highest echelons of decision-making. Their great betrayal was that they had surrendered their autonomy and had become the flunkies of power, as the atomic physicist at the present moment is the flunky of the war lords.

Had Benda known his history, he would have been less angry and less surprised. For it has always been the role of intelligentsia to act as liaison and as mediators between old and new power groups. Most familiar of such groups is the case of the Greek slaves, who were for long the educators and confidential clerks of the Roman power. And it is precisely this servile role of the confidential clerk to the tycoon — commercial, military, or political — that the educator has continued to play in the Western world until the present moment. In England "the Angries" were a group of such clerks who had suddenly emerged from the lower echelons by the educational escape hatch. As they emerged into the upper world of power, they found that the air was not at all fresh or bracing. But they lost their nerve even quicker than Bernard Shaw lost his. Like Shaw, they quickly settled down to whimsy and to the cultivation of entertainment values.

In his *Study of History*, Toynbee notes a great many reversals of form and dynamic, as when, in the middle of the fourth century A.D., the Germans in the Roman service began abruptly to be proud of their tribal names and to retain them. Such a moment marked new confidence born of saturation with Roman values, and it was a moment marked by the complementary Roman swing toward primitive values. (As Americans saturate with European values, especially since TV, they begin to insist upon American coach lamps, hitching posts, and colonial kitchenware as cultural objects.) Just as the barbarians got to the top of the Roman social ladder, the Romans themselves were disposed to assume the dress and manners of tribesmen out of the same frivolous and snobbish spirit that attached the French court of Louis XVI to the world of shepherds and shepherdesses. It would have seemed a natural moment for the intellectuals to have taken over while the governing class was touring Disneyland, as it were. So it must have appeared to Marx and his followers. But they reckoned without understanding the dynamics of the new media of communication. Marx based his analysis most untimely on the machine, just as the telegraph and other implosive forms began to reverse the mechanical dynamic.

The present chapter is concerned with showing that in any medium or structure there is what Kenneth Boulding calls a "break boundary at which the system suddenly changes into another or passes some point of no return in its dynamic processes." Several such "break boundaries" will be discussed later, including the one from stasis to motion, and from the mechanical to the organic in the pictorial world. One effect of the static photo had been to suppress the conspicuous consumption of the rich, but the effect of the speed-up of the photo had been to provide fantasy riches for the poor of the entire globe.

Today the road beyond its break boundary turns cities into highways, and the highway proper takes on a continuous urban character. Another characteristic reversal after passing a road break boundary is that the country ceases to be the center of all work, and the city ceases to be the center of leisure. In fact, improved roads and transport have reversed the ancient pattern and made cities the centers of work and the country the place of leisure and of recreation.

Earlier, the increase of traffic that came with money and roads had ended the static tribal state (as Toynbee calls the nomadic food-gathering culture). Typical of the reversing that occurs at break boundaries is the paradox that nomadic mobile man, the hunter and food-gatherer, is socially static. On the other hand, sedentary, specialist man is dynamic, explosive, progressive. The new magnetic or world city will be static and iconic or inclusive.

In the ancient world the intuitive awareness of break boundaries as points of reversal and of no return was embodied in the Greek idea of *hubris*, which Toynbee presents in his *Study of History*, under the head of "The Nemesis of Creativity" and "The Reversal of Roles." The Greek dramatists presented the idea of creativity as creating, also, its own kind of blindness, as in the case of Oedipus Rex, who solved the riddle of the Sphinx. It was as if the Greeks felt that the penalty for one breakthrough was a general sealing-off of awareness to the total field. In a Chinese work — *The Way and Its Power* (A. Waley translation) — there is a series of instances of the overheated medium, the overextended man or culture, and the peripety or reversal that inevitably follows:

He who stands on tiptoe does not stand firm;
He who takes the longest strides does not walk the fastest . . .
He who boasts of what he will do succeeds in nothing;
He who is proud of his work achieves nothing that endures.

One of the most common causes of breaks in any system is the cross-fertilization with another system, such as happened to print with the steam press, or with radio and movies (that yielded the talkies). Today with microfilm and micro-cards, not to mention electric memories, the printed word assumes again much of the handicraft character of a manuscript. But printing from movable type was, itself, the major break boundary in the history of phonetic literacy, just as the phonetic alphabet had been the break boundary between tribal and individualist man.

The endless reversals or break boundaries passed in the interplay of the structures of bureaucracy and enterprise include the point at which individuals began to be held responsible and accountable for their "private actions." That was the moment of the collapse of tribal collective authority. Centuries later, when further explosion and expansion had exhausted the powers of private action, corporate enterprise invented the idea of Public Debt, making the individual privately accountable for group action.

As the nineteenth century heated up the mechanical and dissociative procedures of technical fragmentation, the entire attention of men turned to the
associative and the corporate. In the first great age of the substitution of machine
for human toil Carlyle and the Pre-Raphaelites promulgated the doctrine of *Work*
as a mystical social communion, and millionaires like Ruskin and Morris toiled
like navvies for esthetic reasons. Marx was an impressionable recipient of these
doctrines. Most bizarre of all the reversals in the great Victorian age of mechanization and high moral tone is the counter-strategy of Lewis Carroll and Edward
Lear, whose nonsense has proved exceedingly durable. While the Lord Cardigans
were taking their blood baths in the Valley of Death, Gilbert and Sullivan were
announcing that the boundary break had been passed.

Hybrid Energy

Les Liaisons
Dangereuses

"For most of our lifetime civil war has been raging in the world of art and entertainment. . . . Moving pictures, gramophone records, radio, talking pictures. . . ."
This is the view of Donald McWhinnie, analyst of the radio medium. Most of
this civil war affects us in the depths of our psychic lives, as well, since the war
is conducted by forces that are extensions and amplifications of our own beings.
Indeed, the interplay among media is only another name for this civil war that
rages in our society and our psyches alike. "To the blind all things are sudden," it
has been said. The crossings or hybridizations of the media release great new
force and energy as by fission or fusion. There need be no blindness in these
matters once we have been notified that there is anything to observe.

It has now been explained that media, or the extensions of man, are "make
happen" agents, but not "make aware" agents. The hybridizing or compounding
of these agents offers an especially favorable opportunity to notice their structural components and properties. "As the silent film cried out for sound, so does
the sound film cry out for color," wrote Sergei Eisenstein in his *Notes of a Film
Director*. This type of observation can be extended systematically to all media:
"As the printing press cried out for nationalism, so did the radio cry out for tribalism." These media, being extensions of ourselves, also depend upon us for their
interplay and their evolution. The fact that they do interact and spawn new prog-
eny has been a source of wonder over the ages. It need baffle us no longer if we
trouble to scrutinize their action. We can, if we choose, think things out before
we put them out.

Plato, in all his striving to imagine an ideal training school, failed to notice
that Athens was a greater school than any university even he could dream up. In

other words, the greatest school had been put out for human use before it had been thought out. Now, this is especially true of our media. They are put out long before they are thought out. In fact, their being put outside us tends to cancel the possibility of their being thought of at all.

Everybody notices how coal and steel and cars affect the arrangements of daily existence. In our time, study has finally turned to the medium of language itself as shaping the arrangements of daily life, so that society begins to look like a linguistic echo or repeat of language norms, a fact that has disturbed the Russian Communist party very deeply. Wedded as they are to nineteenth-century industrial technology as the basis of class liberation, nothing could be more subversive of the Marxian dialectic than the idea that linguistic media shape social development, as much as do the means of production.

In fact, of all the great hybrid unions that breed furious release of energy and change, there is none to surpass the meeting of literate and oral cultures. The giving to man of an eye for an ear by phonetic literacy is, socially and politically, probably the most radical explosion that can occur in any social structure. This explosion of the eye, frequently repeated in "backward areas," we call Westernization. With literacy now about to hybridize the cultures of the Chinese, the Indians, and the Africans, we are about to experience such a release of human power and aggressive violence as makes the previous history of phonetic alphabet technology seem quite tame.

That is only the East side story, for the electric implosion now brings oral and tribal ear-culture to the literate West. Not only does the visual, specialist, and fragmented Westerner have now to live in closest daily association with all the ancient oral cultures of the earth, but his own electric technology now begins to translate the visual or eye man back into the tribal and oral pattern with its seamless web of kinship and interdependence.

We know from our own past the kind of energy that is released, as by fission, when literacy explodes the tribal or family unit. What do we know about the social and psychic energies that develop by electric fusion or implosion when literate individuals are suddenly gripped by an electromagnetic field, such as occurs in the new Common Market pressure in Europe? Make no mistake, the fusion of people who have known individualism and nationalism is not the same process as the fission of "backward" and oral cultures that are just coming to individualism and nationalism. It is the difference between the "A" bomb and the "H" bomb. The latter is more violent, by far. Moreover, the products of electric fusion are immensely complex, while the products of fission are simple. Literacy creates very much simpler kinds of people than those that develop in the complex web of ordinary tribal and oral societies. For the fragmented man creates the homogenized Western world, while oral societies are made up of people differentiated, not by their specialist skills or visible marks, but by their unique emotional mixes. The oral man's inner world is a tangle of complex emotions and feelings that the Western practical man has long ago eroded or suppressed within himself in the interest of efficiency and practicality.

The immediate prospect for literate, fragmented Western man encountering the electric implosion within his own culture is his steady and rapid transformation into a complex and depth-structured person emotionally aware of his total interdependence with the rest of human society. Representatives of the older Western individualism are even now assuming the appearance, for good or ill, of Al Capp's General Bull Moose or of the John Birchers, tribally dedicated to opposing the tribal. Fragmented, literate, and visual individualism is not possible in an electrically patterned and imploded society. So what is to be done? Do we dare to confront such facts at the conscious level, or is it best to becloud and repress such matters until some violence releases us from the entire burden? For the fate of implosion and interdependence is more terrible for Western man than the fate of explosion and independence for tribal man. It may be merely temperament in my own case, but I find some easing of the burden in just understanding and clarifying the issues. On the other hand, since consciousness and awareness seem to be a human privilege, may it not be desirable to extend this condition to our hidden conflicts, both private and social?

The present book, in seeking to understand many media, the conflicts from which they spring, and the even greater conflicts to which they give rise, holds out the promise of reducing these conflicts by an increase of human autonomy. Let us now note a few of the effects of media hybrids, or of the interpenetration of one medium by another.

Life at the Pentagon has been greatly complicated by jet travel, for example. Every few minutes an assembly gong rings to summon many specialists from their desks to hear a personal report from an expert from some remote part of the world. Meantime, the undone paper work mounts on each desk. And each department daily dispatches personnel by jet to remote areas for more data and reports. Such is the speed of this process of the meeting of the jet plane, the oral report, and the typewriter that those going forth to the ends of the earth often arrive unable to spell the name of the spot to which they have been sent as experts. Lewis Carroll pointed out that as large-scale maps got more and more detailed and extensive, they would tend to blanket agriculture and rouse the protest of farmers. So why not use the actual earth as a map of itself? We have reached a similar point of data gathering when each stick of chewing gum we reach for is acutely noted by some computer that translates our least gesture into a new probability curve or some parameter of social science. Our private and corporate lives have become information processes just because we have put our central nervous systems outside us in electric technology. That is the key to Professor Boorstin's bewilderment in *The Image, or What Happened to the American Dream*.

The electric light ended the regime of night and day, of indoors and out-of-doors. But it is when the light encounters already existing patterns of human organization that the hybrid energy is released. Cars can travel all night, ball players can play all night, and windows can be left out of buildings. In a word, the message of the electric light is total change. It is pure information without any content to restrict its transforming and informing power.

If the student of media will but meditate on the power of this medium of electric light to transform every structure of time and space and work and society that it penetrates or contacts, he will have the key to the form of the power that is in all media to reshape any lives that they touch. Except for light, all other media come in pairs, with one acting as the "content" of the other, obscuring the operation of both.

It is a peculiar bias of those who operate media for the owners that they be concerned about the program content of radio, or press, or film. The owners themselves are concerned more about the media as such, and are not inclined to go beyond "what the public wants" or some vague formula. Owners are aware of the media as power, and they know that this power has little to do with "content" or the media within the media.

When the press opened up the "human interest" keyboard after the telegraph had restructured the press medium, the newspaper killed the theater, just as TV hit the movies and the night clubs very hard. George Bernard Shaw had the wit and imagination to fight back. He put the press into the theater, taking over the controversies and the human interest world of the press for the stage, as Dickens had done for the novel. The movie took over the novel and the newspaper and the stage, all at once. Then TV pervaded the movie and gave the theater-in-the-round back to the public.

What I am saying is that media as extensions of our senses institute new ratios, not only among our private senses, but among themselves, when they interact among themselves. Radio changed the form of the news story as much as it altered the film image in the talkies. TV caused drastic changes in radio programming, and in the form of the *thing* or documentary novel.

It is the poets and painters who react instantly to a new medium like radio or TV. Radio and gramophone and tape recorder gave us back the poet's voice as an important dimension of the poetic experience. Words became a kind of painting with light, again. But TV, with its deep-participation mode, caused young poets suddenly to present their poems in cafés, in public parks, anywhere. After TV, they suddenly felt the need for personal contact with their public. (In print-oriented Toronto, poetry-reading in the public parks is a public offense. Religion and politics are permitted, but not poetry, as many young poets recently discovered.)

John O'Hara, the novelist, wrote in *The New York Times Book Review* of November 27, 1955:

You get a great satisfaction from a book. You know your reader is captive inside those covers, but as novelist you have to imagine the satisfaction he's getting. Now, in the theater — well, I used to drop in during both productions of Pal Joey *and watch, not imagine, the people enjoy it. I'd willingly start my next novel — about a small town — right now, but I need the diversion of a play.*

In our age artists are able to mix their media diet as easily as their book diet. A poet like Yeats made the fullest use of oral peasant culture in creating his literary effects. Quite early, Eliot made a great impact by the careful use of jazz and film form. *The Love Song of J. Alfred Prufrock* gets much of its power from an inter-penetration of film form and jazz idiom. But this mix reached its greatest power in *The Waste Land* and *Sweeney Agonistes*. *Prufrock* uses not only film form but the film theme of Charlie Chaplin, as did James Joyce in *Ulysses*. Joyce's Bloom is a deliberate takeover from Chaplin ("Chorney Choplain," as he called him in *Finnegans Wake*). And Chaplin, just as Chopin had adapted the pianoforte to the style of the ballet, hit upon the wondrous media mix of ballet and film in developing his Pavlova-like alternation of ecstasy and waddle. He adopted the classical steps of ballet to a movie mime that converged exactly the right blend of the lyric and the ironic that is found also in *Prufrock* and *Ulysses*. Artists in various fields are always the first to discover how to enable one medium to use or to release the power of another. In a simpler form, it is the technique employed by Charles Boyer in his kind of French-English blend of urbane, throaty delirium.

The printed book had encouraged artists to reduce all forms of expression as much as possible to the single descriptive and narrative plane of the printed word. The advent of electric media released art from this straitjacket at once, creating the world of Paul Klee, Picasso, Braque, Eisenstein, the Marx Brothers, and James Joyce.

A headline in *The New York Times Book Review* (September 16, 1962) trills: There's Nothing Like a Best Seller to Set Hollywood a-Tingle.

Of course, nowadays, movie stars can only be lured from the beaches or science-fiction or some self-improvement course by the cultural lure of a role in a famous book. That is the way that the interplay of media now affects many in the movie colony. They have no more understanding of their media problems than does Madison Avenue. But from the point of view of the owners of the film and related media, the best seller is a form of insurance that some massive new *gestalt* or pattern has been isolated in the public psyche. It is an oil strike or a gold mine that can be depended on to yield a fair amount of boodle to the careful and canny processer. Hollywood bankers, that is, are smarter than literary historians, for the latter despise popular taste except when it has been filtered down from lecture course to literary handbook.

Lillian Ross in *Picture* wrote a snide account of the filming of *The Red Badge of Courage*. She got a good deal of easy kudos for a foolish book about a great

178

film by simply *assuming* the superiority of the literary medium to the film medium. Her book got much attention as a hybrid.

Agatha Christie wrote far above her usual good level in a group of twelve short stories about Hercule Poirot, called *The Labours of Hercules*. By adjusting the classical themes to make reasonable modern parallels, she was able to lift the detective form to extraordinary intensity.

Such was, also, the method of James Joyce in *Dubliners* and *Ulysses*, when the precise classical parallels created the true hybrid energy. Baudelaire, said Mr. Eliot, "taught us how to raise the imagery of common life to first intensity." It is done, not by any direct heave-ho of poetic strength, but by a simple adjustment of situations from one culture in hybrid form with those of another. It is precisely in this way that during wars and migrations new cultural mix is the norm of ordinary daily life. Operations Research programs the hybrid principle as a technique of creative discovery.

When the movie scenario or picture story was applied to the *idea* article, the magazine world had discovered a hybrid that ended the supremacy of the short story. When wheels were put in tandem form, the wheel principle combined with the lineal typographic principle to create aerodynamic balance. The wheel crossed with industrial, lineal form released the new form of the airplane.

The hybrid or the meeting of two media is a moment of truth and revelation from which new form is born. For the parallel between two media holds us on the frontiers between forms that snap us out of the Narcissus-narcosis. The moment of the meeting of media is a moment of freedom and release from the ordinary trance and numbness imposed by them on our senses.

10

Is It Natural That One Medium Should Appropriate and Exploit Another?

Why have the effects of media, whether speech, writing, photography or radio, been overlooked by social observers through the past 3500 years of the Western world? The answer to that question, we shall see, is in the power of the media themselves to impose their own assumptions upon our modes of perception. Our media have always constituted the parameters and the framework for the objectives of our Western world. But the assumptions and parameters projected by the structures of the media on and through our sensibilities have long constituted the overall patterns of private and group association in the West. The same structuring of the forms of human association by various media is also true of the non-Western world, and of the lives of pre-literate and archaic man as well. The difference is that in the West our media technologies from script to print, and from Gutenberg to Marconi, have been highly specialized. Specialism creates not stability and equilibrium, but change and trauma, as one segment of experience usurps and overlays the others in aggressive, brawling sequence and cycle.

All that ends now in the electronic age, whose media substitute all-at-once-ness for one-thing-at-a-timeness. The movement of information at approximately the speed of light has become by far the largest industry of the world. The consumption of this information has become correspondingly the largest consumer function in the world. The globe has become on one hand a community of learning, and at the same time, with regard to the tightness of its interrelationships, the globe has become a tiny village. Patterns of human association based on slower media have become overnight not only irrelevant and obsolete, but a threat to continued existence and to sanity. In these circumstances understanding media must mean the understanding of the *effects* of media. The objectives of new media have tended, fatally, to be set in terms of the parameters and frames of older media. All media testing has been done within the parameters of older media — especially of speech and print.

Today in top-management study and planning, assumptions and objectives are recognized to be distinct entities. Let me quote from a Westinghouse "Long Range Planning" brief of August 3, 1960:

> *Now it is imperative that whenever there is a change so that actual developments do not coincide with your assumptions, you must change your assumptions and*

you must change any plans that were based on the assumption that has now turned out to be erroneous. . . . It is absolutely imperative that you must know what your assumptions are, and that you must recognize that things are not going to develop in the future in accordance with your assumptions. . . . Now, the primary difference between an assumption and an objective is that an assumption pertains to things that are beyond your control, and an objective pertains to things that are achieved through your own effort.

What the writer of this brief does not know is that assumptions can also come within the range of prediction and control just as soon as it is recognized that the new media of communication in any age, as they penetrate and transform the older media, are the source of new assumptions and consequently the causes of change in our objectives.

The study of media constituents and content can never reveal these dynamics of media *effects*. Media study has lagged behind all other fields in this century, even behind economics, as the following quotation from W. W. Rostow's *The Stages of Economic Growth* (Boston: Cambridge University Press, 1960, page 90) will show:

The argument of this book has been that once man conceived of his physical environment as subject to knowable, consistent laws, he began to manipulate it to his economic advantage; and once it was demonstrated that growth was possible, the consequences of growth and modernization, notably its military consequences, unhinged one traditional society after another, pushed it into the treacherous period of preconditions, from which many, but not all of the world's societies have now emerged into self-sustained growth through the take-off mechanism. . . .

Media study has not begun to approach the awareness of this "take-off mechanism" of social change involved in the shaping and speeding of information for eye and for ear and for touch and kinetics.

Our project set out to bring media study within the range of the expanding awareness here indicated by Rostow in economics. My assumptions, then, were:

(a) that nothing had yet been done to bring understanding to the effects of media in patterning human association,

(b) that such understanding was quite possible; media assumptions do not have to remain subliminal,

(c) that the absence of such understanding was eloquent testimony to the power of media to anesthetize those very modes of awareness in which they were most operative.

My objectives were:

(a) to explain the character of a dozen media, illustrating the dynamic symmetries of their operation on man and society,

(b) to do this in a syllabus usable in secondary schools. (Secondary schools were chosen as offering students who had not in their own lives become aware of any vested interest in acquired knowledge. They have very great experience of media, but no habits of observation or critical awareness. Yet they are the best teachers of media to teachers, who are otherwise unreachable.)

WRITING

1. What would be the problems of introducing the phonetic alphabet today into Japan and China?
2. Would the consequences of introducing the phonetic alphabet into China today be as drastic as when the Romans introduced the same alphabet to Gaul?
3. Will the ideogram survive in some new roles in the same way that the printed book finds new work to do in the electronic age?
4. What are some of the advantages of the ideogram over our alphabet?
5. Does a form of writing which involves complex situations at a single glance favor cultural continuity and stability?
6. By contrast, does a form of writing that favors attention to one-thing-at-a-time foster instability and change?
7. In other words, is the man of the ear a conservative, and the man of the eye a liberal?
8. Why should writing weaken the human memory? Pre-literate man, amazed at the efforts of the white man to write down his thoughts and sayings, asks: "Why do you write; can you not remember?"
9. Why should a pre-literate people have no concept of words as referring to things, but only of words as being things?
10. Is the "content" of writing the medium of speech? Is it possible for any medium to have a content except it be another medium?
11. Is the medium the message?
12. Is is possible for a mathematical proposition or demonstration to have content?

PRINT

1. Let us try to discover any area of human action or knowledge unaffected by the forms and pressures of print during the past five centuries.
2. If the forms of print have shaped all the levels of action and organization in

the Western world up until the advent of nuclear technology, does this explain and justify the type of stress which we allow to our printed forms in the educational establishment?

3. If a nuclear technology is now succeeding the mechanical print technology of the past five centuries, what problems does such a transition present to the educator? To the political establishment? To the legal establishment?

4. What would happen to the society that did not recognize or identify these problems at all?

5. What happened to medieval education when it failed to understand the nature of print?

6. Consider why anthropology with its pre-literate concerns should have so much in common with post-literate and nuclear forms of communication?

7. How did the uniformity and repeatability of the print production process affect human arrangements in time and in space?

8. Why should the speeding of information flow for the print reader create historical perspective and background? Why should the much slower information flow of the manuscript make such background impossible?

9. Why should the electronic speed of information flow eliminate historical background in favor of "you are there"?

10. Why is homogeneity of space and time arrangement natural under print conditions of learning?

11. Why was it revolutionary for Columbus to assume that he could keep moving in a straight line, in one direction? Why are there no straight lines in medieval maps? Why was it unthinkable for them that space should be continuous and homogeneous?

12. Why should the Columbus pursuit of the straight line in navigation have been necessary in order to discover the round earth?

13. Are the flat-earthers on strong ground in terms of our Western devotion to Euclidean space?

14. In garment-making and hence in clothing styles, the straight seam was impossible before the sewing machine. Trace some of the implications of the straight line and of mechanism in one or more other fields of human organization.

15. How much is our notion of "content" affected in the case of printing by the blank page as filled with moveable type?

PRESS

1. Does the aspect of newspaper as inclusive image of the community commit the newspaper to the job of exposing private manipulation of the communal thing? Is there an inevitable clash between the public nature and function of a newspaper and the private points of view of many of the interests in a community?

2. Consider the same news story as handled on radio and television, and in the newspaper. Do you think any one of these ways of handling the news especially adapted to any particular kind of news? Does world news, for example, seem most appropriate in headline form? Does local news find its most appropriate form on the radio?

3. Which medium — press, radio, or television — is most effective in gaining the participation of the viewer? Does the newspaper reader tend to be a mere spectator of events? Is the radio listener more closely involved? Is the television viewer most challenged to participate in action?

4. Does the newspaper typically create the outlook of the sidewalk superintendent in all community matters?

5. Is the job of the newspaper to dramatize the issues within a community?

6. How did the news photograph alter the nature of the newspaper and the news story?

7. How had the print affected the nature of news coverage prior to the photograph? (See Ivins' *Print and Visual Communication*.)

8. Has the influence of radio and television been to encourage newspapers to a more editorial attitude to the news? If news can be given by radio and television, does the newspaper see its unique advantage to consist in background to the news?

9. Why should the newspaper find so little sympathy with historical perspective on any matter? (See *Time* magazine as a newspaper trying to achieve historical perspective.)

10. What devices does a newspaper employ to provide a sense of continuity from day to day for its readership?

11. Why should the newspaper, in processing opinion in such ways as to produce homogeneous emotions and attitudes, be a major means of mobilizing the manpower resources of a nation?

TELEPHONE

1. How would a speed-up of information movement to telephone dimension affect the pattern of authority and of decision-making?

2. Ask your friends and parents how the telephone shapes their business and social lives.

3. What, for example, is the effect of the telephone in medical practice? In political life?

4. What has been the role of the telephone in the newspaper world?

5. Consider the way in which the telephone is used in Broadway plays, or in Hollywood movies, as indication of its real force and character.

6. What qualities of drama and action come to mind in relating the telephone to stage and movie and novel?

7. Is it natural that one medium should appropriate and exploit another?
8. Is the use one medium makes of another the clearest testimony to its nature?
9. Why is the telephone so irresistibly intrusive?
10. Why do Europeans and especially English people particularly resent the telephone?
11. Why does an Englishman prefer to manage his appointments by telegraph and postcard rather than person-to-person telephone calls?
12. Why is it difficult to exercise delegated authority in a world supplied with telephones?
13. Is the telephone extremely demanding of individual attention?
14. Is it abrupt, intrusive, and indifferent to human concerns?
15. How does the telephone affect the typewriter? Does it enormously speed up and increase the role of the typewriter? Check this question with the book *Parkinson's Law* by C. Northcote Parkinson.

MOVIES

1. In view of the various cultural backgrounds of England, France, America, Russia, India, and Japan, what qualities would you expect to appear most in the movies made in these countries?
2. In his *Film As Art*, Rudolph Arnheim for example says that the American film-maker excels in the single shot; the Russian in montage. Why should this be?
3. Why should the European and the Russian and the Japanese have regarded the film as an art form from the first? Why should the English-speaking world have such difficulty in seeing popular forms of entertainment as art forms whether the movie, the comic strip, or the common advertisement?
4. How did movies sell the American way of life to the backward countries of the globe? Consider the role of uniformity and repeatability as indispensable to competition and rivalry. How could competition thrive where unique expression and achievement are stressed?
5. Was the picture story borrowed from the cartoon world?
6. Is there any hook-up between magazine picture stories and silent movies? If so, is it in the isolation of one emotion at a time?
7. Magazines like the *Saturday Evening Post* have discovered that idea articles, written like movie scenarios shot by shot, sell better than short stories. Check the technique of such articles.

RADIO

1. What was the effect of the radio on movies? On newspapers? On magazines? On language? On the concept of time?

2. How do P.A. systems relate to radio?
3. Does the P.A. system affect the visual as well?
4. What changes occurred in radio listening and programming after television?
5. Why is radio so intensely visual in effect?
6. What was the relation of radio to the rise of Fascism, politically and psychologically?
7. Why should radio exert such force among the pre-literate and the semi-literate?
8. What was the overall effect of radio among highly literate people?
9. Why does the twelve-year-old tend to turn from the television set to radio?

TELEVISION

1. Engineers claim that a thousand-line television image would provide almost as high definition as the present movie image. Supposing that an equally high definition of retinal impression were achieved for television, what would be the effect of its multi-point mosaic structure over and above the retinal impression?
2. Why should the broken line of the television mosaic emphasize the sculptural contours of objects?
3. Why has sculpture traditionally been spoken of as the voice of silence? Does this mean that the sculptural object exists on the frontier between sight and sound?
4. Is there any possible line of investigation suggested by the fact that sound waves become visible on the wings of jet planes just before they break the sound barrier? Does this suggest that the various human senses are translatable one into the other at various intensities?
5. If sculpture exists on the frontier between sight and sound, does this mean that beyond that frontier is writing and architecture and enclosed or pictorial space? In a word, must the nuclear age civilize those primitive dimensions from which we emerged by means of writing and the visual organization of experience? Can this be done without mere destruction both of the primitive and of the civilized achievement?
6. Consider the power of any medium to impose its own spatial assumptions and structures. Extend your observations to discriminate and distinguish between the kinds of space evoked and constituted by the film on one hand, television on the other.

RECOMMENDATIONS

Communication, creativity, and growth occur together or they do not occur at all. New technology creating new basic assumptions at all levels for all enterprises is wholly destructive if new objectives are not orchestrated with the new technological motifs.

Dr. James E. Russell, of the National Education Association's Educational Policies Committee, commenting on my paper "The New Media and the New Education," felt that I had not included consideration of the computer's effect:

> *What I had in mind is the new dimension forced on education by the existence of computers and teaching machines. This runs at a much deeper level than the distinction between print and nonprint communications. It has to do with a new concept of the nature of thought. . . . All rational propositions can be reduced to binomial terms.*

As Tobias Dantzig revealed in his book on *Number*, primitive, pre-digital counting was binomial. Post-digital computation returns to the pre-digital just as post-literate education returns to the dialogue. However, what the computer means in education is this. As information movement speeds up, information levels rise in all areas of mind and society, and the result is that any subject of knowledge becomes substitutable for any other subject. That is to say, any and all curricula are obsolete with regard to subject matter. All that remains to study are the media themselves, *as forms*, as modes ever creating new assumptions and hence new objectives.

This basic change has already occurred in science and industry. Almost any natural resource has, with the rise in information levels, become substitutable for any other. In the order of knowledge this fact has given rise to Operations Research, in which any kind of problem can be tackled by nonspecialists. The technique is to work backward from effect or result to cause, not from cause to effect. This situation resulting from instantaneous information movement was referred to by A. N. Whitehead in *Science and the Modern World*, when he pointed out that the great discovery of the later nineteenth century was not the invention of this or that, but the discovery of the technique of discovery. We can discover anything we decide to discover.

In education this means the end of the one-way passing along of knowledge to students. For they already live in a "*field*" of knowledge created by new media which, though different in kind, is yet far richer and more complex than any ever taught via traditional curricula. The situation is comparable to the difference between the complexity of a language versus the crudities of traditional grammars used to bring languages under the rule of written forms. Until we have mastered the multiple grammars of the new nonwritten media, we shall have no curriculum relevant to the new languages of knowledge and communication which have come into existence via the new media. These new languages are known to most people but their grammars are not known at all. We have "read" these new languages in the light of the old. The result has been distortion of their character and blindness to their meaning and effects.

Non-Euclidean space, and the dissolution of our entire Western fabric of perception, results from electric modes of moving information. This revolution involves us willy-nilly in the study of modes and media as forms that shape and reshape our perceptions. That is what I have meant all along by saying the "medium is the message," for the medium determines the modes of perception and the matrix of assumptions within which objectives are set.

All of my recommendations, therefore, can be reduced to this one: Study the modes of the media, in order to hoick all assumptions out of the subliminal, non-verbal realm for scrutiny and for prediction and control of human purposes.

Such a program can most readily be instituted today at the level of secondary education.

11

Explorations

STRESS

8 Dr. Hans Selye has come up with the first non-visual disease theory since the Greeks introduced the image of the skin as an envelope enclosing organs. His *stress* theory is entirely a *field* view of disease. The body is part of a total field.

The Greek view of the body as package of organs and humors got cut down, at the Renaissance, to a view of the body as a pumping station. Then with the rise of chemistry in the nineteenth century the body became a chemistry factory. Everybody was loaded with germs. But the rise of field theory in physics now has its medical counterpart in Dr. Hans Selye's stress view. He rejects the idea that each disease has a specific cause which must be found and isolated in order for cure to occur. In a word he regards as unreal and out-dated the lineal view of disease as specific target for which a specific *shot* is indicated.

Dr. Selye wrote in *Explorations* no. 1 that:
experimental work in animals (1936) demonstrated that the organism responds in a stereotyped manner to a variety of factors such as infections, intoxications, trauma, nervous strain, heat, cold, muscular fatigue or X-irradiation . . . Their only common feature was that they placed the body in a state of general (systemic) stress. We therefore concluded that this stereotyped response, which was superimposed

upon the specific effects, represented the somatic manifestations of non-specific stress itself.

The field theory finds unnecessary the cell theory of Schleiden and Schwann (1839), just as in physics it detaches itself from the visual closed system of Newtonian mechanics.

The Selye theory becomes at once intelligible and acceptable in our twentieth century of oral awareness. That "all vital phenomena depend merely upon quantitative variations in the activation of pre-existent elementary targets" is not a superficial view in terms of auditory space.

In the old lineal terms, quantitative relations mean the exclusion of most meaning and of all spiritual complexity. A mere sequence of such effects can contain no vital or analogical drama of proportions. But analogy is itself field theory or vision such as disappeared from philosophy in the sixteenth century.

The analogical drama of being and perception needs no more than the quantitative terms postulated by Selye. With these the living word constitutes and manifests itself in all mental and spiritual complexity.

Analogical proportion is a basic aspect of auditory space and of oral culture. It is the oral equivalent of the golden section in architecture and design.

ORAL⊏⊐ a n a l

9 Otto Fenichel in *The Psychoanalytic Theory of Neuroses* describes the oral concept of Freud as follows:

All positive or negative emphasis on taking and receiving indicates an oral origin. Unusually pronounced oral satisfaction results in a remarkable self-assurance and optimism. . . . Exceptional oral deprivation, on the other hand, determines a pessimistic (depressive) or sadistic (redress-demanding) attitude. If a person remains fixated to the world of oral wishes, he will, in his general behaviour, present a disinclination to take care of himself . . . Thus both marked generosity and marked niggardliness may be attributed to conflicts around oral eroticism. (N.Y. 1945, pp. 488–90)

Fenichel describes the correlative anal character as frugal, orderly, obstinate, likely to be concerned with saving money and with time schedules. Greedy and fond of collecting things for the sake of collecting.

In a culture which for centuries has been as lineally arranged as our own, it is obvious that the habits called "anal" or "oral" by psychologists receive a collective educational stress far in excess of any fashionable biological or psychological emphasis· that could occur in individual training. It is equally obvious that our 3,000-year-old lineal stress did not originate nor terminate in biological bias or in toilet habits.

Gertrude Stein in *The Making of Americans* sets up the anal-oral axis very naturally as the correlative of verbalization:
"I cannot remember not talking all the time and all the same feeling that while I was talking that I was not only hearing but seeing . . .
A history of anyone must be a long one, slowly it comes out from them . . . in the kind of repeating each one does."

What Freud calls "oral" is noted as typical of pre-literate societies and is applied to one by Anthony F. C. Wallace in his study of Iroquois culture (*Symposium on Local Diversity in Iroquois Culture* ed. by W. N. Fenton). Oral cultures in the auditory sense naturally have small time sense because they play by ear. And all time is *now* in oral societies. This auditory space is a physical field and its spherical character really explains the bias and expectations of oral, pre-literate societies. Likewise the visual lineality of scribal and print cultures really includes the anal-oral axis, with strong anal stress, of course. The psychodynamics of sight, sound and language take easy precedence over social biology as concepts and instruments of explanation of these phenomena.

SHERLOCK HOLMES VS THE BUREAUCRAT

10 The popular idea of Holmes, the many-sided man, and of his many triumphs over Scotland Yard is a vivid image of the basic clash of attitudes in Western culture.

Sherlock Holmes is so much the type of the intuitive genius that it is unnecessary to dwell at length on the characteristics of the intuitive mind. It is a mind for which situations are total and inclusive unities. Every facet, every item of a situation, for Holmes, has total relevance. There are no irrelevant details for him. In an organic complex all parts have total relevance, not just *some* relevance to the whole. In the nineteenth century the power of biological metaphor such as obsessed the Holmesian mind of Samuel Taylor Coleridge in his scrutiny of artistic creation, gradually was extended to every phase of human speculation and inquiry.

The concentration on biological analogy with its assumption of total relevance of the least details begins to appear in the joy taken in the new realism, in documenting the most ordinary scenes from daily life in the press, in the novel, in painting.

Flaubert worked in exactly the opposite way from his notion of *le mot juste*. For Flaubert, every word in a long novel had total relevance to the whole novel not just to the local episode. He was the first to return to contrapuntal composition in which all levels of action and implication are simultaneous and in which character becomes theme or motif. Flaubert like Holmes is an instance of the new artist for whom every art situation is total and inclusive of many of the simultaneous levels which occur in actual experience.

THE ARTIST AND THE BUREAUCRAT

For the artist with his organic, vivisectional (or living section) point of view of man and society, the natural enemy is the bureaucrat, the man with the tidy desk, the big file, the orderly mind devoid of simultaneous modes of awareness or observation. It needs no documentation to sustain the view that the admirable administrations of Scotland Yard are hostile to the inclusive and instantaneous grasping of situations. The Yard technology is serial, segmented and circumstantial. They conclude effect from immediately preceding cause in lineal and chronological order. They do not dream of totalities or of the major relevance of details.

In the visual theories of Ruskin as in the poetic theories of Walter Pater the passionate devotion to vivid detail goes with growing awareness that all the arts approach a condition of music; for in music all parts tend to be simultaneous in the sense that narrative progress in musical composition must constantly recapitulate and unify as much as a movie. Toward the end of the last century Theodore Lipps the psychologist was to demonstrate that the single clang of a bell contained all possible sonatas and musical forms. *Anna Livia Plurabelle.*

As all kinds of information flowed from many quarters of the world in greater volume and at greater speed, so similar varieties of knowledge about the inner and outer life of man and society began to co-exist even in semi-literate minds. Biological metaphors of change and existence are necessary means of processing and unifying large bodies of data. Hippolyte Taine on one hand, Gustave Flaubert on the other, took up such biological concepts to revolutionize literary history and the novel. Taine undertook to explain the totality of literature *in* society as an organic and evolutionary process. His view of literature as an organic by-product of massive institutions and nationalisms lasted until recently as the basis for university study of vernacular literatures.

The ordinary man finds a hero in Holmes and in his numerous descendants because the bureaucrat is always putting the finger on each of us in a way which makes us feel like Kafka characters—guilty but mystified.

The Secretariat building at the U.N. is the biggest filing cabinet in the world.

11 Highly literate people are those who have been read aloud to when young? The eye does not move evenly along the line save when retarded and guided by the ear? Ineluctable modality of the visible.

There is an impression abroad that literary folk are fast readers. Wine tasters are not heavy drinkers. Literary people read slowly because they sample the complex dimensions and flavors of words and phrases. They strive for totality not lineality. They are well aware that the words on the page have to be decanted with the utmost skill. Those who imagine they read only for "content" are illusioned.

As Bartlett showed in his classic *Remembering,* an act of attention to any situation is an act of rearranging all the members of that situation. Recall is also restructuring.

Psychologists have shown that the eye does not apprehend while moving or while at rest. Rather there is a tremor while at rest which permits the encompassing of the object. The "reeling and writhing" of Lewis Carroll is close to the action of pre-typewriter reading and writing. The staccato stutter of the typewriter on the other hand is really close to the stutter that is oral speech. The typewriter is part of our oral revolution today. "Bygmeister Finnegan of the stuttering hand" is Joyce's figure of the inventor of spoken words and of architecture. The typist yatters to the script.

Today children have to have radio or gramophone playing in order to attend to visual tasks of reeling and writhing, rocking and rolling, reading and writing. The silent class-room favors only those who have been rigidly swaddled in habits of silent solitary reading. Is class-room swaddling a principal factor in juvenile delinquency? The normal environment with auditory messages carried simultaneously by different media on several levels creates new habits of attention in which the adult world is little-skilled. The fall in the level of literacy goes hand in hand with a great increase in range of oral verbalization. Literacy is the social acceptance of the monopoly of one mode of perception. It would be well to diagnose the total situation before pronouncing a general moral doom. Naturally the professional scribes make it their business to issue moral judgements on this technological change.

> Legal contracts in today's business are just the minutes of the last meeting.
>
> Oil Executive

12 In English libel law, "the greater the truth the greater the libel." The English conception of libel is aristocratic and oral, the American is written. Oral codes have no loop-holes for legal eagles. In oral codes the sanctions are total: ostracism—the duel.

In written, sanctions are lineal and metrical—the fine, the damages.

The Merchant of Venice is the dramatization of a clash between oral and written codes.

BECAUSE PRINT IS A

The ᴘᴀᴛᴛᴇʀᴋɪʟʟᴇʀ

WORD

May ꜰʟᴜᴛᴛᴇʀʙʏ

Oral societies have a code of honor. Charles James Fox was confronted by his tailor one morning when he was piling up gold pieces to pay a gambling debt. The tailor presented his bill. Fox explained the money was for a debt of honor. "Then," said the tailor tearing up his bill, "I make mine a debt of honor also." And Fox paid him on the spot. Even today in the American South order books are taboo.

The Boer general Krueger was quite illiterate, said Roy Campbell. He sat daily under a large tree administering justice. Two brothers presented themselves. They could not agree about the division of their patrimony. They showed him a map of the land. Krueger said to one: "You divide it." To the other: "You choose." The oral is quick, inclusive, total. It considers all aspects in a single instant.

If one were to ask any power group, a corporation or an ad agency: "If, by pressing a button in this room you could instantly achieve all your goals, would you press that button?" The answer would be "NO". This question merely transfers their operations from the written and analytic mode to the oral and simultaneous. It is the difference between the fairy wish and the Puritan will. The world of the oral wish at once reveals the moral quality of the goal.

Somebody said the nineteenth century saw the shift from the dance to the race, from inclusive symmetry to lineal anarchy.

Aristocracies are always oral in tendency, living by gossip and anecdote, games and sports. They make use of the scribe but despise him. Said the Duke of Gloucester to Edward Gibbon on the appearance of his *History*: "Another damned fat book eh, Mr. Gibbon? Scribble scribble scribble eh, Mr. Gibbon?" The use of the fox hunter said Wyndham Lewis, is to keep the business man in his place.

It is not accidental that oral countries like Spain, Italy, France, rely heavily on written legal codes. For the same cause (antithetic polarity) common law and oral tradition in England and America rely heavily on the general literacy of the Anglo-Saxon world.

Mr. Justice Jackson observed that "when the Court moved to Washington in 1800, it was provided with no books, which probably accounts for the high quality of early opinions. In five of Marshall's great opinions he cited not a single precedent."

Young lawyers today are encouraged to keep all books out of sight in their offices. "*You* are the law for your client."

In his "Roman Law and the British Empire" (in *Changing Concepts of Time*) Innis shows how it happens that in print cultures like ours lawyers tend to become legislators, whereas in oral cultures journalists enter the legislature. Innis might have added that the newspaper is essentially an oral form produced by oral types of men. The newspaper via the telegraph provides no explanations but instead an instantaneous global section.

Legal procedure in oral countries is inquisitorial, equally in Russia or France or Ireland. Written tradition favors, instead, the sifting of circumstantial evidence. Because Roman law countries are concerned with principles they attract the highest intellectual ability into the academic field, said Innis, and Roman Law countries are strong in the social sciences for this reason.

Always the totalitarian, inclusive and drastic character of the oral tradition in law and society. Always the fragmentary, loop-holed, and limited aspect of law in the written tradition.

These remarks imply no value judgements, no preferences. To distinguish the properties of these things avoids the confusion of moral clamor. Clarification permits co-existence, and resolution of conflict.

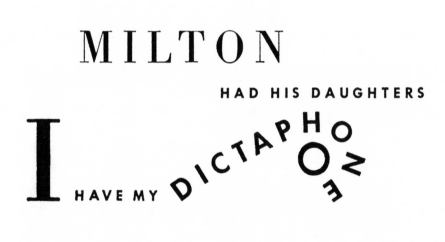

MILTON

HAD HIS DAUGHTERS

I HAVE MY DICTAPHONE

13 Henry James on his death-bed called for his Remington. It was brought and the sound of its keys soothed his delirium. Dictating to a typist during the last 25 years of his life, Henry James revolutionized his prose. Dictation permitted the slow elaboration of those vast periods of *The Golden Bowl*. And dictation changed the style of Wyndham Lewis after his blindness.

Here is the early, visual Lewis:
There are torsos moving with bemused slowness on all sides; their helmet-capped testudinate heads jut this way and that. In their clockwork cadence the exhausted splash of the waves is a sound that is a cold ribbon just existing in the massive heat. The delicate surf

falls with the abrupt clash of glass, section by section.

After his blindness the prose of Lewis became less pigmented, less kinesthetic. It acquired narrative ease:

> Pullman had noticed long before this that both giants had kicked off their shoes, which lay, very minute footwear, not far from where their feet were moving. Their clothes had everywhere burst asunder. But it was at this moment that with enormous splutters and gasps, they suddenly levitated . . . two vast nudities rose into the air and disappeared over the roofs. But they made their exit buttocks uppermost.

Most prominent among American representatives of the oral manner in prose is William Faulkner whose latest novel *The Town* (volume two) opens:

> I wasn't born yet so it was Cousin Gowan who was there and big enough to see and remember and tell me afterward when I was big enough for it to make sense.

The oral tradition of the South is a world in which past and present concert in a babble of chat and memories and observation and complicated kinship relations. An oral world keeps multiple blood relationships in easy acoustic focus in the same way as a pre-literate people have no trouble in managing complex word formations and inflections. James W. Hart in *The Popular Book* notes that:

> Sharing the heritage of England's established religious beliefs, the Southerners were not embroiled in doctrinal dispute which made New Englanders import and print books. . . . As one of the Southern colonists said, they were more inclinable to read men by business and conversation than to dive into books.

The author of *Tom Sawyer* and *Huck Finn* stays in the heart of this oral world as much as the author of *Pogo*.

The new art or science which the electronic

or post-mechanical age has to invent

concerns the alchemy of social change.

14 We can no longer tolerate the irresponsibility of social trial and error. When information moves instantly to all parts of the globe it is chemically explosive. Any chain-reaction which occurs rapidly is explosive, whether in personal or social life.

President Sukarno of Indonesia spoke to the tycoons of Hollywood describing them as revolutionaries. They may have been shocked. But people who are as specialized as they are can't avoid shocks.

New ideas and new attitudes are disruptive. Today the normal movements of information have the effect of armed invasion on some culture or group. Earlier ages entertained themselves with speculation on the historical effect of Cleopatra's nose. We teeter hysterically on the consequences of rumor about President Eisenhower's viscera.

It is the normal aspect of our information-flow which is revolutionary now. The new media normalize that state of revolution which is war. Two hundred years ago it was idea and theory which disrupted the old regimes. Now it is just the packaged information which we call entertainment which transforms living conditions and basic attitudes. It is the ordinary flow of news and pictures from every quarter of the globe which rearranges our intellectual and emotional lives without either struggle or acceptance on our part.

Our present conceptions of what constitutes social cause, effect, and influence are quite unable to cope with this electronic simultaneity of conspicuous co-existence.

We have to know in advance the effect, on all the cultures of the world, of any change whatever. This is necessity not ideal. It is also a possibility. There was never a critical situation created by human ingenuity which did not contain its own solution.

The same technology which has made instantaneous information-flow a chemical danger to every culture in the world has also created the power of total re-construction and pre-construction of models of situations. For nearly a century we have employed reconstruction as historical method. Instead of *a view* of the past we simply re-create a model of it. This method began in detective fiction, and in symbolist poetry. Instead of a theory of a crime, the whole crime reconstructed. Instead of a poetic statement about an experience, the situation which is formula for that experience.

In a movie like *Richard III* by Lawrence Olivier there is expert reconstruction of an Elizabethan play and also reconstruction of the visual and textural and political period about which the play is concerned. The historical expertise of dozens of scholars led to a working model which any school-child could enjoy equally with an adult.

GEOGRAPHY AND TIME ARE NOW CAPSULATED. Our tendency has been to make possible the co-existence of all cultures and also of all pasts. But this means that we can also anticipate the effects of all our present actions and technology. What we must know in order to achieve this is the fact that the media of communication are not mere catalysts but have their own physics and chemistry which enter into every moment of social alchemy and change.

THE PHYSICS OF TYPOGRAPHIC LINEALITY HAVE DOMINATED OUR PERCEPTION

Previously Newtonian mechanics had been a closed system of perception. But we have moved swiftly beyond mechanization in this century, and mechanical metaphors are mostly irrelevant to the physics of our media and the demands which we should now make of our education. Why make the media of light fight on the side of darkened perception?

If we can no longer tolerate trial and error in modern urban and economic life, neither is the fact of traditional time-lag in educational procedure a matter for banal and cynical observation. When all kinds of information flowed slowly in a society, educational irrelevance could be corrected by self-education and by individual brilliance.

THAT WON'T WORK TODAY.

About 1830 Lamartine pointed to the newspaper as the end of book culture.

THE BOOK ARRIVES TOO LATE

At the same time Dickens used the press as base for a new impressionist art which D. W. Griffiths and Sergei Eisenstein studied in 1920 as the foundation of movie art.

Robert Browning took the newspaper as art model for his impressionist epic *The Ring and the Book*; Mallarmé did the same in *Un Coup de Dés*. Edgar Poe, a press man and, like Shelley, a science fictioneer, correctly analysed the poetic process. Conditions of newspaper serial publication led both him and Dickens to the process of writing backwards. This means simultaneity of all parts of a composition. Simultaneity compels sharp focus on *effect* of thing made. Simultaneity is the form of the press in dealing with Earth City. Simultaneity is formula for the writing of both detective story and symbolist poem. These are derivatives (one 'low' and one "high") of the new technological culture. Simultaneity is related to telegraph, as the telegraph to math and physics.

Joyce's *Ulysses* completed the cycle of this technological art form.

LET

the sun and moon go!
let scenery take the applause of the audience!
let there be apathy under the stars!

Let nothing remain but the ashes of teachers,
artists, moralists, lawyers,
and learn'd and polite persons!

Let churches accommodate serpents, vermin,
and the corpses of those who have died
of the most filthy of diseases!

Let there be no unfashionable wisdom!
let such be scorn'd and derided
off from the earth!

Let a floating cloud in the sky —
let a wave of the sea — let growing mint,
spinach, onions, tomatoes — let these be exhibited
as shows, at a great price for admission!

Let shadows be furnished with genitals!
Let substances be deprived of their genitals! . . .

Walt Whitman, Respondez

202

1. We shall sing the love of danger,
the habit of energy and boldness.

2. The essential elements of our poetry
shall be courage, daring and rebellion.

3. Literature has hitherto glorified
thoughtful immobility, ecstasy and sleep:
we shall extol aggressive movement,
feverish insomnia, the double
quick step, the somersault, the box on
the ear, the fisticuff . . .

F. T. Marinetti, Futuristic Manifesto

BEYOND ACTION AND REACTION

WE WOULD ESTABLISH OURSELVES

We start from opposite statements of a chosen world. Set up violent structure of adolescent clearness between two extremes.

We discharge ourselves on both sides.

We fight first on one side, then on the other, but always for the SAME cause, which is neither side or both sides and ours.

Mercenaries were always the best troops.

We are Primitive Mercenaries in the Modern World.

Our *Cause* Is NO-MAN'S.

We set Humor at Humor's throat.

Stir up Civil War among peaceful apes.

We only want Humor if it has fought like Tragedy.

We only want Tragedy if it can clench its side-muscles like hands on its belly, and bring to the surface a laugh like a bomb.

Wyndham Lewis, *Manifesto*

To believe that it is necessary for or conducive to art, to "Improve" life, for instance—make architecture, dress, ornament, in *better taste,* is absurd.

The artist of the modern movement is a savage (in no sense an "advanced," perfected, democratic, Futuristic individual of Mr. Marinetti's limited imagination): this enormous, jangling, journalistic, fiery desert of modern life serves him as Nature did more technically primitive man.

There is violent boredom with that feeble European-ism, abasement of the miserable "intellectual" before anything coming from Paris, Cosmopolitan sentimen-tality, which prevails in so many quarters.

Wyndham Lewis, *Blast*

FUTURISM AND LIFE MAGIC

1. The Futurist theoretician should be a Professor of Hoffman Romance, and attempt the manufacture of a perfect being.

Art merges in Life again everywhere.

Leonardo was the first Futurist, and, incidentally, an airman among Quattro Cento angels.

His Mona Lisa eloped from the Louvre like any woman.

She is back again now, smiling, with complacent reticence, as before her escapade; no one can say when she will be off once more, she possesses so much vitality.

Her olive pigment is electric, so much more so than the carnivorous Belgian bumpkins by Rubens in a neighbouring room, who, besides, are so big they could not slip about in the same subtle fashion.

Rubens IMITATED Life—borrowed the colour of its crude blood, traced the sprawling and surging of its animal hulks.

Leonardo MADE NEW BEINGS, delicate and severe, with as ambitious an intention as any ingenious mediaeval Empiric.

He multiplied in himself, too, Life's possibilities. He was not content to be as an individual Artist alone, any more than he was content with Art.

Life won him with gifts and talents.

2. In Northern Europe (Germany, Scandinavia and Russia) for the last half century, the intellectual world has developed savagely in one direction—that of Life.

His war-talk, sententious elevation and much besides,

MARINETTI picked up from NIETZCHE.

Strindberg, with his hysterical and puissant autobiographies, life-long tragic coquetry with Magic, extensive probing of female flesh and spirit, is the great Scandinavian figure best representing this tendency.

Bergson, the philosopher of Impressionism, stands for this new prescience in France.

EVERYWHERE

LIFE IS SAID

INSTEAD OF

ART

Wyndham Lewis

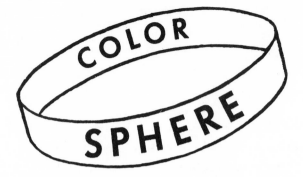

The age-old conflict between the Eastern integrity of the interval and the Western integrity of the object is being resolved in oral culture.

Pound's *Treatise on Harmony* states:

A sound of any pitch, or any combination of such sounds, may be followed by a sound of any other pitch, or any combination of such sounds, providing the time interval between them is properly gauged; and this is true for any series of sounds, chords or arpeggios.

This is a physical fact in color and in design as well.

A superimposed metronomic time or space pattern is intolerable today in verse, in town planning or in music.

Bartok sought new musical order in the rhythms and patterns of folk speech.

The interval is the means of epiphany or revelation.

It is the release which Hopkins called Sprung Rhythm.

It is the instrument of anological intuition of Being.

It is the dynamic symmetry of tensions among proportions which yields the Golden Section in space or time.

The Munsell Color Sphere does not take us into the inclusive auditory world its form implies. The spectator is left outside with one facet of color at a time.

True color experience derives from involvement of all the senses at once—synesthesia.

Man lives in such a sphere of jazzed up rag-time sensuous be-bop.

To bring order into this jangled sphere man must find its center.

A valid color sphere would have the spectator in the center.

Sensation of pure color is only possible through the acoustics of the word.

In actual visual experience of color, perception changes constantly because of factors of background and eye fatigue.

Therefore symmetrical balance and harmony are possible only when man is at the center of the sphere.

In the model sphere colors of strong hue and chroma
will be at the center of the sphere, retreating colors further away.

Today our engineering and town planning permit the extension of such model spheres to every area of physical experience at ground level or from the air.

The color sphere or modulor is cued in with the auditory space of our oral, electronic culture.

THE CITY

no longer exists, except as a cultural ghost for tourists. Any highway eatery with its TV set, newspaper, and magazine is as cosmopolitan as New York or Paris.

The METROPOLIS today is a classroom; the ads are its teachers. The classroom is an obsolete detention home, a feudal dungeon.

The metropolis is OBSOLETE

ASK THE ARMY

The handwriting is on the celluloid walls of Hollywood; the Age of Writing has passed. We must invent a NEW METAPHOR, restructure our thoughts and feelings. The new media are not bridges between man and nature: they are nature.

Gutenberg made all history SIMULTANEOUS: the transportable book brought the world of the dead into the space of the gentleman's library; the telegraph brought the entire world of the living to the workman's breakfast table.

NOBODY yet knows the language inherent in the new technological culture; we are all deaf-blind mutes in terms of the new situation. Our most impressive words and thoughts betray us by referring to the previously existent, not to the present.

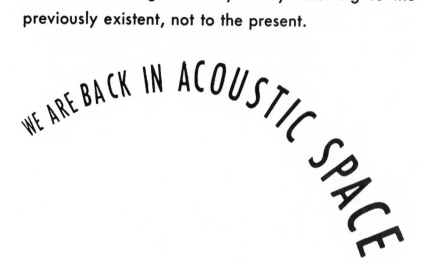

WE ARE BACK IN ACOUSTIC SPACE

We begin again to structure the primordial feelings and emotions from which 3000 years of literacy divorced us.

Counterblast, 1954

POETIC IMAGERY

ONLY a part of an author's imagery comes from his reading. It comes from the whole of his sensitive life since early childhood. Why, for all of us, out of all that we have heard, seen, felt, in a lifetime, do certain images recur, charged with emotion, rather than others? ...

AUDITORY IMAGINATION

What I call the "auditory imagination" is the feeling for syllable and rhythm, penetrating far below the conscious levels of thought and feeling, invigorating every word; sinking to the most primitive and forgotten, returning to the origin and bringing something back, seeking the beginning and the end. It works through meanings, certainly or not without meanings in the ordinary sense, and fuses the old and obliterated and the trite, the current, and the new and surprising, the most ancient and the most civilized mentality.

T. S. ELIOT (From *The Use of Poetry and the Use of Criticism,* 1933)

THE WORLD OF PAPER

We take paper for granted.
We use it and forget it.
We use more than 300 pounds per person every year.
In Asia, the use of paper is less than 9 pounds a year per person.
Every scrap must be salvaged.
It must be used again and again if that is possible.
A torn magazine is a bonanza.
This is serious in the economy and progress of underdeveloped areas.

It is hard to make educational progress when paper is not available.

It is hard to hold an election if there is inadequate paper upon which to print the ballots.

New York Times, Sunday, July 7, '57

Available North American horse power per person . . 800
Available European horse power per person   27
Available Asian horse power per person   2

Buckminster Fuller

We cannot pretend to think *for* others unless we think *with* them . . . "art" involves the whole of the active life, and pre-supposes the contemplative. The disintegration of a people's art is the destruction of their life, by which they are reduced to the proletarian status . . . in the interests of a foreign trader, whose is the *profit*.
We are proud of our museums where we display a way of living that we have made impossible.

A. K. Coomaraswamy

GAUDIER BRZESKA

The sphere is thrown through space, it is the soul and object of the vortex—

The intensity of existence had revealed to man a truth of form — his manhood was strained to the highest potential—his energy brutal—

HIS OPULENT MATURITY WAS CONVEX

Religion pushed him to the use of the

VERTICAL which inspires awe.

His gods were self made, he built them in his image, and RETAINED AS MUCH OF THE SPHERE AS COULD ROUND THE SHARPNESS OF THE PARALLELOGRAM.

M. C. Escher

215

The SEMITIC VORTEX was the lust of war. The men of Elam, of Assur, of Bebel and the Kheta, the men of Armenia and those of Canaan had to slay each other cruelly for the possession of fertile valleys. Their gods sent them the vertical direction, the earth, the SPHERE.

They elevated the sphere in a splendid squatness and created the HORIZONTAL.

From Sargon to Amir-nasir-pal men built man-headed bulls in horizontal flight-wald. Men flayed their captives alive and erected howling lions: THE ELONGATED SPHERE BUTTRESSED ON FOUR COLUMNS, and their kingdoms disappeared.

Oral McLuhan

12

Address at Vision 65

I bring you greetings from the country of the DEW line, or early warning system. Canada carries perhaps a potential role as an early warning system. As the United States becomes a world environment, Canada might serve very well as an early warning system for culture and technology, and on many levels. But this is a whimsy.

We had a delightful story at lunch about the French actor who expressed the delight he had on the stage because of its permitting him to kiss ladies' hands. He said: "You know, you have to begin somewhere." The companion piece to that one is somewhat closer to my predicament — the mosquito in the nudist colony who said: "I don't know where to begin."

The world of humor, as a system of communications, is one that has occasionally interested people, and we live in a time when joke styles have changed very rapidly. I am told by my own children that the latest form of joke concerns the "Poles," and they gave me as an example: "Alexander Graham Kowalski — the first 'telephone Pole.'" This kind of humor is like the slightly older form of the elephant joke and the kind that the computer programmers enjoy — "What is purple and hums?" Of course, the answer is: "An electric grape." "And, why does it hum?" "It

doesn't know the words." This kind of joke appeals enormously to youngsters today.

If you notice, the tendency in these kinds of jokes, or gags, is for the story line to be stripped off. They tend to be deprived of the old story line, and in its place you have a capsule, a compressed overlay, of stories. In fact, there are usually two stories in these little jokes, simultaneously. The older-fashioned jokes had a straight story line. Steve Allen has a theory that the funnyman is a man with a grievance. In French Canada there are a good many jokes going around these days that are by way of being grievance stories. One of them is this: A mouse being pursued around the house by the house cat finally finds a little spot in the floor to creep in and hide. After a while, everything seems quiet, until suddenly there is a kind of "Arf-Arf-Bow-Wow" noise and the mouse feels the dog must have frightened the cat away, so it pops up and the cat grabs it and chews it down. As he chews the mouse down, he says: "You know, it pays to be bilingual." That is the old kind of square joke with a story line around it.

The new stories tend to be much more compressed and on two levels at once, like the sort of *Finnegans Wake* phrase: "though he might have been more humble, there's no police like Holmes." That kind of compressed double-plot story is a very interesting development; and, if you notice, great successes like *My Fair Lady* usually have two plots. One of them is explicit. One is perfectly obvious, like the story of Liza Doolittle acquiring the King's English and becoming a great social success. But there is a subplot in *My Fair Lady* that is much more potent and much concealed. The subplot would seem to be "how to succeed in business without really trying."

The subplot is an environmental one — it includes everybody. The main plot, the little story about Liza Doolittle, appeals to a relatively small group and is not a new story. It is a Cinderella story. But the story of "how to succeed in business without really trying," or, in other words, how to become a huge success by sheer gimmickry, would seem to be the life story, the inside life story, of a very large proportion of the top executives of our world. In other words, *My Fair Lady* has this environmental subplot that is implicit and unverbalized, and that includes the audience. With the subplot, the audience goes right into action. With the main plot, they simply sit outside looking on.

There is a subplot in the famous Hathaway shirt advertisement of the baron with the black patch on his eye. The main plot is simply Hathaway shirts. The subplot, the one that really includes the whole audience, is the black patch which bespeaks the world of aristocratic intrigue, hunts for hidden treasure, and many other mysterious dimensions, all expressed instantaneously by the black patch. The subplot world, the subenvironment, is really that which includes the audience, and it is the power to effect this kind of inclusion that is the mystery of humor, and that explains the rapid change of humor styles — because one style joke will not accommodate a very large proportion of the audience from one period to another.

There is a new book by Jacques Ellul, the Frenchman. The book has recently been published in English. It is called *Propaganda*. Ellul's book has as a theme that propaganda is not ideology; it is not the Hathaway shirt story. It is rather the hidden, but complete, image of a social way of life that is embedded in the social technologies and social patterns, as it is embedded in, say, the English language. Ellul would say the action of the English language, the action of the French language — *that* is propaganda. That presents a total environmental image to men, whereas the ideologies, the explicit verbalized messages, are relatively insignificant compared to this overall image. Ellul's theme in a word is this: Propaganda consists in using all the available means of one's society to create a way of life. Whatever that way may be, is propaganda — that is action that is total and invisible, and invincible.

This is another mysterious feature about the new and potent environment we now live in. The really total and saturating environments are invisible. The ones we notice are quite fragmentary and insignificant compared to the ones we don't see. The English language, for example, as it shapes our perceptions and all our habits of thought and feeling, is quite unperceived by the users of the English language. It becomes much more perceptible if we switch suddenly to

French. But in the case of environments that are created by new technologies, while they are quite invisible in themselves, they do make visible the old environments. We can always see the Emperor's old clothes, but not his new ones.

I want to use this theme a little bit for our purposes here this afternoon. If the new environment is invisible, it does serve to make very visible the receding environment. The obvious and simple illustration of that is the late show. On the late show on television we see old movies. They are very visible; they are very noticeable. Since television, the movie form has been reprocessed. The form of movie that once was environmental and invisible has been reprocessed into an art form, and, indeed, a highly valued art form. Indirectly, the new art films of our time have received an enormous amount of encouragement and impact from the television form. The television form has remained quite invisible — and will only become visible at the moment that television itself becomes the content of a new medium. The next medium, whatever it is — it may be the extension of consciousness — will include television as its content, not as its environment, and will transform television into an art form; but this process whereby every new technology creates an environment that translates the old or preceding technology into an art form, or into something exceedingly noticeable, affords so many fascinating examples I can only mention a few.

There is a wonderful book by Eric Havelock that I delight to refer to, a book called *Preface to Plato*. It is a study of what happened in Greece before Plato. "Preface" means how did the Greeks educate each other before writing? What were the processes by which they educated their young people before Plato? He calls this process that preceded Plato "the tribal encyclopedia." The young were mesmorized by the poets. The poets were operative purveyors of practical wisdom and council. Homer, Hesiod and the rest actually provided the young people with models of perception and models of behavior and strategies for overcoming all sorts of difficulties and obstacles. The great Odysseus was above all a Greek hero because of his resourcefulness — his unfailing initiative and skill in every type of opaque and threatening situation. Havelock describes this education that went on by the poets, the tribal encyclopedia, and then describes the advent of writing and the complete change that came over education as a result of that. With the coming of writing, education shifted from the memorizing of the tribal encyclopedia that made education a sort of "singing commercial." With writing came the classification of knowledge, the ideas, the categories; and Plato's detestation of the poets was mainly a rivalry with the old educational establishment which had naturally failed to come to grips with the new technology of the written word.

Havelock's book has a fascinating quality, because it really tells the story of what we are going through right now. We are playing that tape (the situation he describes) backward — the change from tribal man to individual man. As we move into the world of integral, computerized knowledge, mere classification becomes secondary and inadequate to the speeds with which data can now be processed. As data can be processed very rapidly we move literally into the world of pattern recognition, out of the world of mere data classification. One way of putting this is to say that our children today live in a world in which the environment itself is made of electric information. The environment of the young person today is typically and principally electrically fashioned information. The young person today is a data processor on a very large scale. Some people have estimated that the young person, the infant and the small child, growing up in our world today works harder than any child ever did in any previous human environment — only the work he has to perform is that of data processing. The small child in twentieth-century America does more data processing — more work — than any child in any previous culture in the history of the world, according to Jacques Ellul, among others. We haven't really cottoned on to the fact that our children work furiously, processing data in an electrically structured information world; and when these children enter a classroom — elementary school — they encounter a situation that is very bewildering to them. The youngster today, stepping out of his nursery or TV environment, goes to school and

enters a world where the information is scarce but is ordered and structured by fragmented, classified patterns, subjects, schedules. He is utterly bewildered because he comes out of this intricate and complex integral world of electric information and goes into this nineteenth-century world of classified information that still characterizes the educational establishment. The educational establishment is a nineteenth-century world of classified data much like any factory set up with its inventories and assembly lines. The young today are baffled because of this extraordinary gap between these two worlds.

Paul Goodman has a book recording one aspect of the situation. It is titled *Growing Up Absurd*. To grow up today is to be absurd, because we live in two worlds, and neither one of them inclines us to grow up. I have a friend who once pointed out to me something that struck me with great force. He said, "You know, the only work that royalty has to do is to grow up, and for a young prince or princess growing up and acquiring all the types of knowledge and language necessary for survival is a fantastically difficult job." It would seem that we have paradoxically created on a democratic scale a situation for royalty. Our youngsters today are mainly confronted with the problem of just growing up — that is our new work — and it is total. That is why it is not a job; it is a role. Growing up has become, in the age of electrically processed information, the major task of mankind. We still have our eyes fixed on the rearview mirror looking firmly and squarely at the job that is receding into the nineteenth-century past. The job that we feel we should have by rights belongs to the old mechanical technology of classified data and of fragmented tasks. Yet we are now surrounded by a new environment, of integrated tasks, integrated knowledge, and it demands pattern recognition. The kind of contrast between those two situations creates an absurdity that has launched the theater of the absurd. The theater of the absurd itself is postulated on this kind of dichotomy between these two cultures that never seem to get any closer together.

I have started then with the theme of the imperceptibility of new environments, and that what is perceptible in typical human situations is the old environment. It is plain that the content of Plato's work, of his new written form, was the old oral dialogue. The content of the print technology of the Renaissance was medieval writing. For two hundred years after printing there was hardly anything printed except medieval texts — think of poor Don Quixote! Don Quixote was the victim of the current Renaissance craze for medieval comic books or medieval romances. This went on for another century. What got printed in the main, for two centuries and more after the printing press, was the medieval tale, medieval Books of Hours, medieval liturgies and medieval philosophy. Shakespeare lived in the Renaissance world, and the content of Shakespeare's plays, as everybody knows, is medieval. His

politics, and his world picture — the Elizabethan world picture — present a medieval world picture. They too looked back firmly and squarely at the receding medieval forms. But the Middle Ages were the late show for the Renaissance. By the nineteenth century the Renaissance had come into full view. As the industrial environment formed, this progressive time firmly and squarely confronted the Renaissance. The content of the nineteenth-century mind was the Renaissance; the content of the twentieth-century mind is the nineteenth century. We are obsessed with it. It is not as easy to banish that mirage as one might wish. But one of the most bizarre growths in this development occurred when railways and factories came in. The content of this new industrial, mechanical environment was the old agrarian world, and there was this upsurge of awareness and delight in the old agrarian environment of arts and crafts — the pastoral world. This discovery of the receding age was called the "romantic movement."

The sudden discovery of nature was made possible by the railway and the factories that were so very different from nature. The romantic movement was a product of the mechanical age by way of a contrapuntal environment. It was not a repeat of the mechanical age; rather it was the content of the mechanical age, and the artists and poets turned to processing the old agrarian world into delightful landscapes and delightful pastoral poems. This was in turn altered by the rise of electric technology that went around the old mechanical world of a few decades ago. When the electric technology jacketed the machine world, when circuitry took over from the wheel, and the circuit went around the old factory, the machine became an art form. Abstract art, for example, is very much a result of the electric age going around the mechanical one.

In our time we can see that pop art consists in taking the outer environment and putting it in the art gallery, or indoors somewhere, suggesting that we have reached the stage where we have begun to process the environment itself as an art form. We may be catching up with ourselves. When we begin to deal with our actually existing new environment as an art form, we may be reaching that stage the planet itself seems to have reached. With satellite and electronic antennae as probes, the planet ceases in a way to be the human environment and becomes a satellite itself — a probe into space, creating new space and environments for the planet. If the planet itself has thus become the content of a new space created by its satellites, and its electronic extensions, if the planet has become the content and not the environment, then we can confidently expect to see the next few decades devoted to turning the planet into an art form. We will caress and shape and pattern every facet, every contour of this planet as if it were a work of art, just as surely as we put a new environment around it. Even as the Romantics began to deal with the old pastoral, agrarian world as an art form when machinery was new, so we will now

begin to deal with the planet itself as a work of art.

I think the computer is admirably suited to the artistic programming of such an environment, of taking over the task of programming the environment itself as a work of art, instead of programming the content as a work of art. This situation suggests some considerable changes in the human state. It suggests that the role of art in the past has been not so much the making of environments as making of counterenvironments, or antienvironments. Flaubert, a hundred years ago, said: "Style is a way of seeing." Ever since that time the painters and artists have been quite conscious of their jobs as teaching people how to perceive the world they live in. "It is above all that you may see," said Conrad, apropos the meaning of his work. The training of perception upon the otherwise unheeded environment became the basis of experimentation in what is called modern art and poetry. The artist, instead of expressing himself in various patterns and packages of message, turned his senses and the work of art to the business of probing the environment. The symbolists, for example, broke up the old romantic landscape into fragments that they used as probes to explore the urban and metropolitan environments. Then they turned to probing the inner life of man with the same verbal instruments in hand. Instead of using the verbal as a way of expression, they turned it inward for the purpose of exploring and discovering the contours of the inner life.

The psychiatrist took over in the same pattern and began to erode the unconscious. If the unconscious has an important and irreplaceable function in human affairs, we had best look to it — it is being eroded at a furious pace; it is being invaded by dazzling investigations and insights; and we could quickly reach a stage in which we had no unconscious. This would be like dreaming awake. Such may well be the prophetic meaning of *Finnegans Wake* by James Joyce: his idea, among many others, that tribal man lived a dream and modern man is "back again Finnegan" into the cycle of the tribal involvement, but this time awake. This possibility that we are actively engaged in liquidating the unconscious for the first time in history, behooves us to pay some attention to how it is structured, and to what function it serves in human affairs. It may prove to be indispensable to sanity.

One overall consideration for our time and at a conference like this is to consider how, in the past, the environment was invisible in its operation upon us. Environments are not just containers, but are processes that change the content totally. New media are new environments. That is why the media are the message. One related consideration is that antienvironments, or counterenvironments created by the artist, are indispensable means of becoming aware of the environment in which we live and of the environments we create for ourselves technically. John Cage has a book called *Silence* in which, very early in the book, he explains that silence consists of all of the unintended noises of the environment. All the things that are going on all the time in any environment, but things that were never programmed or intended — that is silence. The unheeded world is silence. That is what James Joyce calls thunder in the *Wake*. In the *Wake* all the consequences of social change — all of the disturbances and metamorphoses resulting from technological change — create a vast environmental roar or thunder that is yet completely inaudible. It is like heat that in organic or other systems creates "noise." If the environment or process of change gets going at a clip consistent with electronic information movement, it becomes very easy to perceive social patterns for the first time in human history. In the pre-Electric Age patterns were imperceptible because change occurred just slowly enough to be invisible. Was it Bertrand Russell who asked, if we were in a bath whose temperature rose half a degree an hour, how would we know when to scream? The pattern recognition that is quite impossible during processes of slow change, becomes quite easy when the same changes are speeded up even to movie or cinematic levels. So, the artist, as a creator of antienvironments, or counterenvironments, created to permit perception of environments, has a very peculiar role in our society.

The artist as a maker of antienvironments becomes the enemy in society. He doesn't seem to be very well adjusted. He does not accept the environment with all its brainwashing functions with any passivity whatever;

he just turns upon it and reflects his antienvironmental perceptions upon it. The artist, for the past century, has increasingly fused or merged with the criminal in popular estimation, as he has become antienvironmental. Since Baudelaire, the artist, the sleuth — the Sherlock Holmes type, the James Bond type, the Raymond Chandler-Marlowe type — these men have turned a vision onto society that is very antienvironmental, very self-conscious, and the artist has mysteriously been hybridized with the criminal or the anti-social figure. By the same token, and I am just beginning to think about this while I stand here, crime has become obsessional in our society as a form of artistic expression. This is not lost on children. The delinquent child is often a very bright and keen, perceptive person. It is not lost on him that the kind of overwhelming, brainwashing forces of his environment really call for a little antisocial or artistic and exploratory activity. The child, by delinquent behavior, is aping the exploratory artist. Dostoevski was aware of this in *Crime and Punishment*. He saw the criminal as a sort of cross between the saint and the artist.

Our newspapers create an information environment, yet without crime as content we would not be able to perceive the environment. The newspapers have to have bad news, otherwise there would be only ads, or good news. Without bad news we could not discern the ground rules of the environment. This does not necessarily mean the environment is bad, but it means its operation upon us is total and ruthless. The environment is always the brainwasher, so that the well-adjusted person, by definition, has been brainwashed. He is adjusted. He's had it. There is a book by Erwin Straus recently that throws new light on Pavlov's operations (the Russian psychologist). He didn't get his conditioning effects by means of stimuli or signals to his experimental subjects. Rather he did it by environmental controls. He put them in environments in which there was no sound, in which the heat and other sensory controls were very carefully adjusted and maintained steadily. Pavlov discovered that if you tried to condition animals in an ordinary environment, it did not work. The environment is the real conditioner, not the stimulus or the content. So the Pavlov story needs to be turned around in order to be observed; but the role of crime as a way of perceiving society is a mysterious one. I am not going to make any moral observations on it whatever. It has increasingly pushed the artist and the scientist into the role of being an enemy.

Let me resume a moment. We have, in the Electric Age, come suddenly to the end of the Neolithic Age. After a good many thousands of years of specialized habits and technology and fragmentary toolmaking, we discovered the electric circuits. It is the circuit that has ended the Neolithic Age. The Neolithic Age, just like its ultimate phase, the factory age in the nineteenth century, was dedicated to specialism, fragmentation, and extensions of this or that limb of man. With circuitry we have, instead of extensions of hand, or foot, or back, or arm, a kind of involvement of the whole nervous system, an extension of the nervous system itself, a most profoundly involving operation. The form and function of the telegraph press can help our observations here. One of the mysterious things about newspapers is that the items in them have no connection except the dateline. The only connecting factor in any newspaper is the dateline, and it is this dateline that enables us to enter the world of the news, as it were, by going through the looking glass. Just as Alice in Wonderland went through the looking glass, when you enter the world of the telegraph or of the circuit, you really become involved in the information process. When you enter through the dateline, when you enter your newspaper, you begin to put together the news — you are producer. And this is a most important fact to understand about the electric time, for it is an age of decentralism. It is hard to face this. We still like to look in the rearview mirror. We still tend to think of the Electric Age as a mechanical age. It is in effect organic and totally decentralist. But the reader of the news, when he goes through his dateline apertures, enters the news world as a maker. There is no "meaning" in the news except what we make — there is no connection between any of the items except the instant dimension of electric circuitry. News items are like the parts of the symbolist structure. The reader is the co-creator, in a newspaper as in a detective story, in which the

reader has to make the plot as he goes. The detective story was one of the very first anticipations of electric technology. Edgar Allan Poe was a considerable innovator in the matter of antienvironments for the Electric Age.

The newspaper is also very much like the world of the delightful films we have been seeing by Mr. Van Der Beek; the world of multiscreen projection is the world of the newspaper where umpteen news stories come at you without any connection, and without connected themes. So, what the new film is doing is stripping off the story line in favor of this mosaic pattern of simultaneous projection, which is very much in accordance with electric technology. It is the film world receiving its baptism by electricity. This hybridizing, this crossing of one technology with another, goes on all the time. The internal combustion engine was a wedding of the old machine and the electric circuit. Perhaps the most startling and most upsetting electric innovation is coming in the matter of xerox and xerography.

Xerography is bringing a reign of terror into the world of publishing because it means that every reader can become both author and publisher. It totally decentralizes the long centralized publishing process. Authorship and readership alike can become production-oriented under xerography. Anybody can take any book apart, insert parts of other books and other materials of his own interest, and make his own book in a relatively fast time. Any teacher can take any ten textbooks on any subject and custom-make a different one by simply xeroxing a chapter from this one and a chapter from that one. The problem is copyrighting, and Congress is now pondering these problems — how to protect the old technology from the new technology by legislation. It will not succeed. There is no possible protection from technology except by technology. When you create a new environment with one phase of a technology, you have to create an antienvironment with the next. But xerography is electricity invading the world of typography, and it means a total revolution in this old sphere, or this old technology, a revolution that is being felt in the classroom itself.

I invite you to consider that perhaps the best way of estimating the impact of any new environmental technology is to notice what happens to the older technologies. You can never perceive the impact of any new technology directly, but it can be done in the manner of Perseus looking in the mirror at Medusa. It has to be done indirectly. You have to perceive the consequences of the new environment on the old environment before you know what the new environment is. You cannot tell what it is until you have seen it do things to the old one. The need, however, to understand the processes and changes brought about by new technology gets strong as the technology does. Therefore, in terms of design or style or shaping of perception, a conference of this sort is very timely in bringing attention to the tremendous new role of design in shaping human perception. "Style is a way of seeing,"

as Flaubert put it.

We are engaged in Toronto in carrying out a unique experiment — it is far too big for us — we need a lot of help and a lot of collaboration. We are carrying out an experiment to establish what are the sensory thresholds of the entire population of Toronto. That is, we are attempting to measure, quantitatively, the levels at which the entire population prefers to set its visual, auditory, tactual, visceral and other senses as a matter of daily use and preference — how much light, how much heat, how much sound, how much movement — as a threshold level. Anything that alters a sensory threshold alters the outlook and experience of a whole society. The sensory thresholds change without warning or indications to the users thereof, for it is new technological environments that shift these levels. We are concerned with what shifts occur in a sensory threshold when some new form comes in. What happens to our sensory lives with the advent of television, the motor car or radio? If we can establish this sort of knowledge quantitatively, we will have something that the computer can really bite into. A child is a genius till he is five because all his senses are in active interrelation. Then his senses shift. The computer will be in a position to carry out orchestrated programming for the sensory life of entire populations. It can be programmed in terms of their total needs, not just in terms of the messages they should be hearing, but in terms of the total experience as picked up and patterned by all the senses at once. For example, if you were to write an ideal sensory program of Indonesia or some area of the world that you wanted to leapfrog across a lot of old technology, this would be possible if you knew in the first place its present sensory thresholds and, second, if you had established what kind of sensory effect a given technology like radio or literacy had upon sensory life as a whole.

On this continent the sensory levels have changed drastically since television. The visual component in our lives has been dropped dramatically and the visceral, the kinetic, the auditory modes of response have shot up to compensate for the drop in the visual component of our culture. This sensory shift has changed the taste in design, in packaging, in every form of entertainment, as well as in every form of vehicle, food and in clothing.

The "Beatles" stare at us with eloquent messages of changed sensory modes for our whole population, and yet people merely think how whimsical, how bizarre, how grotesque. The Beatles are trying to tell us by the antienvironment they present just how we have changed and in what ways.

To repeat, and to make toward a conclusion, the effect of any new environment — every new technology creates a new environment just as the motor car does, as the railway did, or as radio and airplanes do — any new technology changes the whole human environment, and envelops and includes the old environments. It turns these old environments into "art forms" — old Model T's become pre-cious art objects, as do old coach lamps, old anything. The world of Camp, for example, is the world of the nursery of thirty years ago being turned into a conscious art form. By simply taking into the shopwindow old toys, old ornaments, and the things Mom used to wear thirty years ago, you turn them into art forms and you have C-A-M-P, this mysterious new archetype.

The new environment is always creating new archetypes, new art forms, out of the old environment. This process can provide invaluable information for those who want to have some autonomy in controlling their destinies and their environments. I think we are rapidly moving toward a time when we might say, with full awareness of causes and effects: "In our present sensory condition, I don't think we could properly accommodate two hundred more lines on TV." Color TV will considerably change the whole sensory life of the public. It is a much more tactual form than black and white. But what would happen to the North American world if we did as the French and Germans have done; if instead of four hundred and fifty lines on our television, we were to put eight hundred? The results might be most gratifying to the educational establishment. If we raised the visual intensity or the visual component of the TV image, it might serve enormously to ease the transition from the old mechanical age to the electronic age.

What would be the chances of getting an experimental study of such a change in our time? I don't know.

Lindegren would say the chances were not good. Anything that is serious is out of bounds. I think it was David Riesman who said no social scientist would ever study anything important. To be scientific you must study the fragmental, the insignificant. How else can you give assurance of your precision and concentration? Perhaps this attitude explains why, in our world, we tend to substitute moral indignation for observation. Moral vehemence is proof positive of superior perception. For example, we now experience simultaneously the dropout and the teach-in. The two forms are correlative. They belong together. The teach-in represents an attempt to shift education from instruction to discovery, from brainwashing students to brainwashing instructors. It is a big dramatic reversal. Vietnam, as the content of the teach-in, is a very small, misleading Red Herring. It really has nothing to do with the teach-in as such anymore than with the dropout. The dropout represents a rejection of nineteenth-century technology as manifested in our educational establishments. The teach-in represents a creative effort to switch the educational process to discovery, from package to process. As with the Hawthorne experiment, its strategy is to use the audience and the student body as work force — one of the great things that is happening under electric conditions. As the audience becomes participant, involved in the total electric drama, it can become a major work force; and the classroom, as much as any other place, can become a scene in which the audience can perform an enormous amount of work.

The audience as work force has unlimited possibilities. Suppose we were to brief fifty million people on some extremely difficult problems facing top-level scientists. Inevitably, some dozens, hundreds, of the fifty million audience would see instantly through any type of opaque problem, even on the highest scientific levels. Robert Oppenheimer is fond of saying that "there are children playing in the street who could solve some of my top problems in physics, because they have modes of sensory perception that I lost long ago." There are enormous possibilities for using an audience as work force in scientific research, or any other type of research. It is simply that we insist on beaming instruction at them instead of allowing them to participate in the action of discovery.

For example, when printing was new, it created what was known as the Public. In the sixteenth century and after, Montaigne's phrase, *"la publique,"* came into use. The sixteenth century created the public as a new environment. This completely altered politics and altered all social arrangements in education, in work and in every other area. Electric circuitry did not create the public, it created the mass, meaning an environment of information that involved everybody in everybody. Now, to a man brought up in the environment of the public, the mass audience is a horror — it is a mess. In the same way, the public was a many-headed monster to a feudal aristocrat. He never bothered to study its structure any more than we study the mass. Circuitry brings people into relation with each other in total involvement which creates the possibility of dialogue and discovery on an enormous scale. The structure of the public had less of such possibility. The public consisted of fragmented separate individuals with separate points of view. The public was an additive structure. The mass audience is a quite different structure, enormously richer — enormously more capable of integrated creative activity than the old public was. All the old public could do was to enunciate private points of view which they clashed into each other furiously. At the present moment in Canada, if you want a DEW line warning, we are having an election in which no one is interested. There is no involvement because the old political forms do not permit participation. You simply register a fragmented, unrelated-to-anything vote. The population has dropped out of the political setup. Yet when these changing structures are studied they yield enormous meaning.

Let me suggest that it may be possible to write programs for changes, not only in consciousness but in unconsciousness in the future. One could write a kind of science fiction story of the future of consciousness, the future of the unconsciousness, "the future of an erosion." The future of consciousness is already assuming a very different pattern, a very different character. The future of the child is changing beneath our gaze. The small child was an invention of the seventeenth century, according to various historians like Philippe Aries; historically, the child came out of the seventeenth century, did not exist, so to speak, in Shakespeare's day. The child had, up until that time, been so completely merged in the adult world that there was nothing that could be called childhood in our sense at all. And so it is with the family, another seventeenth-century discovery. Suddenly today the child is merging with the total adult environment under electric information processing, and is disappearing from the scene as a child.

The future of child may resemble the future of city. The city under conditions of very rapid movement takes on a totally new meaning. The motor car has served to destroy the city as it existed under the railway conditions. The future of city may be very much like a world's fair — a place to show off new technology — not a place of work or residence whatever.

It is also fascinating to consider the future of language. We know right now some very important structural things about language that are new. The future of language will not be as a system of classified data or meanings. The future of language as a complex structure which can be learned without learning the words at all, is a possibility that the computer presents increasingly. A child does not learn language as a series of meanings of words. He learns language as he learns to walk, or to hear, or to see. He learns language as a way of feeling and exploring his environment. Therefore, he is totally involved. He learns very fast because of this enormous sensuous involvement and the resulting motivation. It will be possible in this generation, I hope, to program the environment in such a way that we can learn a second language as we learned our mother tongue, rapidly and totally, as a means of perception and of discovery. The future of language presents the possibility of a world without words, a wordless, intuitive world, like a technological extension of the action of consciousness.

I had a friend visiting from Harvard the other day who said: "You see, my generation does not have goals." (He is a young architect.) "We are not goal-oriented. We just want to know what is going on." Now that means not a point of view but total ecological awareness. I was reading aloud from *Finnegans Wake* for a moment, and he said: "When you take L.S.D., the whole world takes on a multidimensional and multisensuous character of discovery, and when I listened to *Finnegans Wake* I got the same experience as L.S.D." (Perhaps *Finnegan* would be safer, and also more rewarding.)

The point this person was making was that it is absurd to ask us to pursue fragmentary goals in an electric world that is organized integrally and totally. The young today reject goals — they want roles — R-O-L-E-S — that is, involvement. They want total involvement. They don't want fragmented, specialized goals, or jobs. Now that is not easy to explain or to prescribe for.

I have touched upon the future of language, the future of consciousness, the future of the city, the future, perhaps, finally, of work. As a form of organized human activity, work is undergoing the most drastic changes of all; and there is nobody in the world who knows more about this than the great man sitting down here in front of me who has had a most paralyzing, I am afraid, effect upon my endeavors this afternoon, Professor Buckminster Fuller. I thought of a phrase I came across recently, "Home is where you hang your head." Now, to have in front of me in an audience a man like Buckminster Fuller makes me feel terribly at home in that sense. I really feel shatteringly humble. I am grateful to you for your most genial attention. Thank you.

13

PLAYBOY INTERVIEW

A candid conversation with the high priest of popcult and metaphysician of media

In 1961, the name of Marshall McLuhan was unknown to everyone but his English students at the University of Toronto — and a coterie of academic admirers who followed his abstruse articles in small-circulation quarterlies. But then came two remarkable books — *The Gutenberg Galaxy* (1962) and *Understanding Media* (1964) — and the graying professor from Canada's western hinterlands soon found himself characterized by the *San Francisco Chronicle* as "the hottest academic property around." He has since won a world-wide following for his brilliant — and frequently baffling — theories about the impact of the media on man; and his name has entered the French language as *mcluhanisme*, a synonym for the world of pop culture.

Though his books are written in a difficult style — at once enigmatic, epigrammatic and overgrown with arcane literary and historic allusions — the revolutionary ideas lurking in them have made McLuhan a best-selling author. Despite protests from a legion of outraged scholastics and old-guard humanists who claim that McLuhan's ideas range from demented

to dangerous, his free-for-all theorizing has attracted the attention of top executives at General Motors (who paid him a handsome fee to inform them that automobiles were a thing of the past), Bell Telephone (to whom he explained that they didn't really understand the function of the telephone) and a leading package-design house (which was told that packages will soon be obsolete). Anteing up $5000, another huge corporation asked him to predict — via closed-circuit television — what their own products will be used for in the future; and Canada's turned-on Prime Minister Pierre Trudeau engages him in monthly bull sessions designed to improve his television image.

McLuhan's observations — "probes," he prefers to call them — are riddled with such flamboyantly undecipherable aphorisms as "The electric light is pure information" and "People don't actually read newspapers — they get into them every morning like a hot bath." Of his own work, McLuhan has remarked: "I don't pretend to understand it. After all, my stuff is very difficult." Despite his convoluted syntax, flashy metaphors and word-playful one-liners, however, McLuhan's basic thesis is relatively simple.

McLuhan contends that all media — in and of themselves and regardless of the messages they communicate — exert a compelling influence on man and society. Prehistoric, or tribal, man existed in a harmonious balance of the senses, perceiving the world equally through hearing, smell, touch, sight and taste. But technological innovations are extensions of human abilities and senses that alter this sensory balance — an alteration that, in turn, inexorably reshapes the society that created the technology. According to McLuhan, there have been three basic technological innovations: the invention of the phonetic alphabet, which jolted tribal man out of his sensory balance and gave dominance to the eye; the introduction of movable type in the 16th Century, which accelerated this process; and the invention of the telegraph in 1844, which heralded an electronics revolution that will ultimately retribalize man by restoring his sensory balance. McLuhan has made it his business to explain and extrapolate the repercussions of this electronic revolution.

For his efforts, critics have dubbed him "the Dr. Spock of pop culture," "the guru of the boob tube," a "Canadian Nkrumah who has joined the assault on reason," a "metaphysical wizard possessed by a spatial sense of madness," and "the high priest of popthink who conducts a Black Mass for dilettantes before the altar of historical determinism." Amherst professor Benjamin DeMott observed: "He's swinging, switched on, with it and NOW. And wrong."

But as Tom Wolfe has aptly inquired, "What if he is *right*? Suppose he *is* what he sounds like — the most important thinker since Newton, Darwin, Freud, Einstein and Pavlov?" Social historian Richard Kostelanetz contends that "the most extraordinary quality of McLuhan's mind is that it discerns significance where others see only data, or nothing; he tells us how to measure phenomena previously unmeasurable."

The unperturbed subject of this controversy was born in Edmonton, Alberta, on July 21, 1911. The son of a former actress and a real-estate salesman, McLuhan entered the University of Manitoba intending to become an engineer, but matriculated in 1934 with an M.A. in English literature. Next came a stint as an oarsman and graduate student at Cambridge, followed by McLuhan's first teaching job — at the University of Wisconsin. It was a pivotal experience. "I was confronted with young Americans I was incapable of understanding," he has since remarked. "I felt an urgent need to study their popular culture in order to get through." With the seeds sown, McLuhan let them germinate while earning a Ph.D., then taught at Catholic universities. (He is a devout Roman Catholic convert.)

His publishing career began with a number of articles on standard academic fare; but by the mid-Forties, his interest in popular culture surfaced, and true McLuhan efforts such as "The Psychopathology of *Time* and *Life*" began to appear. They hit book length for the first time in 1951 with the publication of *The Mechanical Bride* — an analysis of the social and psychological pressures generated by the press, radio, movies and advertising — and McLuhan was on his way. Though the book attracted little public notice, it won him the chairmanship of a Ford Foundation seminar on culture and communications and a $40,000 grant, with part of which he started *Explorations*, a small periodical outlet for the seminar's findings. By the late Fifties, his reputation had trickled down to Washington: In 1959, he became director of the Media Project of the National Association of Educational Broadcasters and the United States Office of Education, and the report resulting from this post became the first draft of *Understanding Media*. Since 1963, McLuhan has headed the University of Toronto's Center for Culture and Technology, which until recently consisted entirely of McLuhan's office, but now includes a six-room campus building.

Apart from his teaching, lecturing and administrative duties, McLuhan has become a sort of minor communication industry unto himself. Each month he issues to subscribers a mixed-media report called *The McLuhan Dew-Line*; and, punning on that title, he has also originated a series of recordings called "The Marshall McLuhan Dew-Line Platter-tudes." McLuhan contributed a characteristically mind-expanding essay about the media — "The Reversal of the Overheated Image" — to our December 1968 issue. Also a compulsive collaborator, his literary efforts in tandem with colleagues have included a high school textbook and an analysis of the function of space in poetry and painting. *Counterblast*, his next book, is a manically graphic trip through the land of his theories.

In order to provide our readers with a map of this labyrinthine terra incog-nita, *Playboy* assigned interviewer Eric Norden to visit McLuhan at his spacious new home in the wealthy Toronto suburb of Wychwood Park, where he lives with his wife, Corinne, and five of his six children. (His eldest son lives in New York, where he is completing a book on James Joyce, one of his father's heroes.) Norden reports: "Tall, gray and gangly, with a thin but mobile mouth and an otherwise eminently forgettable face, McLuhan was dressed in an ill-fitting brown tweed suit, black shoes, and a clip-on necktie. As we talked on into the night before a crackling fire, McLuhan expressed his reservations about the interview — indeed, about the printed word itself — as a means of communication, suggesting that the question-and-answer format might impede the in-depth flow of his ideas. I assured him that he would have as much time — and space — as he wished to develop his thoughts."

The result has considerably more lucidity and clarity than McLuhan's readers are accustomed to — perhaps because the Q. and A. format serves to pin him down by counteracting his habit of mercurially changing the subject in mid-stream of consciousness. It is also, we think, a protean and provocative distillation not only of McLuhan's original theories about human progress and social institutions but of his almost immobilizingly intricate style — described by novelist George P. Elliott as "deliberately anti-logical, circular, repetitious, unqualified, gnomic, outrageous" and, even less charitably, by critic Christopher Ricks as "a viscous fog through which loom stumbling metaphors." But other authorities contend that McLuhan's stylistic medium is part and parcel of his message — that the tightly structured "linear" modes of traditional thought and discourse are obsolescent in the new "postliterate" age of the electric media. Norden began the interview with an allusion to McLuhan's favorite electric medium: television.

PLAYBOY: To borrow Henry Gibson's oft-repeated one-line poem on Rowan and Martin's *Laugh-In* — "Marshall McLuhan, what are you doin'?"

McLUHAN: Sometimes I wonder. I'm making explorations. I don't know where they're going to take me. My work is designed for the pragmatic purpose of trying to understand our technological environment and its psychic and social consequences. But my books constitute the *process* rather than the completed product of discovery; my purpose is to employ facts as tentative probes, as means of insight, of pattern recognition, rather than to use them in the traditional and sterile sense of classified data, categories, containers. I want to map new terrain rather than chart old landmarks.

But I've never presented such explorations as revealed truth. As an investigator, I have no fixed point of view, no commitment to any theory — my own or anyone else's. As a matter of fact, I'm completely ready to junk any statement I've ever made about any subject if events don't bear me out, or if I discover it isn't contributing to an understanding of the problem. The better part of my work on media is actually somewhat like a safe-cracker's. I don't know what's inside; maybe it's nothing. I just sit down and start to work. I grope, I listen, I test, I accept and discard; I try out different sequences — until the tumblers fall and the doors spring open.

PLAYBOY: Isn't such a methodology somewhat erratic and inconsistent — if not, as your critics would maintain, eccentric?

McLUHAN: Any approach to environmental problems must be sufficiently flexible and adaptable to encompass the entire environmental matrix, which is in constant flux. I consider myself a generalist, not a specialist who has staked out a tiny plot of study as his intellectual turf and is oblivious to everything else. Actually, my work is a depth operation, the accepted practice in most modern disciplines from psychiatry to metallurgy and structural analysis. Effective study of the media deals not only with the content of the media but with the media themselves and the total cultural environment within which the media function. Only by standing aside from any phenomenon and taking an overview can you discover its operative principles and lines of force. There's really nothing inherently startling or radical about this study — except that for some reason few have had the vision to undertake it. For the past 3500 years of the Western world, the effects of media — whether it's speech, writing, printing, photography, radio or television — have been systematically overlooked by social observers. Even in today's revolutionary electronic age, scholars evidence few signs of modifying this traditional stance of ostrichlike disregard.

PLAYBOY: Why?

McLUHAN: Because all media, from the phonetic alphabet to the computer, are extensions of man that cause deep and lasting changes in him and transform his environment. Such an extension is an intensification, an amplification of an organ, sense or function, and whenever it takes place, the central nervous system appears to institute a self-protective *numbing* of the affected area, insulating and anesthetizing it from conscious awareness of what's happening to it. It's a process rather like that which occurs to the body under shock or stress conditions, or to the mind in line with the Freudian concept of repression. I call this peculiar form of self-hypnosis Narcissus narcosis, a syndrome whereby man remains as unaware of the psychic and social effects of his new technology as a fish of the water it swims in. As a result, precisely at the point where a new media-induced environment becomes all-pervasive and transmogrifies our sensory balance, it also becomes invisible.

This problem is doubly acute today because man must, as a simple survival strategy, become aware of what is happening to him, despite the attendant pain of such comprehension. The fact that he has not done so in this age of electronics is what has made this also the age of anxiety, which in turn has been transformed into its *Doppelgänger* — the therapeutically reactive age of *anomie* and apathy. But despite our self-protective escape mechanisms, the total-field awareness engendered by electronic media is enabling us — indeed, compelling us — to grope toward a consciousness of the unconscious, toward a realization that technology is an extension of our own bodies. We live in the first age when change occurs sufficiently rapidly to make such pattern recognition possible for society at large. Until the present era, this awareness has always been reflected first by the artist, who has had the power — and courage — of the seer to read the language of the outer world and relate it to the inner world.

PLAYBOY: Why should it be the artist rather than the scientist who perceives these relationships and foresees these trends?

McLUHAN: Because inherent in the artist's creative inspiration is the process of subliminally sniffing out environmental change. It's always been the artist who perceives the alterations in man caused by a new medium, who recognizes that the future is the present, and uses his work to prepare the ground for it. But most people, from truck drivers to the literary Brahmins, are still blissfully ignorant of what the media do to them; unaware that because of their pervasive effects on man, it is the medium itself that is the message, *not* the content, and unaware that the medium is also the *massage* — that, all puns aside, it literally works over and saturates and molds and transforms every sense ratio. The content or message of any particular medium has about as much importance as the stenciling on the casing of an atomic bomb. But the ability to perceive media-induced extensions of man, once the province of the artist, is now being expanded as the new environment of electric information makes possible a new degree of perception and critical awareness by nonartists.

PLAYBOY: Is the public, then, at last beginning to perceive the "invisible" contours of these new technological environments?

McLUHAN: People are beginning to understand the nature of their new technology, but not yet nearly enough of them — and not nearly well enough. Most people, as I indicated, still cling to what I call the rearview-mirror view of their world. By this I mean to say that because of the invisibility of any environment during the period of its innovation, man is only consciously aware of the environment that has *preceded* it; in other words, an environment becomes fully visible only when it has been superseded by a new environment; thus we are always one step behind in our view of the world. Because we are benumbed by any new technology — which in turn creates a totally new environment — we tend to make the old environment more visible; we do so by turning it into an art form and by attaching ourselves to the objects and atmosphere that characterized it, just as we've done with jazz, and as we're now doing with the garbage of the mechanical environment via pop art.

The present is always invisible because it's environmental and saturates the whole field of attention so overwhelmingly; thus everyone but the artist, the man of integral awareness, is alive in an earlier day. In the midst of the electronic age of software, of instant information movement, we still believe we're living in the mechanical age of hardware. At the height of the mechanical age, man turned back to earlier centuries in search of "pastoral" values. The Renaissance and the Middle Ages were completely oriented toward Rome; Rome was oriented toward Greece, and the Greeks were oriented toward the pre-Homeric primitives. We reverse the old educational dictum of learning by proceeding from the familiar to the unfamiliar by going from the unfamiliar to the familiar, which is nothing more or less than the numbing mechanism that takes place whenever new media drastically extend our senses.

PLAYBOY: If this "numbing" effect performs a beneficial role by protecting man from the psychic pain caused by the extensions of his nervous system that you attribute to the media, why are you attempting to dispel it and alert man to the changes in his environment?

McLUHAN: In the past, the effects of media were experienced more gradually, allowing the individual and society to absorb and cushion their impact to some degree. Today, in the electronic age of instantaneous communication, I believe that our survival, and at the very least our comfort and happiness, is predicated on understanding the nature of our new environment because unlike previous environmental changes, the electric media constitute a total and near-instantaneous transformation of culture, values and attitudes. This upheaval generates great pain and identity loss, which can be ameliorated only through a conscious awareness of its dynamics. If we understand the revolutionary transformations caused by new media, we can anticipate and control them; but if we continue in our self-induced subliminal trance, we will be their slaves.

Because of today's terrific speed-up of information moving, we have a chance to apprehend, predict and influence the environmental forces shaping us — and thus win back control of our own destinies. The new extensions of man and the environment they generate are the central manifestations of the evolutionary process, and yet we still cannot free ourselves of the delusion that it is how a medium is used that counts, rather than what it does to us and with us. This is the zombie stance of the technological idiot. It's to escape this Narcissus trance that I've tried to trace and reveal the impact of media on man, from the beginning of recorded time to the present.

PLAYBOY: Will you trace that impact for us — in condensed form?

McLUHAN: It's difficult to condense into the format of an interview such as this, but I'll try to give you a brief rundown of the basic media break-throughs. You've got to remember that my definition of media is broad: it includes any technology whatever that creates extensions of the human body and senses, from clothing to the computer. And a vital point I must stress again is that societies have always been shaped more by the nature of the media with which men communicate than by the content of the communication. All technology has the property of the Midas touch; whenever a society develops an extension of itself, all other functions of that society tend to be transmuted to accommodate that new form; once any new technology penetrates a society, it saturates every institution of that society. New technology is thus a revolutionizing agent. We see this today with the electric media and we saw it several thousand years ago with the invention of the phonetic alphabet, which was just as far-reaching an innovation — and had just as profound consequences for man.

PLAYBOY: What were they?

McLUHAN: Before the invention of the phonetic alphabet, man lived in a world where all the senses were balanced and simultaneous, a closed world of tribal depth and resonance, an oral culture structured by a dominant auditory sense of life. The ear, as opposed to the cool and neutral eye, is sensitive, hyperaesthetic and all-inclusive, and contributes to the seamless web of tribal kinship and interdependence in which all members of the group existed in harmony. The primary medium of communication was speech, and thus no man knew appreciably more or less than any other — which meant that there was little individualism and specialization, the hallmarks of "civilized" Western man. Tribal cultures even today simply cannot comprehend the concept of the individual or of the separate and independent citizen. Oral cultures act and react simultaneously, whereas the capacity to act without reacting, without involvement, is the special gift of "detached" literate man. Another basic characteristic distinguishing tribal man from his literate successors is that he lived in a world of *acoustic* space, which gave him a radically different concept of time-space relationships.

PLAYBOY: What do you mean by "acoustic space"?

McLUHAN: I mean space that has no center and no margin, unlike strictly visual space, which is an extension and intensification of the eye. Acoustic space is organic and integral, perceived through the simultaneous interplay of all the senses; whereas "rational" or pictorial space is uniform, sequential and continuous and creates a closed world with none of the rich resonance of the tribal echoland. Our own Western time-space concepts derive from the environment created by the discovery of phonetic writing, as does our entire concept of Western civilization. The man of the tribal world led a complex, kaleidoscopic life precisely because the ear, unlike the eye, cannot be focused and is synaesthetic rather than analytical and linear. Speech is an utterance, or more precisely, an *outering*, of all our senses at once; the auditory field is simultaneous, the visual successive. The modes of life of nonliterate people were implicit, simultaneous and discontinuous, and also far richer than those of literate man. By their dependence on the spoken word for information, people were drawn together into a tribal mesh; and since the spoken word is more emotionally laden than the written — conveying by intonation such rich emotions as anger, joy, sorrow, fear — tribal man was more spontaneous and passionately volatile. Audile-tactile tribal man partook of the collective unconscious, lived in a magical integral world patterned by myth and ritual, its values divine and unchallenged, whereas literate or visual man creates an environment that is strongly fragmented, individualistic, explicit, logical, specialized and detached.

PLAYBOY: Was it phonetic literacy alone that precipitated this profound shift of values from tribal involvement to "civilized" detachment?

McLUHAN: Yes, it was. Any culture is an order of sensory preferences, and in the tribal world, the senses of touch, taste, hearing and smell were developed, for very practical reasons, to a much higher level than the strictly visual. Into this world, the phonetic alphabet fell like a bombshell, installing sight at the head of the hierarchy of senses. Literacy propelled man from the tribe, gave him an eye for an ear and replaced his integral in-depth communal interplay with visual linear values and fragmented consciousness. As an intensification and amplification of the visual function, the phonetic alphabet diminished the role of the senses of hearing and touch and taste and smell, permeating the discontinuous culture of tribal man and translating its organic harmony and complex synaesthesia into the uniform, connected and visual mode that we still consider the norm of "rational" existence. The whole man became fragmented man; the alphabet shattered the charmed circle and resonating magic of the tribal world, exploding man into an agglomeration of specialized and psychically impoverished "individuals," or units, functioning in a world of linear time and Euclidean space.

PLAYBOY: But literate societies existed in the ancient world long before the phonetic alphabet. Why weren't *they* detribalized?

McLUHAN: The phonetic alphabet did not change or extend man so drastically just because it enabled him to read; as you point out, tribal culture had already coexisted with other written languages for thousands of years. But the phonetic alphabet was radically different from the older and richer hieroglyphic or ideogrammic cultures. The writings of Egyptian, Babylonian, Mayan and Chinese cultures were an extension of the senses in that they gave pictorial expression to reality, and they demanded many signs to cover the wide range of data in their societies — unlike phonetic writing, which uses semantically meaningless letters to correspond to semantically meaningless sounds and is able, with only a handful of letters, to encompass all meanings and all languages. This achievement demanded the separation of both sights and sounds from their semantic and dramatic meanings in order to render visible the actual sound of speech, thus placing a barrier between men and objects and creating a dualism between sight and sound. It divorced the visual function from the interplay with the other senses and thus led to the rejection from consciousness of vital areas of our sensory experience and to the resultant atrophy of the unconscious. The balance of the sensorium — or *Gestalt* interplay of all the senses — and the psychic and social harmony it engendered was disrupted, and the visual function was overdeveloped. This was true of no other writing system.

PLAYBOY: How can you be so sure that this all occurred solely because of phonetic literacy — or, in fact, if it occurred at all?

McLUHAN: You don't have to go back 3000 or 4000 years to see this process at work; in Africa today, a single generation of alphabetic literacy is enough to wrench the individual from the tribal web. When tribal man becomes phonetically literate, he may have an improved abstract intellectual grasp of the world, but most of the deeply emotional corporate family feeling is excised from his relationship with his social milieu. This division of sight and sound and meaning causes deep psychological effects, and he suffers a corresponding separation and impoverishment of his imaginative, emotional and sensory life. He begins reasoning in a sequential linear fashion; he begins categorizing and classifying data. As knowledge is extended in alphabetic form, it is localized and fragmented into specialties, creating division of function, of social classes, of nations and of knowledge — and in the process, the rich interplay of all the senses that characterized the tribal society is sacrificed.

PLAYBOY: But aren't there corresponding gains in insight, understanding and cultural diversity to compensate detribalized man for the loss of his communal values?

McLUHAN: Your question reflects all the institutionalized biases of literate man. Literacy, contrary to the popular view of the "civilizing" process you've just echoed, creates people who are much less complex and diverse than those who develop in the intricate web of oral-tribal societies. Tribal man, unlike homogenized Western man, was not differentiated by his specialist talents or his visible characteristics, but by his unique emotional blends. The internal world of the tribal man was a creative mix of complex emotions and feelings that literate men of the Western world have allowed to wither or have suppressed in the name of efficiency and practicality. The alphabet served to neutralize all these rich divergencies of tribal cultures by translating their complexities into simple visual forms; and the visual sense, remember, is the only one that allows us to *detach*; all other senses involve us, but the detachment bred by literacy disinvolves and detribalizes man. He separates from the tribe as a predomi-

nantly visual man who shares standardized attitudes, habits and rights with other civilized men. But he is also given a tremendous advantage over the nonliterate tribal man who, today as in ancient times, is hamstrung by cultural pluralism, uniqueness and discontinuity — values that make the African as easy prey for the European colonialist as the barbarian was for the Greeks and Romans. Only alphabetic cultures have ever succeeded in mastering connected linear sequences as a means of social and psychic organization; the separation of all kinds of experiences into uniform and continuous units in order to generate accelerated action and alteration of form — in other words, applied knowledge — has been the secret of Western man's ascendancy over other men as well as over his environment.

PLAYBOY: Isn't the thrust of your argument, then, that the introduction of the phonetic alphabet was not progress, as has generally been assumed, but a psychic and social disaster?

McLUHAN: It was both. I try to avoid value judgments in these areas, but there is much evidence to suggest that man may have paid too dear a price for his new environment of specialist technology and values. Schizophrenia and alienation may be the inevitable consequences of phonetic literacy. It's metaphorically significant, I suspect, that the old Greek myth has Cadmus, who brought the alphabet to man, sowing dragon's teeth that sprang up from the earth as armed men. Whenever the dragon's

242

teeth of technological change are sown, we reap a whirlwind of violence. We saw this clearly in classical times, although it was somewhat moderated because phonetic literacy did not win an overnight victory over primitive values and institutions; rather, it permeated ancient society in a gradual, if inexorable, evolutionary process.

PLAYBOY: How long did the old tribal culture endure?

McLUHAN: In isolated pockets, it held on until the invention of printing in the 16th Century, which was a vastly important qualitative extension of phonetic literacy. If the phonetic alphabet fell like a bombshell on tribal man, the printing press hit him like a 100-megaton H-bomb. The printing press was the ultimate extension of phonetic literacy: Books could be reproduced in infinite numbers; universal literacy was at last fully possible, if gradually realized; and books became portable individual possessions. Type, the prototype of all machines, ensured the primacy of the visual bias and finally sealed the doom of tribal man. The new medium of linear, uniform, repeatable type reproduced information in unlimited quantities and at hitherto-impossible speeds, thus assuring the eye a position of total predominance in man's sensorium. As a drastic extension of man, it shaped and transformed his entire environment, psychic and social, and was directly responsible for the rise of such disparate phenomena as nationalism, the Reformation, the assembly line and its offspring, the Industrial Revolution, the whole concept of causality, Cartesian and Newtonian concepts of the universe, perspective in art, narrative chronology in literature and a psychological mode of introspection or inner direction that greatly intensified the tendencies toward indivi- dualism and specialization engendered 2000 years before by phonetic literacy. The schism between thought and action was institutionalized, and fragmented man, first sundered by the alphabet, was at last diced into bite-sized tidbits. From that point on, Western man was Gutenberg man.

PLAYBOY: Even accepting the principle that technological innovations generate far-reaching environmental changes, many of your readers find it difficult to understand how you can hold the development of printing responsible for such apparently unrelated phenomena as nationalism and industrialism.

McLUHAN: The key word is "apparently." Look a bit closer at both nationalism and industrialism and you'll see that both derived directly from the explosion of print technology in the 16th Century. Nationalism didn't exist in Europe until the Renaissance, when typography enabled every literate man to *see* his mother tongue analytically as a uniform entity. The printing press, by spreading mass-produced books and printed matter across Europe, turned the vernacular regional languages of the day into uniform closed systems of national languages — just another variant of what we call mass media — and gave birth to the entire concept of nationalism.

The individual newly homogenized by print saw the nation concept as an intense and beguiling image of group destiny and status. With print, the homogeneity of money, markets and transport also became possible for the first time, thus creating economic as well as political unity and triggering all the dynamic centralizing energies of contemporary nationalism. By creating a speed of information movement unthinkable before printing, the Gutenberg revolution thus produced a new type of visual centralized national entity that was gradually merged with commercial expansion until Europe was a network of states.

By fostering continuity and competition within homogeneous and contiguous territory, nationalism not only forged new nations but sealed the doom of the old corporate, noncompetitive and discontinuous medieval order of guilds and family-structured social organization; print demanded both personal fragmentation and social uniformity, the natural expression of which was the nation-state. Literate nationalism's tremendous speed-up of information movement accelerated the specialist function that was nurtured by phonetic literacy and nourished by Gutenberg, and rendered obsolete such generalist encyclopedic figures as Benvenuto Cellini, the goldsmith-*cum-condottiere-cum*-painter-*cum*-sculptor-*cum*-writer; it was the Renaissance that destroyed Renaissance Man.

PLAYBOY: Why do you feel that Gutenberg also laid the groundwork for the Industrial Revolution?

McLUHAN: The two go hand in hand. Printing, remember, was the first mechanization of a complex handicraft; by creating an analytic sequence of step-by-step processes, it became the blueprint of all mechanization to follow. The most important quality of print is its repeatability; it is a visual statement that can be reproduced indefinitely, and repeatability is the root of the mechanical principle that has transformed the world since Gutenberg. Typography, by producing the first uniformly repeatable commodity, also created Henry Ford, the first assembly line and the first mass production. Movable type was archetype and prototype for all subsequent industrial development. Without phonetic literacy and the printing press, modern industrialism would be impossible. It is necessary to recognize literacy as typographic technology, shaping not only production and marketing procedures but all other areas of life, from education to city planning.

PLAYBOY: You seem to be contending that practically every aspect of modern life is a direct consequence of Gutenberg's invention of the printing press.

McLUHAN: Every aspect of Western *mechanical* culture was shaped by print technology, but the modern age is the age of the *electric* media, which forge environments and cultures antithetical to the mechanical consumer society derived from print. Print tore man out of his traditional cultural matrix while showing him how to pile individual upon individual into a massive agglomeration of national and industrial power, and the typographic trance of the West has endured until today, when the electronic media are at last demesmerizing us. The Gutenberg Galaxy is being eclipsed by the constellation of Marconi.

PLAYBOY: You've discussed that constellation in general terms, but what precisely are the electric media that you contend have supplanted the old mechanical technology?

McLUHAN: The electric media are the telegraph, radio, films, telephone, computer and television, all of which have not only extended a single sense of function as the old mechanical media did — i.e., the wheel as an extension of the foot, clothing as an extension of the skin, the phonetic alphabet as an extension of the eye — but have enhanced and externalized our entire central nervous systems, thus transforming all aspects of our social and psychic existence. The use of the electronic media constitutes a break boundary between fragmented Gutenberg man and integral man, just as phonetic literacy was a break boundary between oral-tribal man and visual man.

In fact, today we can look back at 3000 years of differing degrees of visualization, atomization and mechanization and at last recognize the mechanical age as an interlude between two great organic eras of culture. The age of print, which held sway from approximately 1500 to 1900, had its obituary tapped out by the telegraph, the first of the new electric media, and further obsequies were registered by the perception of "curved space" and non-Euclidean mathematics in the early years of the century, which revived tribal man's discontinuous time-space concepts — and which even Spengler dimly perceived as the death-knell of Western literate values. The development of telephone, radio, film, television and the computer have driven further nails into the coffin. Today, television is the most significant of the electric media because it permeates nearly every home in the country, extending the central nervous system of every viewer as it works over and molds the entire sensorium with the ultimate message. It is television that is primarily responsible for ending the visual supremacy that characterized all mechanical technology, although each of the other electric media have played contributing roles.

PLAYBOY: But isn't television itself a primarily visual medium?

McLUHAN: No, it's quite the opposite, although the idea that TV is a visual extension is an understandable mistake. Unlike film or photograph, television is primarily an extension of the sense of touch rather than of sight, and it is the tactile sense that demands the greatest interplay of all the senses. The secret of TV's tactile power is that the video image is one of low intensity or definition and thus, unlike either photograph or film, offers no detailed information about specific objects but instead involves the active participation of the viewer. The TV image is a mosaic mesh not only of horizontal lines but of millions of tiny dots, of which the viewer is physiologically able to pick up only 50 or 60 from which he shapes the image; thus he is constantly filling in vague and blurry images, bringing himself into in-depth involvement with the screen and acting out a constant creative dialog with the iconoscope. The contours of the resultant cartoonlike image are fleshed out within the imagination of the viewer, which necessitates great personal involvement and participation; the viewer, in fact, becomes the screen, whereas in film he becomes the camera. By requiring us to constantly fill in the spaces of the mosaic mesh, the iconoscope is tattooing its message directly on our skins. Each viewer is thus an unconscious pointillist painter like Seurat, limning new shapes and images as the iconoscope washes over his entire body. Since the point of focus for a TV set is the viewer, television is Orientalizing us by causing us all to begin to look within ourselves. The essence of TV viewing is, in short, intense participation and low definition — what I call a "cool" experience, as opposed to an essentially "hot," or high definition–low participation medium like radio.

PLAYBOY: A good deal of the perplexity surrounding your theories is related to this postulation of hot and cool media. Could you give us a brief definition of each?

McLUHAN: Basically, a hot medium *ex*cludes and a cool medium *in*cludes; hot media are low in participation, or completion, by the audience and cool media are high in participation. A hot medium is one that extends a single sense with high definition. High definition means a complete filling in of data by the medium without intense audience participation. A photograph, for example, is high definition or hot; whereas a cartoon is low definition or cool, because the rough outline drawing provides very little visual data and requires the viewer to fill in or complete the image himself. The telephone, which gives the ear relatively little data, is thus cool, as is speech; both demand considerable filling in by the listener. On the other hand, radio is a hot medium because it sharply and intensely provides great amounts of high-definition auditory information that leaves little or nothing to be filled in by the audience. A lecture, by the same token, is hot, but a seminar is cool; a book is hot, but a conversation or bull session is cool.

In a cool medium, the audience is an active constituent of the viewing or listening experience. A girl wearing open-mesh silk stockings or glasses is inherently cool and sensual because the eye acts as a surrogate hand in filling in the low-definition image thus engendered. Which is why boys seldom make passes at girls who wear glasses. In any case, the overwhelming majority of our technologies and entertainments since the introduction of print technology have been hot, fragmented and exclusive, but in the age of television we see a return to cool values and the inclusive in-depth involvement and participation they engender. This is, of course, just one more reason why the medium is the message, rather than the content; it is the participatory nature of the TV experience itself that is important, rather than the content of the particular TV image that is being invisibly and indelibly inscribed on our skins.

PLAYBOY: Even if, as you contend, the medium is the ultimate message, how can you entirely discount the importance of content? Didn't the content of Hitler's radio speeches, for example, have some effect on the Germans?

McLUHAN: By stressing that the medium is the message rather than the content, I'm not suggesting that content plays *no* role — merely that it plays a distinctly subordinate role. Even if Hitler had delivered botany lectures, some other demagog would have used the radio to retribalize the Germans and rekindle the dark atavistic side of the tribal nature that created European fascism in the Twenties and Thirties. By placing all the stress on content and practically none on the medium, we lose all chance of perceiving and influencing the impact of new technologies on man, and thus we are always dumfounded by — and unprepared for — the revolutionary environmental transformations induced by new media. Buffeted by environmental changes he cannot comprehend, man echoes the last plaintive cry of his tribal ancestor, Tarzan, as he plummeted to earth: "Who greased my vine?" The German Jew victimized by the Nazis because his old tribalism clashed with their new tribalism could no more understand why his world was turned upside down than the American today can understand the reconfiguration of social and political institutions caused by the electric media in general and television in particular.

PLAYBOY: How is television reshaping our political institutions?

McLUHAN: TV is revolutionizing every political system in the Western world. For one thing, it's creating a totally new type of national leader, a man who is much more of a tribal chieftain than a politician. Castro is a good example of the new tribal chieftain who rules his country by a mass-participational TV dialog and feedback; he governs his country on camera, by giving the Cuban people the experience of being directly and intimately involved in the process of collective decision making. Castro's adroit blend of political education, propaganda and avuncular guidance is the pattern for tribal chieftains in other countries. The new political showman has to literally as well as figuratively put on his audience as he would a suit of clothes and become a corporate tribal image — like Mussolini, Hitler and F. D. R. in the days of radio, and Jack Kennedy in the television era. All these men were tribal emperors on a scale theretofore unknown in the world, because they all mastered their media.

PLAYBOY: How did Kennedy use TV in a manner different from his predecessors — or successors?

McLUHAN: Kennedy was the first TV President because he was the first prominent American politician to ever understand the dynamics and lines of force of the television iconoscope. As I've explained, TV is an inherently cool medium, and Kennedy had a compatible coolness and indifference to power, bred of personal wealth, which allowed him to adapt fully to TV. Any political candidate who doesn't have such cool, low-definition qualities, which allow the viewer to fill in the gaps with his own personal identification, simply electrocutes himself on television — as Richard Nixon did in his disastrous debates with Kennedy in the 1960 campaign. Nixon was essentially hot; he presented a high-definition, sharply-defined image and action on the TV screen that contributed to his reputation as a phony — the "Tricky Dicky" syndrome that has dogged his footsteps for years. "Would you buy a used car from this man?" the political cartoon asked — and the answer was "no," because he didn't project the cool aura of disinterest and objectivity that Kennedy emanated so effortlessly and engagingly.

PLAYBOY: Did Nixon take any lessons from you the last time around?

McLUHAN: He certainly took lessons from somebody, because in the recent election it was Nixon who was cool and Humphrey who was hot. I had noticed the change in Nixon as far back as 1963 when I saw him on *The Jack Paar Show*. No longer the slick, glib, aggressive Nixon of 1960, he had been toned down, polished, programmed and packaged into the new Nixon we saw in 1968: earnest, modest, quietly sincere — in a word, cool. I realized then that if Nixon maintained this mask, he could be elected President, and apparently the American electorate agreed last November.

PLAYBOY: How did Lyndon Johnson make use of television?

McLUHAN: He botched it the same way Nixon did in 1960. He was too intense, too obsessed with making his audience love and revere him as father and teacher, and too classifiable. Would people feel any safer buying a used car from L. B. J. than from the old Nixon? The answer is, obviously, "no." Johnson became a stereotype — even a parody — of himself, and earned the same reputation as a phony that plagued Nixon for so long. The people wouldn't have cared if John Kennedy lied to them on TV, but they couldn't stomach L. B. J. even when he told the truth. The credibility gap was really a communications gap. The political candidate who understands TV — whatever his party, goals or beliefs — can gain power unknown in history. How he uses that power is, of course, quite another question. But the basic thing to remember about the electric media is that they inexorably transform every sense ratio and thus recondition and restructure all our values and institutions. The overhauling of our traditional political system is only one manifestation of the retribalizing process wrought by the electric media, which is turning the planet into a global village.

PLAYBOY: Would you describe this retribalizing process in more detail?

McLUHAN: The electronically induced technological extensions of our central nervous system, which I spoke of earlier, are immersing us in a world-pool of information movement and are thus enabling man to incorporate within himself the whole of mankind. The aloof and dissociated role of the literate man of the Western world is succumbing to the new, intense depth participation engendered by the electronic media and bringing us back in touch with ourselves as well as with one another. But the instant nature of electric-information movement is decentralizing — rather than enlarging — the family of man into a new state of multitudinous tribal existences. Particularly in countries where literate values are deeply institutionalized, this is a highly traumatic process, since the clash of the old segmented visual culture and the new integral electronic culture creates a crisis of identity, a vacuum of the self, which generates tremendous violence — violence that is simply an identity quest, private or corporate, social or commercial.

PLAYBOY: Do you relate this identity crisis to the current social unrest and violence in the United States?

McLUHAN: Yes, and to the booming business psychiatrists are doing. All our alienation and atomization are reflected in the crumbling of such time-honored social values as the right of privacy and the sanctity of the individual; as they yield to the intensities of the new technology's electric circus, it seems to the average citizen that the sky is falling in. As man is tribally metamorphosed by the electric media, we all become Chicken Littles, scurrying around frantically in search of our former identities, and in the process unleash tremendous violence. As the preliterate confronts the literate in the postliterate arena, as new information patterns inundate and uproot the old, mental breakdowns of varying degrees — including the collective nervous breakdowns of whole societies unable to resolve their crises of identity — will become very common.

It is not an easy period in which to live, especially for the television-conditioned young who, unlike their literate elders, cannot take refuge in the zombie trance of Narcissus narcosis that numbs the state of psychic shock induced by the impact of the new media. From Tokyo to Paris to Columbia, youth mindlessly acts out its identity quest in the theater of the streets, searching not for goals but for roles, striving for an identity that eludes them.

PLAYBOY: Why do you think they aren't finding it within the educational system?

McLUHAN: Because education, which should be helping youth to understand and adapt to their revolutionary new environments, is instead being used merely as an instrument of cultural aggression, imposing upon retribalized youth the obsolescent visual values of the dying literate age. Our entire educational system is reactionary, oriented to past values and past technologies, and will likely continue so until the old generation relinquishes power. The generation gap is actually a chasm, separating not two age groups but two vastly divergent cultures. I can understand the ferment in our schools, because our educational system is totally rearview mirror. It's a dying and outdated system founded on literate values and fragmented and classified data totally unsuited to the needs of the first television generation.

PLAYBOY: How do you think the educational system can be adapted to accommodate the needs of this television generation?

McLUHAN: Well, before we can start doing things the right way, we've got to recognize that we've been doing them the wrong way — which most pedagogs and administrators and even most parents still refuse to accept. Today's child is growing up absurd because he is suspended between two worlds and two value systems, neither of which inclines him to maturity because he belongs wholly to neither but exists in a hybrid limbo of constantly conflicting values. The challenge of the new era is simply the total creative process of *growing up* — and mere teaching and repetition of facts are as irrelevant to this process as a dowser to a nuclear power plant. To expect a "turned on" child of the electric age to respond to the old education modes is rather like expecting an eagle to swim. It's simply not within his environment, and therefore incomprehensible.

The TV child finds it difficult if not impossible to adjust to the fragmented, visual goals of our education after having had all his senses involved by the electric media; he craves in-depth involvement, not linear detachment and uniform sequential patterns. But suddenly and without preparation, he is snatched from the cool, inclusive womb of television and exposed — within a vast bureaucratic structure of courses and credits — to the hot medium of print. His natural instinct, conditioned by the electric media, is to bring all his senses to bear on the book he's instructed to read, and print resolutely rejects that approach, demanding an isolated visual attitude to learning rather than the *Gestalt* approach of the unified sensorium. The reading postures of children in elementary school are a pathetic testimonial to the effects of television: children of the TV generation separate book from eye by an average distance of four and a half inches, attempting psychomimetically to bring to the printed page the all-inclusive sensory experience of TV. They are becoming Cyclops, desperately seeking to wallow in the book as they do in the TV screen.

PLAYBOY: Might it be possible for the "TV child" to make the adjustment to his educational environment by synthesizing traditional literate-visual forms with the insights of his own electric culture — or must the medium of print be totally unassimilable for him?

McLUHAN: Such a synthesis is entirely possible, and could create a creative blend of the two cultures — if the educational establishment was aware that there *is* an electric culture. In the absence of such elementary awareness, I'm afraid that the television child has no future in our schools. You must remember that the TV child has been relentlessly exposed to all the "adult" news of the modern world — war, racial discrimination, rioting, crime, inflation, sexual revolution. The war in Vietnam has written its bloody message on his skin; he has witnessed the assassinations and funerals of the nation's leaders; he's been orbited through the TV screen into the astronaut's dance in space, been inundated by information transmitted via radio, telephone, films, recordings and other people. His parents plopped him down in front of a TV set at the age of two to tranquilize him, and by the time he enters kindergarten, he's clocked as much as 4000 hours of television. As an IBM executive told me, "My children had lived several lifetimes compared to their grandparents when they began grade one."

PLAYBOY: If you had children young enough to belong to the TV generation, how would you educate them?

McLUHAN: Certainly not in our current schools, which are intellectual penal institutions. In today's world, to paraphrase Jefferson, the least education is the best education, since very few young minds can survive the intellectual tortures of our educational system. The mosaic image of the TV screen generates a depth-involving *nowness* and simultaneity in the lives of children that makes them scorn the distant visualized goals of traditional education as unreal, irrelevant and puerile. Another basic problem is that in our schools there is simply too much to learn by the traditional analytic methods; this is an age of information overload. The only way to make the schools other than prisons without bars is to start fresh with new techniques and values.

PLAYBOY: A number of experimental projects are bringing both TV and computers directly into the class-

rooms. Do you consider this sort of electronic educational aid a step in the right direction?

McLUHAN: It's not really too important if there is ever a TV set in each classroom across the country, since the sensory and attitudinal revolution has already taken place at home before the child ever reaches school, altering his sensory existence and his mental processes in profound ways. Book learning is no longer sufficient in any subject; the children all say now, "Let's *talk* Spanish," or "Let the Bard be *heard*," reflecting their rejection of the old sterile system where education begins and ends in a book. What we need now is educational crash programing in depth to first understand and then meet the new challenges. Just putting the present classroom on TV, with its archaic values and methods, won't change anything; it would be just like running movies on television; the result would be a hybrid that is neither. We have to ask what TV can do, in the instruction of English or physics or any other subject, that the classroom cannot do as presently constituted. The answer is that TV can deeply involve youth in the process of learning, illustrating graphically the complex interplay of people and events, the development of forms, the multileveled interrelationships between and among such arbitrarily segregated subjects as biology, geography, mathematics, anthropology, history, literature and languages.

If education is to become relevant to the young of this electric age, we must also supplant the stifling, impersonal and dehumanizing multiversity with a multiplicity of autonomous colleges devoted to an in-depth approach to learning. This must be done immediately, for few adults really comprehend the intensity of youth's alienation from the fragmented mechanical world and its fossilized educational system, which is designed in their minds solely to fit them into classified slots in bureaucratic society. To them, both draft card and degree are passports to psychic, if not physical, oblivion, and they accept neither. A new generation is alienated from its own 3000-year heritage of literacy and visual culture, and the celebration of literate values in home and school only intensifies that alienation. If we don't adapt our educational system to their needs and values, we will see only more dropouts and more chaos.

PLAYBOY: Do you think the surviving hippie subculture is a reflection of youth's rejection of the values of our mechanical society?

McLUHAN: Of course. These kids are fed up with jobs and goals, and are determined to forge their own roles and involvement in society. They want nothing to do with our fragmented and specialist consumer society. Living in the transitional identity vacuum between two great antithetical cultures, they are desperately trying to discover themselves and fashion a mode of existence attuned to their new values; thus the stress on developing an "alternate life style." We can see the results of this retribalization process whenever we look at *any* of our youth — not just at hippies. Take the field of fashion, for example, which now finds boys and girls dressing alike and wearing their hair alike, reflecting the unisexuality deriving from the shift from visual to tactile. The younger generation's whole orientation is toward a return to the native, as reflected by their costumes, their music, their long hair and their sociosexual behavior. Our teenage generation is already becoming part of a jungle clan. As youth enters this clan world and all their senses are electrically extended and intensified, there is a corresponding amplification of their sexual sensibilities. Nudity and unabashed sexuality are growing in the electric age because as TV tattoos its message directly on our skins, it renders clothing obsolescent and a barrier, and the new tactility makes it natural for kids to constantly touch one another — as reflected by the button sold in the psychedelic shops: IF IT MOVES, FONDLE IT. The electric media, by stimulating all the senses simultaneously, also give a new and richer sensual dimension to everyday sexuality that makes Henry Miller's style of randy rutting old-fashioned and obsolete. Once a society enters the all-involving tribal mode, it is inevitable that our attitudes toward sexuality change. We see, for example, the ease with which young people live guiltlessly with one another, or, as among the hippies, in communal ménages. This is completely tribal.

PLAYBOY: But aren't most tribal societies sexually restrictive rather than permissive?

McLUHAN: Actually, they're both. Virginity is not, with a few exceptions, the tribal style in most primitive societies; young people tend to have total sexual access to one another until marriage. But after marriage, the wife becomes a jealously guarded possession and adultery a paramount sin. It's paradoxical that in the transition to a retribalized society, there is inevitably a great explosion of sexual energy and freedom; but when that society is fully realized, moral values will be extremely tight. In an integrated tribal society, the young will have free rein to experiment, but marriage and the family will become inviolate institutions, and infidelity and divorce will constitute serious violations of the social bond, not a private deviation but a collective insult and loss of face to the entire tribe. Tribal societies, unlike detribalized, fragmented cultures with their stress on individualist values, are extremely austere morally, and do not hesitate to destroy or banish those who offend the tribal values. This is rather harsh, of course, but at the same time, sexuality can take on new and richer dimensions of depth involvement in a tribalized society.

Today, meanwhile, as the old values collapse and we see an exhilarating release of pent-up sexual frustrations, we are all inundated by a tidal wave of emphasis on sex. Far from liberating the libido, however, such onslaughts seem to have induced jaded attitudes and a kind of psychosexual *Weltschmerz*. No sensitivity of sensual response can survive such an assault, which stimulates the mechanical view of the body as capable of experiencing specific thrills, but not total sexual-emotional involvement and transcendence. It contributes to the schism between sexual enjoyment and reproduction that is so prevalent, and also strengthens the case for homosexuality. Projecting current trends, the love machine would appear a natural development in the near future — not just the current computerized datefinder, but a machine whereby ultimate orgasm is achieved by direct mechanical stimulation of the pleasure circuits of the brain.

PLAYBOY: Do we detect a note of disapproval in your analysis of the growing sexual freedom?

McLUHAN: No, I neither approve nor disapprove. I merely try to understand. Sexual freedom is as natural to newly tribalized youth as drugs.

PLAYBOY: What's natural about drugs?

McLUHAN: They're natural means of smoothing cultural transitions, and also a short cut into the electric vortex. The upsurge in drug taking is intimately related to the impact of the electric media. Look at the metaphor for getting high: turning on. One turns on his consciousness through drugs just as he opens up all his senses to a total depth involvement by turning on the TV dial. Drug taking is stimulated by today's pervasive environment of instant information, with its feedback mechanism of the inner trip. The inner trip is not the sole prerogative of the LSD traveler; it's the universal experience of TV watchers. LSD is a way of miming the invisible electronic world; it releases a person from acquired verbal and visual habits and reactions, and gives the potential of instant and total involvement, both all-at-onceness and all-at-oneness, which are the basic needs of people translated by electric extensions of their central nervous systems out of the old rational, sequential value system. The attraction to hallucinogenic drugs is a means of achieving empathy with our penetrating electric environment, an environment that in itself is a drugless inner trip.

Drug taking is also a means of expressing rejection of the obsolescent mechanical world and values. And drugs often stimulate a fresh interest in artistic expression, which is primarily of the audile-tactile world. The hallucinogenic drugs, as chemical simulations of our electric environment, thus revive senses long atrophied by the overwhelmingly visual orientation of the mechanical culture. LSD and related hallucinogenic drugs, furthermore, breed a highly tribal and communally oriented subculture, so it's understandable why the retribalized young take to drugs like a duck to water.

PLAYBOY: A Columbia coed was recently quoted in *Newsweek* as equating you and LSD. "LSD doesn't mean anything until you consume it," she said. "Likewise McLuhan." Do you see any similarities?

McLUHAN: I'm flattered to hear my work described as hallucinogenic, but I suspect that some of my academic critics find me a bad trip.

PLAYBOY: Have you ever taken LSD yourself?

McLUHAN: No, I never have. I'm an observer in these matters, not a participant. I had an operation last year to remove a tumor that was expanding my brain in a less pleasant manner, and during my prolonged convalescence I'm not allowed any stimulant stronger than coffee. Alas! A few months ago, however, I was almost "busted" on a drug charge. On a plane returning from Vancouver, where a university had awarded me an honorary degree, I ran into a colleague who asked me where I'd been. "To Vancouver to pick up my LL.D.," I told him. I noticed a fellow passenger looking at me with a strange expression, and when I got off the plane at Toronto Airport, two customs guards pulled me into a little room and started going over my luggage. "Do you know Timothy Leary?" one asked. I replied I did and that seemed to wrap it up for him. "All right," he said. "Where's the stuff? We know you told somebody you'd gone to Vancouver to pick up some LL.D." After a laborious dialog, I persuaded him that an LL.D. has nothing to do with consciousness expansion — just the opposite, in fact — and I was released. Of course, in light of the present educational crisis, I'm not sure there isn't something to be said for making possession of an LL.D. a felony.

PLAYBOY: Are you in favor of legalizing marijuana and hallucinogenic drugs?

McLUHAN: My personal point of view is irrelevant, since all such legal restrictions are futile and will inevitably wither away. You could as easily ban drugs in a retribalized society as outlaw clocks in a mechanical culture. The young will continue turning on no matter how many of them are turned off into prisons, and such legal restrictions only reflect the cultural aggression and revenge of a dying culture against its successor.

Speaking of dying cultures, it's no accident that drugs first were widely used in America by the Indians and then by the Negroes, both of whom have the great cultural advantage in this transitional age of remaining close to their tribal roots. The cultural aggression of white America against Negroes and Indians is not based on skin color and belief in radical superiority, whatever ideological clothing may be used to rationalize it, but on the white man's inchoate awareness that the Negro and Indian — as men with deep roots in the resonating echo chamber of the discontinuous, interrelated tribal world — are actually physically and socially superior to the fragmented, alienated and dissociated man of Western civilization. Such a recognition, which stabs at the heart of the white man's entire social value system, inevitably generates violence and genocide. It has been the sad fate of the Negro and the Indian to be tribal men in a fragmented culture — men born ahead of rather than behind their time.

PLAYBOY: How do you mean?

McLUHAN: I mean that at precisely the time when the white younger generation is retribalizing and generalizing, the Negro and the Indian are under tremendous social and economic pressure to go in the opposite direction: to detribalize and specialize, to tear out their tribal roots when the rest of society is rediscovering theirs. Long held in a totally subordinate socioeconomic position, they are now impelled to acquire literacy as a prerequisite to employment in the old mechanical service environment of hardware, rather than adapt themselves to the new tribal environment of software, or electric information, as the middle-class white young are doing. Needless to say, this generates great psychic pain, which in turn is translated into bitterness and violence. This can be seen in the microcosmic drug culture; psychological studies show that the Negro and the Indian who are turned on by marijuana, unlike the white, are frequently engulfed with rage; they have a low high. They are angry because they understand under the influence of the drug that the source of their psychic and social degradation lies in the mechanical technology that is now being repudiated by the very white overculture that developed it — a repudiation that the majority of Negroes and Indians cannot, literally, afford because of their inferior economic position.

This is both ironic and tragic, and lessens the chances for an across-the-board racial *détente* and reconciliation, because rather than diminishing and eventually closing the sociopsychic differences between the races, it widens them. The Negro and the Indian seem to always get a bad deal; they suffered first because they were tribal men in a mechanical world, and now as they try to detribalize and structure themselves within the values of the mechanical culture, they find the gulf between them and a suddenly retribalizing society widening rather than narrowing. The future, I fear, is not too bright for either — but particularly for the Negro.

PLAYBOY: What, specifically, do you think will happen to him?

McLUHAN: At best, he will have to make a painful adjustment to two conflicting cultures and technologies, the visual-mechanical and the electric world; at worst, he will be exterminated.

PLAYBOY: Exterminated?

McLUHAN: I seriously fear the possibility, though God knows I hope I'm proved wrong. As I've tried to point out, the one inexorable consequence of any identity quest generated by environmental upheaval is tremendous violence. This violence has traditionally been directed at the tribal man who challenged visual-mechanical culture, as with the genocide against the Indian and the institutionalized dehumanization of the Negro. Today, the process is reversed and the violence is being meted out, during this transitional period, to those who are nonassimilable into the new tribe. Not because of his skin color but because he is in a limbo between mechanical and electric cultures, the Negro is a threat, a rival tribe that cannot be digested by the new order. The fate of such tribes is often extermination.

PLAYBOY: What can we do to prevent this from happening to America's Negro population?

McLUHAN: I think a valuable first step would be to alert the Negro, as well as the rest of society, to the nature of the new electric technology and the reasons it is so inexorably transforming our social and psychic values. The Negro should understand that the aspects of himself he has been conditioned to think of as inferior or "backward" are actually *superior* attributes in the new environment. Western man is obsessed by the forward-motion folly of step-by-step "progress," and always views the discontinuous synaesthetic interrelationships of the tribe as primitive. If the Negro realizes the great advantages of his heritage, he will cease his lemming leap into the senescent mechanical world.

There are encouraging signs that the new black-power movement — with its emphasis on Negritude and a return to the tribal pride of African cultural and social roots — is recognizing this, but unfortunately a majority of Negro Americans are still determined to join the mechanical culture. But if they can be persuaded to follow the lead of those who wish to rekindle their sparks of tribal awareness, they will be strategically placed to make an easy transition to the new technology, using their own enduring tribal values as environmental survival aids. They should take pride in these tribal values, for they are rainbow-hued in comparison with the pallid literate culture of their traditional masters.

But as I said, the Negro arouses hostility in whites precisely because they subliminally recognize that he is closest to that tribal depth involvement and simultaneity and harmony that is the richest and most highly developed expression of human consciousness. This is why the white political and economic institutions mobilize to exclude and oppress Negroes, from semiliterate unions to semiliterate politicians, whose slim visual culture makes them hang on with unremitting fanaticism to their antiquated hardware and the specialized skills and classifications and compartmentalized neighborhoods and life styles deriving from it. The lowest intellectual stratum of whites view literacy and its hardware environment as a novelty, still fresh and still status symbols of achievement, and thus will be the last to retribalize and the first to initiate what could easily become a full-blown racial civil war. The United States as a nation is doomed, in any case, to break up into a series of regional and racial ministates, and such a civil war would merely accelerate that process.

PLAYBOY: On what do you base your prediction that the United States will disintegrate?

McLUHAN: Actually, in this case as in most of my work, I'm "predicting" what has already happened and merely extrapolating a current process to its logical conclusion. The Balkanization of the United States as a continental political structure has been going on for some years now, and racial chaos is merely one of several catalysts for change. This isn't a peculiarly American phenomenon; as I pointed out earlier, the electric media always produce psychically integrating and socially decentralizing effects, and this affects not only political institutions within the existing state but the national entities themselves.

All over the world, we can see how the electric media are stimulating the rise of ministates: in Great Britain, Welsh and Scottish nationalism are recrudescing powerfully; in Spain, the Basques are demanding autonomy; in Belgium, the Flemings insist on separation from the Walloons; in my own country, the *Quebecois* are in the first stages of a war of independence; and in Africa, we've witnessed the germination of several ministates and the collapse of several ambitiously unrealistic schemes for regional confederation. These ministates are just the opposite of the traditional centralizing nationalisms of the past that forged mass states that homogenized disparate ethnic and linguistic groups within one national boundary. The new ministates are decentralized tribal agglomerates of those same ethnic and linguistic groups. Though their creation may be accompanied by violence, they will not remain hostile or competitive armed camps but will eventually discover that their tribal bonds transcend their differences and will thereafter live in harmony and cultural cross-fertilization with one another.

This pattern of decentralized ministates will be repeated in the United States, although I realize that most Americans still find the thought of the Union's dissolution inconceivable. The U.S., which was the first nation in history to begin its national existence as a centralized and literate political entity, will now play the historical film backward, reeling into a multiplicity of decentralized Negro states, Indian states, regional states, linguistic and ethnic states, etc. Decentralism is today the burning issue in the 50 states, from the school crisis in New York City to the demands of the retribalized young that the oppressive multiversities be reduced to a human scale and the mass state be debureaucratized. The tribes and the bureaucracy are antithetical means of social organization and can never coexist peacefully; one must destroy and supplant the other, or neither will survive.

PLAYBOY: Accepting, for the moment, your contention that the United States will be "Balkanized" into an assortment of ethnic and linguistic ministates, isn't it likely that the results would be social chaos and internecine warfare?

McLUHAN: Not necessarily. Violence can be avoided if we comprehend the process of decentralism and retribalization, and accept its outcome while moving to control and modify the dynamics of change. In any case, the day of the super state is over; as men not only in the U.S. but throughout the world are united into a single tribe, they will forge a diversity of viable decentralized political and social institutions.

PLAYBOY: Along what lines?

McLUHAN: It will be a totally retribalized world of depth involvements. Through radio, TV and the computer, we are already entering a global theater in which the entire world is a Happening. Our whole cultural habitat, which we once viewed as a mere container of people, is being transformed by these media and by space satellites into a living organism, itself contained within a new macrocosm or connubium of a supraterrestrial nature. The day of the individualist, of privacy, of fragmented or "applied" knowledge, of "points of view" and specialist goals is being replaced by the over-all awareness of a mosaic world in which space and time are overcome by television, jets and computers — a simultaneous, "all-at-once" world in which everything resonates with everything else as in a total electrical field, a world in which energy is generated and perceived not by the traditional connections that create linear, causative thought processes, but by the intervals, or gaps, which Linus Pauling grasps as the languages of cells, and which create synaesthetic discontinuous integral consciousness.

The open society, the visual offspring of phonetic literacy, is irrelevant to today's retribalized youth; and the closed society, the product of speech, drum and ear technologies, is thus being reborn. After centuries of dissociated sensibilities, modern awareness is once more becoming integral and inclusive, as the entire human family is sealed to a single universal membrane. The compressional, implosive nature of the new electric technology is retrogressing Western man back from the open plateaus of literate values and into the heart of tribal darkness, into what Joseph Conrad termed "the Africa within."

PLAYBOY: Many critics feel that your own "Africa within" promises to be a rigidly conformist hive world in which the individual is totally subordinate to the group and personal freedom is unknown.

McLUHAN: Individual talents and perspectives don't have to shrivel within a retribalized society; they merely interact within a group consciousness that has the potential for releasing far more creativity than the old atomized culture. Literate man is alienated, impoverished man; retribalized man can lead a far richer and more fulfilling life — not the life of a mindless drone but of the participant in a seamless web of interdependence and harmony. The implosion of electric technology is transmogrifying literate, fragmented man into a complex and depth-structured human being with a deep emotional awareness of his complete interdependence with all of humanity. The old "individualistic" print society was one where the individual was "free" only to be alienated and dissociated, a rootless outsider bereft of tribal dreams; our new electronic environment compels commitment and participation, and fulfills man's psychic and social needs at profound levels.

The tribe, you see, is not conformist just because it's inclusive; after all, there is far more diversity and less conformity within a family group than there is within an urban conglomerate housing thousands of families. It's in the village where eccentricity lingers, in the big city where uniformity and impersonality are the milieu. The global-village conditions being forged by the electric technology stimulate more discontinuity and diversity and

division than the old mechanical, standardized society; in fact, the global village makes maximum disagreement and creative dialog inevitable. Uniformity and tranquillity are not hallmarks of the global village; far more likely are conflict and discord as well as love and harmony — the customary life mode of any tribal people.

PLAYBOY: Despite what you've said, haven't literate cultures been the only ones to value the concepts of individual freedom, and haven't tribal societies traditionally imposed rigid social taboos — as you suggested earlier in regard to sexual behavior — and ruthlessly punished all who do not conform to tribal values?

McLUHAN: We confront a basic paradox whenever we discuss personal freedom in literate and tribal cultures. Literate mechanical society separated the individual from the group in space, engendering privacy; in thought, engendering point of view; and in work, engendering specialism — thus forging all the values associated with individualism. But at the same time, print technology has homogenized man, creating mass militarism, mass mind and mass uniformity; print gave man private habits of individualism and a public role of absolute conformity. That is why the young today welcome their retribalization, however dimly they perceive it, as a release from the uniformity, alienation and dehumanization of literate society. Print centralizes socially and fragments psychically, whereas the electric media bring man together in a tribal village that is a rich and creative mix, where there is actually *more* room for creative diversity than within the homogenized mass urban society of Western man.

PLAYBOY: Are you claiming, now, that there will be no taboos in the world tribal society you envision?

McLUHAN: No, I'm not saying that, and I'm not claiming that freedom will be absolute — merely that it will be less restricted than your question implies. The world tribe will be essentially conservative, it's true, like all iconic and inclusive societies; a mythic environment lives beyond time and space and thus generates little radical social change. All technology becomes part of a shared ritual that the tribe desperately strives to keep stabilized and permanent; by its very nature, an oral-tribal society — such as Pharaonic Egypt — is far more stable and enduring than any fragmented visual society. The oral and auditory tribal society is patterned by acoustic space, a total and simultaneous field of relations alien to the visual world, in which points of view and goals make social change an inevitable and constant byproduct. An electrically imploded tribal society discards the linear forward-motion of "progress." We can see in our own time how, as we begin to react in depth to the challenges of the global village, we all become reactionaries.

PLAYBOY: That can hardly be said of the young, whom you claim are leading the process of retribalization, and according to most estimates are also the most radical generation in our history.

McLUHAN: Ah, but you're talking about politics, about goals and issues, which are really quite irrelevant. I'm saying that the result, not the current process, of retribalization makes us reactionary in our basic attitudes and values. Once we are enmeshed in the magical resonance of the tribal echo chamber, the debunking of myths and legends is replaced by their religious study. Within the consensual framework of tribal values, there will be unending diversity — but there will be few if any rebels who challenge the tribe itself.

The instant involvement that accompanies instant technologies triggers a conservative, stabilizing, gyroscopic function in man, as reflected by the second-grader who, when requested by her teacher to compose a poem after the first Sputnik was launched into orbit, wrote: "The stars are so big / The earth is so small / Stay as you are." The little girl who wrote those lines is part of the new tribal society; she lives in a world infinitely more complex, vast and eternal than any scientist has instruments to measure or imagination to describe.

PLAYBOY: If personal freedom will still exist — although restricted by certain consensual taboos — in this new tribal world, what about the political system most closely associated with individual freedom: democracy? Will it, too, survive the transition to your global village?

McLUHAN: No, it will not. The day of political democracy as we know it today is finished. Let me stress again that individual freedom itself will not be submerged in the new tribal society, but it will certainly assume different and more complex dimensions. The ballot box, for example, is the product of literate Western culture — a hot box in a cool world — and thus obsolescent. The tribal will is consensually expressed through the simultaneous interplay of all members of a community that is deeply interrelated and involved, and would thus consider the casting of a "private" ballot in a shrouded polling booth a ludicrous anachronism. The TV networks' computers, by "projecting" a victor in a Presidential race while the polls are still open, have already rendered the traditional electoral process obsolescent.

In our software world of instant electric communications movement, politics is shifting from the old patterns of political representation by electoral delegation to a new form of spontaneous and instantaneous communal involvement in all areas of decision making. In a tribal all-at-once culture, the idea of the "public" as a differentiated agglomerate of fragmented individuals, all dissimilar but all capable of acting in basically the same way, like interchangeable mechanical cogs in a production line, is supplanted by a mass society in which personal diversity is encouraged while at the same time everybody reacts and interacts simultaneously to every stimulus. The election as we know it today will be meaningless in such a society.

PLAYBOY: How will the popular will be registered in the new tribal society if elections are passé?

McLUHAN: The electric media open up totally new means of registering popular opinion. The old concept of the plebiscite, for example, may take on new relevance; TV could conduct daily plebiscites by presenting facts to 200,000,000 people and providing a computerized feedback of the popular will. But voting, in the traditional sense, is through as we leave the age of political parties, political issues and political goals, and enter an age where the collective tribal image and the iconic image of the tribal chieftain is the overriding political reality. But that's only one of countless new realities we'll be confronted with in the tribal village. We must understand that a totally new society is coming into being, one that rejects *all* our old values, conditioned responses, attitudes and institutions. If you have difficulty envisioning something as trivial as the imminent end of elections, you'll be totally unprepared to cope with the prospect of the forthcoming demise of spoken language and its replacement by a global consciousness.

PLAYBOY: You're right.

McLUHAN: Let me help you. Tribal man is tightly sealed in an integral collective awareness that transcends conventional boundaries of time and space. As such, the new society will be one mythic integration, a resonating world akin to the old tribal echo chamber where magic will live again: a world of ESP. The current interest of youth in astrology, clairvoyance and the occult is no coincidence. Electric technology, you see, does not require words any more than a digital computer requires numbers. Electricity makes possible — and not in the distant future, either — an amplification of human consciousness on a world scale, without any verbalization at all. **PLAYBOY:** Are you talking about global telepathy?

McLUHAN: Precisely. Already, computers offer the potential of instantaneous translation of any code or language into any other code or language. If a data feedback is possible through the computer, why not a feed-*forward* of thought whereby a world consciousness links into a world computer? Via the computer, we could logically proceed from translating languages to bypassing them entirely in favor of an integral cosmic unconsciousness somewhat similar to the collective unconscious envisioned by Bergson. The computer thus holds out the promise of a technologically engendered state of universal understanding and unity, a state of absorption in the logos that could knit mankind into one family and create a perpetuity of collective harmony and peace. This is the *real* use of the computer, not to expedite marketing or solve technical problems but to speed the process of discovery and orchestrate terrestrial — and eventually galactic — environments and energies. Psychic communal integration, made possible at last by the electronic media, could create the universality of consciousness foreseen by Dante when he predicted that men would continue as no more than broken fragments until they were unified into an inclusive consciousness. In a Christian sense, this is merely a new interpretation of the mystical body of Christ; and Christ, after all, is the ultimate extension of man.

PLAYBOY: Isn't this projection of an electronically induced world consciousness more mystical than technological?

McLUHAN: Yes — as mystical as the most advanced theories of modern nuclear physics. Mysticism is just tomorrow's science dreamed today.

PLAYBOY: You said a few minutes ago that *all* of contemporary man's traditional values, attitudes and institutions are going to be destroyed and replaced in and by the new electric age. That's a pretty sweeping generalization. Apart from the complex psychosocial metamorphoses you've mentioned, would you explain in more detail some of the specific changes you foresee?

McLUHAN: The transformations are taking place everywhere around us. As the old value systems crumble, so do all the institutional clothing and garbage they fashioned. The cities, corporate extensions of our physical organs, are withering and being translated along with all other such extensions into information systems, as television and the jet — by compressing time and space — make all the world one village and destroy the old city-country dichotomy. New York, Chicago, Los Angeles — all will disappear like the dinosaur. The automobile, too, will soon be as obsolete as the cities it is currently strangling, replaced by new antigravitational technology. The marketing systems and the stock market as we know them today will soon be dead as the dodo, and automation will end the traditional concept of the job, replacing it with a *role*, and giving men the breath of leisure. The electric media will create a world of dropouts from the old fragmented society, with its neatly compartmentalized analytic functions, and cause people to drop *in* to the new integrated global-village community.

All these convulsive changes, as I've already noted, carry with them attendant pain, violence and war — the normal stigmata of the identity quest — but the new society is springing so quickly from the ashes of the old that I believe it will be possible to avoid the transitional anarchy many predict. Automation and cybernation can play an essential role in smoothing the transition to the new society.

PLAYBOY: How?

McLUHAN: The computer can be used to direct a network of global thermostats to pattern life in ways that will optimize human awareness. Already, it's technologically feasible to employ the computer to program societies in beneficial ways.

PLAYBOY: How do you program an entire society — beneficially or otherwise?

McLUHAN: There's nothing at all difficult about putting computers in the position where they will be able to conduct carefully orchestrated programing of the sensory life of whole populations. I know it sounds rather science-fictional, but if you understood cybernetics you'd realize we could do it today. The computer could program the media to determine the given messages a people should hear

in terms of their over-all needs, creating a total media experience absorbed and patterned by all the senses. We could program five hours less of TV in Italy to promote the reading of newspapers during an election, or lay on an additional 25 hours of TV in Venezuela to cool down the tribal temperature raised by radio the preceding month. By such orchestrated interplay of all media, whole cultures could now be programed in order to improve and stabilize their emotional climate, just as we are beginning to learn how to maintain equilibrium among the world's competing economies.

PLAYBOY: How does such environmental programing, however enlightened in intent, differ from Pavlovian brainwashing?

McLUHAN: Your question reflects the usual panic of people confronted with unexplored technologies. I'm not saying such panic isn't justified, or that such environmental programing couldn't be brainwashing, or far worse — merely that such reactions are useless and distracting. Though I think the programing of societies could actually be conducted quite constructively and humanistically, I don't want to be in the position of a Hiroshima physicist extolling the potential of nuclear energy in the first days of August 1945. But an understanding of media's effects constitutes a civil defense against media fallout.

The alarm of so many people, however, at the prospect of corporate programing's creation of a complete service environment on this planet is rather like fearing that a municipal lighting system will deprive the individual of the right to adjust each light to his own favorite level of intensity. Computer technology can — and doubtless will — program entire environments to fulfill the social needs and sensory preferences of communities and nations. The *content* of that programing, however, depends on the nature of future societies — but that is in our own hands.

PLAYBOY: Is it really in our hands — or, by seeming to advocate the use of computers to manipulate the future of entire cultures, aren't you actually encouraging man to abdicate control over his destiny?

McLUHAN: First of all — and I'm sorry to have to repeat this disclaimer — I'm not advocating *anything*; I'm merely probing and predicting trends. Even if I opposed them or thought them disastrous, I couldn't stop them, so why waste my time lamenting? As Carlyle said of author Margaret Fuller after she remarked, "I accept the Universe": "She'd better." I see no possibility of a world-wide Luddite rebellion that will smash all machinery to bits, so we might as well sit back and see what is happening and what will happen to us in a cybernetic world. Resenting a new technology will not halt its progress.

The point to remember here is that whenever we use or perceive any technological extension of ourselves, we necessarily embrace it. Whenever we watch a TV screen or read a book, we are absorbing these extensions of ourselves into our individual system and experiencing an automatic "closure" or

displacement of perception; we can't escape this perpetual embrace of our daily technology unless we escape the technology itself and flee to a hermit's cave. By consistently embracing all these technologies, we inevitably relate ourselves to them as servomechanisms. Thus, in order to make use of them at all, we must serve them as we do gods. The Eskimo is a servomechanism of his kayak, the cowboy of his horse, the businessman of his clock, the cyberneticist — and soon the entire world — of his computer. In other words, to the spoils belongs the victor.

This continuous modification of man by his own technology stimulates him to find continuous means of modifying it; man thus becomes the sex organs of the machine world just as the bee is of the plant world, permitting it to reproduce and constantly evolve to higher forms. The machine world reciprocates man's devotion by rewarding him with goods and services and bounty. Man's relationship with his machinery is thus inherently symbiotic. This has always been the case; it's only in the electric age that man has an opportunity to *recognize* this marriage to his own technology. Electric technology is a qualitative extension of this age-old man-machine relationship; 20th Century man's relationship to the computer is not by nature very different from prehistoric man's relationship to his boat or to his wheel — with the important difference that all previous technologies or extensions of man were partial and fragmentary, whereas the electric is total and inclusive. Now man is beginning to wear his brain outside his skull and his nerves outside his skin; new technology breeds new man. A recent cartoon portrayed a little boy telling his nonplused mother: "I'm going to be a computer when I grow up." Humor is often prophecy.

PLAYBOY: If man can't prevent this transformation of himself by technology — or *into* technology — how can he control and direct the process of change?

McLUHAN: The first and most vital step of all, as I said at the outset, is simply to understand media and their revolutionary effects on all psychic and social values and institutions. Understanding is half the battle. The central purpose of all my work is to convey this message, that by understanding media as they extend man, we gain a measure of control over them. And this is a vital task, because the immediate interface between audile-tactile and visual perception is taking place everywhere around us. No civilian can escape this environmental blitzkrieg, for there is, quite literally, no place to hide. But if we diagnose what is happening to us, we can reduce the ferocity of the winds of change and bring the best elements of the old visual culture, during this transitional period, into peaceful coexistence with the new retribalized society.

If we persist, however, in our conventional rearview-mirror approach to these cataclysmic developments, all of Western culture will be destroyed and swept into the dustbin of history. If literate Western man were really interested in preserving the most creative aspects of his civilization, he would not cower in his ivory tower bemoaning change but would plunge himself into the vortex of electric technology and, by understanding it, dictate his new environment — turn ivory tower into control tower. But I can understand his hostile attitude, because I once shared his visual bias.

PLAYBOY: What changed your mind?

McLUHAN: Experience. For many years, until I wrote my first book, *The Mechanical Bride*, I adopted an extremely moralistic approach to all environmental technology. I loathed machinery, I abominated cities, I equated the Industrial Revolution with original sin and mass media with the Fall. In short, I rejected almost every element of modern life in favor of a Rousseauvian utopianism. But gradually I perceived how sterile and useless this attitude was, and I began to realize that the greatest artists of the 20th Century — Yeats, Pound, Joyce, Eliot — had discovered a totally different approach, based on the identity of the processes of cognition and creation. I realized that artistic creation is the playback of ordinary experience — from trash to treasures. I ceased being a moralist and became a student.

As someone committed to literature and the traditions of literacy, I began to study the new environment that imperiled literary values, and I soon realized that they could not be dismissed by moral outrage or pious indignation. Study showed that a totally new approach was required, both to save what deserved saving in our Western heritage and to help man adopt a new survival strategy. I adapted some of this new approach in *The Mechanical Bride* by attempting to immerse myself in the advertising media in order to apprehend their impact on man, but even there some of my old literate "point of view" bias crept in. The book, in any case, appeared just as television was making all its major points irrelevant.

I soon realized that recognizing the symptoms of change was not enough; one must understand the *cause* of change, for without comprehending causes, the social and psychic effects of new technology cannot be counteracted or modified. But I recognized also that one individual cannot accomplish these self-protective modifications; they must be the collective effort of society, because they affect all of society; the individual is helpless against the pervasiveness of environmental change: the new garbage — or mess-age — induced by new technologies. Only the social organism, united and recognizing the challenge, can move to meet it.

Unfortunately, no society in history has ever known enough about the forces that shape and transform it to take action to control and direct new technologies as they extend and transform man. But today, change proceeds so instantaneously through the new media that it may be possible to institute a global education program that will enable us to seize the reins of our destiny — but to do this we must first recognize the kind of therapy that's needed for the effects of the new media. In such an effort, indignation against those who perceive the nature of those effects is no substitute for awareness and insight.

PLAYBOY: Are you referring to the critical attacks to which you've been subjected for some of your theories and predictions?

McLUHAN: I am. But I don't want to sound uncharitable about my critics. Indeed, I appreciate their attention. After all, a man's detractors work for him tirelessly and for free. It's as good as being banned in Boston. But as I've said, I can understand their hostile attitude toward environmental change, having once shared it. Theirs is the customary human reaction when confronted with innovation: to flounder about attempting to adapt old responses to new situations or to simply condemn or ignore the harbingers of change — a practice refined by the Chinese emperors, who used to execute messengers bringing bad news. The new technological environments generate the most pain among those least prepared to alter their old value structures. The literati find the new electronic environment far more threatening than do those less committed to literacy as a way of life. When an individual or social group feels that its whole identity is jeopardized by social or psychic change, its natural reaction is to lash out in defensive fury. But for all their lamentations, the revolution has already taken place.

PLAYBOY: You've explained why you avoid approving or disapproving of this revolution in your work, but you must have a private opinion. What is it?

McLUHAN: I don't like to tell people what I think is good or bad about the social and psychic changes caused by new media, but if you insist on pinning me down about my own subjective reactions as I observe the reprimitivization of our culture, I would have to say that I view such upheavals with total personal dislike and dissatisfaction. I do see the prospect of a rich and creative retribalized society — free of the fragmentation and alienation of the mechanical age — emerging from this traumatic period of culture clash; but I have nothing but distaste for the *process* of change. As a man molded within the literate Western tradition, I do not personally cheer the dissolution of that tradition through the electric involvement of all the senses: I don't enjoy the destruction of neighborhoods by high-rises or revel in the pain of identity quest. No one could be less enthusiastic about these radical changes than myself. I am not, by temperament or conviction, a revolutionary; I would prefer a stable, changeless environment of modest services and human scale. TV and all the electric media are unraveling the entire fabric of our society, and as a man who is forced by circumstances to live within that society, I do not take delight in its disintegration.

You see, I am not a crusader; I imagine I would be most happy living in a secure preliterate environment; I would never attempt to change my world, for better or worse. Thus I derive no joy from observing the traumatic effects of media on man, although I do obtain satisfaction from grasping their modes of operation. Such comprehension is inherently cool, since it is simultaneously involvement and detachment. This posture is essential in studying media. One must begin by becoming extraenvironmental, putting oneself beyond the battle in order to study and understand the configuration of forces. It's vital to adopt a posture of arrogant superiority; instead of scurrying into a corner and wailing about what media are doing to us, one should charge straight ahead and kick them in the electrodes. They respond beautifully to such resolute treatment and soon become servants rather than masters. But without this detached involvement, I could never objectively observe media; it would be like an octopus grappling with the Empire State Building. So I employ the greatest boon of literate culture: the power of man to act without reaction — the sort of specialization by dissociation that has been the driving motive force behind Western civilization.

The Western world is being revolutionized by the electric media as rapidly as the East is being Westernized, and although the society that eventually emerges may be superior to our own, the process of change is agonizing. I must move through this pain-wracked transitional era as a scientist would move through a world of disease; once a surgeon becomes personally involved and disturbed about the condition of his patient, he loses the power to help that patient. Clinical detachment is not some kind of haughty pose I affect — nor does it reflect any lack of compassion on my part; it's simply a survival strategy. The world we are living in is not one I would have created on my own drawing board, but it's the one in which I must live, and in which the students I teach must live. If nothing else, I owe it to them to avoid the luxury of moral indignation or the troglodytic security of the ivory tower and to get down into the junk yard of environmental change and steam-shovel my way through to a comprehension of its contents and its lines of force — in order to understand how and why it is metamorphosing man.

PLAYBOY: Despite your personal distaste for the upheavals induced by the new electric technology, you seem to feel that if we understand and influence its effects on us, a less alienated and fragmented society may emerge from it. Is it thus accurate to say that you are essentially optimistic about the future?

McLUHAN: There are grounds for both optimism and pessimism. The extensions of man's consciousness induced by the electric media could conceivably usher in the millennium, but it also holds the potential for realizing the Anti-Christ — Yeats' rough beast, its hour come round at last, slouching toward Bethlehem to be born. Cataclysmic environmental changes such as these are, in and of themselves, morally neutral; it is how we perceive them and react to them that will determine their ultimate psychic and social consequences. If we refuse to see them at all, we will become their servants. It's inevitable that the world-pool of electronic information movement will toss us all about like corks on a stormy sea, but if we keep our cool during the descent into the maelstrom, studying the process as it happens to us and what we can do about it, we can come through.

Personally, I have a great faith in the resiliency and adaptability of man, and I tend to look to our tomorrows with a surge of excitement and hope. I feel that we're standing on the threshold of a liberating and exhilarating world in which the human tribe can become truly one family and man's consciousness can be freed from the shackles of mechanical culture and enabled to roam the cosmos. I have a deep and abiding belief in man's potential to grow and learn, to plumb the depths of his own being and to learn the secret songs that orchestrate the universe. We live in a transitional era of profound pain and tragic identity quest, but the agony of our age is the labor pain of rebirth.

I expect to see the coming decades transform the planet into an art form; the new man, linked in a cosmic harmony that transcends time and space, will sensuously caress and mold and pattern every facet of the terrestrial artifact as if it were a work of art, and man himself will become an organic art form. There is a long road ahead, and the stars are only way stations, but we have begun the journey. To be born in this age is a precious gift, and I regret the prospect of my own death only because I will leave so many pages of man's destiny — if you will excuse the Gutenbergian image — tantalizingly unread. But perhaps, as I've tried to demonstrate in my examination of the postliterate culture, the story begins only when the book closes.

14

A McLuhan Sourcebook

Key Quotations from the Writings of Marshall McLuhan, Assembled by William Kuhns

McLuhan was the most epigrammatic of writers. His talent for the gemlike insight — in which various facets, from unrelated worlds, flared with brilliant, wholly shared light — was unrivalled. To this day, the French term *McLuhanisme* describes the junction of discrepant worlds that can mingle and intersect, bringing illumination to one another.

His genius for compression was allied to a discursive, non-consecutive, and frequently confounding style. In *Understanding Media*, there are paragraphs more dizzying and gravity-defying than Montreal's fabled roller coaster, Le Monstre. If McLuhan flashed constantly with brilliance, each flash could lurch and twist in a new unexpected direction from the flash that came before. His writings offer remarkable riches, and very little continuity.

Yet one marvel of his aphorisms is that they lend themselves to a continuity and a context all their own. This is the idea behind the Sourcebook. His most provocative and compelling comments on any subject can be assembled in a few pages. Each remark remains discretely its own, a world of

insight unto itself, with no formal continuity between what comes before or after. Yet the combined effect is to converge different sources of luminosity. The quotations interact with one another, becoming a kind of nonlinear essay.

McLuhan's best thought speaks to us in the language of metaphor. In a scientific and logical universe, this makes him suspect: not only do many of his tenets lie beyond present scientific scrutiny; like any voice that speaks primarily in metaphor, McLuhan lends himself to subjective, rather than "objective," understanding.

This may appear a difficulty: it is a remarkable strength. McLuhan's best aphorisms can be described as arcs of thought strikingly like subatomic trajectories: they're startling, constantly transformative, and influenced by the subtle participation of the observer. Understandably, McLuhan's critics shy from this volatility: his final meaning seems pitched for them in ever-changing shades of ambiguity. Yet there can be a fine creative edge in that ambiguity. For example, in 1962 he wrote: "The new reality is in the image and not behind it." This has no predetermined meaning. A fashion designer whose faith rides on label and logo would make one sense of it; a programmer who creates computerized models of aerodynamic flow would make another sense of it. Both are apt. It is the breadth of aptness which we find so unfamiliar.

McLuhan was trained as a literary scholar. Within the realms of poetry, drama, fiction, variable interpretations of the same work are not only allowable: they are a measure of the writer's reach. The world of technology has fostered other rules. Any engineer will tell you that the scanning raster lines of a TV are no more and no less than its scanning raster lines. McLuhan looked at those lines and asked, "Why should the broken lines of the television mosaic emphasize the sculptural contours of objects?" Or, why should the scanning raster lines of the TV behave so much like a human finger?

A question like this brings the gifts of a major poet to the terra incognita of our technological environment. In doing that, McLuhan offered what no one before him had dreamt possible, and what no one since has adequately begun to achieve: a perception of our man-made world which can tap into the richest resources of the imagination.

McLuhan not only speaks through one's intuition, he expands it, and enables it to return to the world with awakened capabilities. What is there to learn from McLuhan? Perception and perception and perception.

I. ABOUT MEDIA

MEDIA AS "THE NEW NATURE"

The new media are not bridges between man and nature; they are nature.

The new media are not ways of relating us to the old "real" world; they are the real world and they reshape what remains of the old world at will. — *1969*

It is the medium that shapes and controls the scale and form of human association and action. — *1964*

The word "medium" was Latin for "public." There not being any reading public before printing, men perhaps tended to think of readers at large as a kind of scattering of currency — a "medium" in that sense. — *1973*

The reader of the newspaper accepts the newspaper not so much as a highly artificial image having some correspondence to reality as he tends to accept it as reality itself. Perhaps the effect is for the media to substitute for reality just in the degree to which they become virtuosos of realistic detail.

The news automatically becomes the real world for the TV user and is not a substitute for reality, but is itself an immediate reality. — *1978*

We must substitute an interest in the media for the previous interest in subjects. This is the logical answer to the fact that the media have substituted themselves for the older world. Even if we should wish to recover that older world we can do so only by an intensive study of the ways in which the media have swallowed it. — *1956*

AS NEW LANGUAGES . . .

Today we are beginning to realize that the new media are not just mechanical gimmicks for creating worlds of illusion, but new languages with new and unique powers of expression. — *1957*

If a language contrived and used by many people is a mass medium, any one of our new media is in a sense a new language, a new codification of experience collectively achieved by new work habits and inclusive collective awareness. — *1960*

New media may at first appear as mere codes of transmission for older achievement and established patterns of thought. But nobody could make the mistake of supposing that phonetic writing merely made it possible for the Greeks to set down in visual order what they had thought and known before writing. In the same way printing made literature possible. It did not merely encode literature. — *1960*

Ads, comics, and movies are not codes in North America but basic languages. That we have not yet begun to teach their grammars is as natural as it is for pre-literate man to ignore the written or visual mode of his language. Grammar comes from the Greek "written." And education would seem to involve the translation of experience into a new mode. — *1960*

It is the framework that changes with each new technology and not just the picture within the frame.

The spoken word was the first technology by which man was able to let go of his environment in order to grasp it in a new way.

We must maximize rather than minimize the various features of our new media. It is easy now to see that they are not mere vehicles for already-achieved experience and insight.

Gramophone and movies were merely the mechanization of speech and gesture. But the radio and TV were not just the electronification of speech and gesture but the electronification of the entire range of human personal expressiveness. With electronification the flow is taken out of the wire and into the vacuum tube circuit, which confers freedom and flexibility such as are in metaphor and in words themselves. — *1955*

Each new technology creates an environment that is itself regarded as corrupt and degrading yet the new one turns its predecessor into an art form. — *1964*

The bias of each medium of communication is far more distorting than the deliberate lie. The form and tone of some press styles may make the very concept of truth irrelevant. The most urgent and reliable facts presented in this way are a travesty of any reality. — *1955*

All media exist to invest our lives with artificial perception and arbitrary values. — *1964*

The effects of new media on our sensory lives are similar to the effects of new poetry. They change not our thoughts but the structure of our world. — *1969*

(To Mike Wallace) If I turn off this mike my relationship to you is changed instantly. — *1966*

BURSTING BOUNDARIES

Today the boundaries between inner and outer forces of the media are confused. And our four-century preoccupation with print has fixed our attention on so limited an aspect of the media that we find it very hard to release our attention to the whole range of media influence. What I wish to show is that today we experience, in reverse, what pre-literate men faced with the advent of writing. — *1955*

Personally, I think that the effect of the telegraph has been . . . to break down the division between our inner and outer worlds. — *1956*

There is no inside or outside under electronic conditions. That is the meaning of our glass buildings, the new banking services. — *1970*

The dichotomy between information and entertainment has ended. — *1962*

What we call entertainment at the present time is really, basically, a form of politics. There is really far more politics in Hollywood in the consumer attitudes and personal preferences and goals as set by casting bureaus and so on, far more political reality in the Hollywood scene than there ever has been in the so-called political scene. — *1966*

The media themselves are the avant-garde of our society. Avant-garde no longer exists in painting and music and poetry, it's the media themselves. — *1973*

With the telegraph and after, we enter the world of interdependence and inter-action, in which no medium has its meaning alone and no product or advertisement has its meaning or use by itself. — *1961*

DEVELOPING THE POTENTIAL OF NEW MEDIA

[F.D.R.] was at great pains to use an unfavourable press to enhance his radio image. The art of politics today requires an orchestral use of the varied instruments of public communication. These instruments do not exist or function in isolation from one another any more than do our senses function in isolation. — *1965*

Circuitry means that every situation must fold back into itself much in the pattern of cognition and its playback, which is "recognition" in the action of human perceiving and knowing. The new technology mimes the prime procedure of human learning and knowing. — *1968*

For rational beings to see or re-cognize their experience in a new material form is an unbought grace of life. Experience translated into a new medium literally bestows a delightful playback of earlier awareness.

It is possible that our new technologies can bypass verbalizing. There is nothing inherently impossible in the computer, or that type of technology, extending consciousness itself — as a universal environment. There is a sense in which the surround of information that we now experience electrically is an extension of consciousness itself. — *1970*

New media are new archetypes, at first disguised as degradations of older media. These degradations happen when new media inevitably use older ones as content. Using the older ones as content hastens the tidying-up process by which a medium becomes an art form. — *1964*

Except for light, all other media come in pairs, with one acting as the "content" of the other, obscuring the operation of both. — *1964*

The art of politics today requires an orchestral use of the varied instruments of public communication. The most ardent Beatlemaniac is quite unable to verbalize the meaning of the Beatles. In the same way a flag cannot involve if its symbols can be spelt out or verbalized. A flag issue that is raised and maintained on the level of editorial debate has no relevance to the function of flag. — *1964*

ENVIRONMENTS

[Environment, from the Greek, peri-vello: to hit from all sides at once]

Environments are not just containers, but are processes that change the content totally. — *1967*

Cab Calloway: "When I walk down Eighth Avenue, man, I see rhythms, I don't see downtown."

A prime feature of the environmental is its invisibility and unawareness. This seems to be involved in the very process of phylogeny. Each new stage of growth becomes the environment for all preceding stages. But we are aware only of the preceding stages, or, as it were, the content of the environment. — *1964*

The new environment reprocesses the old one as radically as TV is reprocessing film. — *1964*

The unconscious is a store of everything at once. When you begin to move information electrically, you begin to create a subconscious outside. — *1967*

We actually live in a world environment that now has the structure of our own subconscious lives . . . — *1967*

The sudden discovery of nature was made possible by the railway.

At electric speeds of data processing, we become aware of environments for the first time. We call them "parameters." It all began in electronic research when it was discovered that the instruments of observation distorted the data. Now we know that any environment acts like the instrument of observation. — *1964*

The simultaneous insists upon the harmonious. — *1957*

The present is always invisible because it's environmental. No environment is perceptible, simply because it saturates the whole field of attention. — *1967*

We can always see the Emperor's old clothes, but not his new ones. — *1965*

Electric technology offers, perhaps for the first time, a means of dealing with the environment itself as a direct instrument of vision and knowing.

All human technology begins as an immediate service or aid to some existing function and this aid quickly develops its own field of associated services and activities which, in turn, create new services and satisfactions. — *1973*

While environments as such have a strange power to elude perception, the preceding ones acquire an almost nostalgic fascination when surrounded by the new. This is nowhere more evident than in the art of photography with its power to invest all human artifacts with the quality of art. — *1967*

One of the features of service environments is that two create less total service than one, or, in other words, the addition of service environments creates not increased service but a decrease of service. — *1970*

Apropos "the medium is the message" I now point out that the medium is not the figure but the ground, not the motor car but the highways and the factories. Also, I point out that in all media the user is the content, and the effects come before the invention.
— *1973*

It may even be that the loss of one's power to recognize new patterns of power in the environment is in direct ratio to the impact of such new powers. We are most nearly numb where impact is most severe . . . A. J. Toynbee has few if any instances of societies meeting the challenge of major change successfully. — *1964*

Whether it be recognized as radio or television or Telstar or the bomb, the new environment of mankind is scarcely "hardware" or physical so much as it is information and the configurations of codified data. — *1966*

HOW NEW ENVIRONMENTS RESHAPE OLDER ENVIRONMENTS

You have to perceive the consequences of the new environment on the old environment before you know what the new environment is.

When a new environment forms, we see the old one as if we lived in a world of the *déjà vu*. This was, of course, Plato's theory of knowledge, that it was a form of recognition of that which we had known in another existence. — *1967*

The history of the arts and sciences could be written in terms of the continuing process by which new technologies create new environments for old technologies. — *1964*

Each technological extension involves an act of collective cannibalism. The previous environment is swallowed by the new environment and reprocessed for whatever values are digestible. Thus, Nature was succeeded by the mechanical environment and became what we call the "content" of the new industrial environment. — *1964*

. . . we now live in a technologically prepared environment that blankets the earth itself. The humanly contrived environment of electric information and power has begun to take precedence over the old environment of "nature." Nature, as it were, begins to be the content of our technology.
— *1965*

And this strange processing of old forms by new forms tends, in some cases, to strengthen the old forms considerably. For example, one of the effects of automation on libraries and catalogs is to enormously increase the whole cataloging activity. Unexpectedly, instead of supplanting it, it has increased it enormously. — *1965*

Xerox makes it possible to present instant recaps of ongoing events — a sort of "story so far" that used to sit above serial publications. As in football instant replays, the recap or *recorso* draws attention to processes rather than product or even goal. The audience is involved in the game in a totally new way — a way that changes the game itself. — *1964*

Xerox has completely changed the nature of conferences and has led to a much higher frequency of meetings. Xerox feeds and speeds the entire environment into the dialogue process of the conference table. — *1971*

HOW TO STUDY MEDIA

You must be literate in umpteen media to be really "literate" nowadays.
— *1966*

If you want to understand the nature of TV, you make a complete inventory of all the things that have changed in the past 12 years, in dress, in social behavior, in program tastes. — *1966*

Understanding several media simultaneously is the best way of approaching any one of them.

Any study of one medium helps us to understand all others. — *1964*

A primary method for studying the effects of anything is simply to imagine ourselves as suddenly deprived of them. If students were to interview physically deprived people about the effects on them of living in a world which has no place for a paraplegic, or a blind man, they would quickly apprehend the menace of our man-made service environment. — *1974*

Bad news reveals the character of change; good news does not. — *1966*

[Joyce showed how to] make an inventory of all the effects of the new thing as it encounters all the older forms of the society. — *1967*

The understanding of media as art forms is achieved by translation of one medium into another. — *1960*

Today we can test the contrast between radio and TV in a variety of ways. We have only to imagine what might be the effects of video-phone on the telephone to perceive the utter diversity of these media. — *1971*

If you wanted to study radio as a medium in its impact on society, you would do well to look at what happens to radio in a movie. What use is there made of radio in the movie? What happens to a telephone in a Broadway play? — *1959*

The best way to study the nature of any medium is to study its effect on other media because you can see them spelled out there. So when you study the effect of TV on sports, then you begin to understand the nature of TV. And when you see its effects on politics, in advertising, and in movies, then you begin to understand it. — *1977*

HYBRID MEDIA

The hypertrophy of written messages, which has been dubbed "Parkinson's law" by its author, would appear to be caused not by paper-shuffling and the typewriter, but by the effort of the typewriter to keep pace with the acceleration of information movement created by the telephone and electronic media. — *1960*

The hybrid or meeting of two media is a moment of truth and revelation from which new form is born. — *1964*

The electric typewriter is a contradiction in terms. It is a hybrid of the fragmentary and the integral. Our world is filled with such hybrids. The internal combustion engine is such a hybrid. — *1964*

The telegraph is an electric form that, when crossed with print and rotary presses, yields the modern newspaper. — *1964*

And the photograph is not a machine, but a chemical and light process that, crossed with the machine, yields the movie. — *1964*

One of the most common causes of breaks in any system is the cross-fertilization with another system, such as happened to print with the steam press, or with radio and movies (which yielded the talkies).

Artists in various fields are always the first to discover how to enable one medium to use or to release the power of another. — *1964*

Dickens, by using the newspaper as the content of the older novel form, created a new hybrid of great power. As usual, when the new medium swallowed an older one, conventional taste protested that vulgarization had occurred. Paradoxically, Dickens, by pushing the camera eye to a point of high fidelity, broke out of the domain of perspective and moved back into the highly tactual and iconic world of surrealism and modern art. — *1964*

MEDIA AS THEY AFFECT MEDIA

A new medium is never an addition to an old one, nor does it leave the old one in peace. It never ceases to oppress the older media until it finds new shapes and positions for them. — *1964*

One of the many effects of television on radio has been to shift radio from an entertainment medium into a kind of nervous information system. News bulletins, times signals, traffic data, above all weather reports, now serve to enhance the native power of radio to involve people in one another. — *1964*

The alphabet was one thing when applied to clay or stone, and quite another when set down on light papyrus. — *1964*

In the age of the photograph, language takes on a graphic or iconic character whose "meaning" belongs very little to the semantic universe, and not at all to the republic of letters. — *1964*

It was the telephone, paradoxically, that sped the commercial adoption of the typewriter. The phrase "send me a memo on that," repeated into millions of phones daily, helped to create the huge expansion of the typist function.
— *1964*

It seems useful to consider the impact of Xerox if only because it illustrates how profoundly one technology can alter traditional patterns of relation between writing and speaking. — *1973*

Xerox extends the function of the typewriter almost to the point where the secret, personal memo is moved into the public domain, as with the Pentagon Papers. When notes for briefing individuals or groups are first typed and then Xeroxed, it is as if a private manuscript were put in the hands of the general reader. The typewriter plus photocopying thus, unexpectedly, restores many of the features of confidential handwritten records. — *1973*

Today the decentralizing of such institutions [as department stores] into a multiplicity of small shops in shopping plazas is partly the creation of the

car, partly the result of TV. — *1964*

The BBC was set up to some extent, according to Innis, under the pressure of newspapers, post office, and various political pressures which felt that this form would be altogether too radical or mutational if it got out of hand.
— *1959*

The newspaper that could advertise every sort of product on one page quickly gave rise to department stores that provided every kind of product under one roof. — *1964*

Yet does General Motors, for example, know, or ever suspect, anything about the effect of the TV image on the users of their motor cars? — *1964*

With the rise of statistics as a means of persuasion in 1830s, parliamentary oratory took a nose dive. Gladstone appears to have been the first to master statistics as a form of oratory. The advent of radio in the same way was fatal to political oratory, for one cannot orate into microphone. — *1957*

MEDIA FUSING FUNCTIONS

The typewriter fuses composition and publication, causing an entirely new attitude to the written and printed word. Composing on the typewriter has altered the forms of the language and literature. — *1974*

Like the typewriter, the telephone fuses functions, enabling the call-girl, for example, to be her own procurer and madame. — *1964*

The very nature of the telephone, as of all electric media, is to compress and unify that which had previously been divided and specialized. Only the authority of knowledge works by telephone because of the speed that creates a total and inclusive field of relations. — *1964*

The poet or novelist now composes on the typewriter. The typewriter now fuses composition and publication, causing an entirely new attitude to the written and printed word. — *1964*

MEDIA REPROCESSING MEDIA

When television becomes an old technology, we will really understand and appreciate its glorious properties.
— *1967*

The history of the arts and sciences could be written in terms of the continuing process by which new technologies create new environments for old technologies. — *1964*

Swift's *A Tale of a Tub* used the new world of print to enclose the preceding world of the sermon and theological exegesis. Swift is aware of the conflict of forms somewhat in the manner of *Mad Magazine* today.
— *1964*

It is not surprising that these new [electrical] forms have beaten the book into the pulps, just as the book destroyed the manuscript and the great

culture linked to it. In 1831 the French poet Lamartine foresaw that the newspaper was the book and the poetry of the future.

THE USER AS CONTENT OF A MEDIUM

When one medium uses another, it is the user that is the "content." When motor cars ride on freight cars, the car is using the railway, and the car is the "content" of the railway, and also of the highway. So it is when print uses the manuscript, or when TV uses the movie, or when movie uses the theatre or when writing uses the voice. Hybridising or piggy-backing creates new chemical compounds like talking pictures or horseless carriages.
— *1971*

In the case of any medium whatever, whether of language or clothing or radio or TV, it is the user himself who is the content, and it is the user alone who constitutes the experience of that service. No matter what is on TV, if the user is a Chinese, it is going to be a Chinese program, just as surely as a movie on TV is experienced as a TV show. — *1974*

You are the content of any extension of yourself, whether it be pin or pen, pencil or sword, be it palace or page, song or dance or speech . . . The meaning of all these is the experience of using these extensions of yourself. Meaning is not "content" but an active relationship. — *1971*

The user is always the content, at least in the traditional Aristotelean view that the "cognitive agent itself becomes and is the thing known."

— *1975*

I. A. Richards's . . . *Practical Criticism* was a series of revelations about what people do when they actually read [a poem]. They turn it into whatever happens to suit them.

— *1978*

The reader "puts on" the poem as a mask. He becomes its "content" by adjusting himself to use the poem as a means of perceiving the world.

— *1974*

II. MEDIA EVOLUTION, MEDIA FORMS

PATTERNS IN MEDIA EVOLUTION

In short, any new technology is an evolutionary and biological mutation opening new doors of perception and new spheres of action to mankind.
— *1964*

Every mode of technology is a reflex of our most intimate psychological experience. — *1947*

The new technology mimes the prime procedure of human learning and knowing. — *1968*

Physiologically, man in his normal use of technology, or his variously extended body, is perpetually modified by it and in turn finds ever new ways of modifying his technology. — *1964*

Until 1700 more than 50 per cent of all printed books were ancient or medieval. Not only antiquity but also the Middle Ages were given to the first reading public of the printed word. And the medieval texts were by far the most popular. — *1964*

At the very beginning, in 1450, the printed word already had all the essential characteristics of modern movies. The movie today is at once a fulfillment and a kind of reversal of the nature of print invented five hundred years ago. — *1959*

The "flickers," as the movies were once called, are really built into the printed form. The printed form is itself a flicker in which you are constantly transferring from this shot to that shot. This shot, the image lingers while you look at that one, and while you look at the next one, there's a fingering, wavering, doubtful no-man's land.
— *1959*

Edwin Schrödinger has explained how he and his fellow physicists had agreed that they would report their new discoveries and experiments in quantum physics in the language of the old Newtonian physics. That is, they agreed to discuss and to report the nonvisual, electronic world in the language of the visual world of Newton.
— *1974*

TV is a new start, like the invention of writing itself. But the movie is in a sense the final stage of the Gutenberg revolution; for the movie is a mechanical, not an electronic, form. And print was the first mechanization of a handicraft, the first form of mass production by exact repetition. — *1958*

Television may be as decisively the successor to writing as oral speech was the predecessor of writing.
— *1955*

The television environment has steadily upgraded the old movie forms into sentimentally valued art forms. The medieval world got the same treatment from the Gutenberg technology. — *1966*

We have here today, the electronic equipment (TV) that is translating us into software instantaneously and enables us to be played back as software instantaneously. — *1978*

The new environment of mankind is scarcely "hardware" or physical so much as it is information and the configurations of codified data. — *1966*

But whereas the age of photo, radio, and movie was the period of fission in media and marketing, with TV we now move into the age of fusion and, even psychically, the hydrogen bomb. The message of TV is of interfusion, implosion, and integral effort. — *1961*

As technology advances, it reverses the characteristics of every situation again and again. The age of automation is going to be the age of "do it yourself." — *1957*

LANGUAGE AND SPEECH

The great and abiding mass medium is not literature but speech. Language is at once the most vulgar of all media and the greatest work of art that ever can be devised by man.

Language does for intelligence what the wheel does for the feet and the body. It enables them to move from thing to thing with greater ease and speed and ever less involvement. — *1964*

Our own mother tongues are things in which we participate totally. They

change our perception. So that if we spoke Chinese we would have a different sense of hearing, smell, and touch. — *1970*

The mother tongue is propaganda. — *1965*

Speech is our principal means of structuring interpersonal distances. And these distances are not just physical, but emotional and cultural. We involuntarily raise our voices when speaking to those who do not understand our language. — *1955*

When does a mechanical code of transmission of information itself become a language? Under what conditions does a language revert to a code of transmission? With our new coding devices today [such as movies] we are setting about to establish whether these means of transmission have themselves so deeply altered human sensibilities and reshaped human institutions and attitudes as to have acquired the status of new languages. — *1960*

For to an infant, English is not a language but a mechanical code. To an adult beginning Russian, it, too, is first a mechanical code. It becomes a language only when it has become subliminal. — *1960*

Traditional vernaculars are themselves the great mass media; that is, specialized frames and vehicles of experience.

Language is metaphor in the sense that it not only stores but translates experi-

ence from one mode to another.
— *1962*

Eliot's discovery that our whole English language was shifting from iambic rising stress to trochaic falling stress goes along with an amazing set of revolutions in English language and literature and a change of human outlook and human association. — *1965*

For language, itself, is the collective mask of a culture, even as its resources and powers for channelling perception are the prime concern of the poet. With language, the poet assumes the corporate mask and manipulates it like a puppet. — *1963*

The English or any other language is itself a massive organization of traditional experience providing a complex view of the world. — *1954*

Human languages are the greatest of all works of art beside which the works of Homer, Virgil, Dante, and Shakespeare are minor variations. — *1954*

Language is really a storage system for the corporate and collective experience of all mankind . . . Every time you play back some of that language, you release a whole charge of these ancient perceptions and memories.
— *1966*

Although we think of speech [in mother tongues] as near and private, there is nothing about us that is so corporate and public. Speech in its subliminal resonance unites us with the most distant ages as well as with the present multitudes. — *1972*

ALPHABET

The phonetic alphabet is unique in being formed by phonemes, or meaningless bits. All other alphabets consist mainly of morphemes, or meaningful bits. The extreme abstraction of meaning from the formal sign . . . releases the visual faculty from its embodiment in the other senses. In separation from sound and touch and semantics, both Euclid and logic become simultaneously possible. — *1973*

The translating of auditory into visual terms set up an inner life in man which separated himself from the exterior world and, in part, from his own senses, as we know from the study of pre-literate societies. — *1953*

The unique power [of the alphabet] is its power to separate sound, sight and meaning. The letters of our alphabet are semantically neutral . . . This divorce . . . has permeated and shaped all the perceptions of Western literate man. — *1964*

The Japanese are about to launch a multi-billion dollar program to impose Western phonetic literacy on the whole of Japan. This program will scrub off the entire face of Japan, eroding its oral culture . . . The ripping-off of the entire Japanese iden-tity will release a fantastic flood of violence and a corporate quest for new identity on a competitive scale unimagined in human history. — *1974*

The phonetic alphabet is the only one in which the letters are semantically neutral, lacking verbal structure or force. Since the visual image presented in these letters is acoustically and semantically neutral, they have had the extraordinary effect . . . of supporting the visual faculty independently. — *1973*

The translation of auditory into visual terms set up an inner life in man which separated him from the external world and, in part, from his own senses, as we know from the study of pre-literate societies. — *1953*

Phonetically literate man, from the Greeks to the present, has been consistently aggressive with his environment. His need to translate his environment into phonetic, literate terms turns him into a conqueror and a cultural bulldozer, or leveller. — *1974*

WRITING AND THE WRITTEN WORD

In large measure [writing] is the spatialization of thought. — *1954*

Writing gives control over space. Writing produces at once the city. The power to shape space in writing brings the power to organize space architecturally. And when messages can be transported, then come the road, and armies, and empires. The empires of Alexander and the Caesars were essentially built by paper routes. — *1954*

In the *Phaedrus*, Plato argued that the new arrival of writing would revolutionize culture for the worst. He suggested that it would substitute reminiscence for thought and mechanical learning for the true dialect of the living quest for truth by discourse and conversation. — *1954*

The written word no longer relates people to the key jobs and functions of our society. The airplane pilot doesn't depend upon written messages. And the same goes for just about everybody. — *1967*

PRINT

A place for everything and everything in its place is a feature not only of the compositor's arrangement of his type fonts, but of the entire range of human organization of knowledge and action from the sixteenth century onward.
— *1964*

. . . the space of the modern classroom is based on the printed book. The kind of uniform, repeatable enclosure of data from the press made it possible for the first time in history to have the same book in front of teacher and student alike . . . . Modern classroom seating plans persist in the spatial layout of the movable types which gave us the printed page. — *1961*

Print provided a vast new memory for past writings that made a personal memory inadequate. — *1964*

In five centuries explicit comment and

awareness of the effects of print on human sensibility are very scarce. — *1964*

The fact that print fosters the consumer habit of mind, the readiness to accept completely processed and packaged goods, is a side of print that has been little considered. — *1958*

Print created the mental habit of communing with another mind. The illusion that you are in close and sympathetic contact with another mind is a natural illusion resulting from quickly following the images on the printed page. It is pure illusion. Nobody had such an illusion before printing, at least, nothing resembling it. — *1959*

We are perhaps too much a part of the civilization which followed the printing industry to be able to detect its characteristics. Education in the words of Laski became the art of teaching men to be deceived by the printed word. — *1964*

Not only does print vividly discover national boundaries, but the print market was itself defined by such boundaries, at least for early printers and publishers. Perhaps also the ability to see one's mother tongue in uniform and repeatable technological dress creates in the individual reader a feeling of unity and power that he shares with all other readers of that tongue. Quite different sentiments are felt by preliterate or semiliterate people. — *1960*

In fact, the discovery of movable type

was the ancestor of all assembly lines and it would be foolish to overlook the impact of the technological form involved in print on the psychological life of readers. To overlook this would be as unrealistic as to ignore rhythm and tempo in music. — *1964*

School and classroom as we know them were the direct extension of the technology of the printed book. And the printed book was the first teaching-machine, whereas the manuscript had been merely a teaching tool. — *1960*

Gutenberg made all history simultaneous: the transportable book brought the world of the dead into the space of the gentleman's library. — *1951*

Mechanization of any process is achieved by fragmentation, beginning with the mechanization of writing by movable type. — *1964*

The ability to see one's mother tongue in uniform . . . dress creates in the individual reader a feeling of unity and power that he shares with all other readers of that tongue. — *1960*

The literate liberal is convinced all real values are private, personal, individual. — *1962*

Perhaps the most potent of all as an expression of literacy is our system of uniform pricing that penetrates distant markets and speeds the turn-over of commodities. — *1964*

THE PHOTOGRAPH

While environments as such have a strange power to elude perception, the preceding ones acquire an almost nostalgic fascination when surrounded by the new. This is nowhere more evident than in the art of photography with its power to invest all human artifacts with the quality of art. This is no mere power of reproduction but a making-new. — *1967*

The photograph revolutionized the human image as much as it changed the patterns and spaces of our cities. Indeed, the photograph gave us a push in the direction of the programmed environment. — *1966*

In the photographic age, fashions have come to be like the collage style in painting. — *1964*

The first blow against nationalism is struck by the photograph, because it ignores all boundaries. It just annihilates the usual space-pockets created by newsprint. But even though it's printed in the newspaper, it's still totally antithetic to the news-story form, because what you see in a photograph is very different from what you read about a given situation in Korea or Cairo or anywhere else. What you see are people. What you read about are Egyptians, Koreans, and so on. — *1959*

The first market effect of the photo was to give new intensity of presence and conspicuousness to products. The new effect was to relate the consumer directly to the product . . . So that whereas the public had once been spectators of the rich consuming conspicuously, the public now became aware of the ordinary man in the act of consuming. — *1957*

The photograph has reversed the purpose of travel, which until now had been to encounter the strange and unfamiliar. — *1964*

A picture of a group of persons of any hue whatever is a picture of people, not of "coloured people." — *1964*

The photograph as an extension of the visual power has the strange property of being a form of statement without syntax. The woodcuts and engravings that preceded the photo were highly syntactical. So is the movie that succeeded the photograph. The syntax of the engraving was from the hand. The syntax of the movie is from the foot. The movie, physiologically, is the union of the eye and the foot. — *1964*

Photography has been one of the major means that compelled men to examine their environments critically. — *1967*

Nobody can commit photography alone. It is possible to have at least the illusion of reading and writing in isolation, but photography does not foster such attitudes. — *1964*

It was the photograph that revealed the secret of bird-flight and enabled man to take off. The photo, in arresting bird-flight, showed that it was based on a principle of wing fixity. Wing movement was seen to be for propulsion, not for flight. — *1964*

Just as the painter Samuel Morse had unintentionally projected himself into the nonvisual world of the telegraph, so the photograph really transcends the pictorial by capturing the inner gestures and postures of both body and mind, yielding the new worlds of endocrinology and psychopathology. — *1964*

THE TELEGRAPH

The telegraph . . . is not the mechanization of writing but the electrification of writing. — *1960*

The telegraph made possible a daily, hourly snap or cross-section of the globe. It killed the 19th-century editorial and the feature writer, who used to shake governments and mount diplomats.

The original telegraph line between Baltimore and Washington promoted chess games between experts in the two cities. Other lines were used for lotteries and play in general, just as early radio existed in isolation from any commercial commitments and was, in fact, fostered by the amateur hams for years before it was seized by big interests. — *1964*

The telegraph had already created new forms of the printed word, in the newspaper and in poetry alike. By making it possible for information to be gathered simultaneously from every quarter of the globe, the telegraph press took on a mosaic and essentially acoustic character of simultaneity that occurred in symbolist poetry as well. — *1974*

THE TELEPHONE

The very nature of the telephone, as all electric media, is to compress and unify that which had previously been divided and specialized. Only the "authority of knowledge" works by telephone because of the speed that creates a total and inclusive field of relations. — *1964*

The absence of image on the telephone is a great big positive potential of that medium that has never been tapped. It could be used for teaching mathematics to disadvantaged children and so on, to people who have no mathematical aptitude and so on. — *1966*

The auditory image of the telephone is of low definition. It elicits maximum attention and cannot be used as background. All the senses rally to strengthen the weak sound of the phone. We even feel the need to be kinetically involved via doodling or pacing. And whereas we complete the strong auditory image of radio by visualizing, we only slightly visualize on the phone. — *1964*

Whereas we accept the phone as an invader of our homes, we are by no means ready to leap outside our homes for socializing in the way which the videophone demands. — *1976*

Why does a phone ringing on the stage create instant tension? Why is that tension so very much less for an unanswered phone in a movie scene? The answer to all of these questions is simply that the phone is a participant form that demands a partner, with all the intensity of electric polarity. — *1964*

The English dislike the telephone so much that they substitute numerous mail deliveries for it. The Russians use the telephone for a status symbol, like the alarm clock worn by tribal chiefs as an article of attire in Africa.
— *1964*

We . . . hijack the [Inuit] group with Anik, with the satellites, and we put them on the air. You heard the story about having telephones put in there, but the people didn't want any private phones. Everybody wanted a party line so they could listen in to everybody else. They refused to have any private phones up in the Eskimo country. They insisted that everybody's conversation be available to everybody simultaneously. — *1973*

Telephone in hand, the decision maker can exercise only the authority of knowledge, not delegated authority.
— *1960*

"Real" is an idea borrowed from the visual world. The word "phony" — which means "unreal" in English slang — originally meant "as unreal as a telephone conversation." In the 1920 dictionary, that's what "phony" meant.
— *1978*

Electric media transport us instantly wherever we choose. When we are on the phone we don't just disappear down a hole, Alice in Wonderland style — we are there and they are here.
— *1971*

French is the "language of love" just because it unites voice and ear in an especially close way, as does the telephone. So it is quite natural to kiss via phone, but not easy to visualize while phoning. — *1964*

The child and the teenager understand the telephone, embracing the cord and the ear-mike as if they were beloved pets. — *1964*

THE TYPEWRITER

The rhythms of typing favour short, concise sentences, sentences with oral form. — *1974*

The typewriter is part of our oral revolution. — *1974*

A typewriter is a means of transcribing thought, not expressing it. — *1974*

At the typewriter, the poet commands the resources of the printing press. The machine is like a public address system immediately in hand. — *1964*

The typewriter fuses composition and publication, causing an entirely new attitude to the written and printed word. Composing on the typewriter has altered the forms of the language and literature. — *1974*

MOVIES

The movie, by sheer speeding up of the mechanical, carried us from the world of sequence and connections into the world of creative configuration and structure. — *1964*

The basic fact to keep in mind about the movie camera and projector is their resemblance to the process of human cognition. — *1954*

Film is still in its Manuscript phase.
— *1964*

When an inexpensive play-back for video tape is available, the film will become as portable as a book after Gutenberg. — *1966*

Every literary form, from the stream of consciousnessness to James Joyce and Virginia Woolf, to the private eye in the whodunit, is a direct import of film technique. One of the principal effects of new art forms is to awaken older forms to new life and manifestation. — *1964*

I can only regard the movie as the mechanization and distortion of this cognitive miracle by which we recreate the exterior world. But whereas cognition provides that dance of the intellect which is the analogical sense of Being, the mechanical medium has tended to provide merely a dream world which is a substitute for reality rather than a means of proving reality.
— *1954*

The movie camera is a means of rolling up the daylight world on a spool. It does this by rapid still shots. The movie projector unrolls the spool and recreates the daylight world as a dark dream world. In reversing the process of perception even the mechanical camera and projector bring about a mysterious change in everyday experience. The movie reconstructs the external daylight world and in so doing provides an interior dream world. — *1954*

You see, the camera extends your feet and your eyes; a movie camera carries your eyes out on your feet into the world — it's mobile. And TV doesn't do that; it doesn't extend your eyes and your feet, it extends your eyes and your hands: it feels, it handles, it scans the environment, by scanning, by handling. — *1966*

TV has processed the old movie into a widely heralded avant-garde form. The movie is no longer an environmental form. It is the "content" of TV. Thus it has become a harmless consumer commodity that is no longer regarded as corrupt and degrading. That designation is always reserved for whatever is actively environmental. — *1965*

In *David Copperfield*, [Dickens] experimented with the eyes of a child as if they were a camera turned on the adult world. To see the adult world as a live process unfolding mysteriously to the child's awareness was a notable degree of anticipation of film form and camera eye. D. W. Griffiths recognized this and habitually carried a volume of Dickens with him on location. He would sit down and open his Dickens in the midst of shooting a film in order to discover new ways of solving his problems. — *1964*

NEWSPAPER

The modern newspaper is a magical institution like the rainmaker. It is written to release feelings and to keep us in a state of perpetual emotion. It is not intended to provide rational schemes or patterns for digesting the news. It never provides insights into events, but merely the thrill of the event.

People don't actually read newspapers, they step into them like a warm bath.

Take the date line off a newspaper and it becomes an exotic and fascinating surrealist poem.

[On bad polling predictions] It's noticed in Britain too; the pollsters had a bad time. In the last two elections, they came off very badly. I think they are asking newspaper questions — high-definition questions about your point of view on this candidate, that candidate. — *1960*

Man uses the press for privacy in public conveyances. — *1967*

Most trivial matters are given considerable additional intensity by being translated into prose at all. That is why no account of anything can be "truthful" in a newspaper. — *1970*

The unformulated message of an assembly of news items from every quarter of the globe is that the world today is one city. All war is civil war. All suffering is our own. — *1954*

It is a paradoxical situation, but the press in literate America has an intensely oral character, while in oral Russia and Europe the press has a strongly literary character and function. — *1964*

It was Poe who invented both the detective story and the symbolist poem as his response to the electric challenge . . . Poe saw that the principle [of working backward for serialization] extended all the way to the daily news report. For, if news came in so fast that no single editorial eye could process the entire contents of the paper, then it was necessary to package the news in a style that made the reader the editor. — *1958*

In pictorial papers and magazines even words take on the character of landscape. — *1952*

What has happened since the old muck-raking days of the 1920s is that espionage, whether political or commercial, has become the largest business in the world, and we take it for granted that the modern newspaper depends on "bugging" the whole community. In fact, we expect the press to "bug" the world and to challenge and penetrate all privacy and identity, whether private or corporate.
— *1974*

Quite independently of good or bad editorial policies, the ordinary man is now accustomed to human-interest stories from every part of the globe. The sheer technique of world-wide news gathering has created a new state of mind which has little to do with local or national political opinion. So that even the frequent sensational absurdity and unreliability of the news cannot annul the total effect, which is to enforce a deep sense of human solidarity. — *1951*

It is the daily communal exposure of multiple items in juxtaposition that gives the press its complex dimension of human interest. — *1964*

The classified ads (and stock-marketed quotations) are the bedrock of the press. Should an alternative source of easy access to such diverse daily information be found, the press would fold. — *1964*

News, far more than art, is artifact. — *1969*

The proud motto "All the news that's fit to print" advertises the fact that news is actually a fiction. From the initial selection of experiences to be written up, to the arbitrary selection of items to be read by the reader as scanner, there is a large factor of choice in looking at the world itself as *something to fit print.* — *1971*

"He made the news" is a strangely ambiguous phrase, since to be in the newspaper is both to be news and to make news. Thus "making the news," like "making good," implies a world of actions and fictions alike. — *1964*

RADIO

Radio was inseparable from the rise of jazz culture as TV has been inseparable from the rise of rock culture. — *1972*

The subliminal depths of radio are charged with the resonating echoes of tribal horns and antique drums . . . this medium has the power to turn the psyche and society into a single echo chamber. — *1964*

Radio provides a speed-up of information that also causes acceleration in other media. It certainly contracts the world to village size, and creates insatiable village tastes for gossip, rumor, and personal malice. — *1964*

Radio will serve as background-sound or as a noise-level control, as when the ingenious teenager employs it as a means of privacy. — *1964*

Radio . . . transforms the relation of everybody to everybody, regardless of programming. — *1974*

The power of radio to involve people in-depth is manifested in its use during homework by youngsters and by many other people who carry transistor sets in order to provide a private world for themselves amidst crowds. — *1964*

Radio provided the first massive experience of electronic implosion, that reversal of the entire direction and meaning of literate Western civilization. — *1964*

Both Hitler and Gandhi, and many others in this century, were made possible by the electric P.A. system and by radio. Anybody who wants to moralize about radio has to dump Gandhi and Hitler into the same pot. — *1970*

[F.D.R.] was at great pains to use an unfavourable press to enhance his radio image. The art of politics today requires an orchestral use of the varied instruments of public communication. These instruments do not exist or function in isolation from one another any more than do our senses function in isolation. — *1965*

It is not easy to explain to a Westerner why oral cultures should be so rabid in their response to radio. The oral man cannot tolerate radio any more than he can tolerate alcohol . . . His very culture is already profoundly involving, and radio and alcohol excite the tribal membrane of the oral cultures to a morbid degree. — *1972*

I live right inside radio when I listen.
— *1964*

Radio, in contrast to the telephone, permits the listener to fill in a good deal of visual imagery. The radio-announcer or disc-jockey stands out loud and clear, while the voice on the telephone resonates in isolation from the visual sense. Nobody ever wrote a lament about "All Alone by the Radio" but "All Alone by the Telephone" is a classic of the twenties that was a resounding prophecy of high-rise living in the present time. — *1971*

XEROGRAPHY

Any notable figure has only to empty his Xeroxed memos into the publisher's office to have a biography available in a few hours. — *1971*

The Pentagon Papers were position papers that probably were never read by anyone. Xerox is responsible for the proliferation of large committees and their position papers. — *1973*

Xerography makes the reader both author and publisher in tendency. The highly centralized activity of publishing naturally breaks down into extreme decentralism when anybody can, by means of xerography, assemble printed, or written, or photographic materials which can be supplied with sound tracks.

But xerography is electricity invading the world of typography, and it means a total revolution in this old sphere, or this old technology, a revolution that is being felt in the classroom itself.
— *1965*

TV

TV is an integral medium, forcing an interaction among components of experience which have long been separate and scattered. — *1961*

The TV screen just pours that energy into you which paralyses the eye; you are not looking at it; it is looking at you. — *1977*

Most people were struck by the TV coverage of the Kennedy assassination. We were all conscious of great depth of involvement, but there was no excitement, no sensationalism. When involvement is maximal, we are nearly numb. — *1964*

TV, then, is not part of the 19th-century art-program for the reconquest of synesthesia. TV is rather the overwhelming and technological success of that program after its artistic exponents have retired. — *1961*

The man with a very private face makes a very bad TV image, whereas somebody that looks like an old peasant, or a very broken-down character, makes good TV. — *1972*

If television is going to strip us of our civilized individuality, of our separate selves, then we should close down TV. Because, as far as I know, television is incompatible with the continuance of Western man. — *1972*

For centuries Americans had gone outside to be alone and had gone inside to be warm and sociable. The basic pattern had reversed the custom of the rest of mankind. Suddenly, TV had brought Americans into line with Europe and Asia. Since TV, the young, at least, tend to go outside to be with people and inside to be alone. — *1973*

Why should the broken line of the television mosaic emphasize the sculptural contours of objects? — *1960*

The TV image is the first technology to project or externalize our tactile sense. — *1961*

In the movie you sit and look at the screen. You are the camera eye. In television you are the screen. You are the vanishing point as in an oriental picture. The picture goes inside you. In the movie, you go outside into the world. In television you go inside yourself. — *1967*

Television . . . is profoundly and subliminally introverting, [creating] an inward depth, meditative, oriental. The television child is a profoundly orientalized being. And he will not accept goals as objects in the world to pursue. — *1967*

[People] don't see movies on TV; they see TV. — *1966*

The ideal show on pay TV would be a great composer rehearsing a symphony, not playing his symphony. — *1967*

TV is a service medium only during a crisis. — *1970*

TV as a today show is a continuous present. There are really no dates. — *1971*

People will not accept war on TV.

They will accept war in movies. They will accept it in newspapers. Nobody will accept war on TV. It is too close.
— *1973*

The Beatle hairdos are another fringe benefit of TV. — *1966*

When the news team seeks to become the news source by means of direct dialogue rather than by remote report of the event, they are being true to the immediacy of the TV medium in which comments outrank the event itself. — *1971*

COMPUTER

It is one of the mysteries of cybernation that it is forever challenged by the need to simulate consciousness.
— *1966*

The real job of the computer in the future is not going to have anything to do with retrieval. It's going to have to do with pure discovery, because we use our memories for many purposes, mostly unconscious . . . When you can recall things at a very high speed, they take on a new mythic and structural meaning that is quite alien to ordinary perception. So the computer . . . has, in spite of itself . . . revealed the knowledge of the mythic, pattern, structures, and profiles, all of which are quite excitedly loaded with discovery. — *1966*

At computer speeds, effect is so closely related to the input that the arranger of computer systems can

scarcely avoid artistic involvement in whatever he is doing. — *1971*

It is a world in which the creative imagination of the artist is now needed by the men who handle the computers.
— *1958*

Circuitry means that every situation must fold back into itself much in the pattern of cognition and its playback, which is "recognition" in the action of human perceiving and knowing. The new technology mimes the prime procedure of human learning and knowing. — *1968*

The programming of computers calls for levels of human awareness about media and ourselves such as we do not yet possess. — *1961*

Computers are still serving mainly as agents to sustain precomputer effects.
— *1973*

The computer is able to take over the whole mechanical age. Everything that was done under mechanical conditions can be computerized with relative ease, and that includes our educational system. — *1966*

In terms of, say, a computer technology we are headed for cottage economics, where the most important industrial activities can be carried on in any individual little shack anywhere on the globe. — *1970*

A computer as a research and communication instrument could enhance information retrieval, obsolesce mass library organization, retrieve the individual's encyclopedic function and flip into a private line to speedily tailored data of a saleable kind. — *1979*

"Come into my parlor," said the computer to the specialist. — *1968*

With electric circuitry, all the mechanical enterprises of mankind tend to acquire reverse characteristics. Just as the educational establishment tends to shift its stress from instruction to discovery with the audience directly involved in the learning process, so all mechanical industry tends to abandon packaging in favor of the tailor-made or custom-built for the individual. This pattern begins to emerge in computer design procedures in architecture.
— *1966*

...AND FUTURE MEDIA

The book is about to cease being a vehicle of self-expression, and is about to become a corporate probe of society. — *1966*

The tendency is for the book to cease to be a package and to become a custom-made information service tailored to the individual needs of the reader. The public was a creation of print technology and largely ceases to exist under electric circuitry. — *1966*

The video cassette is even now awaiting programs and themes to bring to the mass audience. The makers of video cassettes have been baffled by the question of programming. The natural impulse is to repeat, in this new form, the existing shows from older media. That is called "the law of implementation": we use the new to do the old, even if it doesn't need doing at all. — *1975*

The next medium, whatever it is — it may be the extension of consciousness — will include television as its content, not as its environment, and will transform television into an art form.
— *1967*

Survival now would seem to depend upon the extension of consciousness itself as environment. This extension has already begun with the computer and has been anticipated in our obsession with ESP and occult awareness.
— *1972*

It may be worth mentioning the structural features of analogy since with the computer there has risen the possibility of extending consciousness itself as a technological environment. If this is to be done, it cannot be done on the basis of any existing notion of rationality. — *1971*

Having extended or translated our central nervous system into the electromagnetic technology, it is but a further stage to transfer our consciousness to the computer world as well. — *1964*

An external consensus or conscience is now as necessary as private consciousness. — *1964*

[A future medium like a kind of computerized ESP would process] consciousness as the corporate content of the environment — and eventually maybe even [lead to] a small portable computer, about the size of a hearing aid, that would process of private experience through the corporate experience, the way dreams do now.

— *1965*

The technological tendency to do more and more with less and less could now be exceeded only by putting the information directly into the human nervous system. If an age of "brain transplants" lies ahead, it may become possible to supply each new generation with "brain prints" taken live and directly from the intellects of the age. Instead of buying the works of Shakespeare or Erasmus, one might well become electroencephalographically imprinted with the actual brain perception and erudition of Shakespeare or Erasmus. The book . . . could then be bypassed. — *1970*

15

Explorations

The Media Fit the Battle of Jericho

I sabotage the sentence! With me is the naked word.
I spike the verb — all parts of speech are pushed over on their backs.
I am the master of all that is half-uttered and imperfectly heard.
Return with me where I am crying out with the gorilla and the bird.

(One-way Song)

The Western world is living through its own past and the pasts of many forgotten cultures.

We think we are watching the rushes of recently shot film as we let the dreaming historical eye of the projector god entertain us.

Print merely permitted a fixed stereoptic vision of the past. Its imagery-flow was much greater than writing or speech permitted. But it was very far from the simultaneity that came first with the telegraph, and which now characterizes all phases of our culture.

The telegraph gave us the global snap-shot which knocked out the walls between capitals and cultures, and created "open diplomacy", or diplomacy without walls.

Olivier's *Richard III* movie gives as a single experience the specialist knowledge of many historians of English art and society. It would take one person many years to assemble the details of the past that are there made available to the six-year-old and the professor alike. The simultaneous convergence of many kinds of specialist knowledge results in knocking out all specialist walls. It knocks out the walls between historical and biological categories equally. The child can enter the past as easily as the trained archeologist. History is abandoned to the Bridey Murphys.

We can now move into any past on the same terms at least as the cab-driver possesses the present. The upshot of the minute and exact reproduction of a phase of the English past is that it is as vulgarly familiar as the urban features of our own present.

This is not to point a moral.

The same state of affairs resulting from simultaneity of communication appears in our cities. Cities were always a means of achieving some degree of simultaneity of association and awareness among men. What the family and the tribe had done in this respect for a few, the city did for many. Our technology now removes all city walls and pretexts.

The oral and acoustic space of tribal cultures had never met a visual reconstruction of the past. All experience and all past lives were *now*. Pre-literate man knew only simultaneity. The walls between men, and between arts and sciences, were built on the written or visually arrested word.

With the return to simultaneity we enter the tribal and acoustic world once more. Globally.

As primeval man pressed on his acoustic walls and moved forward the visual orientation of experience, he discovered sculpture and painting as sculpture. Sculpture is half-way to architecture and writing.

Sculpture is not the enclosure of space. It is the modelling of space. But to a purely acoustic culture such a means of arresting visually the dynamics of acoustic space must inevitably appear as very astonishing.

Purely acoustic space, the space evoked by the spoken word in a pre-literate world, is equally magical. The complex harmonic structure of the word can never be a sign or reference before writing. It evokes the thing itself in all its particularity. Only after this acoustic magic has been enclosed in the fixed written form can it become a sign.

To capture the dynamics of the phonetic flux or flash in a fixed visual net — that was the achievement of our alphabet. This net proved to be unique. In that net the Western world took all other cultures. No other culture originally took the step of separating the sound of words from their meanings and then of translating the sound into sight.

This fracturing of the integrity of the word split consciousness and culture into many fragments. It transferred the rich organic compound of immemorial speech into a thin abstract cross-section which could be examined at leisure and analysed.

The analysis of visually abstracted speech brought into existence very quickly the now traditional arts and sciences and their divisions. Today, simultaneity and inclusiveness of awareness is rapidly abolishing these divisions.

In the physical world we have the end of the age-old opposition between art and nature, as our technology reaches out to embrace light itself.

In the world of esthetics the poetic process has become the subject, plot and action of works of art. No more divisions of form and content, meaning and experience.

The new media — the new languages — which have increasingly supplemented writing and print, have begun to reassemble the multiple sensuousness of integral speech. Touch, taste, kinesthesia, sight and sound are all recreating that acoustic space which had been abolished by phonetic writing.

Under these conditions, prediction and evaluation are merely substitutes for observation. A basic feature of acoustic space is its inclusiveness. Visual space is exclusive. As our world re-creates acoustic and oral culture by simply pushing on with devices of instantaneity and simultaneity, we need not fear the suppression of visual and written culture.

But the book will acquire, has already acquired, a major new role as tool of perception. It has long lost its monopoly as a channel of information. It can never lose its usefulness as a means of arresting thought and language for study. What the book was to the written manuscript, the LP disc is to music and radio.

Any change in any medium always causes modifications in all other media or languages within the same culture. Today in our simultaneous world such changes are felt as abrupt and drastic. They always were. But now we notice.

Let's now take a quick tour of the walls knocked over by media change.

Writing was the break-through from sound to sight. But with the end of the acoustic wall came chronology, tick-tock time, architecture. Writing, the enclosure of speech and sound space, split off song and dance and music from speech. It split off *harmonia* from *mimesis*.

Writing permitted the visual analysis of the dynamic logos that produced philology, logic, rhetoric, geometry, etc.

Modern physics and mathematics, like modern art before them, gradually abandoned visual for acoustic or non-Euclidean space.

With writing on paper came the road. The road and paper meant organization at a distance: armies, empires, and the end of city walls.

But the manuscript was far from being the printed page. It was nearer to our photographic journalism. It had to be read slowly, aloud. The manuscript reader automatically found it easier to memorize all he read than refer again and again to this form. Until print, readers carried their lore at the tips of their tongues.

With print from movable type (the first application of assembly-line method to a handicraft), came fast, silent reading.

Print knocked down the monastic walls of social and corporate study. The Bible: religion without walls.

But print isolated the scholar. It created the enterprising individual who, like Marlowe's Tamburlaine or Dr. Faustus, could over-run time and history and cultures and peoples.

Print evoked the walls of the classroom.

Print could channel so much information to the individual that had previously been in the mind and memory of the teacher alone, that it upset all existing educational procedures.

It upset the monopoly of Latin by making possible multi-lingual study.

It fostered the vernaculars and enlarged the walls between nations.

It speeded up language, thereby setting new walls between speech and song, and song and instrumentation.

Print led to spoken poetry and silently read poetry, thus changing the nature of verse entirely.

Printed music entirely changed the structures of musical forms.

In America print and book-culture became the dominant form from the beginning, setting walls between literature and art, and art and life, which were less obvious in Europe.

In America print was a technological matrix of all subsequent invention. Its assembly-lines finally reached expression in Detroit and the motor-car: the home without walls.

In America the press moulded public opinion and created a new base for politics.

The press was a means of mobilizing public opinion and made national road systems.

The press became in large measure a substitute for the book. But the press page is not the book page. The press creates new mental habits.

With telegraph only vernacular walls remain. All other cultural walls collapse under the impact of its instantaneous flash. With the wire-photo the vernacular walls are undermined.

The telegraph translates writing into sound. The electrification of writing was almost as big a step back towards the acoustic world as those steps since taken by telephone, radio, TV.

The telephone: speech without walls.

The phonograph: music hall without walls.

The photograph: museum without walls.

The movie and TV: classroom without walls.

Before print the community at large was the centre of education. Today, information-flow and educational impact outside the classroom is so far in excess of anything occurring inside the classroom that we must reconsider the educational process itself.

The classroom is now a place of detention, not attention. Attention is elsewhere.

It is now obvious that as all languages are mass media, so the new media are new languages. To unscramble our Babel we must teach these languages and their grammars on their own terms. This is something quite different from the educational use of audio-visual aids or of closed-circuit TV.

Culture Without Literacy

The ordinary desire of everybody to have everybody else think alike with himself has some explosive implications today. The perfection of the *means* of communication has given this average power-complex of the human being an enormous extension of expression.

The telephone, the teleprinter and the wireless made it possible for orders from the highest levels to be given direct to the lowest levels, where, on account of the absolute authority behind them, they were carried out uncritically; or brought it about that numerous offices and command centres were directly connected with the supreme leadership from which they received their sinister orders without any intermediary; or resulted in a widespread surveillance of the citizen, or in a high degree of secrecy surrounding criminal happenings. To the outside observer this governmental apparatus may have resembled the apparently chaotic confusion of lines at a telephone exchange, but like the latter it could be controlled and operated from one central source. Former dictatorships needed collaborators of high quality even in the lower levels of leadership, men who could think and act independently. In the era of modern technique an authoritarian system can do without this. The means of communication alone permit it to mechanize the work of subordinate leadership. As a consequence a new type develops: the uncritical recipient of orders.[1]

Perfection of the *means* of communication has meant instantaneity. Such an instantaneous network of communication is the body-mind unity of each of us. When a city or a society achieves a diversity and equilibrium of awareness analogous to the body-mind network, it has what we tend to regard as a high culture.

But the instantaneity of communication makes free speech and thought difficult if not impossible and for many reasons. Radio extends the range of the casual speaking voice, but it forbids that many should speak. And when what is said has such range of control it is forbidden to speak any but the most acceptable words and notions. Power and control are in all cases paid for by loss of freedom and flexibility.

Today the entire globe has a unity in point of mutual inter-awareness which exceeds in rapidity the former flow of information in a small city — say Elizabethan London with its eighty or ninety thousand inhabitants. What happens to existing societies when they are brought into such intimate contact by press, picture stories, news-reels and jet propulsion? What happens when the neolithic Eskimo is compelled to share the time and space arrangements of technological man? What happens in our minds as we become familiar with the diversity of human cultures which have come into existence under innumerable circum-

---

[1] Albert Speer, German Armament Minister in 1942, in a speech at the Nuremburg trials, quoted in Hjalmar Schacht, *Account Settled*, London, 1949, p. 240.

stances, historical and geographical? Is not what happens comparable to that social revolution which we call the American melting-pot?

When the telegraph made possible a daily cross-section of the globe transferred to the page of newsprint, we already had our mental melting-pot for cosmic man — the world citizen. The mere format of the page of newsprint was more revolutionary in its intellectual and emotional consequences than anything that could be *said* about any part of the globe.

When we juxtapose news items from Tokyo, London, New York, Chile, Africa and New Zealand we are not just manipulating space. The events so brought together belong to cultures widely separated in time. The modern world abridges all historical times as readily as it reduces space. Every*where* and every *age* have become *here* and *now*. History has been abolished by our new media. If prehistoric man is simply preliterate man living in a timeless world of seasonal recurrence, may not posthistoric man find himself in a similar situation? May not the upshot of our technology be the awakening from the historically conditioned nightmare of the past into a timeless present? Historic man may turn out to have been literate man. An episode.

Robert Redfield in his recent book *The Primitive World and Its Transformations* points to the timeless character of preliterate societies where exclusively oral communication ensures intimacy, homogeneity and fixity of social experience. It is the advent of writing that sets in motion the urban revolution. Writing breaks up the fixity and homogeneity of preliterate societies. Writing creates that inner dialogue or dialectic, that psychic withdrawal which makes possible the reflexive analysis of thought via the stasis of the audible made spatial. Writing is the translation of the audible into the spatial as reading is the reverse of this reciprocal process. And the complex shuttling of eye, ear and speech factors once engaged in this ballet necessarily reshape the entire communal life, both inner and outer, creating not only the "stream of consciousness" rediscovered by contemporary art, but ensuring multiple impediments to the activities of perception and recall.

So far as writing is the spatializing and arrest of oral speech, however, it implies that further command of space made possible by the written message and its attendant road system. With writing, therefore, comes logical analysis and specialism, but also militarism and bureaucracy. And with writing comes the break in that direct, intuitive relationship between men and their surroundings which modern art has begun to uncover.

"Compared with the evidence afforded by living tradition," says Sir James Frazer, "the testimony of ancient books on the subject of the early religion is worth very little. For literature accelerates the advance of thought at a rate which leaves the slow progress of opinion by word of mouth at an immeasurable distance behind. Two or three generations of literature may do more to change thought than two or three thousand years of traditional life."[2] But literature, as we know today, is a relatively conservative time-binding medium compared with press, radio and movie. So the thought is now beginning to occur: How many thousands of years of change can we afford every ten years? May not a spot of culture-lag here and there in the great time-flux prove to be a kind of social and psychological oasis?

Involved with the loss of memory and the psychic withdrawal of alphabetic cultures, there is a decline of sensuous perception and adequacy of social responsiveness. The preternatural sensous faculties of Sherlock Holmes or the modern sleuth are simply those of preliterate man who can retain the details of a hundred-mile trail as easily as a movie camera can record it. Today our detailed knowledge of societies existing within the oral tradition enables us to estimate accurately the advantages and disadvantages of writing. Without writing there is little control of space, but perfect control of accumulated experience. The misunderstandings of Ireland and England can be seen in some basic respects as the clash of oral and written cultures. And the strange thing to us is that the written culture has very little historical sense. The English could never remember; the Irish could never forget. Today the university as a community is in large degree one in which the members are in regular oral communication. And whereas the university has a highly developed time sense, the business community operates on the very short-run and exists mainly by the control of space. The present divorce between these two worlds is only accentuated by the perfection of the media peculiar to each.

Faced with the consequence of writing, Plato notes in the *Phaedrus*:

> *This discovery of yours will create forgetfulness in the learners' souls, because they will not use their memories; they will trust to the external written characters and not remember of themselves. The specific which you have discovered is an aid not to memory, but to reminiscence and you give your disciples not truth but only the semblance of truth; they will be hearers of many things and have learned nothing; they will appear to be omniscient and will generally know nothing; they will be tiresome company, having the show of wisdom without the reality.*

Two thousand years of manuscript culture lay ahead of the Western world when Plato made this observation. But nobody has yet studied the rise and decline of Greece in terms of the change from oral to written culture. Patrick Geddes said

---

[2]Frazer, *Man, God and Immortality*, 1927, p. 318.

that the road destroyed the Greek city-state. But writing made the road possible, just as printing was later to pay for the roads of England and America.

In order to understand the printed-book culture which today is yielding, after four hundred years, to the impact of visual and auditory media, it is helpful to note a few of the characteristics of that manuscript culture which persisted from the 5th century B.C. to the 15th century A.D. I shall merely mention a few of the principal observations of scholars like Pierce Butler and H. J. Chaytor. In the first place, manuscript culture never made a sharp break with oral speech because everybody read manuscripts aloud. Swift, silent reading came with the macadamized surfaces of the printed page. Manuscript readers memorized most of what they read since in the nature of things they had to carry their learning with them. Fewness of manuscripts and difficulty of access made for utterly different habits of mind with regard to what was written. One result was encyclopedism. Men of learning tried, at least, to learn everything. So that if learning was oral, teaching was even more so. Solitary learning and study came only with the printed page. And today when learning and study are switching more and more to the seminar, the round-table and the discussion group, we have to note these developments as due to the decline of the printed page as the dominant art form.

The manuscript page was a very flexible affair. It was not only in close rapport with the oral speech but with plastic design and colour illustration. So the ornate examples of manuscript art easily rival and resemble those books in stone and glass, the cathedrals and abbeys. In our own time James Joyce, seeking a means to orchestrate and control the various verbi-voco-visual media of our own age, resorted to the page format of the *Book of Kells* as a means thereto. And even the early romantic poets, painters and novelists expressed their preference for gothic in terms of rebellion against book culture.

Recently Rosamund Tuve, in elucidating the art of George Herbert, discovered that the characteristic effects of metaphysical wit in the 17th century poetry resulted from the translation of visual effects from medieval manuscript and woodcut into the more abstract form of the printed word. If the 17th century was receding from a visual, plastic culture towards an abstract literary culture, today we seem to be receding from an abstract book culture towards a highly sensuous, plastic pictorial culture. Recent poets have used simultaneously effects from both extremes to achieve witty results not unlike those of the 17th century. The impact of Mr. Eliot's very first lines of poetry has been felt everywhere:

Let us go then, you and I,
When the evening is spread out against the sky
Like a patient etherized upon a table.

It is the overlayering of perspectives, the simultaneous use of two kinds of space which creates the shock of dislocation here. For if all art is a contrived trap for the attention, all art and all language are techniques for looking at one situation through another one.

The printed page is a 16th century art form which obliterated two thousand years of manuscript culture in a few decades. Yet it is hard for us to see the printed page or any other current medium except in contrast to some other form. The mechanical clock, for example, created a wholly artificial image of time as a uniform linear structure. This artificial form gradually changed habits of work, feeling and thought which are only being rejected today. We know that in our own lives each event exists in its own time. Time is not the same for the speaker as for the audience. To the speaker it is too, too brief for what he has to say. For the audience it is a grim foretaste of eternity. Ultimately the medieval clock made Newtonian physics possible. It may also have initiated those orderly linear habits which made possible the rectilinear page of print created from movable type, as well as the methods of commerce. At any rate the mechanization of writing was as revolutionary in its consequences as the mechanization of time. And this, quite apart from thoughts or ideas conveyed by the printed page. Movable type was already the modern assembly line in embryo.

Harold Innis explored some of the consequences of the printed page: the breakdown of international communication; the impetus given to nationalism by the commercial exploitation of vernaculars; the loss of contact between writers and audience; the depressing effect on music, architecture and the plastic arts.

Bela Balazs in his *Theory of the Film* notes some of the changes in visual habits resulting from the printing press on one hand and the camera on the other:

> *The discovery of printing gradually rendered illegible the faces of men. So much could be read from paper that the method of conveying meaning by facial expression fell into desuetude. Victor Hugo wrote once that the printed book took over the part played by the cathedral in the Middle Ages and became the carrier of the spirit of the people. But the thousands of books tore the one spirit . . . into thousands of opinions . . . tore the church into a thousand books. The visual spirit was thus turned into a legible spirit and visual culture into a culture of concepts. . . . But we paid little attention to the fact that, in conformity with this, the face of individual men, their foreheads, their eyes, their mouths, had also of necessity and quite correctly to suffer a change.*

At present a new discovery, a new machine is at work to turn the attention of men back to a visual culture and to give them new faces. This machine is the cinematographic camera. Like the printing press it is a technical device for the multiplication and distribution of products of the human spirit; its effect on human culture will not be less than that of the printing press. . . . The gestures of visual man are not intended to convey concepts which can be expressed in words, but such . . . non-rational emotions which would still remain unexpressed when everything that can be told has been told. . . . Just as our musical experiences cannot be expressed in rationalized concepts, what appears on the face and in facial expression is a spiritual experience which is rendered immediately visible without the intermediary of words.

The printed page in rendering the language of the face and gesture illegible has also caused the abstract media of printed words to become the main bridge for the inter-awareness of spiritual and mental states. In the epoch of print and word culture the body ceased to have much expressive value and the human spirit became audible but invisible. The camera eye has reversed this process in reacquainting the masses of men once more within the grammar of gesture. Today commerce has channelled much of this change along sex lines. But even there the power of the camera eye to change physical attitudes and make-up is familiar to all. In the 90's Oscar Wilde noted how the pale, long-necked, consumptive red-heads painted by Rossetti and Burne-Jones were for a short time an exotic visual experience. But soon in every London salon these creatures sprouted up where none had been before. The fact that human nature, at least, imitates art is too obvious to labour. But the fact that with modern technology the entire material of the globe as well as the thoughts and feelings of its human inhabitants have become the matter of art and of man's factive intelligence means that there is no more nature. At least there is no more external nature. Everything from politics to bottle-feeding, global landscape, and the subconscious of the infant is subject to the manipulation of conscious artistic control — the BBC carries the unrehearsed voice of the nightingale to the Congo, the Eskimo sits entranced by hillbilly music from West Tennessee. Under these conditions the activities of Senator McCarthy belong with the adventures of the Pickwick Club and our talk about the Iron Curtain is a convenient smokescreen likely to divert our attention from much greater problems. The Russians differ from us in being much more aware of the non-commercial impact of the new media. We have been so hypnotized with the commercial and entertainment qualities of press, radio, movie and TV that we have been blind to the revolutionary character of these toys. The Russians after a few years of playing with these radio-active toys have tried to neutralize them by imposing various stereotypes on their content and messages. They have forced their press to stick to an 1850 format. They have imposed similar time-locks on music and literature. They hope, thereby, to abate the revolutionary fury of these instruments. But the fury for change is in the form and not the message of the new media, a fact which seems almost inevitably to escape men trained in our abstract literary culture. The culture of print has rendered people extremely insensitive to the language and meaning of spatial forms — one reason for the architectural and city horrors tolerated by predominantly book cultures. Thus the English and American cultures in particular were overwhelmed by print, since in the 16th century they had only rudimentary defences to set up against the new printed word. The rest of Europe, richer in plastic and oral culture, was less blitzed by the printing press. And the Orient has so far had many kinds of resistance to offer. But the curious thing is that Spaniards like Picasso or Salvador Dali are much more at home amidst the new visual culture of North America than we ourselves.

This division between visual and literary languages is a fact which has also set a great abyss between science and the humanities. Thinking as we do of culture in book terms, we are unable to read the language of technological forms. And since our earliest esthetic responses are to such forms, this has set up numerous cleavages between official and idiomatic cultural response within our own experience. We are all of us persons of divided and sub-divided sensibility through failure to recognize the multiple languages with which our world speaks to us. Above all it is the multiplicity of messages with which we are hourly bombarded by our environment that renders us ineffectual. Karl Deutsch has argued that a people shaped by oral tradition will respond to an alien challenge like a suicidal torpedo. The wild Celtic charge. A people shaped by a written tradition will not charge, but drift, pulled in a thousand different directions.

One obvious feature of the printed book is its republicanism. The page of print is not only a leveller of other forms of expression; it is a social leveller as well. Anyone who can read has at least the illusion of associating on equal terms with anyone who has written. And that fact gave the printed word a privileged place in American society and politics. The Duke of Gloucester could say casually to Edward Gibbon, on the completion of his *History*: "Another damned fat square book. Scribble, scribble, scribble, eh, Mr. Gibbon!" But there were no foxhunters in America to put the literary upstart in his place.

So far as quantity goes the printed book was the first instrument of mass culture. Erasmus was the first to see its meaning and turned his genius to the manufacture of textbooks for the classroom. He saw, above all, that the printing press was a device for reproducing the past in the present, much like a Hollywood movie set. The nouveaux riches of Italy began to enact on a tiny scale the past that was being unearthed and printed. Hastily they ran up villas and palazzas in ancient style. Assisted by the newly printed exemplars they began to imitate the language of Cicero and Seneca. In England the new print mingled with the old oral tradition to produce the new forms of sermon and drama which were hybrids of written and spoken culture. But in the printing press there is one great feature of mass culture which is lacking. Namely, the instantaneous. From one point of view, language itself is the greatest of all mass media. The spoken word instantly evokes not only some recently conceived idea but reverberates with the total history of its own experience with man. We may be oblivious of such overtones as of the spectrum of colour in a lump of coal. But the poet by exact rhythmic adjustment can flood our consciousness with this knowledge. The artist is older than the fish.

Reading the history of the newspaper retrospectively we can see that it was not a mere extension of the art form of the book page. As used by Rimbaud, Mallarmé and Joyce the newspaper page is a revolution in itself, juxtaposing many book pages on a single sheet. And the news page was, moreover, more nearly a mass medium not only in reaching more people than the book, but in being more instantaneous in its coverage and communication. Once linked to the telegraph, the press achieved the speed of light, as radio and TV have done since then. Total global coverage in space, instantaneity in time. Those are the two basic characters that I can detect in a mechanical mass medium. There are other characteristics derivative from these, namely anonymity of those originating the messages or forms, and anonymity in the recipients. But in respect of this anonymity it is necessary to regard not only words and metaphors as mass media but buildings and cities as well.

The modern newspaper page is not a mere extension of the book page because the speed with which the telegraph feeds news to the press today precludes any possibility of organizing a sheet of news by any but the most impressionistic devices. Each item lives in its own kind of space totally discontinuous from all other items. A particularly vigorous item will sprout a headline and provide a kind of aura or theme for surrounding items. So that, if the book page could imitate visual perspective as in Renaissance painting, setting facts and concepts in proportions that reproduced the optical image of the three-dimensional object-world, the uninhibited world of the press and modern advertising abandoned such realistic properties in favor of weighting news and commercial objects by every dynamic and structural device of size and colour bringing words and pictures back into a plastic and meaningful connection. If the book page tends to perspective, the news page tends to cubism and surrealism. So that every page of newspapers and magazines, like every section of our cities, is a jungle of multiple, simultaneous perspectives which make the world of hot-jazz and be-bop seem relatively sedate and classical. Our intellectual world, by virtue of the same proliferation of books (over 18,000 new titles in England alone last year) has achieved the same entanglement which is easier to assess through the complexity of our visual environment. It is not just a quantitative problem, of course. As

Gyorgy Kepes states it in his *Language of Vision*:

The environment of man living today has a complexity which cannot be compared with any environment of any previous age. The skyscrapers, the street with its kaleidoscopic vibration of colours, the window-displays with their multiple mirroring images, the streetcars and motor cars, produce a dynamic simultaneity of visual impression which cannot be perceived in the terms of inherited visual habits. In this optical turmoil the fixed objects appear utterly insufficient as the measuring tape of the events. The artificial light, the flashing of electric bulbs, and the mobile game of the many new types of light-sources bombard man with kinetic colour sensations having a keyboard never before experienced. Man, the spectator, is himself more mobile than ever before. He rides in streetcars, motorcars and aeroplanes and his own motion gives to optical impacts a tempo far beyond the threshold of a clear object-perception. The machine man operates adds its own demand for a new way of seeing. The complicated interactions of its mechanical parts cannot be conceived in a static way; they must be perceived by understanding of their movements. The motion picture, television, and, in a great degree, the radio, require a new thinking, i.e., seeing, that takes into account qualities of change, interpenetration and simultaneity.

That situation can be snapshotted from many angles. But it always adds up to the need to discover means for translating the experience of one medium or one culture into another, of translating Confucius into Western terms and Kant into Eastern terms. Of seeing our old literary culture in the new plastic terms in order to enable it to become a constitutive part of the new culture created by the orchestral voices and gestures of new media. Of seeing that modern physics and painting and poetry speak a common language and of acquiring that language at once in order that our world may possess consciously the coherence that it really has in latency, and which for lack of our recognition has created not new orchestral harmonies but mere noise.

Perhaps the terrifying thing about the new media for most of us is their inevitable evocation of irrational response. The irrational has become the major dimension of experience in our world. And yet this is a mere by-product of the instantaneous character in communication. It can be brought under rational control. It is the perfection of the means which has so far defeated the end, and removed the time necessary for assimilation and reflection. We are now compelled to develop new techniques of perception and judgement, new ways of reading the languages of our environment with its multiplicity of cultures and disciplines. And these needs are not just desperate remedies but roads to unimagined cultural enrichment.

All the types of linear approach to situations past, present or future are useless. Already in the sciences there is recognition of the need for a unified field theory which would enable scientists to use one continuous set of terms by way of relating the various scientific universes. Thus the basic requirement of any system of communication is that it be circular, with, of course, the possibility of self-correction. That is why presumably the human dialogue is and must ever be the basic form of all civilization. For the dialogue compels each participant to see and recreate his own vision through another sensibility. And the radical imperfection in mechanical media is that they are not circular. So far they have become one-way affairs with audience research taking the place of the genuine human vision, heckling and response. There is not only the anonymity of press, movies and radio but the factor of scale. The individual cannot discuss a problem with a huge, mindless bureaucracy like a movie studio or a radio corporation. On the other hand a figure like Roosevelt could mobilize the networks for a war with the press. He could even make the microphone more effective by having the press against him, because the intimacy of the microphone preserved his human dimension while the national scale of the press attack could only appear as a tank corps converging on a telephone booth.

Thus the microphone invites chat, not oratory. It is a new art form which transforms all the existing relations between speakers and their audiences and speakers and their material of discourse. "The great rhetorical tradition, which begins with Halifax and runs through Pitt to Channing, sent up its expiring flash in Macaulay."[3] The modern manner was less declamatory and more closely reasoned. And the new manner which Gladstone handled like a Tenth Muse was based on facts and figures. Statistics represents a branch of pictorial expression. If the rise of bureaucracy and finance changed the style of public and private speech, how much more radical a change is daily worked in our habits of thought and discourse by the microphone and the loudspeaker.

Perhaps we could sum up our problem by saying that technological man must betake himself to visual metaphor in contriving a new unified language for the multiverse of cultures of the entire globe. All language or expression is metaphorical because metaphor is the seeing of one situation through another one. Right on the beam. I'll take a rain check on that.

One's vernacular is best seen and felt through another tongue. And for us, at least, society is only appreciated by comparing and contrasting it with others. Pictorial and other experience today is filled with metaphors from all the cultures

---

[3]G. M. Young, *Victorian England*, 1944, p. 31.

of the globe. Whereas the written vernaculars have always locked men up within their own cultural monad, the language of technological man, while drawing on all the cultures of the world, will necessarily prefer those media which are least national. The language of visual form is, therefore, one which lies to hand as an unused Esperanto at everybody's command. The language of vision has already been adopted in the pictograms of scientific formula and logistics. These ideograms transcend national barriers as easily as Chaplin or Disney and would seem to have no rivals as the cultural base for cosmic man.

Cicero and the Renaissance Training for Prince and Poet

In his *European Literature and the Latin Middle Ages* (New York: Pantheon Books for Bollingen Foundation Inc., 1953), Ernst Robert Curtius points out that "in ancient Greece there is hardly any idea of the sacredness of the book" (p. 304). Homer and Hesiod are preliterates and "Pindar and the tragedians are the first to conceive of memory as a written record" (p. 304). Curtius further explains (p. 305) why the idea of the "'erudite poet' (*doctus poeta* among the Romans)" only entered Greek culture in the Hellenistic period. It was during the Augustan period that book culture became the basis of the new kind of encyclopedism such as Cicero propagated which was represented by Virgil and the other Roman poets. St. Augustine, a teacher of grammar and rhetoric himself, took it for granted that the Christian student of Scripture would avail himself of the new encyclopaedic learning made available by the new Augustan libraries and schools. The *translatio studii* or transmission of traditional pagan learning was mainly accomplished by the uniting of the ideals of *doctus poeta* and *doctus orator* to the functions of scriptural exegesis and preaching.

Robert Hollander in *Allegory in Dante's Commedia* (Princeton: Princeton University Press, 1969), using the work of Henri de Lubac (*Exégèse Médiévale: Les Quatre Sens De L'Ecriture*, 4 vols., Paris: Editions Montaigne, 1959-1964), shows how Dante became heir to this entire tradition of multi-level exegesis. He does not concern himself with the role of the poet as *doctus orator*, but this major current is carried abundantly in the manuals of instruction for a Christian prince, which were exceedingly popular and influential.

It is worth mentioning another work which is of great relevance to the student of Dante as well as to the history of eloquence. I refer to Rosalie L. Colie's *Paradoxia Epidemica: The Renaissance Tradition of Paradox* (Princeton: Princeton University Press, 1966). The tradition of paradox from ancient through mediaeval and renaissance times called for the utmost erudition and virtuosity from the *doctus orator*. Dante's *Divina Commedia* is the central Christian paradox of the happy fall on which Dante lavishes the same scope of learning and exegesis as the Fathers had done. The great paradoxes in this tradition are, of course, familiar in Erasmus' *The Praise of Folly*, and Rabelais' *Gargantua*, to both of which and to many others, she devotes attention. John Donne's *Biathanatos* as a defence of suicide for Christians is only one of his paradoxes defended with great learning.

Since Homer was not a *doctus poeta* but a pre-literate bard, he could not, if only for this reason, have occupied the place of Virgil in the *Divina Commedia*. The student will be grateful to Eric Havelock for his definitive study of pre-literate encyclopaedism of the Homeric Age (*Preface to Plato*, Cambridge: Harvard University Press, 1963). It was a training designed to encode the wisdom and experience of the entire community but it was directed toward a training of practical perceptions in affairs of daily life and had no relevance to literary or scriptural problems, so the eminence of Homer for Dante is only equalled by his irrelevance. There are, of course, other reasons why Dante chose Virgil to be his guide.

Perhaps the most expeditious way of illustrating the powerful continuity of the Ciceronian concept of eloquent wisdom is simply to point to the long tradition of statesmen's manuals. Many of these are cited by L. K. Born in his useful introduction to his translation of Erasmus' *Education of a Christian Prince*: "That there is a continuous line of succession at least from the time of Isocrates with his *Ad Nicoclem* to the twentieth century is beyond question."[1] Unfortunately, Born has not seen that the Ciceronian-Augustine concept of the *doctus orator* is what really gives consistency to the tradition. Thus Plato and Aristotle, on whom he fruitlessly dwells, have really no place in the central discussion, while Machiavelli is consciously antipodal to the tradition. No better evidence both of Machiavelli's full knowledge of the Ciceronian tradition and his deliberate flouting of it could be found than in the *Contre-Machiavel* of Gentillet (trans. by Simon Patericke, London, 1577), who sets forth the traditional princely ideal of education based on morality and eloquent wisdom.[2] The Machiavellians despised civic or public eloquence and favored the cryptic or curt style which M. W. Croll has studied for us. Thus, the stylistic disputes of Ramus and Nashe are based on the most radical opposition of views.[3]

---

[1] New York: Columbia University Press, 1936, p. 99.

[2] See Patericke's translation, ed. 1608, pp. 1; 12-13; 34; 189-190; 240-242; 309; 366.

[3] L. K. Born (op. cit.) offers no insights into these matters, and does not consider Rabelais' *Gargantua*, both a blow at the dialecticians and a defense of the Ciceronian concept of princely education. More's *Utopia* really belongs in the same tradition quite as much as Elyot's *Governour*, Castiglione's *Courtier*, Ascham's *Scholemaster*, or Spenser's *Faerie Queene*. In this connection, almost the whole of Ruth Kelso's *Doctrine of the English Gentleman in the Sixteenth Century* (Urbana: University of Illinois Press, 1929, reprinted Gloucester, Mass.: Peter Smith, 1964) is relevant to a perspective of the Ciceronian tradition.

Born, however, in tracing the history of the princely manuals, unconsciously attests to the integrity of the encyclopaedic tradition. Isidore of Seville and Alcuin contributed to this literature (pp. 102-104). Peter Damian and John of Salisbury were notable representatives (pp. 109-114). And the *De Eruditione Filiorum Nobilium* of Vincent of Beauvais is a classic instance (ed. by A. Steiner, Cambridge, Mass., 1938).

The treatises which Woodword published under the title *Vittorino da Feltre and other Humanist Educators* (Cambridge, 1931) all contribute to the picture of the Ciceronian ideal of eloquence. Vittorino and the other successors of Petrarch are patristic to a man. The Fathers certify their Ciceronianism and usually modify it considerably: "The purely imitative treatment of Cicero was not the aim of Barzizza and of the scholars whom he typifies, such as Zabarella, Vergerio, and Vittorino. In the widest sense, these men set before themselves the reconciliation of the ancient learning with the Christian life, thought and polity of their own day; they had no dream of a dead reproduction of the past."[4] Nothing is more indicative of the patristic sympathies of Vittorino than his aversion to dialectics except as an incidental preparation for rhetoric (p. 60). Likewise Aeneas Sylvius warns us to "beware of logicians who waste time and ingenuity in verbal subtleties, in whose hands Logic is a thing not of living use but of intellectual death. You will remember that Cicero reproached Sextus Pompey for too great devotion to Geometry, and affirmed that far too much time was spent in his day upon Civil Law and Dialectic . . . which withdraws our energies from fruitful activity, is unworthy of the true Citizen." (*Ibid.*, p. 153)

This concept of the completely rounded citizen, the versatile and encyclopaedic individual, which all historians have agreed is the Renaissance ideal, is nothing if not Cicero's ideal orator: "To sum up what I have endeavoured to set forth. That high standard of education to which I referred at the outset is only to be reached by one who has seen many things and read much. Poet, Orator, Historian, and the rest, all must be studied, each must contribute a share. Our learning thus becomes full, ready, varied and elegant, available for action or for discourse in all subjects. But to enable us to make effectual use of what we know we must add to our knowledge the power of expression." (d'Arezzo, *ibid.*, p. 132) Like Roger Bacon, Aeneas Sylvius puts moral philosophy over mathematics and the physical sciences in the formation of the ideal prince: "There is a danger lest in our interest in natural, or external, objects we find but a lower place for those weightier things which concern character and action." (*Ibid.*, p. 156)

Approaching the question of how rhetoric could have become such a dominant interest of the sixteenth century, it is necessary to consider the fact that the Ciceronian ideal necessarily gave first place in education to the means of achiev-

---

[4]W. H. Woodward, *Vittorino da Feltre*, Cambridge, 1921, p. 10. See also pp. 21; 27; 67; 185 for the fact that Vittorino's position was patristic. Woodward's failure to see the patristic tradition at work in these humanists is easily excusable when it is considered that, forty years later, many specialists in the field are still oblivious of it. Leonardo d'Arezzo, defining true learning and eloquence, strikes at the dialecticians: "True learning, I say: not a mere acquaintance with that vulgar, threadbare jargon which satisfies those who devote themselves to theology, viz., the knowledge of realities — Facts and Principles — united to a perfect familiarity with Letters and the art of expression. Now this combination we find in Lactantius, in Augustine, or in Jerome; . . . " (*ibid.*, pp. 123-124). The Fathers are the types of the *doctus orator*, the statesmen of Cicero.

ing eloquence. For eloquence was indispensable to the administrator and the prince. We have seen that this concept of learning was cherished throughout the Middle Ages because it had been baptized by St. Augustine and grafted into the main stem of patristic culture. Thus the sixteenth century was far from having rediscovered the Ciceronian concept, although the new commercial developments greatly enlarged the scope of its application.[5] L. K. Born's statement concerning the concept of the perfect prince in the thirteenth and fourteenth centuries is really applicable to the entire Middle Ages and to the Renaissance, as well: "In the political thought of the thirteenth and fourteenth centuries, the central figure about which the whole revolves is the prince. This emphasizes the personal view toward rulership, which is characteristic of the period. Furthermore, in accordance with the mediaeval attitude, the writers of these centuries considered the real in terms of the ideal, and were interested in nothing less than in the pattern of the perfect prince."[6]

Machiavelli and Castiglione are at the end of a long line of writers. However, Machiavelli still awaits the historical scholarship which is necessary to put him in his true perspective. Most writers have recognized that his Satanocratism or his violent fission of nature and grace, in which he is at one with Luther and Calvin, is thoroughly Christian. That is, Machiavelli, like Hobbes, Swift, or Mandeville, cannot be explained except in terms of Christian culture. There is nothing pagan about this scepticism concerning human nature.[7] He rather looked on nature as shut off from grace and as shut in upon itself, and abandoned to the

---

[5]Samuel Daniel's summing up of the ways in which the increasing commercialization of society enhanced the educational avenues to power, is excellent: "A time not of that virilitie as the former, but more subtile, and let out into wider motions . . . A time wherein began a greater improvement of the soveraigntie, and more came to be effected by wit then the sword: Equal and just incounters, of State and State in forces, and of Prince and Prince in sufficiencie. The opening of a new world, which strangely altered the manner of this . . . by the induction of infinite Treasure, and opened a wider way to corruption, whereby Princes got much without their swords. . . . Leidger Ambassadors first imployed abroad for intelligences, Common Banks erected, to return and furnish moneys for these businesses. Besides strange alterations in the State Ecclesiasticall: religion brought forth to bee an Actor in the greatest Designs of Ambition and Faction." (*The Complete Works in Verse and Prose of Samuel Daniel*. Edited, with memorial introduction and a glossarial index embracing notes and illustrations. By the Rev. Alexander B. Grosart. London: Aylesbury, 1895-96. Vol. 4, p. 77.) It was in this world that scholars and schoolmasters came to assume the functions of civil prudence. Ruth Kelso points out that in the sixteenth century: "Of all professions, then, the fittest for gentlemen and those aspiring to become gentlemen was the law" (op. cit., p. 51). This was basically Ciceronian. The difficulties encountered in extending the Ciceronian ideal of the learned statesman to the feudal aristocracy are evident in many arguments urged against those who held that studies are effeminate. See Elyot's *Governour* (London: J. M. Dent & Co.; New York: E. P. Dutton & Co., 1907. Everyman ed. by Ernest Rhys, pp. 49 ff.) and Spenser's *Tears of the Muses*, 11.79-90, and Roger Ascham's *Scholemaster*, ed. J. E. B. Mayor, London, 1934, p. 40.
[6]L. K. Born "The Perfect Prince" in *Speculum III* (1928), p. 470.
[7]See J. Maritain's *True Humanism*, New York, 1938, pp. 95-96; 147 ff.; 208; 220. J. Allen shows

interplay of its own distorted forces. Within this dying order, however, Machiavelli envisaged the ideal prince as a man devoted to political action, impressing his character upon the flux of events, and living solely for the commonwealth which alone is the expression of the integral laws of our now fallen nature.[8] There is much of the Old Testament attitude in Machiavelli — the attitude of trust in the prince as one who cooperates with God to bring good out of evil, having regard to the passionate and blind violence of men. Whether Machiavelli finally confounded political action with mere political technique and made of the latter an end in itself is not a question which can be easily determined. It is only necessary to insist that Machiavelli is anti-Ciceronian, and consciously so. He has no place for eloquence in his education since he has no trust in men's capacity to be persuaded to follow right reason, or any reason. The state must compel man to espouse a useful life free from the anarchy of the passions, and for this purpose eloquence is useless.

It is certainly not on these lines that the characters of Prince Hal and Hamlet were developed. Castiglione, however, cannot be regarded as the "source" of Hamlet's character, since the concepts of Castiglione were universally current in his century. One might as justly say that Castiglione was the source of Sir Philip Sidney.[9] On the other hand, Castiglione would certainly not have had the enormous vogue he did in the sixteenth century had he not been the spokesman for a large party. Hoby compares Cicero and Castiglione at some length, saying, among other things: "Cicero an excellent Oratour, in three bookes of an Oratour unto his brother, fashioneth such a one as never was, nor yet is like to be: Castilio an excellent Courtier, in three bookes of a Courtier unto his deare friend, fash-

---

Marsilio of Padua states Machiavelli's and Hobbes' theory of the state long before them (*Great Medieval Thinkers*, ed. F. J. C. Hearnshaw, London, 1921: pp. 176-177). Significantly, too, Wycliffe anticipates the same theories (pp. 217 ff).

[8]See H. Butterfield's *The Statecraft of Machiavelli*, London, 1940.

[9]The obvious parallels between Hamlet and Castiglione have been indicated by W. B. D. Henderson in "A Note on Castiglione and English Literature," in the Everyman edition of Hoby's translation (London: J. M. Dent & Co., 1928, pp. xi-xiv). Ascham highly approved Castiglione (*Scholemaster*, ed. Mayor, p. 119). In *The Advancement of Learning* Bacon significantly conjoins the concept of the ideal courtier to that of prince and orator: "But as Cicero, when he setteth down an idea of a perfect orator, doth not mean that every pleader should be such; and so likewise, when a prince or a courtier hath been described by such as have handled those subjects, the mould hath used to be made according to the perfection of the art . . . " (New York: E. P. Dutton & Co.; London: J. M. Dent & Co., 1915. Edited by G. W. Kitchin, p. 203).

One of the most emphatic testimonies to the recognition of the function of the prince in uniting wisdom and eloquence is the *Papyrus Geminus*, published at Cambridge in 1522 as *Eleatis Hermathena seu de eloquentia victoria*, an entertainment in which Eloquence, Wisdom's child, with the help of Caesar, Cicero, and Servius Sulpicius, pleading in the Elysian fields for the release of her mother Wisdom, long kept in bondage by her enemies, nobles, women, sophists, and lawyers, wins a truce. Eloquence brings Wisdom to England where she is welcomed by Henry VIII and admired by the people. Henry, quite as much as James I, was a scholar-prince.

ioneth such a one as is hard to find . . . " (p. 3). Castiglione himself says: "I am content, to err with Plato, Xenophon, and M. Tullius . . . in imagination of a perfect commune weale, and of a perfect king, and of a perfect Oratour . . ."[10]

It is perfectly natural, therefore, that Elyot should have devoted two thirds of his *Governour* to discussing the virtues that became a gentleman who had authority in the commonwealth. It is equally natural that an educational system which arose in the sixteenth century to provide members for a governing class should be primarily concerned with "character" or the achievement of the social and political virtues. It is pointless to rehearse Elyot's familiar insistence on the need for eloquence and his encyclopaedic program for the attaining of this traditional ideal. It is perhaps less commonly recognized how thoroughly Elyot envisaged that ideal in the light of the patristic tradition, as seen, for example, in his enthusiasm for *The Institution of a Christian Prince* of Erasmus (Everyman, p. 48). Finally, in Elyot's wake, the long series of manuals for intending statesmen, mostly written by schoolmasters, the professional rhetoricians of the day, need only be referred to in order to focus the great influence of the rhetorical tradition.[11]

---

[10]Everyman, p. 13. Cicero's basic insistence that the orator be a versatile or encyclopedic amateur blended into Castiglione's major condition for the Courtier that he "eschue as much as a man may, and as a sharpe and dangerous rocke, too much curiousnesse and affectation and (to speake a new word) to use in everything a certain disgracing to cover art withall, and seem whatsoever he doth and saith, to doe it without paine, and (as it were) not minding it" (p. 46). The habits of understatement and of easy nonchalance about one's attainments were incorporated in the gentlemanly code of the sixteenth century, thanks to Cicero. See Hamlet's

I'll be your foil, Laertes. In mine ignorance
Your skill shall, like a star i' the darkest night
Stick fiery off indeed. (V, ii, 255-257)

Compare Hamlet's speech to the players with Castiglione pp. 56-57. Compare his jests with p. 58. Compare his cautious fearfulness in accusing Claudius with p. 171. It is part of the civil prudence of an ideal prince. It is also noteworthy that the full rhetorical doctrine of decorum enters the sphere of courtly manners, so that rhetorical and social decorum are identical: ". . . we have given the Courtier a knowledge in so many things, that hee may well varie his conversation, and frame himselfe according to the inclination of them he accompanieth himselfe withall. . ." (p. 121). It was conceived that one function of the aristocratic governor was "to maintain civil obedience by gaining the good will of the lower classes to the upper." Kelso, *op. cit.*, p. 88.

[11]Ruth Kelso deals with these, pp. 118 ff. Lyly's *Euphues* is, of course, prominent in the list. She doesn't include Brinsley's *Ludus Literarius*, whose advice on theme writing is pointed up with reference to the Ciceronian ends of education: "The principal end of making Theams, I take to be this, to furnish schollers with all store of the choicest matter, that they may thereby learn to understand, speak or write of any ordinary theame, Morale or Politicall, such as usually fall into discourse amongst men and in practice of life; and especially concerning virtues and vices" (Campagnac's reprint, London, 1917, p. 172).

16
From Cliché to Archetype

Archetype

Archetypal enjoyed a "highbrow" popularity, ca. 1946-55; nor is it unknown today.

(Eric Partridge, Usage and Abusage)

E. S. Carpenter, the anthropologist, wrote about the inability of Robert Graves to grasp the multi-leveled structures. The conventional literary mind naturally tries to "connect" and to classify mythic and symbolic materials by reduction of oral to visual forms of order. Carpenter takes Graves merely as typical of the literary approach to all nonliterate culture. What Carpenter refers to as "adding Omissions" is the habit of the visually oriented person to try to find connections where the nonliterate person seeks to create intervals, gaps, and interfaces:

> *Graves, not incidentally, has "corrected" Greek mythology in two volumes, elimi-nating contradictions, adding omissions, arranging lineally, and generally "straightening out." What I am getting at is that they first turn these myths into what they are not; by arranging symbols they create "content": then they pigeon-hole these various "contents" and come up with archetypes. None of this interests me save the fact that, like Frye, they direct their attention towards a most important problem and, like a hedgehog, build humourless, water-tight systems (with faithful supporters reading "the Book"), that, instead of answering the problem or even illuminating it, block access to it.*

Graeme Wilson, introducing his translation of the poems of Hagiwara Sakutaro, cites from the 1882 Japanese translations of early-nineteenth-century English poems:

> *The Preface sharply attacked the cramping brevity of traditional forms ("How can a consecutive thought be expressed in such tight forms?"); . . .*

The West was discovering the power of discontinuity just when the East was taking on the excitement of the novelty of the Western continuum.

Lauriat Lane, Jr., provides a more conventional version of the archetypal question:

"The primordial image or archetype is a figure, whether it be daemon, man, or process, that repeats itself in the course of history wherever creative fantasy is fully manifested. Essentially, therefore, it is a mythological figure. If we subject these images to a closer investigation, we discover them to be the formulated resultants of countless typical experiences of our ancestors. They are, as it were, the psychic residua of numberless experiences of the same type" (Jung, "On the Relation of Analytical Psychology to Poetic Art," London, 1928).

The crux of Jung's statement lies in the phrase "psychic residua," which seems to imply the presence of inherited characteristics in the mind. Complete scientific proof of such an assumption would be impossible, but it is important to recognize that just as Jung's psychology is continually on the point of becoming philosophy, so this scientific-sounding statement of what Jung feels to be true is essentially metaphysical and must be judged as such. What is of as much value as Jung's definition of the archetype, and much more susceptible to investigation, is his distinction between the introvertive and the extravertive writer, a distinction central to any discussion of the use of literary archetypes by a particular author.

It might be asked why the word "archetype" should seem to relate so exclusively to literature. The same question can be asked of "cliché": why is it almost exclusively verbal in its association? When I. A. Richards was lecturing at the University of Wisconsin, he was accidentally immersed in the very cold waters of Lake Mendota while canoeing. He was rescued in an unconscious condition still clinging to the thwart of the canoe. The student paper *The Cardinal* in a feature cartoon ran the caption: "Saved by a stock response."

Most of us are saved by stock responses in all the nonverbal situations of our lives. It is necessary to consider the incident of the cliché-archetype theme in its nonverbal forms. Language as gesture and cadence and rhythm, as metaphor and image, evokes innumerable objects and situations which are in themselves nonverbal. The extent to which the nonverbal world is shared by language is obscure but no more so than the effect of human artifacts and technological environments on language. We are taking for granted that there is at all times interplay between these worlds of percept and concept, verbal and nonverbal. Anything that can be observed about the behavior of linguistic cliché or archetype can be found plentifully in the nonlinguistic world.

Those masterful images because complete
Grew in pure mind, but out of what began?
A mound of refuse or the sweepings of a street,
Old kettles, old bottles, and a broken can,
Old iron, old bones, old rags, that raving slut
Who keeps the till. Now that my ladder's gone,

I must lie down where all the ladders start,
In the foul rag-and-bone shop of the heart.
(W. B. Yeats, "The Circus Animals' Desertion")

The human city in all its complexity of functions is thus "a center of paralysis," a waste land of abandoned images. The clue that Yeats offers to the relation between the verbal and the nonverbal cliché and archetype is, in a word, "complete." The most masterful images, when complete, are tossed aside and the process begins anew. Language is a technology which extends all of the human senses simultaneously. All the other human artifacts are, by comparison, specialist extensions of our physical and mental faculties. Written language at once specializes speech by limiting words to one of the senses. Written speech is an example of such specialism, but the spoken word resonates, involving all the senses. The ancient saying, "Speak that I may see thee," was a popular way of citing this integral and inclusive quality of the spoken word.

If the world of kettles and bottles and broken cans and the world of commerce and money in the till are fragmentary specialisms of man's powers, it becomes easier to see the bond that remains between verbal and nonverbal cliché or archetype. The specialist artifact form has the advantage over language of intensification and amplification far beyond the limits of word or phrase. The archetype is a retrieved awareness or consciousness. It is consequently a retrieved cliché — an old cliché retrieved by a new cliché. Since a cliché is a unit extension of man, an archetype is a quoted extension, medium, technology, or environment.

The following are examples of archetypes which have been chosen to stress the normal tendency of a cliché to cross-quote from one technology to another:

a flagpole flying a flag
a cathedral adorned by a stained-glass window
pipeline carrying oil
cartoon with a caption
story with an engraved illustration
advertisement of a perfume with a sachet of perfume
electric circuit feeding an electric log fire
ship with a figurehead
a mold and its casting

A flagpole flying a flag may become a complex retrieval system. The flag could be the Russian flag, with its hammer and sickle. As flagcloth, the flag could retrieve an entire textile industry. By virtue of the fact that the flag is a national flag, it can retrieve flags of other nations.

The cliché, in other words, is incompatible with other clichés, but the archetype is extremely cohesive; other archetypes' residues adhere to it. When we consciously set out to retrieve one archetype, we unconsciously retrieve others; and this retrieval recurs in infinite regress. In fact, whenever we "quote" one consciousness, we also "quote" the archetypes we exclude; and this quotation of excluded archetypes has been called by Freud, Jung, and others "the archetypal unconscious."

Examples of retrieval systems occur in the Phoenician alphabet, dictionaries, indexes, computers, tables of engineering standards, etc. What these forms retrieve are archetypes or old processes.

It has been observed that civilization has to be recollected by every citizen. Education, whatever guise it takes, is retrieval of the archetype. A dream is a "quoted" experience, that is, it is archetypal — a dream purge rather than a conscious probe.

The common usage of the word "archetype" in literary criticism today has been to consider it more or less under the banner of psychoanalysis. For recent literary criticism it has been a primordial symbol or, as in Yeats, an ancestral symbol. Jung and his disciples have been careful to insist that the archetype is to be distinguished from its expression. Strictly speaking, a Jungian archetype is a power or capacity of the psyche. Nevertheless even in Jung's writings the term is used with interchangeable senses. In *Psyche and Symbol* Jung declares that "the archetype is an element of our psychic structure and thus a vital and necessary component in our psychic economy. It represents or personifies certain instinctive data of the dark primitive psyche; the real, the invisible *roots of consciousness.*" Jung is careful to remind literary critics to consider the archetype as a primordial symbol:

> *The archetypes are by no means useless archaic survivals or relics. They are living entities, which cause the praeformation of numinous ideas or dominant representations. Insufficient understanding, however, accepts these praeformations in their archaic form, because they have a numinous appeal to the underdeveloped mind. Thus Communism is an archaic, primitive and therefore highly insidious pattern which characterizes primitive social groups. It implies lawless chieftainship as a vitally necessary compensation, a fact which can only be overlooked by means of a rationalistic one-sidedness, the prerogative of the barbarous mind.*
>
> *It is important to bear in mind that my concept of the "archetypes" has been frequently misunderstood as denoting inherited patterns of thought or as a kind of philosophical speculation. In reality they belong to the realm of the activities of the instincts and in that sense they represent inherited forms of psychic behaviour. As such they are invested with certain dynamic qualities which, psychologically speaking, are designated as "autonomy" and "numinosity."*

Jung accounts for his theory of archetypes by means of the hypothesis of a collective race memory, although he is well aware that there is no scientific acceptance for such an idea. His justification, however, for using the concept of a collective memory is based on the recurrence over a wide area of archetypal patterns in artifacts, literatures, arts, etc., apart from the shaky scientific basis.

José Argüellas, writing on "Compute and Evolve" alludes to the power of the new computer in restoring to contemporary relevance the ancient *I Ching*:

> *The I Ching is becoming popular not because it is a refuge from modern life, but because its structure is once again understandable; it is now understandable because men have invented and understand computers — for the way the I Ching works when consulted, with its simple but mathematically flawless system, is much the same way that the computer works. No matter what language system an electronic computer is dependent upon, its functioning is based on the binary system — the same system which, in a simplified way, governs the manipulation of the yarrow stalks or coins which are used in consulting the I Ching. It is not too extravagant to say that, in terms of the nature of the input of the programmerquerent, and of the output, the I Ching can be viewed as a psychic computer. Given the development of computers with all the attendant implications (such as we mentioned earlier on, in referring to ethics), it is not at all odd that many people today are finding the I Ching strangely satisfying. . . .*
>
> *The I Ching functions as a computer, and its functioning is only according to the truth of the programming. The truth of the programming depends on how the person who consults the Book of Changes responds to its messages.*

Introduction

Between the ancient and the modern worlds there has been a kind of reversal of roles for cliché and archetype. The inventor, the discoverer of new forms and new technologies, was for archaic man someone who was more than a man. "Surely some power more than human gave things their first names," says Socrates in the *Phaedrus*. A modern Eskimo said to Professor E. S. Carpenter, "How could I know stone if there were no word 'stone'?" To archaic man language is an immediate evoker of reality, a magical form. In the same way, he thinks of the "apple of his eye" as constituting his visual world, not as receiving it.

The idea of words as merely corresponding to reality, the idea of matching, is characteristic only of highly literal cultures in which the visual sense is dominant. Today in the age of quantum mechanics, for which the "chemical bond" is, according to Heisenberg and Linus Pauling and others, a "resonance," it is perfectly natural to resume a "magical" attitude to language. The poetry of statement became the crux of one of the great critical upheavals of the twentieth century. This change corresponds to the discovery that consciousness is also a multileveled event with its roots in the "deepest terrors and desires."

It might be argued that a main cause of the merging of the archaic attitude to cliché with the modern notion of archetype as a more intense reality resulted from our great variety of new techniques of retrieval. Both past cultures and primal individual experiences are now subject to ready and speedy access. The ancient world had fewer means and fewer motives for retrieving the past just in the degree to which it considered all past events as present. The medieval need for the retrieval of ancient Greek and Latin and Hebrew for scriptural study began a cult of historical scholarship under modest conditons of manuscript culture. Today the means of retrieval of historical cultures and events is so extensive that it involves our time in depth in ancient cults and mysteries.

As we meditate upon the ancient clichés or sacro-breakthroughs, the literal man is inclined to consider them as "archetypes." For example, Northrop Frye in *Anatomy of Criticism* defines archetype as "a symbol, usually an image, which recurs often enough in literature to be recognizable as an element of one's literary experience as a whole." Of course this particular definition is most unJungian in suggesting that archetypes are human artifacts produced by much repetition — in other words, a form of cliché. For the literary archetypalist there is always a problem of whether *Oedipus Rex* or *Tom Jones* would have the same effect on an audience in the South Sea Islands as in Toronto. With the new means of plenary cultural retrieval, ancient clichés are taking their place as transcendental or archetypal forms.

This raises a central matter that will be discussed more fully. It is the process by which new clichés or new technological probes and environments have the effect of liquidating or scrapping the preceding clichés of cultures and environments created by preceding technologies. The world of archaeology and musicology today is entirely concerned with classifying these rejected fragments of obsolete and broken cultures. It is in "The Circus Animals' Desertion" that Yeats reviews this whole process, which was inherent in his entire creative procedure, as can be seen in "Leda and the Swan."

If we can consider form the reversing of archetype into cliché, as for example, the use of an archetypal Ulysses in James Joyce's novel to explore contemporary consciousness in the city of Dublin, then we may ask what would be the status of this pattern in primordial times, in the medieval period, and today. The answer would seem to be that in primordial times and today this archetype-into-cliché process is perfectly normal and accepted but that in the medieval period it is exceptional and unusual. The Balinese say, "We have no art, we do everything as well as possible." The artist in the Middle Ages, Renaissance, or the era up to the nineteenth century was regarded as a unique, exceptional person because he used an exceptional, unusual process. In primordial times, as today, the artist uses a familiar, ordinary technique and so he is looked upon as an ordinary, familiar person. Every man today is in this sense an artist — the administrator, the scientist, the doctor, as well as the man who uses paint or sculpts stone. Just as the archaic man had to follow natural processes of rhythms in order to influence and to purge, cleanse them by *ricorso*, so modern electric technologies require such timing and precision that only the following of processes in nature can be tolerated. The immediately preceding centuries of mechanization had been able to bypass these processes by fragmentation and strip-mining kinds of procedures. The very word "cliché" derives from the mechanical processes of printing, as we have noted. The Gutenberg technology of imposing and impressing by means of fragmented and repeatable units was the cue for all succeeding mechanization of the social and educational and political establishments. As various technologies have succeeded print, it has become more and more the home of the archetype.

Any breakthrough, whether for the poet or for the engineer, such as Daedalus or Hermes or Prometheus, seemed to reverberate with the divine thunder. The ceaseless use and repetition of these discoverers was sacralized. Eliade, in *Cosmos and History*, states:

> *In the particulars of his conscious behavior, the "primitive," the archaic man, acknowledges no act which has not been previously posited and lived by someone else, some other being who was not a man. What he does has been done before. His life is the ceaseless repetition of gestures initiated by others.*

For archaic or tribal man there was no past, no history. Always present. Today we experience a return to that outlook when technological breakthroughs have become so massive as to create one environment upon another, from telegraph to radio to TV to satellite. These forms give us instant access to all pasts. As for tribal man, there is for us no history. All is present, including the tribal man studied by Eliade.

The assumption of cliché as a breakthrough, as a probe into a new dimension, is challenged by Plato. His cave is the first "rag-and-bone shop," to use Yeats's phrase, the first archetypal storehouse. The sacralizing of the archetype was the work of civilized man with his literate, historical perspective. Petrarch, "the first modern man," stood on the border between two worlds: as one student put it, "With one foot firmly planted in the Middle Ages, while with the other he saluted the rising star of the Renaissance." His *Ruins of Rome* began the humanist cult of the rag-and-bone shop. The very small part of antiquity accessible to the twelfth-century historian was brought to bear upon the task of the exegesis of scripture. The sacralizing of the archetype, or ancient form, was not characteristic of the pagan world. For that world the words of Eliade describe the role of the archetype:

> *What does living mean for a man who belongs to a traditional culture? Above all, it means living in accordance with extrahuman models, in conformity with archetypes. Hence it means living at the heart of the real since . . . there is nothing truly real except the archetypes. Living in conformity with the archetypes amounted to*

respecting the "law," since the law was only a primordial hierophany, the revelation in illo tempore of the norms of existence, a disclosure by a divinity or a mystical being. And if, through the repetition of paradigmatic gestures and by means of periodic ceremonies, archaic man succeeded, as we have seen, in annulling time, he none the less lived in harmony with the cosmic rhythms; we could even say that he entered into these rhythms (we need only remember how "real" night and day are to him, and the seasons, the cycles of the moon, the solstices).

Naturally, the Old Testament repudiated this archetypal world as understood by pagan man. It repudiated all technologies as pagan deities, from the Tower of Babel to the Golden Calf. For Christian culture the scrapping or superannuation of the formulas and rituals and technologies sacred to pagan man became a natural form of behavior; but the door was now wide open for technological innovation in a merely humanist context. Christian contempt for the world and its works has had much to do with shaping attitudes toward cliché and formulaic models of organizing experience. In the same way Christian indifference to the "supernatural" claims of human invention and arts of the Muses encouraged meditation on the world as a vast ruin. Paradoxically, it was this indifference to the traditional that permitted novelty and innovation to thrive unhindered by religious observations. A single book serves to illuminate this entire theme: Lynn White's *Medieval Technology and Social Change* is an account of a wide range of technical inventions unknown to archaic man. Such inventions as the horse collar quickly led to the development of the modern world. Archaic man, as presented to us by Eliade and a host of contemporary anthropologists, had a huge stake in fixity and in an unchanging order, like the French Academy scrutinizing neologisms. Stasis is a strange facet of tribal and oral cultures, as revealed in *The Lore and Language of School Children* by Iona and Peter Opie.

Christian indifference to the pagan rituals of stability and renewal, as well as Christian contempt for the world as a wreck or middenheap, tended to reverse the pattern of cliché and archetype that characterized prehistoric man. This reversal stands out clearly today when we experience a return to the prehistoric attitudes to both cliché and archetype. Our technological breakthroughs are on a superior human scale, re-creating total new environments, greatly enlarging the Emperor's wardrobe, and making possible a reprogramming of the totality of existence on the planet. It is these developments that have restored cliché-as-probe and put invention in a position of dominance over the archetype.

Since we have already raised the theme of printing as related to cliché and archetype, the complexities of this innovation can be seen in *Finnegans Wake*, where Joyce is not only discussing the subject but illustrating the linguistic means for tackling it on several levels at once (see below).

Line 1 indicates that the process of creating a cliché for use or probe begins in taking something petite or pretty as a means of extending its action to include the *holos*. This is cliché in its sacroarchaic character and it is also cliché in the sense of dull habituation. The *part* may be a tooth. In a sense, teeth are not only the feature of the animal body where repetition and lineality concur, but when followed by "an allforabit" (alphabet) as their issue, recall the fable of King Cadmus and "the dragon's teeth which sprang up armed men." The letters of the alphabet in their early mode were pictograms that offered many relationships to the *holos*, as the famous phrase "alpha and the plough." Letters permitted specialism in human organization, which is inseparable from the military life. It also creates a social order or hierarchy (as in line 2 — "please to stoop"). The use of an alphabet is a great drop in dignity from the full magical power of the spoken word in archaic ritual. It is "stooping to conquer," in many senses. "Stoop" is "step" and in cliché technology a step that can be up or down. It is a means of control and power. Joyce is saying that no cliché or technology can be accepted without great loss to the integral being of the *holos*, and proceeds to a witty evocation of the psychic and social consequences of the "allforabit" beginning with the effect on human identity.

"Selveran" (line 2) resonates with the modalities of the individual self in relation to the little module bits ("peteet peas"). Throughout the *Wake* the theme of the mass-man, whether preliterate or postliterate, is alluded to many times via the "mush of porter pease." The condition of the self as merged in tribe or society is like that of the individual pea mashed. It is the mashing, of course, that creates (line 4) the pay roll. Money, as repetitive module, is only one of the many side effects of the allforabit. "Tomtummy's" (line 4) recalls that an army of Tommies not only marches on its tummy, but is roused by the roll of drums and tomtoms. "Wisha, wisha" (line 5) introduces the driving emotion in all technological cliché development. It is alluded to under many forms in the *Wake*: "a burning would is come to dance inane," and of course, "the willingdone museyroom" — a massive collection of human cliché and weaponry by which "a burning would" manifests itself in ever new environments and power.

"Wisha, wisha" alludes also to another theme that goes with "peteet peas" (line 2), namely "mishe, mishe," the Celtic for "I am" and the tribal mishe of the wild Irish, or "a mush and a wish."

The query (line 6) "Whydidtha?" follows the chain of consequences resulting from a single bit, or bite (line 2) "allforabit." The "a" is for "apple," as it were. The image of the "thorn that's thuck in its thoil" (line 6) is one of the punishments for the bite — his toil in the garden that has now become a mess. The word "mness" (line 7) mimes the mouth full of apple, as it were. "A middenhide hoard of objects" (line 8) recalls the impulse of fallen man to cover himself (hides, skins). Instead of plucking the fruit as it grows, he now specializes in

1 When a part so ptee does duty for the holos we soon grow to use of an
2 allforabit. Here (please to stoop) are selveran cued peteet peas of
3 quite a pecuniar interest inaslittle as they are the pellets that make
4 the tomtummy's pay roll. Right rank ragnar rocks and with these
5 rox orangotangos rangled rough and rightgorong. Wisha, wisha,
6 whydidtha? Thik is for thorn that's thuck in its thoil like thum-
7 fool's thraitor thrust for vengeance. What a mnice old mness it
8 all mnakes! A middenhide hoard of objects! Olives, beets, kim-
9 mells, dollies, alfrids, beatties, cormacks and daltons. Owlets' eegs
10 (O stoop to please!) are here, creakish from age and all now
11 quite epsilene, and oldwolldy wobblewers, haudworth a wipe o
12 grass. Sss! See the snake wurrums everyside! Our durlbin is
13 sworming in sneaks. They came to our island from triangular
14 Toucheaterre beyond the wet prairie rared up in the midst of the
15 cargon of prohibitive pomefructs but along landed Paddy Wip-
16 pingham and the his garbagecans cotched the creeps of them
17 pricker than our whosethere outofman could quick up her whats-
18 thats. Somedivide and sumthelot but the tally turns round the
19 same balifuson. Racketeers and bottloggers.
20　　Axe on thwacks on thracks, axenwise. One by one place one
21 be three dittoh and one before. Two nursus one make a plaus-
22 ible free and idim behind. Starting off with a big boaboa and three-
23 legged calvers and ivargraine jadesses with a message in their
24 mouths. And a hundreadfilled unleavenweight of liberorumqueue
25 to con an we can till allhorrors eve. What a meanderthalltale to
26 unfurl and with what an end in view of squattor and anntisquattor
27 and postproneauntisquattor! To say too us to be every tim, nick
28 and larry of us, sons of the sod, sons, littlesons, yea and lealittle-
29 sons, when usses not to be, every sue, siss and sally of us, dugters
30 of Nan! Accusative ahnsire! Damadam to infinities!
31.　　True there was in nillohs dieybos as yet no lumpend papeer
32 in the waste and mightmountain Penn still groaned for the micies
33 to let flee. All was of ancientry. You gave me a boot (signs on
34 it!) and I ate the wind. I quizzed you a quid (with for what?) and
35 you went to the quod. But the world, mind, is, was and will be
36 writing its own wrunes for ever, man, on all matters that fall
37 under the ban of our infrarational senses . . .

THIS IS
A PRINTING OFFICE

CROSSROADS OF CIVILIZATION
REFUGE OF ALL THE ARTS
AGAINST THE RAVAGES OF TIME
ARMOURY OF FEARLESS TRUTH
AGAINST WHISPERING RUMOUR
INCESSANT TRUMPET OF TRADE

FROM THIS PLACE WORDS MAY
FLY ABROAD
NOT TO PERISH ON WAVES OF SOUND
NOT TO VARY WITH THE
WRITER'S HAND
BUT FIXED IN TIME HAVING BEEN
VERIFIED IN PROOF

FRIEND YOU STAND ON
SACRED GROUND

THIS IS A PRINTING OFFICE

the production of the hoard of objects and a diversity of diets. Man becomes a producer and a consumer, organizing trade and markets with ensuing wars ("cormacks and daltons" [line 9] . . . "Racketeers and bottloggers" [line 19]). It's the money economy, i.e. "allforabit" where "the tally turns round the same balifuson" (lines 18-19).

The entire page is devoted to tracing the "meanderthalltale" (line 25), the labyrinthine ways of the alphabet technology as a kind of prototype of all cliché or breakthroughs. One of the principal effects of "allforabit" specialism is not only the production of a "hoard of objects" (line 8) but the endless tossing of same onto the middenheap. New technology as an automatic means of scrapping or rejecting the preceding culture creates the "liberorumqueue" (line 24), the endless production "to con an we can" (line 25).

Writing as a means of retrieving "ancientry" (line 33) led to a vast scrap heap of retrieved data even before the advent of "lumpend paper" (line 31). The middenhide grows mountainous with the castoffs of cultures and technologies. One theme in "middenhide" is the popular invisible quality of the environments created by new cliché or techniques. The forms of these technologies are imprinted not only on human language but on the outer world as well: "But the world, mind, is, was and will be writing its own wrunes for ever, man, on all matters" (lines 35-36) gave us the "ruins," the deciphering and retrieval of which fascinates the literate humanist.

Vico, in his *Scienza Nuova*, which Joyce found so useful, stresses that all ancient fables and tales are really records of moments of technical breakthrough to which the ancients assigned the status and name of a god, but Vico also insisted that the effects of such breakthroughs were recorded in the new "wrunes" (line 36), writing into the patterns of human speech and sensibility. Vico, like Joyce, insists that new technology is not added to culture, but it "ruins" whole societies, tossing them into the middenhide or heap, whence they are forever being retrieved and refurbished by succeeding generations.

This page of the *Wake*, like many others, is an approach to Yeats's "rag-and-bone shop of the heart." It is the tradition from which the individual talent must filch the fragments that he will shore against his own ruins. For Joyce, as for Yeats, the rag-and-bone shop is a collection of abandoned clichés.

It is the clichés that are the invented probes of artists and society, enabling them to ascend or descend the ladder of human accomplishment: "please to stoop" (line 2) and "O stoop to please" (line 10). The need of the poet for ever-new means of probing and exploration of experience sends him back again and again to the rag-and-bone shop of abandoned cliché. The testimony of artists in this matter is impressive. The stages by which the literary archetype became substituted for the technical cliché as the means of creation is one of the subjects of this book.

As a case in point, Yeats begins "The Circus Animals' Desertion" by saying:

I sought a theme and sought for it in vain,
I sought it daily for six weeks or so.
Maybe at last, being but a broken man,
I must be satisfied with my heart, although
Winter and summer till old age began
My circus animals were all on show,
Those stilted boys, that burnished chariot,
Lion and woman and the Lord knows what.

This poem is a *ricorso* or rehearsal, a retrieval of Yeats's entire career. Seeing himself as an old man, he has thrown himself on the scrap heap. He has archetypalized himself, but first he rehearses all the clichés of his art, all the innovations that he had introduced into the drama and poetry of his time.

What can I but enumerate old themes?

Having surveyed these stages of his art, his innovations and experiments, he simply says,

Those masterful images because complete,
Grew in pure mind, but out of what began?

His answer presents the main theme of *From Cliché to Archetype*: the new poetic techniques and images are retrieved from

A mound of refuse or the sweepings of a street,
Old kettles, old bottles, and a broken can,
Old iron, old bones, old rags, that raving slut
Who keeps the till. . . .

Yeats brings in here the whole theme of commerce as part of the poetic process. His poetic exhibitionism onto the big top is done. The images retrieved from "the rag-and-bone-shop" out of which he built his ladder for the high-wire act are now complete and cast aside. His "Jacob's ladder" is gone.

"I must lie down where all the ladders start." Our theme in *From Cliché to Archetype* is simply the scrapping of all poetic innovation and cliché when it has reached a certain stage of use. Masterful forms and images, when complete, are cast aside to become "the rag-and-bone shop of the heart" — that is, the world of the archetype.

What about Jacob's ladder? Jacob lay down only to climb a ladder, or to dream, at least, of a ladder of angels ascending and descending in heavenly hierarchy. Yeats regards the moment of poetic breakdown as a new breakthrough, the beginning again of the ascent and descent of Jacob's ladder of heavenly vision.

As his poetic clichés collapse and are scrapped, he turns to the retrieval of old forms for new clichés. It is the worn-out cliché that reveals the creative or archetypal processes in language as in all other processes and artifacts.

J. Seznec in *The Survival of the Pagan Gods* provides an entire study of the process of desacralization of the gods by literary humanism from the third century B.C. to the Renaissance. The process consisted in accepting the gods as technology heroes, or geniuses, who devoted their lives to the good of their fellow men. The recognition of the human element in the gods tended at first to be used against them, but beginning with Isadore of Seville's *Etymologiae*, a seventh-century encyclopedia, authors had begun to accept a desacralized view of the gods. The new strategy was followed throughout the Middle Ages and until the *Scienza Nuova* of Giambattista Vico. Like Isidore of Seville, Vico saw the history of cultural evolution in the etymologies of words as recording responses to technological innovations.

The encyclopedic tradition of classical rhetoric accepted the gods on a multileveled exegesis basis. This "grammatical" method of literary analysis via the figurative, tropological (moral), and anagogical (high mysteries) retained the old tribal and magical tradition of the "gods" approach by literary techniques of retrieval. It follows that the sixteenth- and seventeenth-century Puritans, in rejecting the multi-leveled literary approach also rejected the pagan "gods." The insistence on the single level of literal interpretation is the one that led Milton to toss the whole caboodle of pagan deities into his Hell, just as Plato had tossed all the multi-leveled phenomena of the world into his cave.

There may be something odd about the Paleolithic cave culture being dismissed by Plato into a Spenserian Cave of Error. But just as the plenary retrieval techniques of Gutenberg print created the Puritan ideal of a recovery of a purified and primitive Christianity, so the modern anthropologist, using plenary methods of retrieval, has rejected the traditional humanistic or literary view of the gods in favor of a complete resacralizing of pagan art and ritual. The resacralizing of the ancient clichés of ancient technology by anthropologists places the literary archetypalist in a very embarrassing position. The archetypalist, having come to regard the gods as a neutered or "spayed" bunch of moralized entities, now confronts the anthropologist, who insists on accepting them as real wild environmental forces completely beyond literary occurrence or control. The gods as cliché technologies are not susceptible to literary classification.

W. K. Wimsatt in "Horses of Wrath" details the conventional procedure of the literary man when he turns to the *Anatomy of Criticism* by Northrop Frye:

> *Some of the ideas of the arch-mythopoeist of our time have been foreshadowed, in fact appropriated, in the preceding paragraph. Northrop Frye's* Fearful Symmetry *(1949) announced in the last chapter the Blakean inspiration of an apocalyptic*

construct which came to realization in is Four Essays entitled Anatomy of Criticism *(1957). Earlier drafts and later applications are collected in his* Fables of Identity *(1963). The* Anatomy, *especially in its "Polemical Introduction," is written from an exceedingly keen awareness of the history of criticism and of the problems for criticism which we have just been surveying. It intends to escape from the main problem of criticism — that of literary evaluation — by the announcement of a very bold separation — that is, simply a separation of the act of "criticizing" literature from the act of valuing it.*

This is something like what both Eliot and Richards at moments in their thought during the 1920's had touched upon, but it now appears with a surpassing starkness and insistence. I refrain from saying "with systematic insistence," because, although the whole volume is an astonishing invention, I believe that the confrontation of the concepts of value and criticism is never in fact squarely made, and not only that the Four Essays themselves are in fact heavily charged with value assertions and implications, but that the Polemical Introduction, where the main argument about value is carried on, is notable for a series of finely disguised contradictions in this respect.

Homer's Ulysses descended into Hell to consult the ancients, oracle-style (cf. Eliot's "Tradition and the Individual Talent"). Plato, with the help of the new technological cliché of the written word, tossed the whole world of becoming into the middenhide of his cave. Virgil's Book VI is in the Homeric tradition of consulting the wisdom of the tribe.

Dante's Hell, complete with a few celebrated historical figures, is a sort of social register of his society. His Hell is a minutely discriminating structure of psychological states. Critics have commented upon the grandeur of the vagueness of Milton's Hell in comparison with the concretely imagined Hell of Dante. Considered as a scrap heap of rejected pagan technologies or clichés, Milton's Hell is amazingly specific, cataloguing a great many of the pagan deities and characterizing them with revelatory attributes. It is not difficult to see how Milton has junked the entire pagan cultures, even what to him must have been the attractive technologies of eloquence and poetry and speculative philosophy. Even his favorite art, music, is dispensed with for its technological seductiveness.

In *Paradise Lost* we have a later and fuller version of the youthful Milton's "On the Morning of Christ's Nativity," in which Milton sees the infant Christ almost like a new technology, superannuating the pagan ones. Whereas the pagans' hells omitted the gods of the technologies and of the arts, Milton's Hell receives all the whole company and seems almost to be designed for that purpose. Dante's Hell is a place of physical and psychological torment, but Milton's Hell is an Apollonian museum of pagan antiquity and of the arts and senses.

There is a sort of parallel between the world of Plato's cave as the recipient of a rejected world, where Plato had been replaced by Euclidean rational space and the Socratic probe (derivative from the new cliché of the written word) and the world of the seventeenth century, where Gutenberg print played the role of the earlier phonetic script. The seventeenth-century mechanist tossed aside the whole human past, relegating it to Milton's Hell.

To wanton with the Sun her lusty Paramour.

. . . . . .

She crown'd with Olive green, came softly sliding
Down through the turning sphear
His ready Harbinger,
With Turtle wing the amorous clouds dividing,
And waving wide her mirtle wand,
She strikes a universall Peace through Sea and Land.
(John Milton, "On the Morning of Christ's Nativity")

Public Archetype as Cliché

I was very much impressed to discover how the public in a big city is actually formed. It lives in a tumult of money making and dispersive activities and what we call emotion can neither be expressed nor communicated. All the pleasures, even the theatre, must simply distract . . . I seem to have noted an aversion to poetic productions, at least to the degree in which they are poetic, which seems to me quite natural precisely for these reasons. Poetry demands meditation, isolates man against his will, it crops up again and again, and in the vast world (not to say the large one) it is as uncomfortable as a faithful mistress.

(Goethe to Schiller, August 9, 1797)

Discussing the question of how the readers of fiction may use it to gain access to a finer code than their own, Q. D. Leavis cites a letter that puts cliché and archetype in a new relation of complementarity, explaining:

. . . what the cheaper forms of literature really do achieve for those to whom they appeal. (Speaking as one of the herd to whom Priestley and Walpole have meant a good deal, these last five years, and Eliot and Lawrence practically nil, and who can quite honestly read P. G. Wodehouse with profit) I am not sure that you do not underestimate the extent to which the existence of any real channel of "communication" between any artist and his public depends on his managing a symbolisation of something which was previously the property of that public: in this sense the crime of "giving the public what it wants" has another and not necessarily evil meaning (though this does not justify the usual or Northcliffe idea of doing so). I think the intrinsic qualities of a work of art are impotent unless they can symbolise, reflect, and focus in a convenient form, something that is already

to some extent present in the mind of the man who hears, sees, or reads the work.
Thus any art that I appreciate appeals because it symbolises (not necessarily for-
mulates explicitly) something that is already in my fund of experience. That is why
a writer like Walpole, who is probably not sensitive to more than the common
doings of rather common people, is to me a very great man, whose greatness is
never really likely to be approached by artists whose work can only symbolise, or
evoke the response of, a sensitivity that I and the vast majority have never experi-
enced. I have been enormously impressed by Priestley's latest book because, I
think, it succeeds in symbolising, and thus coheres and concentrates, some knowl-
edge I already had in a dim and confused way, e.g. that most people, as
uneducated as myself, are a curious mixture of the comic, the pathetic, and the
tragic, are moved chiefly by little things of which they ought to take no notice, are
preoccupied constantly and frequently inspired or terrified, by the unnecessary,
the trivial and the accidental, and have no conscious sense of values about any-
thing, and most of all dislike trying to think about anything subtle.

Throughout the entire discussion of *Fiction and the Reading Public* Mrs. Leavis makes the assumption of a "higher code" which it is the function of literature to make accessible. Entrée via this code is presumed sufficient to enable the reader to "place" the products and activities of any culture at all. Mrs. Leavis is making the familiar literary assumption that matching, rather than making, is the function of literary training. In a world of rapid innovation and environmental development the "finer code" permits the classification of novelties and the rejection of vulgar- ity, but for the creation of new codes from new cultural materials, the finer code, as a mere matching or checking device, is quite ineffectual. Indeed, the "finer code" that Mrs. Leavis finds so adequately manifested in the homogeneous tonali- ties of eighteenth-century prose is an interesting example of the environmental form being moved up to nostalgic archetypal status by a nineteenth-century mind. It is the nineteenth century that discovers rich cultural values in the ritual gestures and corporate decorum of eighteenth-century discourse. The twentieth century, on the other hand, has discovered many new values in the popular art and literature of the nineteenth century. Hopkins, for example, abandoned the corporate uses of language as social mask, or manner, using words and phrases as heuristic probes with which to explore and to restore the hidden sinews of English.

What appears to elude the Leavis approach is the role of ever-new art and lit- erature in creating new perception for new environments. Such environments are invisible and invincible except as they are raised to consciousness by new artistic styles and probes. With the advent of new styles or instruments of perception, the effect of the new environment is to mirror the image of the old one. The indus- trial nineteenth century developed a considerable empathy for anthropology and the study of nonliterate societies. Industrial and print technology have a pro- foundly fragmenting effect on human sensibilities. It was not, therefore, very realistic to use nonliterate societies as a "mirror of Perseus" in which to observe the hated face of the industrial Gorgon. The great merit of *Fiction and the Reading Public* is in its concentration upon the changing audiences for fiction. It is a piece of audience research that has done much to get attention for literature as a changing social mask. Literature as a consumer commodity is an inevitable development of an age of industrial mass production. Such a world is ingenious in devising ever-new packages:

> *In effect, every magazine is a package, labelled and authoritatively sealed with the symbol of the editor's approval. . . . The young author is often confused by a rejection which simply says, "This is not a* Harper *story." That does not mean it is not a good story; it simply means that the tale does not, in the editor's trained mind, conform to the type of fiction which his magazine has established.*

Exploration of the function of audience forms is not easy for literary people who can understand only "content." The poet, or creator, more than the critic, tries to exploit new technology in order to establish new plateaus for perception. The critic tends rather to look at the values of the preceding age which have been eroded by the new developments. The critic is like the accountant adding up profits and losses. He is tempted to admonish the young to hold their fingers firmly in the eighteenth-century dike of a society with critical standards firmly imposed by the mandarinate. It was essentially an aristocratic culture, so that the mere idea of any serious challenge to it was almost unthinkable. The eighteenth century had, in its turn, derived the habit of seriousness from the seventeenth:

> *The Puritan conscience implied a seriousness, an habitual occupation of the mind by major questions, and this had been the shaping factor in the lives of the middle-class and respectable poor from Bunyan's age till well on into the nineteenth century, when, as we have seen, it was side-tracked into a path which has more and more widely diverged from that of the arts. . . .*

It should be clear, however, that standards imposed from above can have little value in relating people to one another in environments that have never existed before. The creative value of commercial stereotypes appears in the portrait of Gerty MacDowell in Joyce's *Ulysses*. Gerty is a mosaic of banalities that reveals the effect of these forms in shaping and extending our lives. Joyce enables the reader to exult and triumph over the trivia by letting him in on the very process by which they dramatize our lives. In the same way, in the Newspaper, or "Aeolus," episode of *Ulysses*, Joyce deploys for us the world of verbal gimmicks as well as the mechanical operations upon which they depend. He floods the entire newsmaking situation with an intelligibility that provides a catharsis for the accumulated effects of the stereotypes in our lives.

There are various nostalgic perspectives in *Fiction and the Reading Public* that are relevant to an understanding of the processes of cliché and archetype:

> . . . it would not be true to suggest a stratification of novel writers and novel read-
> ers in 1760, for example, when any one who could read would be equally likely to
> read any novel, or every novel, published, and the only division of the novelists of
> that age that can be made is between good and indifferent (effective and ineffec-
> tive); even a century later the same conditions hold, for though at that time
> Dickens, Reade, and Wilkie Collins were the idols of the man in the street and
> George Eliot and Trollope of the educated, yet each class read or perfectly well
> might have read the entire output of all the contemporary novelists, who all live in
> the same world, as it were, understand each other's language, live by the same
> code, and employ a common technique presenting no peculiar difficulty to the
> reader.

Is it not strange that Mrs. Leavis should find values in the past cultural uniformity of a mechanical society just when much greater integration of the public
had occurred via telegraph? The quality of past industrial homogeneity has now
acquired archetypal status, thanks to the powerful electric environment of retribalized man. This new electric service environment of oral culture enables us to
perceive value in archaic communities where everybody shares a large body of
traditional lore and experience. Plainly, however, an integral society, whether
tribal or civilized, oral or literate, is possible only under conditions of much
continuity of external organization.

The function of art in a tribal society is not to orient the population to novelty
but to merge it with the cosmos. Value does not inhere in art as object but in its
power to educate the perceptions. In a homogeneous mechanized society, the
individualist role of the training of perception scarcely exists. The primitive role
of art of serving as consolidator and as liaison with the hidden cosmic powers
again comes to the fore in popular art. Paradoxically, it is the most vulgar art that
has the most in common with the integral societies of preliterate man. It is unfortunate, therefore, to invoke homogeneity as a distinct excellence of so civilized a
society as that of the eighteenth century.

This merely tends to draw attention to the process of typographic fragmentation by which the eighteenth century achieved its homogeneity. Such was the
process by which uniform prices and extensive markets were created. The same
market processes were extended to literature. They had begun in the first place in
print technology, without which neither industry nor markets could exist. It is not
very satisfactory to concur in one part of this process and to reject the rest.

Regarding Tragedy and Comedy, any factor that alienates an individual from
his environment archetypalizes him as tragic. Job loses his possessions and his
family. Any individual bereaved by a traffic accident is similarly alienated from

his environment: viz., *The Stranger* by Camus, *The Outsider* by Colin Wilson, Oedipus, etc. Comedy, on the other hand, seems to imply the reverse movement of the individual toward the group. The individual becomes environmental. Like W. B. Yeats in Auden's poem, "He became his admirers."

The complaint about Virginia Woolf — "Why, you can't read her unless your mind is absolutely fresh!" — draws attention to the print medium in a very special way. The mere act of reading is itself a lulling and semi-hypnotic experience. The further fact that print has long been a major environmental factor renders it invisible save to the artist. When the Symbolists began to deal with words as things, they bypassed the print process and accepted words as pigment, as textures, as structures with auras of many kinds. All of these strategies were necessary in order to encounter words at all in the typographic environment.

Mrs. Leavis' complaint about the world of Ethel M. Dell (or Tarzan) as programming for the print medium is irrelevant since these kinds of "content" are in fact perfectly adjusted to the quality of print itself, as it affects the sensibilities of our time. Why has it never occurred to the literary public that a monotonous and hypnotic use of print might be the main cause attracting content to suit? It was already clear to Alexander Pope at the beginning of the eighteenth century that, as print became more environmental, an inky fog had settled down over the human consciousness.

Is it not natural that, as any form whatever becomes environmental and unconscious, it should select as "content" the most common and vulgar and environmental of materials? As any form becomes environmental, it tends to be soporific. That is why its content must also become innocuous in order to match the effects of the medium. Any medium whatever, as it becomes pervasive, is to that degree common and vulgar and therefore attracts and demands only common and vulgar materials. To the artist this vulgarity is an opportunity so far as he is competent to set it in opposition to another equally pervasive form. Since the artist is typically interested in revealing forms, he never balks at contact with the most vulgar materials. The play within the play in *Hamlet* is a tissue of sixteenth-century banalities and clichés, as indeed was most of *Hamlet* to the Elizabethan. The encounter of one kind of environmental cliché with another leads to revolution as an art form. Michael Harrington sees the consequences:

This accidental revolution is the sweeping and unprecedented technological transformation of the Western environment which has been, and is being carried out in a casual way. . . . Conservatives made a revolution, but it was not the one the revolutionists had predicted, and the antagonists were mutually bewildered. . . . Literacy increased, making many educators fearful, since its uses seemed anticultural; the people asserted themselves and the traditional democrats became uneasy. There was perplexity on all sides.

17
The Emperor's New Clothes

In his poem "Esthétique du Mal" Wallace Stevens writes:

This is the thesis scrivened in delight,
The reverberating psalm, the right chorale.

One might have thought of sight, but who could
think
Of what it sees, for all the ill it sees?
Speech found the ear, for all the evil sound,
But the dark italics it could not propound.
And out of what one sees and hears and out
Of what one feels, who could have thought to make
So many selves, so many sensuous worlds,
As if the air, the mid-day air, was swarming
With the metaphysical changes that occur,
Merely in living as and where we live,

He indicates that the slightest shift in the level of visual intensity produces a subtle modulation in our sense of ourselves, both private and corporate. Since technologies are extensions of our own physiology, they result in new programs of an environmental kind. Such pervasive experiences as those deriving from the encounter with environments almost inevitably escape perception. When two or more environments encounter one another by direct interface, they tend to manifest their distinctive qualities. Comparison and contrast have always been a means of sharpening perception in the arts as well as in general experience. Indeed, it is upon this pattern that all the structures of art have been reared. Any artistic endeavor includes the preparing of an environment for human attention. A poem or a painting is in every sense a teaching machine for the training of perception and judgment. The artist is a person who is especially aware of the challenge and dangers of new environments presented to human sensibility. Whereas the ordinary person seeks security by numbing his perceptions against the impact of new experience, the artist delights in this novelty and instinctively creates situations that both reveal it and compensate for it. The artist studies the distortion of sensory life produced by new environmental programing and tends to create artistic situations that correct the sensory bias and derangement brought about by the new form. In social terms the artist can be rewarded as a navigator who gives adequate compass bearings in spite of magnetic deflection of the needle by the changing play of forces. So understood, the artist is not a peddler of ideals or lofty experiences. He is rather the indispensable aid to action and reflection alike.

Therefore the question of whether art should be taught in our schools can easily be answered: of course it should be taught, but not as a subject. To teach art as a subject is to insure that it will exist in a state of classification serving only to separate art off from the other activities of man. As Adolf von Hildebrand points out in *The Problem of Form*, "Deflected thus from his natural course, the child develops his artificial rather than his natural resources and it is only when he reaches full maturity that the artist learns to think again in terms of the natural forces and ideas which in his childhood were his happiest possession." In the space age of information environments, art necessarily takes on new meaning and new functions. All previous classifications of these matters lose their interest and relevance.

In his *Approach to Art* E. H. Gombrich notes the extraordinary shift from making to matching that began for Western art in fifth-century Athens. In discovering the joys of matching or of realistic representation, the Greeks were not behaving like free men, but like robots. In the representation of reality stress is laid upon the visual sense usually at the expense of all the other senses. Such representation began with the rise of phonetic literacy and cannot occur at any time or at any place without the presence of a technology that favors the visual sense at the expense of all the other senses. For many people it is one of the horrors of our present age that we must live amidst the effects of technologies that do not favor the visual sense in anything like the degree that phonetic literacy does. The phonetic alphabet, as explained in *The Gutenberg Galaxy*, is the only form of writing that abstracts sight and sound from meaning. This fact is stressed by David Diringer in *The Alphabet*. By contrast, pictographic writing tends to unite the senses and semantics in a kind of gestalt. When the visual sense is played up above the other senses, it creates a new kind of space and order that we often call "rational" or pictorial space and form. Only the visual sense has the properties of continuity, uniformity and connectedness that are assumed in Euclidean space. Only the visual sense can create the impression of a continuum. Alex Leighton has said, "To the blind all things are sudden." To touch and hearing each moment is unique, but to the sense of sight the world is uniform and continuous and connected. These are the properties of pictorial space which we often confuse with rationality itself.

Perhaps the most precious possession of man is his abiding awareness of the analogy of proper proportionality, the key to all metaphysical insight and perhaps the very condition of consciousness itself. This analogical awareness is constituted of a perpetual play of ratios among ratios: A is to B what C is to D, which is to say that the ratio between A and B is proportioned to the ratio between C and D, there being a ratio between these ratios as well. This lively awareness of the most exquisite delicacy depends upon there being no connection whatever between the components. If A were linked to B, or C to D, mere logic would take the place of analogical perception. Thus one of the penalties paid for literacy and a high visual culture is a strong tendency to encounter all things through a rigorous story line, as it were. Paradoxically, connected spaces and situations exclude participation whereas discontinuity affords room for involvement. Visual space is connected and creates detachment or noninvolvement. It also tends to exclude the participation of the other senses. Thus the New York World's Fair defeated itself by imposing a visual order and story line that offered little opportunity for participation by the viewer. In contrast, Expo Canada presented not a story line but a mosaic of many cultures and environments. Mosaic form is almost like an X-ray compared to pictorial form with its connections. The Canadian mosaic aroused extraordinary enthusiasm and participation, mystifying many people.

The same difference exists between movie and TV. The movie is highly pictorial, but kinematically it is discontinuous and nonvisual, and thus demands participation. This discontinuous quality has been very much played up in such movies as *The Seventh Seal* and *Blow-Up*, to name only two in a rapidly developing métier. A movie is a succession of discrete images which are separated by extremely small spans of time. Because of their rapid succession, the images are fused in the conscious mind and appear connected. Our relatively recent insights into the power of the preconscious in both the creation and the apprehension of works of art indicate that the subliminal is in fact a strong force in psychic reorganization. It is in this sense that the movie form can be described as a medium which deals in disconnected spaces.

TV, on the other hand, is a kind of X-ray. Any new technology, any extension or amplification of human faculties, when given material embodiment, tends to create a new environment. This is as true of clothing as of speech, or script, or wheel. This process is more easily observed in our own time when several new environments have been created. In the latest one, TV, we find a handful of engineers and technicians in the 10 percent area, as it were, creating a set of radical changes in the 90 percent area of daily life. The new TV environment is an electric circuit that takes as its content the earlier environment, the photograph and the movie in particular. The interplay between the old and the new environments generates an innumerable series of problems and confusions which extend all the way from how to allocate the viewing time of children and adults to pay-TV and TV in the classroom. The new medium of TV as an environment creates new occupations. As an environment, it is imperceptible except in terms of its content. That is, all that is seen or noticed is the old environment, the movie. But even the effects of TV on the movie go unnoticed, and the effects of the TV environment in altering the entire character of human sensibility and sensory ratio are completely ignored. The viewer is in the situation of being X-rayed by the image. Typically, therefore, the young viewer acquires a habit of depth involvement which alienates him from the existing arrangements of space and organized knowledge, whether at home or in the classroom. However, this condition of alienation extends to the entire situation of Western man today.

The function of the artist in correcting the unconscious bias of perception in any given culture can be betrayed if he merely repeats the bias of the culture instead of readjusting it. In fact, it can be said that any culture which feeds merely on its direct antecedents is dying. In this sense the role of art is to create the means of perception by creating counterenvironments that open the door of perception to people otherwise numbed in a nonperceivable situation. In Françoise Gilot's book *Life with Picasso* the painter notes that: "When I paint, I always try to give an image people are not expecting and, beyond that, one they reject. That's what interests me. It's in this sense that I mean I always try to be subversive. That is, I give a man an image of himself whose elements are collected from among the usual way of seeing things in traditional painting and then reassembled in a fashion that is unexpected and disturbing enough to make it impossible for him to escape the questions it raises."

Under the heading "What exists is likely to be misallocated" Peter Drucker in *Managing for Results* discusses the structure of social situations: "Business enterprise is not a phenomenon of nature but one of society. In a social situation, however, events are not distributed according to the 'normal distribution' of a natural universe (that is, they are not distributed according to the bell-shaped Gaussian curve). In a social situation a very small number of events *at one extreme* — the first 10 per cent to 20 per cent at most — accounts for 90 per cent of all results." What Drucker is presenting here is the environment as it presents itself for human attention and action. He is confronting the phenomenon of the imperceptibility of the environment as such. Edward T. Hall tackles this same factor in *The Silent Language*. The ground rules, the pervasive structure, the over-all pattern elude perception except insofar as an antienvironment or a countersituation is constructed to provide a means of direct attention. Paradoxically, the 10 percent of the typical situation that Drucker designates as the area of effective cause and as the area of opportunity, this small factor, is the environment. The other 90 percent is the area of problems generated by the active power of the 10 percent environment. For the environment is an active process pervading and impinging upon all the components of the situation. It is easy to illustrate this.

The content of any system or organization naturally consists of the preceding system or organization, and in that degree the old environment acts as a control on the new. It is useful to notice that the arts and sciences serve as antienvironments that enable us to perceive the environment. In a business civilization we have long considered liberal study as providing necessary means of orientation and perception. When the arts and sciences themselves become environments under conditions of electric circuitry, conventional liberal studies, whether in the arts or sciences, will no longer serve as an antienvironment. When we live in a museum without walls, or have music as a structural part of our sensory environment, new strategies of attention and perception have to be created. When the highest scientific knowledge creates the environment of the atom bomb, new controls for the scientific environment have to be discovered, if only in the interest of survival.

The structural examples of the relation of environment to antienvironment need to be multiplied in order to understand the principles of perception and activity involved. The Balinese, who have no word for art, say, "We do everything as well as possible." This is not an ironic but a factual remark. In a preliterate society art serves as a means of merging the individual and the environment, not as a means of training perception of the environment. Archaic or primitive art looks to us like a magical control built into the environment. Thus to put the artifacts from such a culture into a museum or antienvironment is an act of nullification rather than of revelation. Today what is called "Pop Art" is the use of some object from our own daily environment as if it were antienvironmental. Pop Art serves to remind us, however, that we have fashioned for ourselves a world of artifacts and images that are intended not to train perception or awareness but to insist that we merge with them as the primitive man merges with his environment. Therefore, under the terms of our definition of art as antienvironmental, this is nonart except insofar as the illumination of the interior environment of the human mind can be regarded as an artistic stance.

The world of modern advertising is a magical environment constructed to maintain the economy, not to increase human awareness. We have designed schools as antienvironments to develop the perception and judgment of the printed word, but we have provided no training to develop similar perception and judgment of any of the new environments created by electric circuitry. This is not accidental. From the development of phonetic script until the invention of the electric telegraph, human technology had tended strongly toward the furtherance of detachment and objectivity, detribalization and individuality. Electric circuitry has quite the contrary effect. It involves in depth. It merges the individual and the mass environment. To create an antienvironment for such electric technology would seem to require a technological extension of both private and corporate consciousness. The awareness and opposition of the individual are in these circumstances as irrelevant as they are futile.

The structural features of environment and antienvironment appear in the age-old clash between professionalism and amateurism, whether in sport or in studies. Professional sport fosters the merging of the individual in the mass and in the patterns of the total environment. Amateur sport seeks rather the development of critical awareness of the individual and, most of all, critical awareness of the ground rules of the society as such. The same contrast exists for studies. The professional tends to specialize and to merge his being uncritically in the mass. The ground rules provided by the mass response of his colleagues serve as a pervasive environment of which he is uncritical and unaware.

The party system of government affords a familiar image of the relations of environment and antienvironment. The government as environment needs the opposition as antienvironment in order to be aware of itself. The role of the opposition seems to be, as in the arts and sciences, that of creating perception. As the government environment becomes more cohesively involved in a world of instant information, opposition would seem to become increasingly necessary but also intolerable. It begins to assume the rancorous and hostile character of a Dew Line, or a Distant Early Warning System. It is important, however, to consider the role of the arts and sciences as Early Warning Systems in the social environment. The models of perception they provide can give indispensable orientation to future problems well before they become troublesome.

The legend of Humpty-Dumpty suggests a parallel to the 10-90 percent distribution of causes and effects. His fall brought into play a massive response from the social bureaucracy. But all the King's horses and all the King's men could not put Humpty-Dumpty back together again. They could not re-create the old environment; they could only create a new one. Our typical response to a disrupting new technology is to re-create the old environment instead of heeding the new opportunities of the new environment. Failure to notice the new opportunities is also failure to understand the new powers. This means that we fail to develop the necessary controls or antienvironments for the new environment. This failure leaves us in the role of mere automata.

W. T. Easterbrook has done extensive exploration of the relations of bureaucracy and enterprise, discovering that as soon as one becomes the environment, the other becomes an antienvironment. They seem to bicycle along through history alternating their roles with all the dash and vigor of Tweedledum and Tweedledee. In the eighteenth century when *realism* became a new method in literature, what happened was that the external environment was put in the place of antienvironment. The ordinary world was given the role of art object by Daniel Defoe and others. The environment began to be used as an perceptual probe. It became self-conscious. It became an "anxious object" instead of being an unperceived and pervasive pattern. Environment used as probe or art object is satirical because it draws attention to itself. The Romantic poets extended this technique to external nature, transforming nature into an art object. Beginning with Baudelaire and Rimbaud and continuing in Hopkins and Eliot and James Joyce, the poets turned their attention to language as a probe. Long used as an environment, language became an instrument of exploration and research. It became an antienvironment. It became Pop Art along with the graphic probes of Larry Rivers, Rauschenberg and many others.

The artist as a maker of antienvironments permits us to perceive that much is newly environmental and therefore most active in transforming situations. This would seem to be why the artist has in many circles in the past century been called the enemy, the criminal.

Pablo shook his head. "Kahnweiler's right," he said. "The point is, art is something subversive. It's something that should not be free. Art and liberty, like the fire of Prometheus, are things one must steal, to be used against the established order. Once art becomes official and open to everyone, then it becomes the new academicism." He tossed the cablegram down onto the table. "How can I support an idea like that? If art is ever given the keys to the city, it will be because it's been so watered down, rendered so impotent, that it's not worth fighting for."

I reminded him that Malherbe had said a poet is of no more use to the state than a man who spends his time playing ninepins. "Of course," Pablo said. "And why did Plato say poets should be chased out of the republic? Precisely because every poet and every artist is an antisocial being. He's not that way because he wants to be; he can't be any other way. Of course the state has the right to chase him away — from its point of view — and if he is really an artist it is in his nature not to want to be admitted, because if he is admitted it can only mean he is doing something which is understood, approved, and therefore old hat — worthless. Anything new, anything worth doing, can't be recognized. People just don't have that much vision."

(Françoise Gilot and Carlton Lake, *Life with Picasso*)

It helps to explain why news has a natural bias toward crime and bad news. It is this kind of news that enables us to perceive our world. The detective since Poe's Dupin has tended to be a probe, an artist of the big town, an artist-enemy, as it were. Conventionally, society is always one phase back, is never environmental. Paradoxically, it is the antecedent environment that is always being upgraded for our attention. The new environment always uses the old environment as its material.

In the Spring, 1965, issue of the *Varsity Graduate* of the University of Toronto, Glenn Gould discussed the effects of recorded music on performance and composition. This is a reversal or chiasmus of form that occurs in any situation where an environment is pushed up into high intensity or high definition by technological change. A reversal of characteristics occurs, as in the case of bureaucracy and enterprise. An environment is naturally of low intensity or low definition. That is why it escapes observation. Anything that raises the environment to high intensity, whether it be a storm in nature or violent change resulting from a new technology, turns the environment into an object of attention. When it becomes an object of attention, it assumes the character of an antienvironment or an art object. When the social environment is stirred up to exceptional intensity by technological change and becomes a focus of much attention, we apply the terms "war" and "revolution." All the components of "war" are present in any environment whatsoever. The recognition of war depends upon their being stepped up to high definition.

Under electric conditions of instant information movement, both the concept and the reality of war become manifest in many situations of daily life. We have long been accustomed to war as that which goes on between publics or nations. Publics and nations were the creation of print technology. With electric circuitry publics and nations became the content of the new technology: "The mass audience is not a public as environment but a public as content of a new electric environment." And whereas "the public" as an environment created by print technology consisted of separate individuals with varying points of view, the mass audience consists of the same individuals involved in depth in one another and involved in the creative process of the art or educational situation that is presented to them. Art and education were presented to the *public* as consumer packages for their instruction and edification. The members of the mass audience are immediately involved in art and education as participants and co-creators rather than as consumers. Art and education become new forms of experience, new environments, rather than new antienvironments. Pre-electric art and education were antienvironments in the sense that they were the content of various environments. Under electric conditions the content tends, however, toward becoming environmental itself. This was the paradox that Malraux found in *The Museum Without Walls*, and that Glenn Gould finds in recorded music. Music in the concert hall had been an antienvironment. The same music when recorded is *music without halls*, as it were.

Another paradoxical aspect of this change is that when music becomes environmental by electric means, it becomes more and more the concern of the private individual. By the same token and complementary to the same paradox, the pre-electric music of the concert hall (the music made for a public rather than a mass audience) was a corporate ritual for the group rather than the individual. This paradox extends to all electric technology. The same means which permit a universal and centralized thermostat in effect encourage a private thermostat for individual manipulation. The age of the mass audience is thus far more individualistic than the preceding age of the *public*. It is this paradoxical dynamic that confuses every issue about "conformity," "separatism" and "integration" today. Profoundly contradictory actions and directions prevail in all these situations. This is not surprising in an age of circuitry succeeding the age of the wheel. The feedback loop plays all sorts of tricks to confound the single-plane and one-way direction of thought and action as they had been constituted in the pre-electric age of the machine.

Applying the foregoing to the Negro question, one could say that the agrarian South has long tended to regard the Negro as environment. As such, the Negro is a challenge, a threat, a burden. The very phrase "white supremacy," quite as much as the phrase "white trash," registers this environmental attitude. The environment is the enemy that must be subdued. To the rural man, the conquest of nature is an increasing challenge. It is the Southerner who contributed the cowboy to the frontier. The Virginian, the archetypal cowboy, as it were, confronts the environment as a hostile, natural force. To man on the frontier, other men are environmental and hostile. By contrast, to the townsmen, men appear not as environmental but as content of the urban environment.

Parallel to the Negro question is the problem of French Canada. The English Canadians have been the environment of French Canada since the railway and Confederation. However, since the telegraph and radio and television, French Canada and English Canada alike have become the content of this new technology. Electric technology is totally environmental for all human communities today. Hence the great confusion arising from the transformation of environments into antienvironments, as it were. All the earlier groupings that had constituted separate environments before electricity have now become antienvironments or the content of the new technology. Awareness of the old unconscious environments therefore becomes increasingly acute. The content of any new environment is just as unperceived as that of the old one had been initially. As a merely automatic sequence, the succession of environments and the dramatics accompanying them tend to be rather tiresome, if only because the audience is very prone to participate in the dramatics with an enthusiasm proportionate to its lack of awareness. In the electric age all former environments whatever become antienvironments. As such the old environments are transformed into areas of self-awareness and self-assertion, guaranteeing a very lively interplay of forces.

The visual sense, alone of our senses, creates the forms of space and time that are uniform, continuous and connected. Euclidean space is the prerogative of visual and literate man. With the advent of electric circuitry and the instant movement of information, Euclidean space recedes and the non-Euclidean geometries emerge. Lewis Carroll, the Oxford mathematician, was perfectly aware of this change in our world when he took Alice through the looking glass into the world where each object creates its own space and conditions. To the visual or Euclidean man, objects do not create time and space. They are merely fitted into time and space. The idea of the world as an environment that is more or less fixed is very much the product of literacy and visual assumptions. In his book *The Philosophical Impact of Contemporary Physics* Milic Capek explains some of the strange confusions in the scientific mind that result from the encounter of the old non-Euclidean spaces of preliterate man with the Euclidean and Newtonian spaces of literate man. The scientists of our time are just as confused as the philosophers, or the teachers, and it is for the reason that Whitehead assigned: they still have the illusion that the new developments are to be fitted into the old space or environment.

One of the most obvious changes in the arts of our time has been the dropping not only of representation, but also of the story line. In poetry, in the novel, in the movie, narrative continuity has yielded to thematic variation. Such variation in place of story line or melodic line has always been the norm in native societies. It is now becoming the norm in our own society and for the same reason, namely, that we are becoming a nonvisual society.

In the age of circuitry, or feedback, fragmentation and specialism tend to yield to integral forms of organization. Humpty-Dumpty tends to go back together again. The bureaucratic efforts of all the King's horses and all the King's men were naturally calculated to keep Humpty-Dumpty from ever getting together again. The Neolithic age, the age of the planter after the age of the hunter, was an age of specialism and division of labor. It has reached a somewhat startling terminus with the advent of electric circuitry. Circuitry is a profoundly decentralizing process. Paradoxically, it was the wheel and mechanical innovation that created centralism. The circuit reverses the characteristics of the wheel, just as Xerography reverses the characteristics of the printing press. Before printing, the scribe, the author and the reader tended to merge. With printing, author and publisher became highly specialized and centralized forms of action. With Xerography, author and publisher and reader tend to merge once more. Whereas the printed book had been the first mass-produced product, creating uniform prices and markets, Xerography tends to restore the custom-made book. Writing and publishing tend to become services of a corporate and inclusive kind. The printed word created the Public. The Public consists of separate individuals, each with his own point of view. Electric circuitry does not create a Public. It creates the Mass. The Mass does not consist of separate individuals, but of individuals profoundly involved in one another. This involvement is a function not of numbers but of speed.

The daily newspaper is an interesting example of this fact. The items in the daily press are totally discontinuous and totally unconnected. The only unifying feature of the press is the date line. Through that date line the reader must go, as Alice went, "through the looking glass." If it is not today's date line, we cannot get in. Once he goes through the date line, he is involved in a world of items for which he, the reader, must write a story line. He makes the news, as the reader of a detective story makes the plot. In the same way the relatively open-ended movie at the Czech pavilion in Expo allowed for intense audience participation through the easy availability of the consensus.

Just as the printing press created the Public as a new environment, so does each new technology or extension of our physical powers tend to create new environments. In the age of information, it is information itself that becomes environmental. The satellites and antennae projected from our planet, for example, have transformed the planet from being an environment into being a probe. This is a transformation which the artists of the past century have been explaining to us in their endless experimental models. Modern art, whether in painting or poetry or music, began as a probe and not as a package. The Symbolists literally broke up the old packages and put them into our hands as probes. And whereas the package belongs to a consumer age, the probe belongs to an age of experimenters.

One of the peculiarities of art is to serve as an antienvironment, a probe that makes the environment visible. It is a form of symbolic, or parabolic, action. Parable comes from a word that means literally "to throw against," just as symbol comes from one meaning "to throw together." As we equip the planet with satellites and antennae, we tend to create new environments of which the planet is itself the content. It is peculiar to environments that they are complex processes which transform their content into archetypal forms. As the planet becomes the content of a new information environment, it also tends to become a work of art. Where railway and machine created a new environment for agrarian man, the old agrarian world became an art form. Nature became a work of art. The Romantic movement was born. When the electric circuit enveloped the mechanical environment, the machine itself became a work of art. Abstract art was born.

As information becomes our environment, it becomes mandatory to program the environment itself as a work of art. The parallel to this appears in Jacques Ellul's *Propaganda*, where he sees propaganda not as an ideology or content of any medium, but as the operation of all the media at once. The mother tongue is propaganda because it exercises an effect on all the senses at once. It shapes our entire outlook and all our ways of feeling. Like any other environment, its operation is imperceptible. When an environment is new, we perceive the old one for the first time. What we see on the Late Show is not TV, but old movies. When the Emperor appeared in his new clothes, his courtiers did not see his nudity, they saw his old clothes. Only the small child and the artist have the immediacy of approach that permits perception of the environmental. The artist provides us with antienvironments that enable us to see the environment. Such antienvironmental means of perception must constantly be renewed in order to be efficacious. That basic aspect of the human condition by which we are rendered incapable of perceiving the environment is one to which psychologists have not even referred. In an age of accelerated change, the need to perceive the environment becomes urgent. Acceleration also makes such perception of the environment more possible. Was it not Bertrand Russell who said that if the bath water got only half a degree warmer every hour, we would never know when to scream? New environments reset our sensory thresholds. These, in turn, alter our outlook and expectations.

The need of our time is for a means of measuring sensory thresholds and a means of discovering exactly what changes occur in these thresholds as a result of the advent of any particular technology. With such knowledge in hand, it would be possible to program a reasonable and orderly future for any human community. Such knowledge would be the equivalent of a thermostatic control for room temperatures. It would seem only reasonable to extend such controls to all the sensory thresholds of our being. We have no reason to be grateful to those who haphazardly juggle the thresholds in the name of innovation.

Redesign of the so-called "light shows" so that they cease to be merely bombardment and become probes into the environment would be most beneficial in an educational sense.

The Two Cultures by C. P. Snow is a handy instance of our contemporary dilemma between visual and nonvisual methods of codifying and processing reality (C. P. Snow seems to be blowing both horns of the dilemma). The dilemma is the same as that which confronted Alice in *Through the Looking Glass*. Before she went through the looking glass, she was in a visual world of continuity and connected space where the appearance of things matched the reality. When she went through the looking glass, she found herself in a nonvisual world where nothing matched and everything seemed to have been made on a unique pattern. (As a matter of fact, because of electric technology we do have two cultures. They are the culture of our children and that of ourselves; we don't dialogue.) The work of Robert Ardrey in *The Territorial Imperative* is a kind of report from Alice after she had gone through the looking glass. Territoriality is the power of things to impose their own assumptions of time and space by means of our sensory involvement in them. Again, it is a world of making rather than of matching. Modern physics in general carries us into an unvisualizable territory. The speeds as well as the submicroscopic character of its particles are beyond visual representation. John R. Platt in *The Step to Man* explains how it would be possible to incorporate the twenty million books in the world today into an electronic library no larger than the head of a pin.

The present concern with "the death of God" is very much related to the decline in visual culture. The theologian Altizer tells us that the death of God happened roughly two hundred years ago "when the understanding of history grew to supplant an old God-concept. The Christ preserved by the Church has been so progressively dissolved and the God it preached so far decomposed that it is not possible to begin to see Jesus as the core of faith and as incarnate in humanity wherever there is life, and to see God as the opposite of humanity, life, progress — that is, as death." (James Heisig, *The Wake of God*, Divine Seminary, 1967.) In a visual sense God is no longer "up there" and "out there" any more than twenty million books in a pinhead could be said to be "in there." Visual orientation has simply become irrelevant. Some feel that Christianity's existence must always stand in the tension between being in the world and standing outside it. Kierkegaard was keenly aware of this, as were St. Paul and, later, Martin Luther. But the tension between inner and outer is a merely visual guideline, and in the age of the X-ray inner and outer are simultaneous events.

As the Western world goes Oriental on its inner trip with electric circuitry, it is not only the conventional image of God that is deposed; the whole nature of self-identity enters a state of crisis. God the clockmaker and engineer of the universe is no more an essential visual image to the West than is the identity card or the visual classification as an image of private personal status. The problem of personal identity first arose in the West with King Oedipus, who went through the crisis of detribalization, the loss of corporate involvement in the tribal group. To an ancient Greek the discovery of private identity was a terrifying and horrible thing that came about with the discovery of visual space and fragmentary classification. Twentieth-century man is traveling the reverse course, from an extreme individual fragmentary state back into a condition of corporate involvement with all mankind. Paradoxically, this new involvement is experienced as alienation and loss of private selfhood. It began with Ibsen and the Russian writers like Dostoyevsky, for whom there remained a much larger degree of awareness of the old tribal and corporate life than anything available to other European writers in the nineteenth century. The novelists and dramatists who began the quest to discover "Who am I?" have been succeeded by the existentialist philosophers, who meditate upon the meaninglessness of private lives in the contemporary world:

> One can say, in sort, that meaninglessness is spreading before our eyes. A strange inner mutation is thereby produced which takes on the aspect of a genuine uprooting. Entirely new questions are being asked, they insist upon being asked, where one hitherto seemed to be in an order which contained its own justification; it is the very order to which the barracks man belonged in the days when he was still a living being, when he was in the present.
>
> He for whom reflection has become a need, a primordial necessity, becomes aware of the precarious and contingent character of the conditions which constitute the very framework of his existence. The word "normal," which he once made use of in a way which now seems to him so imprudent, is emptied of its significance — let us say at least that it is suddenly, as it were, marked by a sign which makes it appear in a new and disturbing light.

> (Gabriel Marcel, *Problematic Man,* Herder and Herder, 1967)

Marcel is quite aware that there are no concepts or categories that can resolve this crisis:

> Let us now go back to the questions which the barracks man was asking himself: Who am I? What sense does my life have? *It is obvious that one does not resolve these questions by saying to this man (or to myself if I ask them of myself): You are a rational animal. An answer of this kind is beside the point. I said earlier that meaninglessness was spreading: that is to say that I, who have a profession, a country, means of existence, etc., cannot help but turn these questions somehow towards myself. Why is this so? Let us reason* a contrario, *and suppose that I shut myself up prudently, jealously, in that favored category where these questions do not arise. But if I have really managed, by an effort of imagination, to put myself in the place of the barracks man, it is through his eyes that I will be brought to consider the step by which I placed myself once and for all in the category of the privileged, who know who they are, and what they are living for. In other words,*

by the combined action of imagination and reflection, I have been able to bring about a change which bears not only upon the object, but upon the subject himself, the subject who questions.

However, he seems to favor the illusion that these dilemmas are ideological in origin rather than a consequence of a reprograming of the human environment in its sensory modes. The rear-view mirror is the favorite instrument of the philosophical historian:

In particular, one can hardly contest the fact that nationalism in its modern, post-revolutionary form is the product of an ideology that developed in the eighteenth century and combined, under conditions very difficult to state precisely, with a pre-romanticism whose origins seem to be found in Rousseau. Abandoned to its own inclination, this ideology led to a kind of cosmopolitanism of reason. The nationalism which issued from the French Revolution built itself to a large extent upon the ruins of the basic communities which had persisted until the end of the ancien régime, *but which the individualism of the philosophy of the Enlightenment inevitably helped to dissolve. One cannot deny, on the other hand, that there was a close connection between this fact and the devitalization of religion which occurred in the same period. But the industrial revolution, at least during the first part of the nineteenth century, was destined to play a part in considerably aggravating this tendency — to a large extent, moreover, under the influence of a liberalism which on the economic plane (as we know all too well) was destined to engender the most inhuman consequences, the individual being reduced to a more and more fragmentary condition, under the cover of an optimism which seems to us today to have been the height of hypocrisy.*

Marcel occasionally entertains the possibility of considering existence not as a classification or category, but as a total environment:

The profound justification of the philosophies of existence has perhaps consisted above all in the fact that they have brought out the impossibility of considering an existent being without taking into consideration his existence, his mode of existence. But regarding this very existence, the words rational animal *furnish us no genuine enlightenment.*

But in general he is aware of the futility of history. In the electric age, however, history no longer presents itself as a perspective of continuous visual space, but as an all-at-once and simultaneous presence of all facets of the past. This is what T. S. Eliot calls "tradition" in his celebrated essay "Tradition and the Individual Talent." Eliot's concept seemed quite revolutionary in 1917, but it was in fact a report of an immediate and present reality. Awareness of all-at-once history or tradition goes with a correlative awareness of the present as modifying the entire past. It is this vision that is characteristic of the artistic perception which is necessarily concerned with making and change rather than with any point of view or any static position.

The bourgeois nineteenth century referred only to those faces and features which were most strikingly visual in their tidiness and order. That world now persists in some degree in suburbia with the Educational Establishment as its sustaining bulwark. Antithetic to suburbia is the beatnik world, which in the nineteenth century was Bohemia. This is a world in which visual values play a very minor role. One hippie was heard to say, "I have no use for this Cromwell character. I'm a Cavalier!" Cromwell was a sort of *avant-garde* program of visual values. His "Ironsides" were an advance image of industrial production and weaponry. Their "Roundheads" are now the "square" citizens of the upper executive world. "Square," of course, simply means visual and uninvolved.

The transition between worlds may have occurred at the moment of the hula hoop. Mysteriously, people were fascinated by the hula hoops as an invitation to involvement and gyration, but nobody was ever seen rolling one in the approved style of the hoop and stick of yesteryear. When exhorted by their elders to roll these hoops down a walk, children simply ignored the request. An equivalent situation today is the disappearance of the word "escapism" in favor of the word "involvement." In the twenties all popular art, whether written or photographed for the movies, was branded as pure escapism. It has not occurred to anybody to call TV viewing escapist any more than it had occurred to anybody to roll the hula hoop as though it were a wheel. Today popular art is intensely involving, and it contains none of the visual values that characterized respectable art a century ago. Popular art has indeed swamped Bohemia and enlarged its territories many times. The aesthete, 1967 model, does not affect any nineteenth-century elegance, but in the interest of involvement presents a shaggy and multisensuous image. Upon meeting him we may well be inclined to say, "You're putting me on!" This is indeed the case. The image to which both beatnik and Beatle aspire is that of "putting on" the corporate audience. It is not a private need of expression that motivates them, but a corporate need of involvement in the total audience. This is humanism in reverse, instead of the corporate image of an integral society.

The revolt against the exclusively humanistic concept of art has been long in gestation, but it first comes into visible existence in the painting of Cézanne, and Cézanne's fundamental importance in the history of this revolution is due precisely to the fact that he was the first who dared assert that the purpose of art is not to express an ideal, whether religious or moral or humanistic, but simply to be humble before nature, and to render the forms which close observation could disentangle from vague visual impressions. The consequences of this peculiar kind of honesty were hardly such as Cézanne himself would have expected. First came cubism, and then a gradual purification of form which reached its logical conclusion in the abstract or nonfigurative art of Piet Mondrian or Ben Nicholson. This formalist type of art is now widespread among artists in every medium, and whether you like it or not, like technology it has come to stay.

(Herbert Read, *The Redemption of the Robot*, Trident Press, 1966)

A somewhat different approach to the problem of the transforming action of new environments upon older ones can be taken by the study of cliché and archetype. The world of the cliché is itself environmental since nothing can become a cliché until it has pervaded some world or other. It is at the moment of pervasiveness that the cliché becomes invisible. In their study of *The Popular Arts* Stuart Hall and Paddy Whannel have provided many illustrations of the principle by which a world of cliché, by the art of enveloping an older cliché, seems to turn the older cliché into an archetype or art form. They point to the world of Mickey Spillane, in which the free-lance avenger saves the law by working outside it. Raymond Chandler is much more sophisticated:

As Chandler's work develops, his themes emerge with greater clarity. When he died he was still at work on The Poodle Springs Story. *This was to be only incidentally a thriller. Marlowe, married to a wealthy girl, is in danger of becoming her "poodle," confined to the empty round of California cocktail parties. "The contest between what she wants Marlowe to do and what he will insist on doing will make a good sub-plot. I don't know how it will turn out, but she'll never tame him. Perhaps the marriage won't last, or she might even learn to respect his integrity," Chandler wrote, ". . . a struggle of personalities and ideas of life": the thriller becoming the novel of manners.*

It is not only that a new medium creates a new environment, which acts upon the sensory life of its inhabitants. The same new environment acts upon the older literary and artistic forms as well:

As these various satirical modes are more fully employed we begin to understand Chandler's real achievement. Like the true satirist, his gift lies in a disenchanted view of life, and depends upon a highly artificial style. Like the mock-heroic writers and poets, who made play with "heroism," Chandler makes play with the notion of "toughness." He inverts the thriller conventions, draws attention to their artificiality. A hard, polished prose surface permits his wit to play freely. Where the lesser practitioners in the field break their necks to build up the arch-hero, the superman, at the centre of their work, Chandler sets out to portray the most practised of anti-heroes. Apart from Marlowe, who is keeper of both conscience and consciousness in the novel, and through whose elliptical eye every detail is

observed and placed, few of the other characters have true "depth." They are con-
sciously two-dimensional, like the characters in a Ben Jonson play or in a
Restoration comedy. Perhaps, like the latter, a Chandler novel is a decadent work
of art, and there are signs of this in the language (for one thing the similes tend to
be over-elaborate and ornate or bizarre). But his use of the witticism or the wise-
crack has the same pointed "surface" effect as the rhymed couplet or the epigram
in Restoration comedy. There are countless effects of a literary kind which lesser
novelists, practising in the more major literary genres, are able to achieve, but
which escaped Chandler. But there are many compensating pleasures which are
not to be found in their work. Few writers have used so compromised and over-
worked a popular literary form with such skill, craftsmanship and tact.

The hero of the modern thriller puts on the audience, as it were, in a typical
gesture of total involvement, whereas the hero of the older adventure story was
an aristocratic individual. The new hero is a corporate rather than a private individual figure:

As Orwell showed in his comparison between Raffles *and* Miss Blandish, *the*
modern thriller-hero can no longer afford to stand aside from the action in his
story with that aristocratic detachment which was possible in his immediate pre-
decessors. Unlike Sherlock Holmes or Lord Peter Wimsey or that meticulous deus
ex machina *Hercule Poirot, the thriller-hero must finally enter the action as the*
main protagonist. The omniscience of the earlier detective-heroes provided some
distance between them and the mere mortals caught up in the drama and confu-
sion of the crime. But now this hero, of all the figures in the novel, must be the
most *exposed to the play of passion and violence, the one most intimately caught*
up with the actual experience of punishment. And if we ask why this change has
come about we are forced to give a complex set of reasons, all of which suggest
how deeply rooted the literature is in the social imagination. Perhaps it is because
we can no longer accept the figure who stands outside the action and yet knows
all the answers: we demand greater verisimilitude today. Perhaps it is because
these impersonal figures seem now too superhumanly remote: since the revolution
in our thinking effected by Freud and psychoanalysis, we take a different view of
crime, punishment and violence which the thriller reflects. We cannot believe in
the hero who is himself wholly free from the inner compulsions of violence and
lawlessness — we demand that he should stand closer to the villain, exposed to
the very evils he is dedicated to remove: "there, but for the grace of God . . ."
Certainly, the philosopher would argue that the thriller also shows a collapse in
the belief in an abstract and incorruptible justice.

What Hall and Whannel are saying is that the new hero is constituted differently
by virtue of being representative of the entire reading public.

The Mike Hammer and James Bond stories are, of course, fantasies — but fantasies which communicate a graphic and heightened realism. Characters may be overdrawn, situations stereo-typed, resolutions predictable. But the fictional life of these stories is convincing at the very level at which the modern reader, especially the young reader, is likely to find himself most under pressure: at the level of the sensations. In a quite precise sense, the thriller novel is a novel of the sensations. Its power lies in its experiential quality, in the absence of relieving factors and the starkness of the action, and in the image of human behaviour which it offers.

In exactly the same way the modern painting does not allow for the single point of view or the dispassionate survey. The modern painter offers an opportunity for dialogue within the parameters inherent in an art form which is moving away from the rational-visual and into the total world of man's sensory involvement.

18

Pro-log to Exploration

There is, it seems to us,
At best, only a limited value
In the knowledge derived from experience.
The knowledge imposes a pattern, and falsifies,
For the pattern is new in every moment
And every moment is a new and shocking
Valuation of all we have been. We are only undeceived
Of that which, deceiving, could no longer harm. . . .

Old men ought to be explorers . . .

(T. S. Eliot, *Four Quartets*)

Probing and ECO-sounding

The art and science of this century reveal and exploit the resonating bond in all things. All boundaries are areas of maximal abrasion and change. The interval or gap constitutes the resonant or musical bond in the material universe. This is where the action is. To naïve classifiers a gap is merely empty. They will look for connections instead of bonds. They will seek the authors' points of view instead of their probing of processes. Such readers will expect value judgments instead of understanding. With medieval dread they abhor vacuums. But by directing perception on the interfaces of the processes in ECO-land, all gaps become prime sources of discovery. Today's ecological awareness is echo recognition in boundless acoustic space (Greek *echo*: returned sound, personified in mythology as a mountain nymph).

Nothing has its meaning alone. Every *figure* must have its *ground* or environment. A single word, divorced from its linguistic *ground*, would be useless. A note in isolation is not music. Consciousness is corporate action involving *all* the senses (Latin *sensus communis* or "common sense" is the translation of all the senses into each other).

The "meaning of meaning" is relationship. When young activists harp on "relevance," they are asking for interface or the abrasion of dialogue; they are ECO-sounding to discover *where it's at*.

Truth is not matching. It is neither a label nor a "mental reflection." It is something we make in the encounter with a world that is making us. We "make sense," not in cognition but in recognition or re-*play*: Swimming as a cause of drowning is dubious, but only poor fish need boats.

This book tells of hang-ups and explorations. The dropouts today are those determined to keep *in touch* with a fast-changing scene. Touch, as the Japanese know best of all, is created by space between and around figures and situations. The natural interval between the wheel and axle is where action and "play" are one. The aware executive is the one who "steps down" when the action begins to "seize up." He maintains his autonomy and his flexibility. This strategy may well be the key to understanding the "generating gap" of our entire epoch.

Looking to the role rather than to the individual, we can see that specialized jobs of managers are universal casualties of the age of electric-information speed.

"DIE HARD" (General Inglis)

(Diehards: Appellation of the Fifty-seventh Regiment of Foot in the British Army)

Dying hard is the worst way of keeping in touch. The new way is dropping out:
"He who fights and runs away will live to fight another day."

Until now management studies have involuntarily supported the "diehards" and have been concerned with improvement of performance in servicing the physical needs of essentially nineteenth-century producers and consumers. At electric speeds the consumer becomes producer as the public becomes participant role player. At the same time, the old "hardware" is *etherealized* by means of "design" or "software."

Meanwhile, within the very same structure in which the public has become participant, the old management cast finds itself merely holding a fort that is no longer on the frontier of action. They automatically become "diehard" defenders of an old "movie set," as it were, expertly assuming a heroic stance and grimace: "Theirs not to reason why." Meantime, "the reason why" has become both plain and accessible to the new actors. The new cast is inclined to switch roles, as costumes, in order to keep in touch with the new action. The old cast of "diehards," on the other hand, is holding a "phony fort," much as the administrative "establishment" now finds itself in the role of "office boy" and "caretaker" of an abandoned operation.

What's Your Bag?

In passing, it might be noted that Women Liberationists seek to direct their energies toward capture of this abandoned fort of male prerogatives. They thus become the "diehards" of the moment. They might be succeeded by Children Liberationists at any time as heads of fate and state.

> *Beneath the bludgeonings of Chance,*
> *My head is bloody but unbowed.*
> *I am the master of my Fate.*
> *I am the captain of my soul.*
>   (W. E. Henley, "Invictus")

The "diehard" as anesthetized man becomes the *touchstone*, the means of anticipating change. *In every situation metamorphosis depends on the frozen arrest of an action.* The "diehard," paradoxically, can be read as an epitaph on his own tombstone.*

The problem of the "diehard" is that he is unable to attain the role of continuing the complex process of transmitting tradition. He freezes on the controls.

VERTEX V. VORTEX

Fallacies of the Paraphernalia of Power

If the "diehard" fails to understand the *processes of power*, the "revolutionary," in seizing the *positions of power*, mistakes "the state apparatus" for the actual controls of power. The *effect* is the setting up of a "police state" regardless of ideology or intent. Power is always a relationship, the putting on of the vortex of the living community by becoming an acceptable service environment. The components that go into this *mask of power* must, therefore, vary according to the character of the communities. A wearable or bearable "mask of power" must comprise all the principal features and postures inherent in the life of the community. Today, on the other hand, it is a natural mistake of revolutionaries to take over the new service environments of press, radio, and TV. These cannot possibly wear the recognizable visage of deep currents of experience or feeling.

Numerous shortcuts to power now loom as we learn to do more with less. Actually, this is the time when more and more awareness is demanded of everybody. When everyone is more and more involved in the information environment and in the creative process of discovery and innovation, the old divisions of work, play, and idleness disappear. The creative worker is never more powerful or more at leisure, never more the dropout from the specialist job, than when using all his faculties. We are entering a time of dialogue and heightened human awareness

---

*For more on this theme of transformation and innovation, see "Narcissus and Narcosis" in *Understanding Media* by Marshall McLuhan.

that plagues many as the specter of "pollution." The etymology of this word (from Latin *pro-luere*: wash forth) reveals a hidden process that is entirely applicable to the present situation: pushed to extreme, dilution becomes pollution. It is like the rich Texan: whenever he cashed a check, the bank "bounced." *Every process pushed far enough tends to reverse or flip suddenly.* This is the *chiasmus pattern*, perhaps first noted by ancient Chinese sages in *I Ching: The Book of Changes.**

EVITABLE FATE

Since the satellite surround, beginning with Sputnik in 1957, there has come the sudden awareness that nature itself has dropped out. Old experience is no longer relevant, and man must now assume responsibility for the total programming of his planetary environment through new knowledge. "Experience," said Erasmus, "is the schoolmaster of fools." That is, the rates charged by this ruthless pedagogue are outrageous, and few have ever survived his instruction. As the criminal said on his way to execution: "This will teach me a lesson!" Today, effects and causes merge because they almost coincide in time and space in the new information environment. *Change itself has become the main staple.*

The literate Greeks abstracted visual order out of preliterate oral chaos and called their artifact "Nature" (*phusis*). This "natural" order consciously relegated the ancient gods and magic to the irrational "unconscious" and "chaotic." Magic played existence by ear. In today's electric world, man becomes aware that this artificial "Nature" of the Greeks is an extension of himself, just as he is an extension of nature — *all* that exists.

In this book there is no intent to endorse or condemn what has happened. Our concern is to explore and to reveal the process patterns of current happenings. Since it is no longer safe to wait for the harsh judgment of results, we must discover how to *anticipate effects with their causes* in order to avoid the "inevitable" by "programming Fate."

* * *

The intent of our book is to discuss and illustrate the sudden change from the industrial world of assembly-line "hardware" and visual space into the electric world of orchestrated programming. Twenty-five hundred years of rational culture are in the process of dissolution. Age-old habits of conceptualization will not serve to train observation on the *effects* of the new man-made forms of energy. Since Plato, philosophers and scientists have attributed constant forms and patterns of action only to the world of "Nature." Both Plato and Aristotle,

---

*The laws and history of chiastic patterns of action are traced through the Old Testament and classical Greek literature by Nils W. Lund in *Chiasmus in the New Testament*.

and their followers, as well as all the other schools of philosophy, have refused to recognize any patterns of energy arising from man-made technologies. Having invented "Nature" as a world of rigorous order and repetition, they studied and observed only "natural" forms as having power to shape and influence psyche and society. The world of man's artifacts was considered neutral until the electric age. As the electric environment increasingly engulfed the old Greek "Nature," it became apparent that "Nature" was a *figure* abstracted from a *ground* of existence that was far from "natural." Greek "Nature," which sufficed until Einstein, excluded most of the chaotic resonance of the great Sound-Light Show of existence itself. Most of the pre-Socratic magic and ESP and all the Oriental and "Primitive" Natures were pushed into the "subconscious." Civilized man exists by dumping most of his experience into *that* convenient bin. Electric man has discovered that it is his major resource center.

Perceiving Process Patterns by Inventories of Their Effects

While dealing with the old Greek and Newtonian Nature, men found concepts and points of view useful for the framing of theories of causes that could be tested by measurement. At electric speeds, points of view disappear automatically and concepts have to yield to percepts, for concepts arise from endlessly repeated percepts — ossifications of percepts, as it were, which frequently obscure discovery. Percepts are not hypotheses that can be tested quantitatively, but percepts and observations do yield patterns which can be regarded as "causes" although, in fact, they are *processes*. Paradoxically, electronic man has no choice but to understand processes, if he is to be free. To free himself from servitude to his own artifacts has become the main program of the new ecological age that began with Sputnik. For twenty-five hundred years Western science and philosophy have ignored everything that we now consider to be ecological and mandatory.

The new information environment tends to supplant Nature, whereas the old mythic wisdom tried to explain nature. Thus modern man has to *live* mythically, in contrast to his ancient forebears, who sought to *think* mythically. Myth is the record of a simultaneous perception of effects with causes in a complementary process. It is possible to see a history of world art today in thirty seconds. A newspaper under a single date line gives you "Your World Today." These are mythic forms by virtue of speed and compression. When we hear that King Cadmus sowed the dragon's teeth and they sprang up armed men, we are given an instantaneous history of the effects of the phonetic alphabet on man and society. Myth does not limp but leaps.

In this book we turn to the study of new patterns of energy arising from man's physical and psychic artifacts and social organizations. The only method of perceiving process and pattern is by *inventory of effects* obtained by the comparison and contrast of developing situations.

Beyond Exposition for Exploration

Civilized, rationally educated people expect and prefer to have problems described and analyzed sequentially. They try to *follow* your argument to a conclusion. They expect the conclusion to be your *point of view*, illustrative of your *values*. In contrast to the method of exposition is the method of exploration. This begins by the admission of ignorance and difficulties. Such statement will tend to be a tentative groping. The blind man's cane picks up the *relation* of things in his environment by the quality of resonance. His tapping tells him what objects are adjacent to his stick. If his stick were *connected* to any of these objects, he would be helpless so far as orientation was concerned. This is always the plight of the logical method. It is useless for exploration. Its very strength makes it irrelevant. "Proof" of sanity is available only to those discharged from mental institutions.

"Seeing Them Off the Premises"

It is difficult to make a mistake in logic, once the premises are granted. Psychologists report that madmen are rigorously logical, but their premises are irrelevant. The method of exploration seeks to discover adequate premises. This book does not question the structures existing in our world as much as the hidden premises that are supposed to support them. When the *ground* changes, the *figures* may disappear. The *expository method* of system presentation serves very well to package preconceptions. The *exploratory method* encounters surprise and discovery at every turn. Only dead processes can be packaged.

> BRIDGES ARE INTERVALS OF RESONANCE AS MUCH
> AS MEANS OF CONNECTION. LIKE ANY RESONATING INTERVAL,
> THEY TRANSFORM BOTH AREAS THEY TOUCH.

The popular game of "bridge" originated in a major social breakdown. When suburbia was new, community was buried. "Bridge," like booze, served as a ghostly paradigm of community. Bridges mark breakdowns in human communication. Every new slang phrase marks wit's end. It is a frantically devised bridge over an unexpected break in the order of human perception. In "hardware" terms, it is obvious that where roads end, bridges begin. Confronting the wide diversity of breaks in the organization structures of our time, this book throws bridges across every kind of gap in our social fabric.

Consider human artifacts as bridges between areas of experience. Bridges are metaphors (from Greek *metaferein*: "to carry across"). *Bridges as extensions of man are resonating vortices of power.*

362

THE GREATEST BRIDGE KNOWN TO MAN IS SPEECH AND LANGUAGE. AS CLICHÉS, WORDS ABRIDGE TIME AND SPACE BY RECORDING AND STORING THE MULTITUDINOUS MATTERS OF PRIVATE AND CORPORATE IMPRESSION.

The language of a people is not only the resonant bridge that binds them in space and time; it is also the medium that shapes and processes their sensory and mental lives. The poet is concerned with releasing and controlling the corporate linguistic and traditional experience of the race by ever-new resonance and rhythms. He bridges the latest and most ancient awareness by the interface that T. S. Eliot speaks of in *The Use of Poetry and the Use of Criticism.*

THE AUDITORY IMAGINATION

What I call the "auditory imagination" is the feeling for syllable and rhythm, penetrating far below the conscious levels of thought and feeling, invigorating every word: sinking to the most primitive and forgotten, returning to the origin and bringing something back, seeking the beginning and the end. It works through meanings, certainly, or not without meanings in the ordinary sense, and fuses the old and obliterated, and the trite, the current, and the new and the surprising, the most ancient and the most civilized mentality.

Auditory imagination is the mind's ear — the complement of visual imagination. Less familiar as "bridge" is the "tragic flaw" (hamartia), of which Aristotle speaks in the *Poetics.* Without this interval of ignorance or awareness in his character, the tragic hero cannot bridge one state to another. The flaw is an area of interface and mutation, without which he cannot get better, but can only be hung up.

When Lewis Carroll's Alice went through the looking glass, she bridged the inner and outer worlds of fancy and imagination just at the time when the French biologist Claude Bernard bridged the inner and outer fields of medical science by his exploration of *le milieu intérieur*, creating internal medicine. Alice went through the vanishing point into the "total field" that bridges the worlds of visual and acoustic, civilized and primal space.

SYMBOLISM IS PRE-EMINENTLY THE WORLD OF THE INTERVAL, OR RESONANT EFFECTS MINUS CAUSES (Greek *sym-ballein*: "to put together without connection"). Edgar Allan Poe's discovery of the transforming power of the interval was a retrieval of the Ovidian technique of metamorphosis by the use of double plots or actions. W. B. Yeats had discussed it as the technique for creating "the emotion of multitude." This "magical" parallelism was the mode beloved by Dante and Shakespeare. It is the pattern used by James Joyce in *Ulysses* to bridge the ancient and modern worlds by a continuous parallel of interface between myth and realism, order and anarchy. In the detective story Poe discovered the missing clue as the bridge for all scientific research: the Cyclopean and encyclopedic scanning of the total field by the omission of the private point of view. The bridge between the corporate scientific probe and the personal viewpoint was made by the deliberate organization of ignorance, by the suppression of data. The detective sets out to re-create an action that is perceived as flawed or breached. IT IS THE MISSING LINK THAT INSPIRES THE PARTICIPATION OF THE READER, AS IT IS THE ANARCHY OF DISEASE AND DISORDER THAT INSPIRES THE SCIENTIFIC QUEST.

Since Heisenberg and Linus Pauling, the only remaining material bond is resonance. The continuum of visual space of the Euclidian kind is not to be found in the material universe. There are no connections among "particles of being" such as appear in mechanical models. Instead, there is a wide range of resonating intensities that constitute an equally wide variety of "auditory" spaces. Ancient philosophers have often imagined God as a Being whose center was everywhere with boundaries nowhere. Such also is the nature of puns and of acoustic space itself.

To define is to kill,
To suggest is to create.
     (Stéphane Mallarmé)

Walter Pater recognized that "the arts aspire to the condition of music," just as Poe invented the symbolist interval or gap that became the bridge between the structures of art and science in the twentieth century. The Japanese view the artist as one who makes bridges between old and new experience. So, in a changing world, new art is always needed to tune our perceptions to "where it's at." The artist of the preliterate society is a bridge between the visible and the invisible worlds. He is a "pontiff." His work may be in dance, music, or varied materials. His art is to create designs, masks, or vortices of power and energy, which "put on" the public.

As the detective reconstructs events, so the artist by retracing the processes of cognition (mimesis) bridges the world of sense and the world of awareness. James Joyce presents this cognitive bridge in monumental and dramatic form in *Finnegans Wake*: the entire tribal cycle of society now begins again, but awake. ENVIRONMENTAL AWARENESS CREATES A BRIDGE BETWEEN THE OLD ACCIDENTAL AND THE NEWLY PROGRAMMED EVENTS OF HUMAN EXISTENCE FOR ENRICHMENT THROUGH DIVERSITY.

Hypnotized by their rear-view mirrors, philosophers and scientists alike tried to focus the *figure* of man in the old *ground* of nineteenth-century industrial mechanism and congestion. They failed to bridge from the old *figure* to the new. It is man who has become both *figure* and *ground* via the electrotechnical extension of his awareness. *With the extension of his nervous system as a total information environment, man bridges art and nature.*

TODAY "NATURE" IS THE MESS-AGE
BUT MAN IS STILL THE CONTENT

19

Laws of Media

[From Chapter 2]
CULTURE AND COMMUNICATION:
The Two Hemispheres

To the Inuit, truth is given, not by "seeing is believing," but through oral tradition, mysticism, intuition, all cognition — in other words, not simply by observation and measurement of physical phenomena. To the Inuit, the ocularly visible apparition is not nearly so common as the purely auditory one; "hearer" would be a better name than "seer" for their holy men.

Robert Trotter, writing on "The Other Hemisphere" in *Science News*,[1] reports an investigation of brain-hemisphere dominance and patterns of behaviour "among the Inuit or Eskimo people of Baffin Island in northeastern Canada." The project discovered, among the Inuit people, a language that reflected "a high degree of spatial, right-hemispheric orientation. Linguistic studies rate it as being the most synthetic of languages. American English is at the other end of the same scale, and is rated as the most analytic (left-hemisphere)." Inuit sculptures, lithographs, and tapestries are "without apparent linear or three-dimension analytic orientation." That is, they have never developed any measure of visual bias such as is normal to Western culture.

Left Hemisphere (Right side of body)	Right Hemisphere (Left side of body)
Speech/Verbal	Spatial/Musical
Logical, Mathematical	Holistic
Linear, Detailed	Artistic, Symbolic
Sequential	Simultaneous
Controlled	Emotional
Intellectual	Intuitive, Creative
Dominant	Minor (Quiet)
Worldly	Spiritual
Active	Receptive
Analytic	Synthetic, Gestalt
Reading, Writing, Naming	Facial Recognition
Sequential Ordering	Simultaneous Comprehension
Perception of Significant Order	Perception of Abstract Patterns
Complex Motor Sequences	Recognition of Complex Figures

Reproduced courtesy of R.H. Trotter

---

[1] R. H. Trotter, "The Other Hemisphere," 218. The chart above is taken from this article, and is reproduced courtesy of R. H. Trotter.

To the Inuit, nature's forms "lie hidden" until man reveals them one by one. Their language makes little distinction between "nouns" and "verbs"; rather, all words are forms of the verb "to be," which is itself lacking in Eskimo. "Eskimo isn't a nominal language; it doesn't name things which already exist, but brings things/action (nouns/verbs) into being as it goes along . . . when the mother is in labor, an old woman stands around and says as many different eligible names as she can think of. The child comes out of the womb when its name is called" (Edmund Carpenter, *Eskimo Realities*, 39).

In the beginning was the word. The primitive is a phenomenologist who equates reading aloud the Book of Nature with the making process. As a man speaks, his language is in a state of birth, as is also the thing about which he is talking. Such parentage confers responsibilities. In this sense, every man is artist. Primitives have no need, as we have, of a special and unique group (artists) that uses special processes and perceptions. Carvings are often discarded after being made, just as "words fade away." "When Orpingalic says, 'And we will fear to use words,' he doesn't mean he's afraid of the words themselves. He means he's in awe of their power to bring the universe into existence. Words must 'shoot up of themselves.' They must arise naturally out of experience. To impose words of his own would be sacrilegious. 'Many are the words that rush over me, like the wings of birds out of darkness'" (*Eskimo Realities*, 52).

Prior to writing and to print, words and utterances were still endowed with the magical power to form and transform existence. The difference between the two states is clearly reflected in the hemispheric differences in the brain. Trotter's chart of the characteristics of the left and right hemispheres presents a pattern of basic contrasts.[2] Because the dominant feature of the left hemisphere is linearity and sequentiality, there are good reasons for calling it the "visual" (quantitative) side of the brain; and because the dominant features of the right hemisphere are

---

[2]The chart reflects the scientific understanding of the cortical hemispheres, gained mainly in the last twenty years. The cortex of the ordinary human brain has two hemispheres, joined by a massive bundle of fibres called the *corpus callosum*, which seems to be the agency of dialogue between the hemispheres. It was only in the 1950s that these forebrain commissures in man were first deliberately severed, allowing the hemispheres to be studied independently. "The first important finding was that the interhemispheric exchange of information was totally disrupted following commissurotomy. The effect was such that visual, tactual, proprioceptive, auditory, and olfactory information presented to one hemisphere could be processed and dealt with in that half-brain, but each of these activities went on outside the realm of awareness of the other half-cerebrum. This observation confirmed the animal work done earlier by Myers and Sperry, except that in a sense the results were more dramatic. Since it is the left hemisphere that normally possesses the natural language and speech mechanisms, all processes ongoing in the left hemisphere could easily be verbally described by the patients; information presented to the right hemisphere went undescribed" (Michael S. Gazzaniga, "Review of the Split Brain," 91). In subsequent tests of patients that had undergone commissurotomy, the complementarity of the two hemispheres became increasingly evident. Most surprising was the range of activities proper to the right hemisphere, which in the nineteenth century carried the label of "minor"

the simultaneous, holistic, and synthetic, there are good reasons for indicating it as the "acoustic" (qualitative) side of the brain.

We are not Argus-eyed, but Argus-eared.

Visual space is the result of left-hemisphere dominance in a culture, and its use is restricted to those cultures that have immersed themselves in the phonetic alphabet and thereby suppressed the activity of the right hemisphere.

Since, as Jeremy Campbell points out in *Grammatical Man*,[3] alphabetic consonants and much of syntax are products of the left hemisphere, visual space is an extrapolation into the environment of the left brain in high definition — abstract, structured as a figure minus a ground. Acoustic space has the basic character of a dynamic sphere whose focus or centre is simultaneously everywhere and whose margin or periphery is nowhere. As it is multisensory, involving both the interval of tactility and kinetic equilibrium-pressure, it is one of the many figure/ground right-hemisphere forms of space. Ordinarily, the two hemispheres are in constant dialogue through the *corpus callosum*, and each hemisphere uses the other as its ground except when one (i.e., the left) is habitually dominant. Each hemisphere, as it were, provides a particular type of information processing less available to the other. As Dr. J. E. Bogen notes, "the type of cognition proper to the right hemisphere has been called *appositional*, a usage parallel to the common use by neurologists of *propositional* to encompass the left hemisphere's dominance for speaking, writing, calculation and related tasks."[4]

The individual features of the face, as isolated figures, are easily noted by the left hemisphere, which cannot handle them together as a pattern. It is the "acoustic" power of simultaneous comprehension that gives the right hemisphere the ability to recognize faces. By the same token, the sense of touch creates the space of the "resonant interval": interval defines the relation of figure to ground and provides the structure, the con-figuration of ground. Synesthetic interplay

---

or "quiet." So complete was our culture's visual bias at that time, it was seriously proposed that the right hemisphere made no contribution to human intellection or activity.

[3]Page 224: "It is well known that the right brain is poor at comprehending consonants and does not do well at syntax, which is the left brain's special province. How far this is a sheer absence of function, and how far it is an effect of the left brain inhibiting the right across the *corpus callosum* is still not clear." If the right brain cannot even handle consonants they must have had their genesis in the left brain: this adds point to the mystery of what it was that urged the Greeks to invent them in the first place.

[4]Joseph E. Bogen. "Some Educational Implications of Hemispheric Specialization," 138. Bogen observes further: "What distinguished hemispheric speculation is not so much certain kinds of material (e.g. words for the left, faces for the right) but the way in which the material is processed. In other words, hemispheric differences are more usefully considered in terms of *process specificity* rather than material specificity."

among all the senses would seem to relate mainly to the right hemisphere. That Trotter, in "The Other Hemisphere," selects a Third World or non-literate society for observation and illustration points to the fact that societies that have not developed the use of the phonetic alphabet tend to adopt the same Third World posture. While the Third World is mainly oral/aural, even when it cultivates some non-phonetic form of writing such as Sanskrit, the First World (Western) countries tend to be visual (left hemisphere), even when most of their population is declining into a semi-literate state via the information environment of electronic technologies.

Technologies themselves, regardless of content, produce a hemispheric bias in the users.

Herbert Krugman performed brain-wave studies, comparing the response of subjects to print and television. One subject was reading a book as the TV came on. As soon as she looked up, her brain waves slowed significantly. In less than two minutes, she was in a predominantly alpha state — relaxed, passive, unfocused. Her brain-wave response to three different types of TV content was basically the same, even though she told Krugman she "liked" one, "disliked" another, and "was bored by" the third. As a result of a series of such experiments, Krugman argues that this predominantly alpha state is characteristic of how people respond to TV — any TV. He recently remarked, "the ability of respondents to show high right brain response to even familiar logos, their right brain response to stories even before the idea content has been added to them, the predominantly right brain response to TV, and perhaps even to what we call print advertising — all suggests that in contrast to teaching, the unique power of the electronic media is to *shape* the content of people's imagery, and in that particular way determine their behavior and their views."[5]

Krugman's investigations were, he admitted, initially undertaken to disprove that "the medium is the message." His quantitative results point to the massive and subliminal erosion of our culture through right-hemisphere indoctrination by TV in all its forms, including VCRs, video games, computer monitors, and word-processors. In a wider sense, all electric media, as a new ground, give salience only to the right hemisphere. There is no way to quantify the right hemisphere, which emphasizes inner and qualitative aspects of experience.

How paradoxical that the hardware channels of radio and telephonic communication contribute to an extraordinary software effect. Nathaniel Hawthorne was

---

[5]Herbert Krugman, from a paper delivered to the annual conference of the Advertising Research Foundation, October 1978. *Cf.* also, Barry Siegel, "Stay Tuned for How TV Scrambles Your Brain," in *The Miami Herald*, C10. Krugman's original report was presented as a paper to the annual conference (1970) of the American Association for Public Opinion Research.

particularly sensitive to the implications of electric information and not infrequently remarked on them, as in *The House of the Seven Gables*: "Is it a fact that . . . by means of electricity the world of matter has become a great nerve, vibrating thousands of miles in a breathless point of time? Rather, the round globe is a vast head, a brain, instinct with intelligence! Or, shall we say, it is itself a thought, and no longer the substance which we deemed it!" When people are on the telephone or on the air, they have no physical bodies but are translated into abstract images. Their old physical beings are entirely irrelevant to the new situations. The discarnate user of electric media bypasses all former spatial restrictions and is present in many places simultaneously as a disembodied intelligence. This puts him one step above angels, who can only be in one place at a time. Since, however, discarnate man has no relation to natural law (or to Western lineality), his impulse is towards anarchy and lawlessness. Minus his body, the user of telephone or radio or TV also is minus his private identity, an effect that is becoming increasingly evident.

In another experiment, an audience was equally divided, with each half seated facing a translucent-opaque screen placed in the middle of a room. A movie was shown, and then the audience was asked to write a brief response. One group saw light reflected from the screen in the usual manner; the other group saw light passing through the screen, as with television. In their remarks, the "light-on" group adopted an objective, detached tone, and was analytic as to narrative, continuity, cinematography, editing and workmanship, and so on. Whereas they reported "how the movie looked," by contrast, the "light-through" group was mainly concerned with "how the movie felt." Their responses were subjective and emotional: they discussed themselves, how they felt, and the mystical or archetypal significance of characters or actions. The differences between the light-on and the light-through situations (immediate ground) were sufficiently potent to cause one group to have a right-hemisphere experience and the other to have a left-hemisphere experience. With the low-intensity mosaic TV image, this effect is greatly amplified.

Cultural dominance by either the left or the right hemisphere is largely dependent upon environmental factors.

The lineality of the left hemisphere is supported by an alphabet-based service environment of roads and transportation, and by logical or rational activities in social and legal administration. Dominance of the right hemisphere, however, depends upon a cultural milieu or environment of a simultaneous resonating character. Such dominance is normal in oral societies, and today our universal environment of simultaneous electric information has entirely subverted the dominance of the left hemisphere. By tuning in on the new audible-tactile aware-ness made available by our electric ground, Fritjof Capra found that modern physics was, unwittingly, retrieving a world-view harmonious with ancient Eastern wisdom. His problems in reconciling the two were entirely those of the hemispheres:

> *I had gone through a long training in theoretical physics and had done several years of research. At the same time, I had become very interested in Eastern mysti-cism and had begun to see the parallels to modern physics. I was particularly attracted to the puzzling aspects of Zen, which reminded me of the puzzles in quantum theory. At first, however, relating the two was a purely intellectual exer-cise. To overcome the gap between rational, analytical thinking and the meditation experience of mystical truth, was, and still is, very difficult for me.*
>
> (The Tao of Physics, 9-10)

The alphabet created visual space, and with it a lineal and visual "outer world" environment of services and experiences (everything from architecture and highways to representational art), which contributed to the ascendancy or dominance of the left, or lineal, hemisphere. This observation is consistent with the findings of the Russian neurophysiologist A. K. Luria, who found that the area of the brain which controls linear sequencing, and, hence, mathematical and scientific thinking, is located in the pre-frontal region of the left hemisphere: "The mental process for writing a word entails still another specialization: putting the letters in the proper sequence to form the word. Lashley discovered many years ago that sequential analysis involved a zone of the brain different from that employed for spatial analysis. In the course of our extensive studies we have located the region responsible for sequential analysis in the anterior regions of the left hemisphere" ("The Functional Organization of the Brain," 71-2). Luria's results show that the expression "linear thinking" is not merely a figure of speech, but a mode of activity peculiar to the left hemisphere of the brain. His results support the observation that the use of the alphabet, with its emphasis on linear sequence, stimulates dominance of this area of the brain in cultural pat-terns.

Luria's observations provide an understanding of how the written alphabet, with its lineal structure, was able to create conditions conducive to the develop-ment of Western science, technology, and rationality. Many left-hemisphere stroke patients become aphasic, losing some or all of their ability to speak or to write, in some cases also losing the capacity for sustained (sequential) thought. They seem to become "astonied" (fifteenth-century English), or "stunned" — the experience is not unlike being "stoned" on drugs. In part, this may be the result of a loss of muscular motor control. But much of it is directly related to the inner-outer split between the hemispheres and to linearity as a feature of the left side of the brain. Speech and writing have to be *uttered* in a *sequence*. Just as all forms of sequential activity (as contrasted to configuration or pattern) are functions of the left hemisphere, so too all forms of utterances (and artefacts), whether technological or verbal or written, are functions of the left hemisphere. This extends to private identity — and to entrepreneurial aggression of all kinds. Conversely, all technologies that emphasize the outer or the abstract or sequentiality in organizing experience, contribute to left-hemisphere dominance in a culture. Harold Innis remarked on the Oriental (right-hemisphere) antipathy to sequence and abstraction and our sort of precision:

> Social time, for example, has been described as qualitatively differentiated according to the beliefs and customs common to a group and as not continuous but as subject to interruption of actual dates. It is influenced by language which constrains and fixes prevalent concepts and modes of thought. It has been argued by Marcel Granet that the Chinese are not equipped to note concepts or to present doctrines discursively. The Word does not fix a notion with a definite degree of abstraction or generality but evokes an indefinite complex of particular images. It is completely unsuited to formal precision. Neither time nor space is abstractly conceived: time proceeds by cycles and is round.
>
> (*The Bias of Communication*, 62)

Dr. Bogen noted, appositely, "what may well be the most important distinction between the left and right hemisphere modes is the extent to which a linear concept of time participates in the ordering of thought" (*The Human Brain*, 141).

The visual power of the phonetic alphabet to translate other languages into itself is part of its power to invade right-hemisphere (oral) cultures.

Tribal, right-hemisphere "closed" cultures are holistic and entire and resistant to penetration by other preliterate cultures. But the specialist qualities of the left-hemisphere phonetic alphabet have long provided the only means of invading and taking over oral societies. "Propaganda cannot succeed where people have no trace of Western culture." These words of Jacques Ellul in *Propaganda* draw attention to one of the crucial features of Western history. It is no accident that the Christian church, dedicated to propaganda and propagation, adopted Graeco-Roman phonetic literacy from the earliest days. The impact of alphabetic literacy is strong enough not only to break the tribal bond, but to create individualized (left-hemisphere) consciousness as well. Phonetic literacy — our alphabet — alone has this power.

The spread of Graeco-Roman literacy and civilization became inseparable from Christian missionary and educational activity. Paradoxically, people are not only unable to receive, but are unable to retain doctrinal teaching without a minimum of phonetic or Western culture. Here is the observation of Ellul on this matter:

In addition to a certain living standard, another condition must be met: if a man is to be successfully propagandized, he needs at least a minimum of culture. Propaganda cannot succeed where people have no trace of Western culture. We are not speaking here of intelligence; some primitive tribes are surely intelligent, but have an intelligence foreign to our concepts and customs. A base is needed — for example, education; a man who cannot read will escape propaganda, as will a man who is not interested in reading. People used to think that learning to read evidenced human progress; they still celebrate the decline of illiteracy as a great victory: they condemn countries with a large proportion of illiterates: they think that reading is a road to freedom. All this is debatable, for the important thing is not to be able to read, but to understand what one reads, to reflect on and judge what one reads. Outside of that, reading has no meaning (and even destroys certain automatic qualities of memory and observation). But to talk about critical faculties and discernment is to talk about something far above primary education and to consider a very small minority. The vast majority of people, perhaps 90 percent, know how to read, but they do not exercise their intelligence beyond this. They attribute authority and eminent value to the printed word, or, conversely, reject it altogether. As these people do not possess enough knowledge to reflect and discern, they believe — or disbelieve — in toto what they read. And as such people, moreover, will select the easiest, not the hardest, reading matter, they are precisely on the level at which the printed word can seize and convince them without opposition. They are perfectly adapted to propaganda.[6]

The dominance of the left hemisphere (analytic and quantitative) entails the submission or suppression of the right hemisphere; and so, for example, our intelligence tests exist only for measuring left-hemisphere achievement, and take no cognizance of the existence of the (qualitative) right hemisphere.

---

[6]Jacques Ellul, *Propaganda: The Formation of Men's Attitudes*, 108-9. Harold Innis comments on the moment of transition: "For a brief period the Greeks escaped from the oral tradition and the written tradition. The oral tradition was sufficiently strong to check complete submergence in the written. The oral tradition supported Greek skepticism and evaded monopolies of religious literature" (*The Bias of Communication*, 111).

[From Chapter 3]
LAWS OF MEDIA

Sir Karl Popper's (right-brain) statement that a scientific law is one so stated as to be capable of falsification made it both possible and necessary to formulate the laws of the media.

All of man's artefacts — whether language, or laws, or ideas and hypotheses, or tools, or clothing, or computers — are extensions of the physical human body or the mind. Man the tool-making animal has long been engaged in extending one or another of his sense organs in such a manner as to disturb all of his other senses and faculties. But having made these experiments, men have consistently omitted to follow them with observations:

J. Z. Young, in *Doubt and Certainty in Science*, notes:

> *The effect of stimulations, external or internal, is to break up the unison of action of some part or the whole of the brain. A speculative suggestion is that the disturbance in some way breaks the unity of the actual pattern that has been previously built up in the brain. The brain then selects those features from the input that tend to repair the model and to return the cells to their regular synchronous beating. I cannot pretend to be able to develop this idea of models in our brain in detail, but it has great possibilities in showing how we tend to fit ourselves to the world and to the world to ourselves. In some way the brain initiates sequences of actions that tend to return it to its rhythmic pattern, this return being the act of consummation, or completion. If the first action performed fails to do this, fails that is to stop the original disturbance, then other sequences may be tried. The brain runs through its rules one after another, matching the input with its various models until somehow unison is achieved. This may perhaps only be after strenuous, varied, and prolonged searching. During this random activity further connexions and action patterns are formed and they in turn will determine future sequences.* (pages. 67-8)

The inevitable drive for "closure," "completion," or equilibrium occurs with both the suppression and the extension of human sense or function. It was Edward T. Hall who in our time first drew attention to the fact that all human artefacts are extensions of man. In *The Silent Language*, he wrote:

> *Today man has developed extensions for practically everything he used to do with his body. The evolution of weapons begins with the teeth and the fist and ends with the atom bomb. Clothes and houses are extensions of man's biological temperature-control mechanisms. Furniture takes the place of squatting and sitting on the ground. Power tools, glasses, TV, telephones, and books which carry the voice across both time and space are examples of material extensions. Money is a way of extending and storing labor. Our transportation networks now do what we used to do with our*

feet and backs. In fact, all man-made material things can be treated as extensions of what man once did with his body or some specialized part of his body.[7]

Hans Hass, in *The Human Animal*, sees this power to create additional prosthetic organs as "an enormity from the evolutionary standpoint . . . an advance laden with unfathomable consequences" (page 101).

Our *laws of media* are observations on the operation and effects of human artefacts on man and society, since a human artefact "is not merely an implement for working upon something, but an extension of our body, effected by the artificial addition of organs; . . . to which, to a greater or lesser degree, we owe our civilization."[8] Hass considered the advantages of our bodily extensions to be five:

(a) *They have no need of constant nourishment, thus saving energy.*

(b) *They can be discarded or stored rather than carried (a further saving of energy).*

(c) *They are exchangeable, enabling man to specialize and to play multiple roles: when carrying a spear, he can be a hunter, or with a paddle he can move across the sea.*

(d) *All of these instruments can be shared communally.*

(e) *They can be made in the community by "specialists" (giving rise to handicrafts).*

(The Human Animal, 103-4)

One thing Hass overlooks is the absence of biological or psychological means of coping with the effects of our own technical ingenuity. The problem is clearly indicated by A. T. W. Simeons in *Man's Presumptuous Brain*:

But when, about half a million years ago, man began very slowly to embark upon the road to cultural advance, an entirely new situation arose. The use of implements and the control of fire introduced artifacts of which the cortex could avail itself for purposes of living. These artifacts had no relationship whatever to the organization of the body and could, therefore, not be integrated into the functioning of the brain stem.

---

[7] E. T. Hall, *The Silent Language*, 56-7. However, the notion is of a respectable age: Two generations ago, Emerson made the observation, "The human body is the magazine of inventions, the patent office where are the models from which every hint was taken. All the tools and engines on earth are only extensions of its limbs and senses. One definition of man is 'an intelligence served by organs'" ("Works and Days," 151).

[8] Hass, *The Human Animal*, 101. In the same vein, Karl Popper wrote, "the kind of extra-personal or exosomatic evolution that interests me here is this: instead of growing better memories and brains, we grow paper, pens, typewriters, dictaphones, the printing press and libraries. These add to our language . . . what may be described as new dimensions. The latest development . . . is the growth of computers" (*Objective Knowledge*, 238-9).

The brain-stem's great body-regulating centre, the diencephalon, continued to function just as if the artifacts were non-existent. But as the diencephalon is also the organ in which instincts are generated, the earliest humans found themselves faced with a very old problem in a new garb. Their instinctive behaviour ceased to be appropriate in the new situations which the cortex created by using artifacts. Just as in the pre-mammalian reptiles the new environment in the trees rendered many ancient reflexes pointless, the new artificial environment which man began to build for himself at the dawn of culture made many of his animal reflexes useless. (page 43)

To put it briefly, man cannot trust himself when using his own artefacts. For example, Konrad Lorenz argues (*On Aggression*) that if man had more weaponry and armour as an organic part of himself, if he had tusks and horns, he would be less likely to kill his fellow men. Heavily armed animals have strong inhibitions against hurting their own species. Men, however, have few built-in restraints against turning their artificial weapons (extensions) upon one another. Firearms and bombs, which permit deadly action at great distances, seem to relieve the user of responsibility. Anthony Storr in *Human Aggression* observes:

It is obviously true that most bomber pilots are no better and no worse than other men. The majority of them, given a can of petrol and told to pour it over a child of three and ignite it, would probably disobey the order. Yet, put a decent man in an aeroplane a few hundred feet above a village, and he will, without compunction, drop high explosives and napalm and inflict appalling pain and injury on men, women and children. The distance between him and the people he is bombing makes them into an impersonal target, no longer human beings like himself with whom he can identify. (page 112)

Lorenz speaks in a similar fashion:

Humanity would have indeed destroyed itself by its first inventions, were it not for the very wonderful fact that inventions and responsibility are both the achievements of the same specifically human faculty of asking questions.

The deep, emotional layers of our personality simply do not register the fact that the crooking of the forefinger to release a shot tears the entrails of another man. No sane man would even go rabbit-hunting for pleasure if the necessity of killing his prey with his natural weapons brought home to him the full emotional realization of what he is actually doing.

The same principle applies to an even greater degree to the use of modern remote-control weapons.   (*On Aggression*, page 242)

Quite apart from the use of weaponry at a distance, there is the effect of the changes in man himself that result from using his own devices to create environments of service.[9] Any new service environment, such as those created by the alphabet or railways or motor cars or telegraph or radio, deeply modifies the very nature and image of people who use it. As electric media proliferate, whole societies at a time became discarnate, detached from mere bodily or physical "reality" and relieved of any allegiance to or sense of responsibility to or for it.

Radical changes of identity, happening suddenly and in very brief intervals of time, have proved more deadly and destructive of human values than wars fought with hardware weapons.

In the electric age, the alteration of human identity by new service environments of information has left whole populations without personal or community values to a degree that far exceeds the effects of food- and fuel- and energy-shortages.

Sir Peter Medawar has written a fine essay entitled "What's Human about Man Is His Technology" in which he offers the straight hardware approach to considering microscopes and radio telescopes as sensory accessories, whereas cutlery, hammers, and automobiles "are not sensory but motor accessories." All such sensory and motor organs "receive their instructions from ourselves." Moreover, Medawar considers that although "we are integrated psychologically with the instruments that serve us," there is no question in his mind of our serving these instruments: to him they are neutral. He does not consider the total change of social surround created by environments of services brought into existence by these extensions of our bodily organs. Man and society remain essentially unchanged by these extensions which merely serve to enhance convenience or to lessen hardship. Such, at least, is Medawar's implication.

The main characteristic of man "is not so much the devising of tools as the communication from one human being to another of the know-how to make them." We cannot transmit our newly acquired "organs" by any process of biological heredity: "By no manner of means can the blacksmith transmit his

---

[9]Emerson put it similarly: "These tools have some questionable properties. They are reagents. Machinery is aggressive. The weaver becomes a web, the machinist a machine. All tools are in one sense edge-tools, and dangerous. A man builds a fine house; and now he has a master, and a task for life: he is to furnish, watch, show it, and keep it in repair, the rest of his days. A man has a reputation, and is no longer free, but must respect that. A man makes a picture or a book, and, if it succeeds, 'tis often the worse for him. I saw a brave man the other day, hitherto as free as the hawk or the fox of the wilderness, constructing his cabinet of drawers for shells, eggs, minerals and mounted birds. It was easy to see that he was amusing himself with making pretty links for his own limbs . . . The machine unmakes the man. Now that the machine is so perfect, the engineer is nobody" ("Works and Days," 157–8).

brawny arms to his children, but there is nothing to stop him from teaching his children his trade, so that they grow up to be as strong and skillful as himself." That is as far as Medawar is prepared to go. "The evolution of this learning process . . . represents a fundamentally new biological stratagem — more important than any that preceded it — and totally unlike any other transaction of the organism with its environment." The transformational effects of our artificial organs — they generate totally new conditions of environmental service and of life — these are the concerns of *Laws of Media*.

The artist is the person who invents the means to bridge between biological inheritance and the environments created by technological innovation.

Without the artist's intervention man merely *adapts* to his technologies and becomes their servo-mechanism. He worships the Idols of the Tribe, of the Cave, and of the Market. The canoeist or the motorist achieves his equilibrium by the cultivation of reflexes, becoming an extension of these situations. In *Men without Art*, Wyndham Lewis explained that the role of art is to liberate man from the robot status imposed by "adjusting" to technologies. Rimbaud had put the matter simply: the job of the artist is "le dérèglement de tous les sens," the upsetting of enslavements of equilibrium and homeostasis by awakening the faculties to full awareness. In "The Caliph's Design II," Lewis described art as perfecting the evolutionary process: "The creation of a work of art is an act of the same description as the evolution of wings on the sides of a fish, the feathering of its fins; or the invention of a weapon within the body of a hymenopter to enable it to meet the terrible needs of its life" (*Wyndham Lewis the Artist: From "Blast" to Burlington House*, 257). Lewis added: "The artist is older than the fish, having access to primal sources of insight and design."

Media, that is, the ground-configurations of effects, the service environments of technologies, are inaccessible to direct examination since their effects are mainly subliminal. Ferdinand de Saussure in his *Course in General Linguistics* makes the same point in saying that "the concrete entities of language are not directly accessible," and like media "everywhere and always there is the same complex equilibrium of terms that mutually condition each other" (page 110).

Our laws of media are intended to provide a ready means of identifying the properties of and actions exerted upon ourselves by our technologies and media and artefacts. They do not rest on any concept or theory, but are empirical, and form a practical means of perceiving the action and effects of ordinary human tools and services. They apply to all human artefacts, whether hardware of software, whether bulldozers or buttons, or poetic styles or philosophical systems. The four laws are framed as questions:

- What does the artefact enhance or intensify or make possible or accelerate? This can be asked concerning a wastebasket, a painting, a steamroller, or a zipper, as well as about a proposition in Euclid or a law of physics. It can be asked about any word or phrase in any language.
- If some aspect of a situation is enlarged or enhanced, simultaneously the old condition or unenhanced situation is displaced thereby. What is pushed aside or obsolesced by the new "organ"?
- What recurrence or retrieval of earlier actions and services is brought into play simultaneously by the new form? What older, previously obsolesced ground is brought back and inheres in the new form?
- When pushed to the limits of its potential (another complementary action), the new form will tend to reverse what had been its original characteristics. What is the reversal potential of the new form?

This tetrad of the effects of technologies and artefacts presents not a sequential process, but rather four simultaneous ones. All four aspects are inherent in each artefact from the start. The four aspects are complementary, and require careful observation of the artefact in relation to its ground, rather than consideration in the abstract. Usually, "media study" (and equally, promotion) covers only the first two aspects, enhancement and obsolescence, and these lightly.

In tetrad form, the artefact is seen to be not neutral or passive, but an active logos or utterance of the human mind or body that transforms the user and his ground.

Enhancement and obsolescence are obviously complementary actions. Any new technique or idea or tool, while enabling a new range of activities by the user, pushes aside the older ways of doing things. Money speeds transactions and gives rise to uniform pricing systems, obsolescing haggle and barter and much of the human relation to commodities. The motor car enhances private mobility, and pushes aside the old organization of the city in favour of the suburb. "No-fault divorce" enhances the corporate sharing of risk and responsibility and displaces private responsibility. "The pill" tends to banish insecurity and uncertainty, while enhancing the "programmable machine" approach to the body and numbing the user to its more human (fallible) dimensions, thus providing an amoral base for promiscuity. The photograph enhances pictorial realism and obsolesces portrait painting. The vacuum cleaner obsolesces the broom and the beater; the dryer pushes aside the clothes-line, and the washer the washboard and tub; the refrigerator replaces the icebox and the root cellar. Some forms are so evanescent they have their own built-in obsolescence. Nothing is as stale as yesterday's newspaper — until it can be retrieved as valuable documentary evidence or nostalgic treat. The computer speeds calculation and retrieval, obsolescing the "Bob Cratchit" bookkeepers. Romanticism in poetry gave impetus to individual hyperaesthesia and pushed aside the eighteenth-century rationalist sensibility (left-hemisphere). "In every fixed definition there is obsolescence or failed insight" (George Steiner, *After Babel*, 234). These are fairly easy aspects of the tetrad. The relation between obsolescence and retrieval is much more subtle. *From Cliché to Archetype* was written on this theme.

As outlined on the dust-jacket, the theme is "new" archetype is "ye olde cliché writ large." Obsolescence is not the end of anything; it's the beginning of aesthetics, the cradle of taste, of art, of eloquence and of slang. That is, the cultural midden-heap of cast-off clichés and obsolescent forms is the matrix of all innovation. Petrarch's *Ruins of Rome* was the fount of a new humanist culture. Gutenberg technology retrieved the entire ancient world, while obsolescing the scriptoria and scholasticism of the Middle Ages. The needs of poet, musician, and artist for ever-new means of probing and exploring experience send them back again and again to the rag-and-bone shop of abandoned cliché.

*The testimony of artists in this matter is impressive. The stages by which the literary archetype became substituted for the technical cliché as the means of creation is one of the subjects of this book [*From Cliché to Archetype*].*

As a case in point, Yeats begins "The Circus Animals' Desertion" by saying:

I sought a theme and sought for it in vain
I sought it daily for six weeks or so.
Maybe at last, being but a broken man,
I must be satisfied with my heart, although
Winter and summer till old age began
My circus animals were all on show,
Those stilted boys, that burnished chariot,
Lion and woman and the Lord knows what.

This poem is a ricorso *or rehearsal, a retrieval of Yeats's entire career. Seeing himself as an old man, he has thrown himself on the scrap heap. He has archetypalized himself, but first he rehearses all the clichés of his art, all the innovations that he had introduced into the drama and poetry of his time.*

"What can I but enumerate old themes?"

Having surveyed these stages of his art, his innovations and experiments, he simply says,

Those masterful images because complete,
Grew in pure mind, but out of what began?

His answer presents the main theme of From Cliché to Archetype*: the new poetic techniques and images are retrieved from:*

A mound of refuse or the sweepings of a street,
Old kettles, old bottles, and a broken can,
Old iron, old bones, old rags, that raving slut
Who keeps the till . . .

Yeats brings in here the whole theme of commerce as part of the poetic process. His poetic exhibitionism under the big top is done. The images retrieved from "the rag-and-bone shop" out of which he built his ladder for the high-wire act are now complete and cast aside. His "Jabob's ladder" is gone.

"I must lie down where all the ladders start." The theme in From Cliché to Archetype *is simply the scrapping of all poetic innovation and cliché when it has reached a certain stage of use. Masterful forms and images, when complete, are cast aside to become "the rag-and-bone shop of the heart" — that is, the world on the archetype.*

What about Jacob's ladder? Jacob lay down only to climb a ladder, or to dream, at least, of a ladder of angles ascending and descending in heavenly hierarchy. Yeats regards the moment of poetic breakdown as a new breakthrough, the beginning again of the ascent and descent of Jacob's ladder of heavenly vision.

As his poetic clichés collapse and are scrapped, he turns to the retrieval of old forms for new clichés. It is the worn-out cliché that reveals the creative or archetypal processes in language as in all other processes and artifacts.

(*From Cliché to Archetype,* 126-7)

Brunelleschi and Alberti introduced the mathematical science of perspective-illusion drawing to Renaissance Europe, obsolescing the medieval symbolist style of multiple perspective, and carefully retrieving the linear perspective of Ptolemy in the second century. Samuel Edgerton Jr. has detailed this retrieval and its development as an updating of medieval and scholastic sensibility in his *The Renaissance Rediscovery of Linear Perspective*. Retrieval is not simply a matter of hauling the old thing back onto stage, holus-bolus. Some translation or metamorphosis is necessary to place it into relation to the new ground — as anyone can testify who has experienced "revivals" in our culture, whether in fashion or music or any other form. The old thing is brought up to date, as it were. For archaic or tribal man, in acoustic space, there is no past, no history — always present. Today we experience a return to that outlook when technological breakthroughs have become so massive as to bring one environment into collision with another, from telephone to radio to TV to satellite to computer.

Interface, of the resonant interval as "where the action is" in all structures, whether chemical, psychic, or social, involves touch.

Touch, as the resonant interval or frontier of change and process, is indispensable to the study of structures. It involves also the idea of "play," as in the action of the interval between wheel and axle, as the basis of human communication. Since electronic man lives in a world of simultaneous information, he finds himself increasingly excluded from his traditional (visual) world, in which space and reason seem to be uniform, connected and stable. Instead, Western (visual and left-hemisphere) man now finds himself habitually relating to information structures that are simultaneous, discontinuous, and dynamic. Hearing, as such, is from all directions at once, a 360-degree sphere. Electrically, knowing is now from all directions at once in a 360-degree sphere, so that knowing itself has been recast or retrieved in acoustic form, as it were.

In 1917, T. S. Eliot in his "Tradition and the Individual Talent" stressed the view that all art from Homer to the present formed a simultaneous order and that this order was perpetually motivated, renewed, and retrieved by new experience. His symbolist approach to language and art and communication is well indicated in his celebrated definition of the auditory imagination.

> *What I call the "auditory imagination" is the feeling for syllable and rhythm, penetrating far below the conscious levels of thought and feeling, invigorating every word: sinking the most primitive and forgotten, returning to the origin, and bringing something back, seeking the beginning and the end. It works through meanings, certainly, or not without meanings in the ordinary sense, and fuses the old and obliterated, and the trite, the current, and the new and the surprising, the most ancient and the most civilized mentality.*
>
> *(The Use of Poetry and the Use of Criticism,* 118-19)

The definition points to the endless process of change and transformation and retrieval implicit in this simultaneous and homeostatic structure, which is dedicated to eternal stability. Much of the confusion of our present age stems naturally from the divergent experience of Western literate man, on the one hand, and his new surround of simultaneous or acoustic knowledge, on the other. Western man is torn between the claims of visual and auditory cultures or structures.

Neo-acoustic space gives us simultaneous access to all pasts. As for tribal man, for us there is no history. All is present, and the mundane becomes mythic:

If we can consider form the reversing of archetype into cliché, as for example the use of an archetypal Ulysses in James Joyce's novel to explore contemporary consciousness in the city of Dublin, then we may ask what would be the status of this pattern in primordial times, in the medieval period, and today. The answer would seem to be that in primordial times and today this archetype-into-cliché process is perfectly normal and accepted but that in the medieval period it is exceptional and unusual. The Balinese say, "We have no art, we do everything as well as possible." The artist in the Middle Ages, Renaissance, or the era up to the nineteenth century was regarded as a unique, exceptional person because he used an exceptional, unusual process. In primordial times, as today, the artist uses a familiar, ordinary technique and so he is looked upon as an ordinary, familiar person. Every man today is in this sense an artist — the administrator, the scientist, the doctor, as well as the man who uses paint or sculpts stone. Just as the archaic man had to follow natural processes of rhythm in order to influence and to purge, cleanse them by ricorso, so modern electric technologies require such timing and precision that only the following of processes in nature can be tolerated. The immediately preceding centuries of mechanization had been able to bypass these processes by fragmentation and strip-mining kinds of procedures.

(*From Cliché to Archetype*, 118-19)

The fall or scrapping of a culture world puts us all into the same archetypal cesspool, engendering nostalgia for earlier conditions.

Perhaps previous phases of culture seem more secure because they are fixed and processed in memory. Initially, any cliché is a breakthrough into a new dimension of experience. Alfred North Whitehead mentions in *Science and the Modern World* that the great discovery of the nineteenth century was that of the technique of discovery. The art of discovery, the art of acoustic, probing awareness, is now a cliché, and creativity has become a stereotype of the twentieth century. Discovery, or uncovering, is a form of retrieval.

The archetype is retrieved awareness or consciousness. It is consequently a retrieved cliché — an old cliché retrieved by a new cliché. Since a cliché is a unit extension of man, an archetype is a quoted extension, medium, technology, or environment, an old ground seen as figure through a new ground. The cliché, in other words, is incompatible with other clichés, but the archetype is extremely cohesive; the residues of other archetypes adhere to it. When we consciously set out to retrieve one archetype, we unconsciously retrieve others; and this retrieval recurs in infinite regress. In fact, whenever we "quote" one consciousness, we also "quote" the archetypes we exclude; and this quotation of excluded archetypes has been called by Freud, Jung, and others "the archetypal unconscious" (see *From Cliché to Archetype*, 21-2).

Jung and his disciples have been careful to insist that the archetype is to be distinguished from its expression. Strictly speaking, a Jungian archetype is a power or capacity of the psyche. Nevertheless, even in Jung's writings the term is used with interchangeable senses. In *Psyche and Symbol* Jung declares that "the archetype is an element of our psychic structure and thus a vital and necessary component in our psychic economy. It represents or personifies certain instinctive data of the dark primitive psyche: the real, the invisible *roots of consciousness*." Jung is careful to remind literary critics to consider the archetype as a primordial symbol:

> *The archetypes are by no means useless archaic survivals or relics. They are living entities, which cause the praeformation of numinous ideas or dominant representations. Insufficient understanding, however, accepts these praeformations in their archaic form, because they have a numinous appeal to the underdeveloped mind. Thus Communism is an archaic, primitive and therefore highly insidious pattern which characterizes primitive social groups. It implies lawless chieftainship as a vitally necessary compensation, a fact which can only be overlooked by means of a rationalistic one-sidedness, the prerogative of the barbarous mind.*
>
> *It is important to bear in mind that my concept of the "archetypes" has been frequently misunderstood as denoting inherited patterns of thought or as a kind of philosophical speculation. In reality they belong to the realm of the activities of the instincts and in that sense they represent inherited forms of psychic behaviour. As such they are invested with certain dynamic qualities which, psychologically speaking, are designated as "autonomy" and "numinosity."*
>
> (*Psyche and Symbol*, xvi)

Jung accounts for his theory of archetypes by means of the hypothesis of a collective race memory, although he is well aware that there is no scientific acceptance for such an idea. His justification, however, for using the concept of a collective memory is based on the recurrence over a wide area of archetypal patterns in artefacts, literatures, arts, and so on, apart from the shaky scientific basis (see *From Cliché to Archetype*, 22-3). While a new form or technology pervades the host culture as a new cliché, it simultaneously consigns the former and now obsolete cliché or homeostasis to the cultural rag-and-bone shop.

Older clichés are retrieved both as inherent principles that inform the new ground and new awareness, and as archetypal nostalgia figures with transformed meaning in relation to the new ground.

The automobile ended the age of the horse and buggy, but these returned with new significance and experience as the movie "Western." The tetrad — the four laws considered simultaneously, as a cluster — is an instrument for revealing and predicting the dynamics of situations and innovations. Nevertheless the usual "archetypal" explanations are inadequate because they regard the archetype as a figure minus a ground. In this regard, Jean Piaget observed:

> *Before we go on, we should stress the importance of this notion of equilibration, which enables us to dispense with an archetypal explanation for the prevalence of good forms. Since equilibration laws are coercive, they suffice to account for the generality of such processes of form selection; heredity need not be called in at all. Moreover, it is equilibration which makes Gestalten reenter the domain of structure . . . for whether physical or physiological, equilibration involves the idea of transformation within a system and the idea of self-regulation. Gestalt psychology is therefore a structuralist theory more on account of its use of equilibration principles than because of the laws of wholeness it proposes.*[4]

Both the retrieval and reversal aspects of the tetrad involve metamorphosis. The tired cliché, movies, became available as an art form when TV replaced them as the entertainment surround. Likewise the entire planet has been retrieved as a programmable resource and art form (i.e., ecology) as a side-effect of the new satellite ground. Money obsolesces barter, but retrieves potlatch in the form of

---

[4]*Structuralism* 57. Harold Innis, in *The Bias of Communication* and in *Empire and Communications*, made many historical observations on the differing Gestalt patterns and structures in human organization as they related to different means available for shaping situations. One of his most frequent illustrations of this principle concerned the types of bureaucracy that grew from the use of stone, on the one hand, and paper, on the other hand, as materials for writing. When stone or brick or clay are used as writing materials, the bureaucracy or human organization of interests and energies tends to take a priestly form dedicated to stability in time. When paper is available, the bureaucracy tends to become military, with a strong interest in the control of space. Innis was not only concerned with the study of changes in the outer patterns of human organization resulting from different means of communication in time and space, but he was much interested in the changes that took place in the perceptual lives of the people involved in these changes. He played the inner and outer aspects of innovation and change back and forth across each other as a figure/ground interface.

conspicuous consumption. The digital watch displaces the old circular dial, and retrieves the sundial form, which likewise used light itself to tell the time and which also had no moving parts. In the West, electronic technology displaces visual space and retrieves acoustic space in a new form, as the ground now includes the detritus of alphabetic civilization. However, the effect in the East is quite different, to the degree that its culture does not include a ground of phonetic literacy and industrial hardware. Harold Innis showed (*Empire and Communications*) how a shift in the media of writing, from clay tablets or stone to papyrus, was sufficient to displace temple bureaucracies by military ones with expansionist programs of conquest. The new speed of the lightweight medium was enough to release left-hemisphere outward drive and aggression. At present, Iran is enjoying the impact of electric media and driving inward at a furious rate, having shifted from a military- to a temple-controlled government, and spearheading a revival of ancient Islamic mores that is more than latent in many of Iran's neighbours.

The principle that during the stages of their development all things appear under forms opposite to those that they finally present is an ancient doctrine. Interest in the power of things to reverse themselves by evolution is evidenced by a great diversity of observations, sage and jocular. Alexander Pope wrote, in "Essay on Man" (Epistle II):

Vice is a monster of such frightful mien
As to be hated needs but to be seen;
But seen too oft, familiar with its face,
We first endure, then pity, then embrace.

The resonant juxtapositions of Pope's epigrammatic style automatically induce comprehensive awareness of whole situations: alert readers will have noted that Pope has covered all four of the tetrad processes.

In *Take Today: The Executive as Dropout* the main themes were the three principal reversals of Western form wrought by electric information: from hardware to software, from job-structure to role-playing, and from centralism to decentralism. In the age of electric information and programmed production, commodities themselves assume more and more the character of information, although this trend appears mainly in the advertising budget. In his *A Study of History* Arnold Toynbee notes a great many reversals of form and dynamic, as when, in the middle of the fourth century AD, the Germans in the Roman service began abruptly to be proud of their tribal names and to retain them.

Such a moment marked new confidence born of saturation with Roman values, and it was a moment marked by the complementary Roman swing toward primitive values. (As Americans saturate with European values, especially since TV, they begin to insist upon American coach lamps, hitching posts, and colonial kitchenware as cultural objects.) Just as the barbarians got to the top of the Roman social ladder, the Romans themselves were disposed to assume the dress and manners of tribesmen out of the same frivolous and snobbish spirit that attached the French court of Louis XVI to the world of shepherds and shepherdesses. It would have seemed a natural moment for the intellectuals to have taken over while the governing class was touring Disneyland, as it were. So it must have appeared to Marx and his followers. But they reckoned without understanding the dynamics of the new media of communication. Marx based his analysis most untimely on the machine, just as the telegraph and other implosive forms began to reverse the mechanical dynamic.

. . . in any medium or structure there is what Kenneth Boulding calls a "break boundary at which the system suddenly changes into another or passes some point of no return in its dynamic processes" . . .

One effect of the static photo had been to suppress the conspicuous consumption of the rich, but the effect of the speed-up of the photo had been to provide fantasy riches for the poor of the entire globe.

Today the road beyond its break boundary turns cities into highways, and the highway proper takes on a continuous urban character. Another characteristic reversal . . . is that the country ceases to be the center of all work, and the city ceases to be the center of leisure. In fact, improved roads and transport have reversed the ancient pattern and made cities the centers of work and the country the place of leisure and recreation.

Earlier, the increase of traffic that came with money and roads had ended the static tribal state (as Toynbee calls the nomadic food-gathering culture). Typical of the reversing that occurs at break boundaries is the paradox that nomadic mobile man, the hunter and food-gatherer is socially static. On the other hand, sedentary, specialist man is dynamic, explosive, progressive. The new magnetic or world city will be static and iconic or inclusive.

(*Understanding Media*, 37-8)

The reversal aspect of the tetrad is succinctly exemplified in a maxim from information theory: data overload equals pattern recognition. Any word or process or form, pushed to the limits of its potential, reverses its characteristics and becomes a complementary form, just as the airplane reverses its controls when it passes the "sound barrier." Money (hardware), pushed to its limit, reverses into the lack of money, that is, credit (software or information), and the credit card. At high speed or in great quantity, the motor car reverts to nautical form, and traffic (or a crowd) "flows." By repetition, an archetype can become a cliché again; or an individual man a crowd (with no private, but rather corporate, identity). Breakdown becomes breakthrough.

In "'Labour-Saving' Means More Work," Ruth S. Cowan points to the reversal that every labour-saving device is a new and larger form of work in disguise.

"Homemakers," she writes, "log about the same number of hours at their work as their grandmothers did in 1910, 1920, and 1930. The average homemaker, now armed with dozens of motors and thousands of electronic chips, can still spend up to 50 hours a week doing housework" (page 77). All four aspects of the tetrad can be found in her discussion of the vacuum cleaner, which is a grotesque extension of lungs:

> For decades prior to the turn of the century, inventors had been trying to create a carpet-cleaning system that would improve on the semiannual ritual of hauling rugs outside and beating them.
>
> But the vacuum cleaner's introduction coincided almost precisely with the virtual disappearance of the domestic servant. For the most economically comfortable segment of the population, this meant one thing: The female head of the household was doing more housework than she had ever done before. What Maggie had once done with a broom, Mrs. Smith was now doing with a vacuum cleaner.
>
> . . . As living quarters grew, standards for their upkeep increased; rugs had to be vacuumed daily or weekly, rather than semiannually. The net result was that when armed with a vacuum cleaner, homemakers could keep more space cleaner than their mothers and grandmothers would have believed possible. (page 78)

Another reversal occurs because of the proliferation of "household technology": the homemaker leaves the home:

> And then there is the automobile. We do not usually think of our cars as household appliances, but that is precisely what they are, since housework, as currently understood, could not be performed without them. The average homemaker is now more likely to be found behind a steering wheel than in front of a stove. She may have to drive her children to school and after-school activities, her husband to work or to public transport. She must shop for groceries. Meanwhile, as more homemakers acquired cars, more businessmen discovered the profitable joys of dispensing with delivery services.
>
> The iceman, in other words, no longer cometh. Nor doth the baker, the butcher, the grocer, the knife sharpener, the seamstress, nor the doctor. Thus a new category has been added to the homemaker's job description: chauffeur. (pages 78-9)

The next stage in reversal is the "working homemaker" who retrieves either the job or the home as the aesthetic base.

Annotated Contents

Part I
Culture as Business

1. "American Advertising": reprinted from *Horizon* (October 1947). A pivotal piece in McLuhan's scholarly life in which he treats popular culture seriously, if somewhat ironically. This essay leads directly to *The Mechanical Bride* (1951), a work of cultural anthropology examining the value system of North America through the business of advertising. "American Advertising" marks the beginning of the serious study of mass media.

2. *The Mechanical Bride*: "Preface," "The Mechanical Bride," and "From Da Vinci to Holmes," reprinted from *The Mechanical Bride: Folklore of Industrial Man* (1951). A book widely noticed in 1951 (e.g., by *Time* magazine) as an intellectually engaging and entertaining study of a subject normally thought frivolous or trivial. McLuhan later perceived a too-concentrated focus on the content of the ads that nevertheless afforded him scope for social criticism and some witty insightful wordplay in deconstructing the ads.

3. "Culture Is Our Business": reprinted from the book of the same title (1970). The money-making ethos of North American advertising is examined in this continuation of serious interest in popular culture and the arts. In respect to the growth of our mass consumer society, McLuhan reminds us that even T. S. Eliot once addressed 14,000 people in a sports stadium. This book traces the truth about North American culture — its obsession with business. (Curiously, this book was hastened through the publication process so rapidly that the author never got to proofread it or correct errors. It is reproduced here as first printed, errors intact.)

4. "Joyce, Mallarmé, and the Press": reprinted from *The Interior Landscape: The Literary Criticism of Marshall McLuhan*, edited by Eugene McNamara (1969). This prescient essay, which originally appeared in the *Sewanee Review*, 1953, marries the most serious literary considerations with the study of mass media. It is an excellent example of McLuhan's ability to find serious meaning in contemporary culture. The collected essays, often ignored by critics, are a stunning reminder that in McLuhan we are dealing with a first-rate scholarly mind, one of the finest and most innovative of his age.

5. "To Harold Adams Innis": reprinted from *Letters of Marshall McLuhan*, selected and edited by Matie Molinaro, Corinne McLuhan, and William Toye (1989). This important letter shows the two communications scholars coming at their central focus from different sides: Innis as economic historian whose interest in early colonial business led him to discover the significance of media forms for understanding a people; McLuhan as literary critic probing the relations between the psycho-social complex and media. This letter was probably prompted by McLuhan's discovery that Innis had assigned *The Mechanical Bride* for student reading in his famous course.

6. "Postures and Impostures of Managers Past": reprinted from *Take Today: The Executive as Dropout*, Marshall McLuhan and Barrington Nevitt (1972). The authors examine the

problem of "the end of history" and the obsolescence of the management concept of progress. While the world cries out for more and more jobs, McLuhan shows the necessity of thinking instead about roles. Notice also the subtle stylistic adaptations McLuhan makes to a co-author's needs. These two worked together on a number of projects.

Part II
Print and the Electric Revolution

7. Media and Cultural Change: reprinted from McLuhan's introduction to the 1964 edition of *The Bias of Communication* by Harold A. Innis. McLuhan's perceptive introduction drew considerable attention to this book. When he says that he is pleased to think of his own *The Gutenberg Galaxy* "as a footnote to the observations of Innis," it is a classic piece of McLuhanesque deferential litotes — as any careful reader of his analysis of Innis can see. This material also presents some of the most richly provocative insights one can find anywhere in McLuhan's work. At one level it is an imploded and comprehensive history of media and cultural change.

8. *The Gutenberg Galaxy*: reprinted from *The Gutenberg Galaxy: The Making of Typographic Man* (1962), perhaps the most important book ever written on the revolution of print technology. The insights into the process of print and its effects are profoundly significant. *The Gutenberg Galaxy* is McLuhan's masterpiece and the *sine qua non* of literate understanding of the power of a technology to create the conditions for Western civilized power. It may look like an anti-book in its structure, an array of parts like a mosaic, but there is more traditional internal structure than may at first appear. Certainly there is less argument here and more pattern recognition.

9. *Understanding Media*: reprinted from *Understanding Media: The Extensions of Man* (1964). This is the book that set the world on its ear. Everyone was reading it, quoting it, joking about it, trying to understand it, especially people making their living in the media. From this point on, McLuhan had international celebrity. In France he became "McLuhanisme"; in 1968 the U.S. President was elected following his new approaches to understanding media. In North America, McLuhan was ubiquitous as a television reference; he became a household word even to those who had no idea what his work was about.

10. "Is It Natural That One Medium Should Appropriate and Exploit Another?": essay by McLuhan reprinted from *McLuhan: Hot and Cool*, edited by Gerald E. Stearn (1967). McLuhan's controversial worldview made the appearance of this sort of book inevitable. The title page warns the reader that this is "A Primer For The Understanding Of & A Critical Symposium With A Rebuttal By McLuhan." The best adversaries and supporters are lined up for an intellectual battle rarely if ever seen under one cover.

11. "Explorations" from *Explorations*, no. 8, items 8-14 (1967). Something Else Press, Inc., New York. *Explorations* was one of the most influential little magazines of its time. In a relatively short period of existence *Explorations* published such luminaries as Robert Graves, David Riesman, Karl Polanyi, Peter Drucker, Hans Selye, Northrop Frye,

Siegfried Giedion, Jacques Maritain, Ashley Montagu, Harold Innis, Buckminster Fuller, Glenn Gould, and Barrington Nevitt, among many others. McLuhan is the first to interpret fully how print technology, under pressure from electric technology, is managing to reshape itself. All media have now become aspects of the electromagnetic wave spectrum, which results in an "auditory" shift in perception. This condition stresses resonant electronic connections over physical linkage. No transmissions can be seen, though their effects may be visible. Each medium has its own characteristic frequencies and each range of frequencies changes the rhythm of the brain's reception. Increasingly, print reflects many of these changes. Under electric pressure language tends to implode, putting words in an invisible vice. Ideas become slogans as sentences and paragraphs get shorter and shorter. Books take on visual embellishments to attract and aid the mass-media-trained reader. Typography swirls and dances across the page jamming sentiments together with ads in chaotic environmental profusion. Overall, the impression of *Explorations* is that art and science have "amalgamerged" into the synthesis of Verbi-Voco-Visual "all-at-once-ness" that electronic formats create, as anyone with a shelf of books, a CD player, a telephone, a Walkman, a radio, a fax, a computer, and sixty channels of television knows.

Part III
Oral McLuhan

12. "Address at Vision 65": reprinted from *The American Scholar* (1966). This important number of the well-known journal included contributors like Buckminster Fuller, J. Bronowski, Lynn White, Jr., and Walter Rosenblith on the theme of "The Electronic Revolution." Though the talk seems casual and oral, these themes were worked out carefully and McLuhan gave other versions of this talk during 1965 (in May, for example, at the Buffalo Spring Festival of the Arts). The theme is communications "environments," as ecologists never conceived them.

13. "Playboy Interview: Marshall McLuhan — A Candid Conversation with the High Priest of Popcult and Metaphysician of Media": reprinted from *Playboy* (March 1969). People are sometimes surprised that McLuhan would have appeared in this magazine. A good deal less overtly erotic in 1969, *Playboy* was publishing outstanding interviews with world figures. This interview captures McLuhan at his conversational best. Here one finds an almost comprehensive and accessible overview of the entire body of his thought. It is rare as well because it contains the "feel" of McLuhan when he was most himself, dialoguing away during a moment of exceptional interpretive powers.

14. "A McLuhan Sourcebook: Key Quotations from the Writings of Marshall McLuhan": garnered from an unpublished work by William Kuhns, who has graciously consented to our use of his material. Each snippet has the value of a meditation and shows in another way the aphoristic style that McLuhan loved, in which each saying stands on its own, but also in relation to the big picture rather like pieces in a mosaic. A very strong voice pervades these utterances.

15. "Explorations": "The Media Fit the Battle of Jericho" in *Explorations*, no. 6, pp. 15-19, University of Toronto (July 1956). This densely rich and imploded array of aphoristic perception condenses an astounding amount of useful and revolutionary insight into less than five pages. One of the important themes here illustrates how electric conditions force us to live mythically and in depth. Myth is the experience of events as occurring in collapsed time and space, McLuhan suggests. His work demonstrates that this is precisely the effect on the senses of electric media. Each of these pithy utterances is as worthy of consideration as a Tantric meditation on the nature of reality.

"Culture Without Literacy": from *Explorations*, no. 1, pp. 117-27, University of Toronto (December 1953). This prophetic work that comes rather early in McLuhan's career shows his vision intact and unfolding as early as 1953. In this indispensable article, McLuhan prepares his audience for the main message: that literacy, print, the book are undergoing revolutionary changes that affect all Western culture. The competition between media for user attention is heating up and the relations between forms of communication involve the shift in ratios across all human institutions, social, political, and economic. Print is not fated to die, but to change; it has already done so and with more change to come. Culture, which was once completely synonymous with high degrees of literacy, has now to be measured more against the full array of media. The availability of many forms of media expands the reach at least of those who pursue all forms of information available to them.

"Cicero and the Renaissance Training for Prince and Poet": from *Renaissance and Reformation*, vol. vi, no. 3, Victoria, B.C. (1970). In this brief piece we get a taste of the kind of erudition that so impresses the reader of McLuhan's Cambridge University Ph.D. dissertation. The distinctive battle between the old Rhetorical emphasis on form and the new Dialectic concern for content always amused and engaged McLuhan as an important historical and cultural force. Ramus and Nashe? Thereby hangs the tale of our modern world: reason and specialist logic, science and technology, Protestantism and Capitalism, in Western imperial agenda. The rich density of McLuhan's thought is powerfully in evidence here. This is an encyclopedic *tour de force* in three pages, the sketch of a complete Renaissance education in the compass of the average preface. This rewarding little epic of an article must be read carefully and unfolded at length through research.

Part IV
Culture and Art: Figures and Grounds

16. *From Cliché to Archetype*: "Archetype," "Introduction," "Paradox," and "Public as Cliché": reprinted from *From Cliché to Archetype*, Marshall McLuhan with Wilfred Watson (1970). This enigmatic and deeply engaging study probes the relations between cultural objects and their deep archetypal grounds or processes. Jung understood the transpersonal power of the archetype as carrying the genetic continuity of the memory of the race. McLuhan adds this paradoxical insight: that a style of perception when pushed to its limits is

discarded in favour of a new way of seeing which is actually an old way retrieved. Any cliché participates in the hidden power of its archetypal base. Technologies are instrumental in continually reversing this process.

17. "The Emperor's New Clothes": reprinted from *Through the Vanishing Point: Space in Poetry and Painting*, Marshall McLuhan and Harley Parker (1968). The role of art in culture is examined here in a fresh way. Art subverts existing order by insisting always on "making" things in the face of society's demand that things "match" pre-existent categories and models. As McLuhan puts it: "The artist is a person who is especially aware of the challenge and dangers of new environments presented to human sensibility." The operative force in such environmental change is always new technology producing new perception.

18. "Prolog to Exploration": reprinted from *Take Today: The Executive as Dropout* (1972). This is a later statement, with Barrington Nevitt, of the scholar as explorer. Probing the common assumptions will create breakthroughs that may be opportunities for change. "Prolog to Exploration" is a crucial study of how "specialized jobs have become casualties, displaced by the electric world of software and programming."

19. *Laws of Media*: reprinted from *Laws of Media: The New Science*, Marshall McLuhan and Eric McLuhan (1988). The discovery of a set of relations that inhere in all cultural transformation has made it possible to trace the lines of dynamic change of any technology or human artifact, past, present, or future. This book, McLuhan's last, began as a project to update *Understanding Media*; it is a summing-up and a fresh departure. McLuhan had accepted the challenge to make his work "scientific." The book begins with an extended essay on the senses and in particular on the new forms of sensibility provided by the new media. It recapitulates McLuhan's approach to studying media, relates it to evidence then emerging from the field of neurology, and launches into completely new territory: the laws. At the same time, he claimed that the book completed a longstanding project: one begun in the seventeenth century by Sir Francis Bacon in his *The New Science*, and resumed in the eighteenth century by Giambattista Vico in his *The New Science*. McLuhan maintained that the four laws he discovered were related in a particular way, one that revealed the grammar not just of media but every human innovation from levers and clubs to concertos, computers, cliches, and cosmology. The laws remove any basis for continuing to separate the arts and sciences since they both demonstrably belong to poetics. Because of what they reveal about human language, the laws and their implications challenge the validity of work done in a range of fields, including semiotics and linguistics. The laws apply, he found, to all things human, and exclusively to human innovation and utterance — creating implications for philosophy and the humanities. Here at last is a full-blown, mature "theory of communication," paradoxically minus — because rooted in perception and observation — minus the "theory."

Books by Marshall McLuhan

Currently in print

*The Gutenberg Galaxy: The Making of Typographic Man.*Toronto: University of Toronto Press, 1962. Reprinted often.

Laws of Media: The New Science. With Eric McLuhan. Toronto: University of Toronto Press, 1988.

*War and Peace in the Global Village.*With Quentin Fiore. Produced by Jerome Angel. New York: Bantam Books, 1968. Reprinted, New York: Touchstone Books, 1989.

The Medium Is the Massage: An Inventory of Effects. With Quentin Fiore. Produced by Jerome Agel. New York: Bantam Books, 1967. Reprinted, New York: Touchstone Books, 1989.

Understanding Media: The Extensions of Man. Cambridge, Mass., and London, England: The MIT Press, 1994.

Marshall McLuhan: The Man and His Message. With others. Edited by George Sanderson and Frank Macdonald. Introduction by John Cage. Golden, Colorado: Fulcrum, 1989.

Out of print

The Mechanical Bride: The Folklore of Industrial Man. New York: Vanguard Press, 1951.

Explorations in Communication. Edited by Edmund Carpenter and Marshall McLuhan. Boston: Beacon Press, 1960 (paperback, 1966).

Voices of Literature, vol. 1. Toronto and Montreal: Holt, Rinehart and Winston of Canada, 1964.

Voices of Literature, vol. 2. Toronto and Montreal: Holt, Rinehart and Winston of Canada, 1965.

Verbi-Voco-Visual Explorations. (Reprint of *Explorations*, no. 8.) New York: Something Else Press, 1967.

McLuhan: Hot and Cool. Edited by Gerald E. Stern. New York: New American Library, Signet Books, 1967.

Through the Vanishing Point: Space in Poetry and in Painting. With Harley Parker. New York: Harper and Row, 1968.

The Interior Landscape: The Literary Criticism of Marshall McLuhan, 1943–1962. Compiled, edited, and introduced by Eugene McNamara. New York: McGraw-Hill, 1969.

Counterblast. (Designed by Harley Parker.) Toronto: McClelland and Stewart, 1969.

Sounds, Masks, Roles. (Paperback version of *Voices of Literature,* vol. 1.) Toronto and Montreal: Holt, Rinehart and Winston of Canada, 1969.

McLuhan: Pro and Con. Edited by Raymond Rosenthal. New York: Pelican Books, 1969.

From Cliché to Archetype. With Wilfred Watson. New York: Viking Press, 1970.

Culture Is Our Business. New York: McGraw-Hill, 1970.

Take Today: The Executive as Dropout. With Barrington Nevitt. New York: Harcourt Brace Jovanovitch, 1972.

City as Classroom: Understanding Language and Media. With Kathryn Hutchon and Eric McLuhan. Agincourt, Ontario: The Book Society of Canada, 1977.

Letters of Marshall McLuhan. Edited by Matie Molinaro, Corinne McLuhan, and William Toye. Toronto: Oxford University Press, 1987.

The Global Village. With Bruce Powers. New York and Oxford: Oxford University Press, 1989.

In French only (and also out of print)

Mutations 1990. Translated by François Chesneau. Maison Mame, 1969.

D'oeil à oreille. Translated by D. de Kerckhove. Montréal: Editions Hurtubise HMH, 1977.

Autre homme autre chrétien à l'âge électronique. With Pierre Babin. Lyon: Editions du Chalet, 1977.

A Marshall McLuhan
Reading List

Allegro, John. *The Sacred Mushroom and the Cross.* New York: Doubleday & Co., 1970.

Anshen, R. N. *Language: An Inquiry into Its Meaning and Function.* Science of Culture Series, vol. 3. New York: Harper, 1957.

Aquinas, Thomas. *Summa Theologica,* pt. 3. Taurini, Italy: Marietti, 1932.

Atherton, James S. *Books at the Wake.* London: Faber & Faber, 1959.

Auerbach, Erich. *Mimesis: The Representation of Reality in Western Literature.* Translated by Willard R. Trask. Princeton: Princeton University Press, 1953.

Bacon, Francis. *The Advancement of Learning.* 1605. New York: Dutton, Everyman ed., n.d.

———. *Essays or Counsels, Civil and Moral.* Edited by R. F. Jones. New York: Odyssey Press, 1939.

Barnouw, Erik. *Mass Communication.* New York: Rinehart, 1956.

Barzun, Jacques. *The House of Intellect.* New York: Harper, 1959.

Békésy, Georg von. *Experiments in Hearing.* Edited and translated by E. G. Weaver. New York: McGraw-Hill, 1960.

———. "Similarities Between Hearing and Skin Sensation." *Psychological Review* 66, no. 1 (January 1959).

Berkeley, Bishop. *A New Theory of Vision.* 1709. New York: Dutton, Everyman ed., n.d.

Bierce, Ambrose. *The Devil's Dictionary.* New York: Hill & Wang, 1957.

Blake, William. *The Poetry and Prose of William Blake.* Edited by Geoffrey Keynes. London: Nonsuch Press, 1932.

Boguslaw, Robert. *The New Utopians.* Englewood Cliffs, N.J.: Prentice-Hall, 1968.

Boorstin, Daniel J. *The Image: Or, What Happened to the American Dream.* New York: Atheneum Publishers, 1962.

Boulding, Kenneth E. "Failures and Successes in Economics." *Think* (May-June 1965).

———. *The Image: Knowledge in Life and Society.* Ann Arbor: University of Michigan Press, 1956.

Broglie, Louis de. *The Revolution in Physics.* New York: Noonday Press, 1953.

Brown, Norman O. *Life Against Death: Technology as Neurotic Sublimation and Alienation of the Body.* New York: Random House, 1959.

Burke, Edmund. *Reflections on the Revolution in France.* 1790. New York: Dutton, Everyman ed., n.d.

Bushnell, George Herbert. *From Papyrus to Print.* London: Grafton, 1947.

Butler, Samuel. *Erewhon.* New York: Random House, Modern Library, n.d.

Canetti, Elias. *Crowds and Power.* Translated from German by Carol Stewart. New York: Penguin, 1973.

Caponigri, A. Robert. *Time and Idea: The Theory of History in Giambattista Vico.* London: Routledge & Kegan Paul, 1953.

Carlyle, Thomas. *Past and Present.* Boston: Houghton Mifflin Co., 1965.

Carothers, J. C. "Culture, Psychiatry and the Written Word." *Psychiatry* (November 1959).

Carpenter, Edmund. *Eskimo.* Identical with *Explorations,* no. 9. Toronto: University of Toronto Press, 1960.

——. "The New Languages." In *Explorations in Communication.* Boston: Beacon Press, 1960.

Carroll, Lewis. *Alice in Wonderland* and *Through the Looking Glass.* New York: Grosset & Dunlap, 1946.

Carter, T. F. *The Invention of Printing in China and Its Spread Westward.* Edited by L. C. Goodrich. 2d ed. New York: Ronald, 1955.

Cassirer, Ernst. *Language and Myth.* Translated by S. K. Langer. New York: Harper, 1946.

Chardin, Pierre Teilhard de. *Phenomenon of Man.* Translated by Bernard Wall. New York: Harper, 1959.

Chaytor, H. J. *From Script to Print.* Cambridge: Heffer & Sons, 1945.

Chesterton, G. K. *Collected Poems of G. K. Chesterton.* London: Cecil Palmer, 1927.

Cicero. *De oratore.* Loeb Classical Library, n.d.

Clarke, Arthur C. *Profiles of the Future.* New York: Harper & Row, Publishers, 1963.

Colie, Rosalie. *Paradoxica Epidemica: The Renaissance Tradition of Paradox.* Princeton: Princeton University Press, 1966.

Diringer, David. *The Alphabet.* New York: Philosophic Library, 1948.

Drucker, Peter. *The Age of Discontinuity.* New York: Harper & Row, 1963.

——. *The Concept of the Corporation.* New York: John Day Co., 1946.

Einstein, Albert. *Where Is Science Going?* London: George Allen & Unwin, 1933.

Eisenstein, Sergei. *Film Form.* New York: Harcourt Brace & Co., 1949.

Eliot, T. S. *The Complete Poems and Plays, 1909-1950.* New York: Harcourt Brace & Co., 1952.

——. *The Sacred Wood: Essays on Poetry and Criticism.* London: Methuen & Co., 1948.

——. *Selected Essays.* New York: Harcourt Brace & Co., 1950.

——. *The Use of Poetry and the Use of Criticism.* New York: Barnes & Noble, 1955.

Eliade, Mircea. *The Sacred and the Profane: The Nature of Religion.* Translated by W. R. Trask. New York: Harcourt Brace & Co., 1959.

Ellul, Jacques. *Propaganda: The Foundation of Man's Attitudes.* New York: Alfred A. Knopf, 1965.

Erasmus, Desiderius. *The Praise of Folly.* Princeton: Princeton University Press, 1941.

Fenellosa, Ernst. "The Chinese Written Character as a Medium for Poetry." Translated by Ezra Pound. Washington: Square $ Series, n.d.

Frazer, Sir James. *The Golden Bough.* 3d ed. London: Macmillan, 1951.

Friedenberg, Edgar Z. *The Vanishing Adolescent.* Boston: Beacon Press, 1959.

Fries, Charles Carpenter. *American English Grammar.* New York: Appleton, 1940.

Frye, Northrop. *Anatomy of Criticism.* Princeton: Princeton University Press, 1957.

Fuller, R. Buckminster. *Operating Manual for Spaceship Earth.* Carbondale, Ill.: Southern Illinois University Press, 1969.

Gabor, Dennis. *Innovations.* New York: Oxford University Press, 1971.

Galbraith, John Kenneth. *The New Industrial State.* New York: New American Library, Signet Books, 1967.

Giedion, Siegfried. *The Beginnings of Art.* Quoted in *Explorations in Communication* (Boston: Beacon Press, 1960), 65-6.

———. *The Eternal Present.* 2 vols. New York: Pantheon Books, Bollingen Series, vol. 35, no. 6, 1962-64.

———. *Mechanization Takes Command.* New York: Oxford University Press, 1948.

———. *Space, Time and Architecture.* 4th ed. Cambridge, Mass.: Harvard University Press, 1967.
Goedel, Kurt. *Goedel's Theorem: On Formally Undecidable Propositions.* New York: Basic Books, 1963.

Gombrich, Ernst H. *Art and Illusion.* New York: Pantheon Books, 1960.

Hall, Edward T. *The Hidden Dimension.* New York: Doubleday & Co., Anchor Books, 1969.

Havelock, Eric A. *Preface to Plato.* Cambridge, Mass.: Harvard University Press, 1963.

Heisenberg, Werner. *The Physicist's Conception of Nature.* Translated by Arnold J. Pomerans. Westport, Conn.: Greenwood Press, 1958.

Hildebrand, Adolf von. *The Problem of Form in the Figurative Arts.* Translated by Max Meyer and R. M. Ogden. New York: G. E. Stechert, 1907. Reprint, 1945.

Hobbes, Thomas. *Leviathan.* Edited by Francis Randall. New York: Washington Square Press, 1969.

Hopkins, Gerard Manley. *Poems of Gerard Manley Hopkins.* New York: Oxford University Press, 1950.

Huizinga, Johan. *Homo Ludens: A Study of the Play Element in Culture.* Boston: Beacon Press, 1955.

I Ching. Translated by R. Wilhelm and C. F. Baynes. London: Routledge & Kegan Paul, 1951.

Innis, Harold. *The Bias of Communication.* Toronto: University of Toronto Press, 1951.

———. *Empire and Communications.* Oxford: University of Oxford Press, 1950.

———. *Essays in Canadian Economic History.* Toronto: University of Toronto Press, 1956.

———. *The Fur Trade in Canada.* New Haven: Yale University Press, 1930.

Ivins, William, Jr. *Art and Geometry: A Study in Space Intuitions.* Cambridge, Mass.: Harvard University Press, 1946.

———. *Prints and Visual Communication.* London: Routledge & Kegan Paul, 1953.

Jacobs, Jane. *The Economy of Cities.* New York: Random House, 1969.

James, William. *The Principles of Psychology.* 2 vols. 1890. New York: Dover Publications, n.d.

Joyce, James. *Finnegans Wake.* London: Faber & Faber, 1939.

———. *Ulysses.* New York Modern Library, 1934; New York: Random House, 1961.

Kepes, Gyorgy. *The Language of Vision.* Chicago: Paul Theobald, 1939.

Klee, Paul. *The Pedagogical Sketchbook.* Translated by Sibyl Moholy-Nagy. London: Faber & Faber, 1953.

———. *The Thinking Eye.* N.p.: George Wittenborn, 1961.

Kuhn, Thomas S. *The Structure of Scientific Revolutions.* Chicago: University of Chicago Press, 1962.

Lee, Dorothy. "Lineal and Non-lineal Codifications of Reality." Reprinted in *Explorations in Communication*. Boston: Beacon Press, 1960.

Lewis, Percival Wyndham. *The Art of Being Ruled*. London: Chatto & Windus, 1926.

——. *The Lion and the Fox*. London: Grant Richards, 1927.

——. *Men Without Art*. London: Cassell & Co., 1934.

——. *The Human Age*. London: Methuen & Co., n.d.

——. *Time and Western Man*. London: Chatto & Windus, 1927.

Lord, Albert B. *The Singer of Tales*. Cambridge, Mass.: Harvard University Press, 1960.

McHale, John. *The Future of the Future*. New York: George Braziller, 1969.

Mumford, Lewis. *Technics and Civilization: The Interplay of Artefact and Culture*. New York: Harcourt Brace & World, 1934.

——. *The Urban Prospect*. New York: Harcourt Brace & World, 1969.

Olson, Charles. *Proprioception*. Berkeley, Calif.: Four Seasons, 1965.

Ong, Walter. "Ramist Classroom Procedure and the Nature of Reality." *Studies in English Literature, 1500-1900* 1, no. 1 (winter 1961).

——. "Ramist Method and the Commercial Mind." *Studies in the Renaissance* 8 (1961).

——. *Ramus: Method and the Decay of Dialogue*. Cambridge, Mass.: Harvard University Press, 1958.

Opie, Iona, and Peter Opie. *Lore and the Language of Schoolchildren*. Oxford: Oxford University Press, 1959.

Orwell, George. *1984*. Edited by Irving Howe. New York: Harcourt Brace & World, 1962.

Panofsky, Irwin. *Gothic Architecture and Scholasticism*. 2d ed. New York: Meridian Books, 1957.

Plato. *Dialogues*. Translated by B. Jowett. New York: n.p., 1895.

Polanyi, Karl. *The Great Transformation*. New York: Farrar Strauss, 1944; Boston: Beacon Press paperback, 1957.

Polanyi, Karl, Conrad M. Arenberg, and Harry W. Pearson, eds. *Trade and Market in Early Empires*. Glencoe, Ill.: The Free Press, 1957.

Pope, Alexander. *The Dunciad*. Edited by James Sutherland. 2d ed. London: Methuen & Co., 1953.

Popper, Karl R. *The Open Society and Its Enemies*. Princeton: Princeton University Press, 1950.

Pound, Ezra. *The Spirit of Romance*. Norfolk, Conn.: New Directions Press, 1929.

Riesman, David J. with Reuel Denney and Nathan Glazer. *The Lonely Crowd*. New Haven: Yale University Press, 1950.

Ruskin, John. *Modern Painters*. New York: Dutton, Everyman ed., n.d.

Russell, Bertrand. *ABC of Relativity*. 1925. Rev. ed. London: Allen & Unwin, 1958; New York: Mentor paperback, 1959.

——. *History of Western Philosophy*. London: Allen & Unwin, 1946.

Samuelson, Paul A. *Economics*. New York: McGraw-Hill, 1961.

Selye, Hans. *From Dream to Discovery: On Being a Scientist*. New York: McGraw-Hill, 1964.

——. *The Stress of Life*. New York: McGraw-Hill, 1956.

Spengler, Oswald. *The Decline of the West*. London: Allen & Unwin, 1918.

Tawney, R. H. *Religion and the Rise of Capitalism*. Holland Memorial Lectures, 1922. New York: Pelican Books, 1947.

Tocqueville, Alexis de. *Democracy in America*. Translated by Phillips Bradley. New York: Knopf paperback, 1944.

Tuve, Rosamund. *Elizabethan and Metaphysical Imagery*. Chicago: University of Chicago Press, 1947.

Usher, Abbott Payson. *History of Mechanical Inventions*. Boston: Beacon Press paperback, 1959.

Verblen, Thorstein. *Theory of the Leisure Class*. New York: Random House, Modern Library, 1934.

Von Bertalanffy, Ludwig, and Anatol Rapoport, eds. *General Systems*. Yearbook of the Society for General Systems Theory, vol. 1. 1956.

White, John. *The Birth and Rebirth of Pictorial Space*. London: Faber & Faber, 1957.

White, Leslie A. *The Science of Culture*. New York: Grove Press, n.d.

White, Lynn. "Technology and Invention in the Middle Ages." *Speculum* 15 (April 1940).

Whitehead, A. N. *Science and the Modern World*. New York: Macmillan, 1926.

Whittaker, Sir Edmund. *Space and Spirit*. Hinsdale, Ill.: Henry Regnery, 1948.

Whyte, Lancelot Law. *The Unconscious Before Freud*. New York: Basic Books, 1960.

Willey, Basil. *The Seventeenth Century Background*. London: Chatto & Windus, 1934.

Williams, Aubrey. *Pope's Dunciad*. Baton Rouge, La.: Louisiana State University Press, 1955.

Williams, Raymond. *Culture and Society, 1780-1950*. New York: Columbia University Press, 1958; Anchor Books, 1959.

Williamson, George. *Senecan Amble*. London: Faber & Faber, 1951.

Young, J. Z. *Doubt and Certainty in Science*. Oxford: Oxford University Press, 1961.

Index